Optimizing NFS Performance

Tuning and Troubleshooting
NFS on HP-UX Systems

ISBN 013042816-7

90000

9 780130 428165

Hewlett-Packard® Professional Books

OPERATING SYSTEMS

Diercks	MPE/iX System Administration Handbook
Fernandez	Configuring CDE: The Common Desktop Environment
Lund	Integrating UNIX and PC Network Operating Systems
Madell	Disk and File Management Tasks on HP-UX
Mosberger, Eranian	IA-64 Linux Kernel: Design and Implementation
Poniatowski	HP-UX Virtual Partitions
Poniatowski	HP-UX 11i System Administration Handbook and Toolkit
Poniatowski	HP-UX 11.x System Administration Handbook and Toolkit
Poniatowski	HP-UX 11.x System Administration "How To" Book
Poniatowski	HP-UX System Administration Handbook and Toolkit
Poniatowski	Learning the HP-UX Operating System
Poniatowski	UNIX User's Handbook, Second Edition
Rehman	HP Certified, HP-UX System Administration
Roberts	UNIX and Windows 2000 Interoperability Guide
Sauers, Weygant	HP-UX Tuning and Performance
Stone, Symons	UNIX Fault Management
Weygant	Clusters for High Availability: A Primer of HP Solutions, Second Edition
Wong	HP-UX 11i Security

ONLINE/INTERNET

Amor	The E-business (R)evolution: Living and Working in an Interconnected World, Second Edition
Caldwell	The Fast Track to Profit: An Insider's Guide to Exploiting the World's Best Internet Technologies
Chandler , Hyatt	Customer-Centered Design: A New Approach to Web Usability
Greenberg, Lakeland	A Methodology for Developing and Deploying Internet and Intranet Solutions
Greenberg, Lakeland	Building Professional Web Sites with the Right Tools
Klein	Building Enhanced HTML Help with DHTML and CSS
Werry, Mowbray	Online Communities: Commerce, Community Action, and the Virtual University

NETWORKING/COMMUNICATIONS

Blommers	OpenView Network Node Manager: Designing and Implementing an Enterprise Solution
Blommers	Practical Planning for Network Growth
Bruce, Dempsey	Security in Distributed Computing: Did You Lock the Door?
Lucke	Designing and Implementing Computer Workgroups

Optimizing NFS Performance

Tuning and Troubleshooting NFS on HP-UX Systems

Dave Olker

Hewlett-Packard Company

www.hp.com/hpbooks

Prentice Hall PTR
Upper Saddle River, New Jersey 07458
www.phptr.com

Library of Congress Cataloging-in-Publication Data

A CIP catalog record for this book can be obtained from the Library of Congress.

Editorial/production supervision: *Mary Sudul*
Cover design director: *Jerry Votta*
Cover design: *DesignSource*
Manufacturing manager: *Alexis Heydt-Long*
Acquisitions editor: *Jill Harry*
Editorial assistant: *Katie Wolf*
Marketing manager: *Dan DePasquale*

Publisher, Hewlett-Packard Books: *Patricia Pekary*

Published by Prentice Hall PTR
Prentice-Hall, Inc.
Upper Saddle River, New Jersey 07458

Prentice Hall books are widely used by corporations and government agencies for training, marketing, and resale.
The publisher offers discounts on this book when ordered in bulk quantities. For more information, contact Corporate Sales Department, Phone: 800-382-3419; FAX: 201-236-7141;
E-mail: corpsales@prenhall.com
Or write: Prentice Hall PTR, Corporate Sales Dept., One Lake Street, Upper Saddle River, NJ 07458.

(trademark info)
Other product or company names mentioned herein are the trademarks or registered trademarks of their respective owners.

Printed in the United States of America
10 9 8 7 6 5 4 3 2 1

ISBN 0-13-042816-7

Pearson Education LTD.
Pearson Education Australia PTY, Limited
Pearson Education Singapore, Pte. Ltd.
Pearson Education North Asia Ltd.
Pearson Education Canada, Ltd.
Pearson Educación de Mexico, S.A. de C.V.
Pearson Education — Japan
Pearson Education Malaysia, Pte. Ltd.

*To my loving wife Kimberly
and my sons Daniel and Matthew —*

*without your support and patience
this book would not be possible.*

CONTENTS

LIST OF FIGURES

LIST OF TABLES

LIST OF KEY IDEAS AND NFS PERFORMANCE EXAMPLES

LIST OF NFS DIFFERENCES BETWEEN HP-UX 11.0 AND 11i

ACKNOWLEDGEMENTS

I would like to express my gratitude to the following individuals for their tireless efforts in reviewing the contents of this book: Ric Mackie, Tom McNeal, Michael Ehrig, and Rick Jones. They worked diligently to ensure the technical accuracy of the material, and their suggestions and feedback improved the readability of the book tremendously. I hasten to add that any mistakes remaining in the book are mine, not theirs.

I'm especially grateful to Hewlett-Packard engineers, and fellow HP Press authors, Bob Sauers and Rob Lucke, for the advice and encouragement I needed to undertake this project. I also wish to thank my manager, Katy Jenkins, for being supportive of this venture from the beginning and for allowing me the flexible work schedule I needed to write the book.

There are several people who helped with the logistical aspects of the book that I would like to acknowledge. Susan Wright and Pat Pekary of Hewlett-Packard Retail Publishing Press provided a great deal of assistance and direction. Jill Pisoni and Jim Markham of Prentice Hall supported me throughout the production process and endured my numerous schedule changes with patience and good humor. I also owe a special debt of gratitude to Patti Guerrieri of Prentice Hall, for painstakingly explaining the many intricacies of FrameMaker® templates.

Finally, I wish to thank my family: my wife, Kimberly, for her constant encouragement and for putting up with countless late night writing sessions; and for my sons, Daniel and Matthew, for always understanding when Daddy needed to spend time working on "The Book." I couldn't have accomplished this without their love and support.

INTRODUCTION

Network File System (NFS) has been the industry standard protocol for remote file access on the UNIX operating system platform for many years. It is part of the Open Network Computing software family originally developed by Sun Microsystems.

In a nutshell, NFS is a client-server network-based protocol that allows one system to seamlessly access files and directories that physically reside on another system. At one time or another, most UNIX users have used NFS — whether they realized it or not — to access resources such as: data files, home directories, e-mail folders, and application binaries. NFS has become a staple in most large UNIX-based environments and is therefore considered a critical component of every flavor of UNIX, as well as many non-UNIX based operating systems.

Why another book about NFS?

While there are several books available today that describe the NFS protocol itself, there is very little information in those books that specifically describes how to properly tune NFS systems for optimal performance. Of the performance related information that is available, the vast majority pertains only to tuning NFS servers. People sometimes forget that without well-tuned NFS clients it doesn't matter how fast your server is; you'll still end up with poor performance. In order to achieve optimal NFS performance, both clients and servers need to be considered.

Admittedly, no book could possibly hope to accurately explain how best to configure every vendor's NFS systems. Thus, this book concentrates specifically on tuning HP-UX systems. While most of the concepts discussed in this book would apply to any vendor's NFS implementation, this book contains numerous HP-UX-specific tuning recommendations, including describing undocumented command-line options and undocumented kernel parameters, that can dramatically influence NFS behavior and performance on HP-UX systems.

Another factor driving the demand for NFS performance information is the recent shift in the storage industry from Direct Access Storage Devices (DASD) to centralized or consolidated storage models, including Storage Area Networks (SAN) and Network-Attached Storage (NAS). Many hardware vendors, HP included, are releasing storage solutions specifically designed to compete in the SAN and NAS arenas. NFS is a central component in HP's NAS offerings, which has spurred an increase in demand for information about how to properly configure and tune HP's NFS implementation.

Finally, HP recently released HP-UX version 11i, which included support for the new Superdome hardware platform. HP implemented numerous NFS changes in this release of HP-UX; however, most of these differences are not currently described in any customer-viewable documentation. These NFS implementation differences are explained throughout this book.

Who is the intended audience for this book?

The target audience for this book includes system administrators, network administrators, and storage administrators who want to learn how to configure their NFS client and server systems for optimal performance. Other interested parties include anyone wanting to learn more about HP's NFS implementation, or anyone wanting a better understanding of the various kernel and user-space components that make up the NFS product family.

This book is not intended as a replacement for the HP-UX *"Installing and Administering NFS Services"* manual.[1] Some familiarity with basic UNIX and NFS concepts is assumed.

NFS performance tuning methodology used in this book

There is much more to tuning NFS for performance than making sure the right number of nfsds are running on the server. In many ways, NFS is similar to any other network-based application in that it competes for critical system resources such as disk, network, memory, and kernel tables, with all other running processes. In order to optimize NFS performance, many facets of the client and server systems must be interrogated and properly configured.

NFS is heavily dependent upon many different subsystems (i.e. filesystems, network, buffer cache memory, hostname resolution, etc.) and is therefore susceptible to performance problems in these subsystems. In other words, if the performance of the network is slow, NFS throughput will most likely suffer. If local filesystem read and write performance on the NFS server is slow, there is a good chance that NFS read and write throughput to this server will be slow. Thus, when investigating any NFS performance issue it is important to perform a "sanity check" of the overall environment in which the clients and servers reside, in addition to analyzing the NFS-specific configuration of the systems themselves.

The tuning methodology prescribed in this book involves looking at the overall NFS environment and then analyzing the various individual NFS components.

---

1.   The *NFS Services* manual, as well as all other HP-UX documentation, is available online at: *http://docs.hp.com*.

Organization of this book

In keeping with the tuning methodology outlined above, the book begins by discussing two primary environmental factors that can directly influence NFS performance: the network and the configuration of the NFS server's filesystems.

- **Chapter 1 — "Network Considerations"** discusses the importance of understanding the underlying network topology separating your clients and servers, as well as gauging the throughput capabilities of your network.
- **Chapter 2 — "Local Filesystem Considerations"** describes the many factors that can influence the behavior and performance of local filesystems, as well as provides tools and tips for gauging the throughput capabilities of your filesystems.

The next several chapters drill down into the various NFS client and server elements that make up the NFS protocol family, including the optional AutoFS and CacheFS components. The behavior of these components and their effect on NFS performance is discussed. In addition, each of these chapters includes a troubleshooting section designed to help isolate, identify, and resolve problems specific to each of these critical pieces.

- **Chapter 3 — "biod Daemons"** explains the significance of the client-side block I/O daemons, and how to determine the best number of biods to run on a given client.
- **Chapter 4 — "nfsd Daemons and Threads"** discusses the various user-space daemons and kernel-space threads used by the server system to process inbound NFS requests. It offers insight into how HP-UX manages the nfsd daemons that service UDP requests differently than the nfsktcpd threads used to service TCP requests. It also explains how to identify the proper number of daemons and threads to configure on a specific server.
- **Chapter 5 — "rpc.mountd"** describes the server-side daemon used by HP-UX to implement the MOUNT protocol. It explains the many services this daemon performs, and it outlines the many factors that can influence rpc.mountd behavior and performance.
- **Chapter 6 — "rpc.lockd and rpc.statd"** discusses the daemons used by HP-UX to implement the Network Lock Manager (NLM) and Network Status Monitor (NSM) protocols, which allow NFS clients to obtain and recover locks on remote files. This chapter explains how these two daemons work to service lock requests, and it offers suggestions for configuring your systems to avoid potential NFS file lock hangs and to ensure optimal file locking performance.
- **Chapter 7 — "Automount and AutoFS"** describes the two client-side protocols offered on HP UX systems that allow NFS filesystems to be automatically mounted when referenced and automatically unmounted when they become idle. It explains the many differences between the legacy Automount product and the new AutoFS protocol, and it outlines the many configuration factors to consider when using either of these products to ensure optimal NFS behavior and performance.

- **Chapter 8 — "CacheFS"** provides an overview of the CacheFS protocol, which is a client-side filesystem caching mechanism. It explains how CacheFS works, the benefits it can provide, and how to configure it for optimal performance. Also described is an HP-specific enhancement — the *rpages* mount option — that can dramatically increase the effectiveness of CacheFS when caching NFS-mounted application binaries.

The next two chapters deal specifically with how the NFS protocol has evolved over time, and how the new features and functionality introduced in newer versions of NFS, including support for network transport protocols other than UDP, can benefit NFS performance.

- **Chapter 9 — "NFS Protocol Version 2 vs. NFS Protocol Version 3"** describes the many differences between version 2 and version 3 of the NFS protocol, and how these differences can directly affect NFS behavior and performance. It explains why an NFS PV3 filesystem will usually outperform a PV2 filesystem. It also lists several corner-case scenarios where a PV2 filesystem could potentially outperform a PV3 filesystem, and how to re-configure the PV3 filesystem to match or beat the PV2 performance in these situations.
- **Chapter 10 — "NFS/UDP vs. NFS/TCP"** explains the many differences between the UDP/IP and TCP/IP network transport protocols and how NFS behaves differently depending upon which underlying protocol it uses.

The final chapters focus on two critical aspects of HP-UX — buffer cache memory and kernel parameters — and how these components can dramatically affect NFS performance.

- **Chapter 11 — "Buffer Cache"** describes the HP-UX buffer cache memory subsystem and how NFS clients and servers use buffer cache resources to improve performance. It explains the differences between the "static" and "dynamic" cache allocation mechanisms and the reasons for choosing one method over the other. It also offers recommendations for sizing this critical system resource on NFS client and server systems.
- **Chapter 12 — "Kernel Parameters"** provides a detailed description of the numerous HP-UX kernel parameters that can directly influence NFS performance. It offers sizing recommendations for each parameter, and describes the many tools available for inspecting the current values of these parameters and monitoring their utilization.

Additional information is included in two appendices located at the back of the book.

- **Appendix A — "Summary of Tuning Recommendations"** summarizes the numerous recommendations made throughout the book.
- **Appendix B — "Patching Considerations"** explains the critical importance of keeping the operating system on your NFS client and server systems up-to-date with available patches. Keeping your systems properly patched can not only improve NFS performance, in many cases patches are required in order to enable specific NFS functionality.

## CHAPTER 1

Network Considerations

NFS is an acronym for "Network File System," so it should come as no surprise that NFS performance is heavily affected by the latency and bandwidth of the underlying network. Before embarking on a detailed investigation into a specific area of NFS, it is a good idea to first verify that the underlying network is performing as expected.

This chapter focuses on three main areas: analyzing the physical layout of the network that separates your NFS clients and servers, measuring the throughput capabilities of the network, and network troubleshooting concepts.

This chapter describes a recommended methodology and set of tools available for understanding the physical layout of your network, measuring its throughput, and performing routine network troubleshooting tasks. This chapter does not discuss the myriad of networking topologies and interface cards that are currently available for HP-UX systems. NFS runs on most any networking link supporting Internet Protocol (IP), and it typically performs better on faster links.[1]

1.1 Analyze Network Layout

An important early step in troubleshooting any NFS performance issue is to learn as much as possible about the physical layout of the underlying network topology. Some of the questions you should be trying to answer at this stage are:

---

1. There is a wealth of information about the latest and greatest networking technologies, such as Gigabit Ethernet, Auto Port Aggregation (APA), etc., available from HP's IT Resource Center web site. *http://itrc.hp.com*, and HP's online documentation repository: *http://docs.hp.com*.

- How many network hops (i.e. bridges, hubs, routers, switches, etc.) do network packets traverse between the client and the server systems?
- What is the speed of each link separating these systems?
- Does your network equipment use auto-negotiation to set speed and duplex settings?
- Are your network interfaces configured for half-duplex or full-duplex mode?
- Do your switch port settings match the speed and duplex settings of your host interfaces?
- What is the maximum transmission unit (MTU) size of the links between these systems?
- If the links are using different MTU sizes, how are the packets being translated? For example, if the NFS client resides in an FDDI ring and uses an MTU size of 4352 and the NFS server uses a 100BT interface with an MTU size of 1500, how are the 4352 byte packets from the client being fragmented into 1500 byte packets for the server?
- Do packets sent from the client to the server take the same route through the network as the packets sent from the server to the client?
- Are your NFS client and server members of a simple Local Area Network (LAN), such as the example shown in Figure 1.1, where the systems are connected to the same switch?

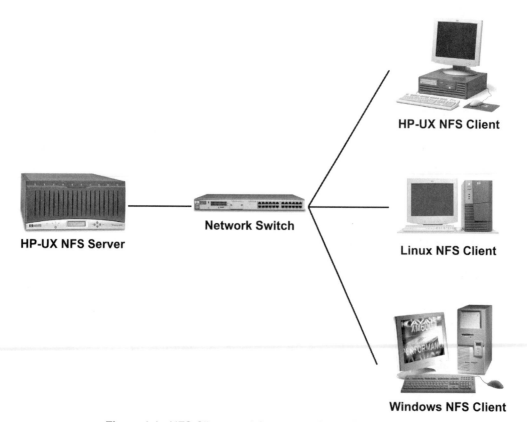

Figure 1.1   NFS Clients and Servers on Same Physical LAN

• Are the systems geographically separated by a Wide Area Network (WAN) such as the example shown in Figure 1.2, where NFS requests and replies must traverse many network switches, routers, and firewalls?

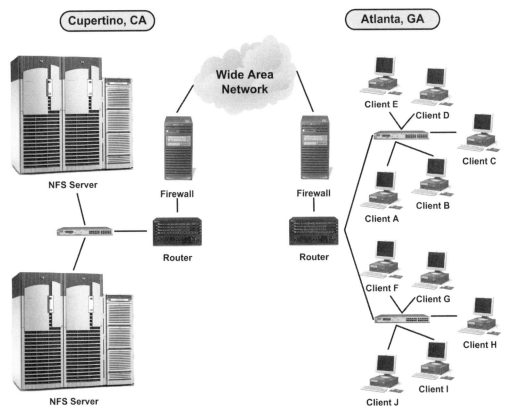

Figure 1.2 NFS Clients and Servers Separated by a WAN

While network administrators should be the best source of knowledge about the layout and capabilities of the underlying network, even they are not always up-to-date on the current state of the network. In many large corporate environments, the physical network is constantly evolving as new equipment replaces old, new backbone technologies replace antiquated technologies, new systems are added to existing networks, new subnets are created, etc. Whenever there is any uncertainty as to the physical layout of the network separating the NFS clients and servers, a network layout analysis should be performed.

Among the best tools available for analyzing network capabilities is the HP OpenView suite of products, such as Network Node Manager.[2] Even without using a full-blown network

2.   For more information about the OpenView product family, visit *http://openview.hp.com*.

management tool such as OpenView, you can still collect a good deal of information about your network topology using tools that ship with HP-UX.

1.1.1 `traceroute(1M)`

The `traceroute(1M)` tool provides a simple means of determining the path through the network taken by packets sent from one system to another. HP's version of `traceroute` is based on the source code originally developed by Van Jacobson. Since `traceroute` is considered "contributed" software, it resides in the `/usr/contrib/bin` directory.

Figure 1.3 shows a sample screen shot of `traceroute` output displaying the physical path taken between a system located in Roseville, CA and a system located in Cupertino, CA. In this example, and the sample shown in Figure 1.4, `traceroute` is run with the "-n" option, instructing `traceroute` to display IP address information for each network hop without performing address-to-hostname translation.[3]

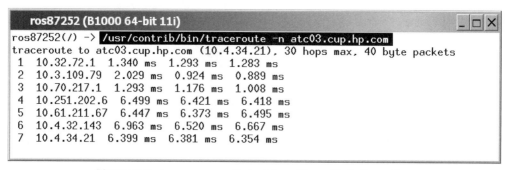

```
ros87252 (B1000 64-bit 11i)                                      _ □ X
ros87252(/) -> /usr/contrib/bin/traceroute -n atc03.cup.hp.com
traceroute to atc03.cup.hp.com (10.4.34.21), 30 hops max, 40 byte packets
 1   10.32.72.1   1.340 ms   1.293 ms   1.283 ms
 2   10.3.109.79  2.029 ms   0.924 ms   0.889 ms
 3   10.70.217.1  1.293 ms   1.176 ms   1.008 ms
 4   10.251.202.6 6.499 ms   6.421 ms   6.418 ms
 5   10.61.211.67 6.447 ms   6.373 ms   6.495 ms
 6   10.4.32.143  6.963 ms   6.520 ms   6.667 ms
 7   10.4.34.21   6.399 ms   6.381 ms   6.354 ms
```

Figure 1.3 `traceroute` Output from Roseville to Cupertino

Figure 1.4 reveals the network path taken by `traceroute` packets sent from the Cupertino system to the Roseville system.

```
atc03 (L2000 64-bit 11i)                                         _ □ X
atc03(/) -> /usr/contrib/bin/traceroute -n ros87252.rose.hp.com
traceroute to ros87252.rose.hp.com (10.32.72.105), 30 hops max, 40 byte packets
 1   10.4.34.1     0.556 ms   0.355 ms   0.339 ms
 2   10.75.208.10  0.259 ms   0.231 ms   0.225 ms
 3   10.61.211.72  0.347 ms   0.420 ms   0.346 ms
 4   10.251.202.5  5.854 ms   5.870 ms   5.910 ms
 5   10.70.216.1   5.695 ms   5.680 ms   5.922 ms
 6   10.43.214.210 6.889 ms   6.466 ms   6.816 ms
 7   10.32.72.105  6.195 ms   6.144 ms   6.128 ms
```

Figure 1.4 `traceroute` Output from Cupertino to Roseville

---

3.   For more information about available traceroute command-line options, refer to the traceroute(1M) man page.

In this example there are six network links separating these two systems (the last line in the `traceroute` output is the actual destination system). The output shows the cumulative latency experienced as the packets transition through the various network links on their way to the final destination. By comparing these two `traceroute` outputs you can see the number of network hops taken in both directions is the same, but the physical path through the network is different in each direction. For example, going to Cupertino the packets went through "10.4.32.143" while on the way to Roseville the packets went through "10.75.208.10." The latencies experienced in both directions appear comparable.

1.1.2 `ping(1M)`

Another tool shipping with HP-UX that can simplify the process of collecting network topology information is `ping(1M)`. Michael Muuss originally developed the `ping` program at the US Army Ballistics Research Lab (BRL) in the early 1980's. It has since become one of the most widely used UNIX networking commands. Most every UNIX administrator has used `ping` at one time or another to quickly verify connectivity between two network nodes. When used with the "`-o`" option, `ping` inserts an IP Record Route[4] option into its outgoing packets, allowing `ping` to track and display the physical network path taken between two nodes.

Figure 1.5 shows the "`ping -o`" command displaying the network path taken by packets sent between the same systems used in the earlier `traceroute` example. The "`-n 1`" option was also used to instruct `ping` to only send a single packet to the remote system.[5]

```
ros87252 (B1000 64-bit 11i)                              _ □ X
ros87252(/) -> ping -o atc03.cup.hp.com -n 1
PING atc03.cup.hp.com: 64 byte packets
64 bytes from 10.4.34.21: icmp_seq=0. time=10. ms

----atc03.cup.hp.com PING Statistics----
1 packets transmitted, 1 packets received, 0% packet loss
round-trip (ms)  min/avg/max = 10/10/10
1 packets sent via:
        10.43.214.210
        10.70.217.1
        10.251.202.5
        10.61.211.67
        10.75.208.10
        10.4.34.1
        10.4.34.21
```

Figure 1.5 `ping -o` between Roseville and Cupertino Systems

---

4.   Many network hardware vendors allow the IP Record Route feature to be disabled, effectively making these hops *invisible* to the "ping -o" command.

5.   For more information about available ping command-line options, refer to the ping(1M) man page.

Comparing this output against the `traceroute` screen shot in Figure 1.3, you can see that the `ping` packet took the same number of hops to get from Roseville to Cupertino as the `traceroute` packet. However, the `ping` traffic took a different route through the HP network than the `traceroute` traffic. These differences in the network path are most likely the result of dynamic routing tables kept in the routers and bridges used in corporate network backbone.

Unlike `traceroute`, `ping` does not report the individual latencies experienced at each location in the topology. While this information may not be as useful as the `traceroute` output, it provides an easy way of determining the network topology separating two systems.

Once you've determined the physical layout of the network separating your NFS clients and servers, there are several other questions to ask yourself:

- Does the layout make sense to you? In other words, is the network laid out as you expected or were you surprised by what `traceroute` and `ping` revealed?
- Did the physical layout change recently? If so, why?
- Are packets taking the most efficient path through the network? If not, can you force them to take the most efficient path?
- Can any of the network hops separating the clients and servers be eliminated?

If there is any way to optimize the physical layout of the network (i.e. minimize the number of network hops and use the most efficient route between the systems) it can help NFS performance tremendously.

1.2 Measure Network Throughput Capabilities

Once the layout of the physical network is understood, the next step in validating your network is to measure the throughput of the connection separating the client and server. Generally speaking, the faster your network throughput, the better your NFS performance will be.

When testing the performance of the network for NFS purposes, it is essential to eliminate the NFS layer from consideration by simply testing the network transport layer using non-NFS protocols. If a network throughput problem exists between an NFS client and server, the problem would likely affect any network-based application, not just NFS.[6] It is also important to measure the throughput going in both directions (i.e. client to server, server to client) to make sure the performance is comparable. Similarly, when attempting to characterize network throughput, it is important to eliminate any influence of the local filesystems. It is therefore necessary to select measurement tools that are not dependent upon NFS or filesystem resources.

Several tools exist to help system and network administrators measure the throughput of their network connections. Two of the more prominent tools are `ttcp(1)` and netperf.

---

6.   A minor packet loss problem may not affect TCP/IP applications such as FTP or NFS/TCP filesystems, but may cause problems for NFS/UDP filesystems. For a detailed explanation of how packet loss affects NFS/UDP and NFS/TCP filesystems differently, refer to Section 10.3 "Managing Retransmissions and Timeouts."

1.2.1 `ttcp(1)`

`ttcp(1)` is a simple, lightweight program that measures the throughput of any network connection without relying on the filesystem layer. It can generate either UDP or TCP traffic and the packet size is adjustable, allowing it to simulate the behavior of different applications.

Mike Muuss (the author of the `ping` command) and Terry Slattery, of the US Army Bal-listics Research Lab (BRL), developed the `ttcp` (Test TCP Connection) program in the early 1980's. The program now resides in the public domain and is freely available to download from *http://ftp.arl.mil/ftp/pub/ttcp*. The `ttcp` man page is also available from this site, which docu-ments the many available command-line arguments.

A sample `ttcp` session is shown in Figure 1.6.

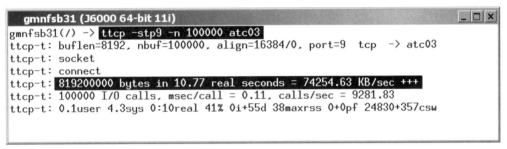

Figure 1.6 `ttcp` Sending TCP Traffic from Client to Server

In this example, `ttcp` is run on the NFS client system and sends TCP/IP traffic to the NFS server's discard port (9) across a Gigabit Ethernet connection. This output shows the client can send over 72MB/sec. on this link. Figure 1.7 shows the server using `ttcp` to send TCP/IP traffic back to the client across the same link and getting roughly the same throughput.

```
atc03 (L2000 64-bit 11i)                                        _ □ x
atc03(/) -> ttcp -stp9 -n 100000 gmnfsb31
ttcp-t: buflen=8192, nbuf=100000, align=16384/0, port=9  tcp  -> gmnfsb31
ttcp-t: socket
ttcp-t: connect
ttcp-t: 819200000 bytes in 10.97 real seconds = 72914.02 KB/sec +++
ttcp-t: 100000 I/O calls, msec/call = 0.11, calls/sec = 9114.25
ttcp-t: 0.1user 4.4sys 0:10real 42% 0i+45d 38maxrss 0+0pf 22997+338csw
```

Figure 1.7 `ttcp` Sending TCP Traffic from Server to Client

The system or network administrator now has a fairly good idea what the capabilities are of the network link between these two systems. Of course, this does not imply that the NFS throughput should be 72-73MB/sec. across this link, since the NFS protocol relies much more on CPU, filesystem, and memory resources than `ttcp` does.

1.2.2 netperf

netperf is a benchmark utility that can measure the performance of many different types of networks. It provides tests for both unidirectional throughput and end-to-end latency. Like ttcp, netperf measures throughput without relying on any filesystem resources. However, it is a far more sophisticated network-measuring tool, compared to ttcp.

Rick Jones, of HP's Infrastructure Solutions and Partners group, developed netperf in 1991 and he has continued to add new features and capabilities to the program as new networking technologies became available. The best source of information is the official netperf web site: *http://netperf.org*. The latest version of the source code is available at the following location: *ftp://ftp.cup.hp.com/dist/networking/benchmarks/netperf*.

Figure 1.8 shows the screen output of netperf sending TCP and UDP data from system "atc03.cup.hp.com" (Cupertino, CA) to three different network destinations:

- Gigabit Ethernet connection to "atc01.cup.hp.com" (Cupertino, CA)
- 100Mb Ethernet connection to "atc01.cup.hp.com" (Cupertino, CA)
- WAN connection to "ros87252.rose.hp.com" (Roseville, CA)

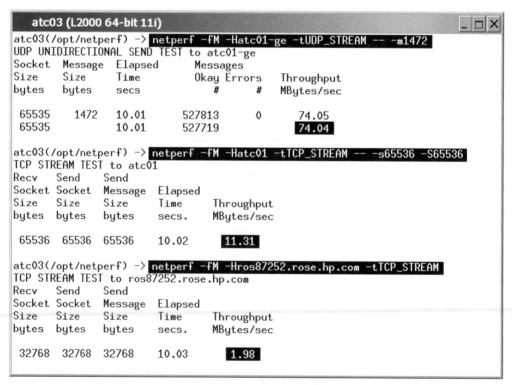

Figure 1.8 netperf Throughput from Different Network Connections

In this example, the UDP traffic sent over a Gigabit Ethernet connection to a neighbor system in Cupertino yielded a throughput of over 74 MB/sec. Sending TCP traffic to the same Cupertino-based system over a 100BT link yielded over 11MB/sec. Finally, sending TCP traffic across HP's network from Cupertino to Roseville (via the six hops identified earlier with `ping` and `traceroute`) yielded just under 2 MB/sec.

Also evident from this example is the fact that netperf has a myriad of command-line options, both for the netperf command itself and for the specific type of test you are performing. Be sure to read the netperf manual, available at *ftp://ftp.cup.hp.com/dist/networking/benchmarks/netperf*, very carefully to understand which options are available and their proper usage, as the throughput numbers can vary greatly depending upon how the tests are run.

Just as with the `ttcp` example earlier, netperf numbers do not directly translate into the expected NFS throughput values. However, they do provide a good means of estimating the upper bounds of a given network connection's bandwidth.

1.3 Network Troubleshooting Tools

At this point, you should be very familiar with the network topology separating the NFS client and server, and have verified that IP packets are taking the appropriate route through the network in both directions. If you have not yet performed these critical steps, refer to the earlier Section 1.1 "Analyze Network Layout" for instructions on how to collect this information. After running network throughput tests using the tools described in Section 1.2 "Measure Network Throughput Capabilities," if you believe your network is experiencing a performance throughput issue then it is time to troubleshoot the network itself.

 KEY IDEA — Common Causes of Dropped Network Packets

In many cases, network throughput problems are caused by packets being dropped somewhere on the network, either by the NFS client or server system itself or at some intermediate point in the network separating the two systems. Some of the more common reasons network packets are dropped include:

- Defective hardware (i.e. network interface cards, cables, switch ports, etc.)
- Mismatching configuration settings between interface cards and switch equipment. The most common configuration issue is where one side of a connection is set to half-duplex and the other side to full-duplex, causing "late" collisions to be logged on the half-duplex side and FCS or CRC errors logged on the full-duplex side.[a]
- Network interconnect device buffer memory exhaustion (described in Section 10.4)
- UDP socket overflows occurring on the NFS server, indicating that not enough daemons are running to handle the inbound requests for a specific port

---

a.   The lanadmin(1M) tool, described in Section 1.3.5, displays duplex settings and reports any link-level errors.

The goal of this phase of the investigation is to determine if the network throughput problem is affecting all IP traffic or only NFS. In some cases, the only tools that can detect these types of problems are external analyzers and reporting tools specific to your network hardware. HP does provide a number of software-based tools to help detect and analyze network problems. Two frequently used network troubleshooting tools are netstat(1) and lanadmin(1M).

1.3.1 netstat -s

The netstat(1) command can be used to display statistics for network interfaces and protocols, it can list active network connections, print routing tables, etc. When executed with the "-s" option, netstat returns a complete list of all network transport statistics (TCP, UDP, IP, ICMP, and IGMP) arranged by protocol.

A portion of "netstat -s" output is shown in Figure 1.9 and Figure 1.10. These two screen shots illustrate how this single command returns an enormous amount of information about the underlying network protocols, including the number of TCP packets sent and received, the number of UDP socket overflows and checksum failures that occurred, etc. Also readily available are statistics such as the total number of IP packets received, the ICMP port unreachable and source quench messages generated, etc. All of this information can be extremely useful when troubleshooting a network or protocol layer problem.

Using netstat and diff to troubleshoot a network problem   Listed below is an example of how to use the "netstat -s" command to help determine if packets are being lost somewhere in your network The <u>underlined</u> steps are the commands you type.

1. Initialize the "before" file with the current date and time.
   # <u>date > netstat.before</u>

2. Collect a baseline set of netstat -s statistics on both the NFS client and server and append the output to the "before" file created in step 1.
   # <u>netstat -s >> netstat.before</u>

3. Perform a test that exhibits the performance problem using the TCP protocol (such as ttcp or netperf).
   # <u>ttcp -stp9 -n 100000 server</u>

4. Initialize the "after" file with the current date and time.
   # <u>date > netstat.after</u>

5. Collect a second set of netstat -s statistics on both the NFS client and server and append the output to the "after" file created in step 4.
   # <u>netstat -s >> netstat.after</u>

6. Locate any differences between the "before" and "after" netstat outputs to identify which statistics were incrementing during the test.
   # <u>diff netstat.before netstat.after</u>

An example of the type of output returned by diff(1) from such an exercise is shown in Figure 1.11. Some of the TCP statistics to monitor are "data packets retransmitted," "completely duplicate packets," and "segments discarded for bad checksum." If these statistics are steadily increasing over time it would indicate that packet loss is occurring somewhere in the network or that a possible network hardware problem is causing TCP checksum failures.

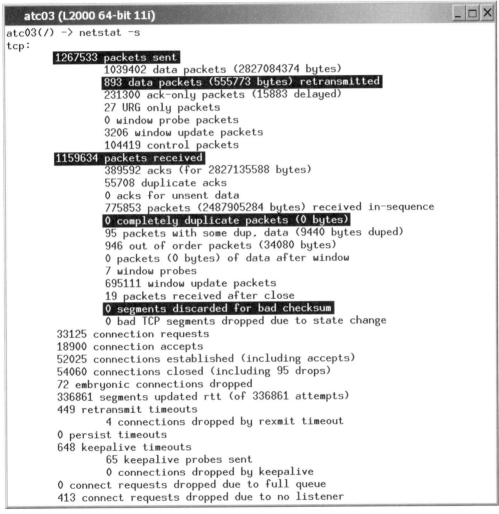

Figure 1.9 netstat -s Output Showing TCP Statistics

Also of concern would be an increasing number of UDP "bad checksums," as this could indicate that an IP level device in the network (perhaps a router performing IP fragmentation) is not correctly fragmenting UDP datagrams as it forwards them. These datagrams would be discarded by the receiving system, forcing the sending system to re-send this data. UDP "socket overflows" usually indicates that an application, such as NFS, is receiving requests on a particular UDP socket faster than it can process them, and consequently discarding requests.[7]

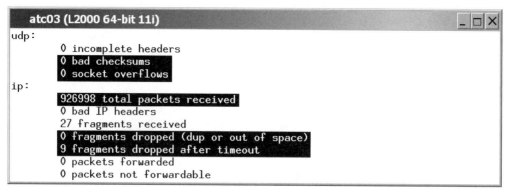

Figure 1.10 `netstat -s` Output Including UDP and IP Statistics

Of the IP statistics reported, "fragments dropped" and "fragments dropped after timeout" would indicate packet loss is occurring in the network.

```
ros87252 (B1000 64-bit 11.0)                                        _ □ ×
ros87252(/) -> diff netstat.before netstat.after
1c1
< Mon Sep 17 14:13:00 PDT 2001
---
> Mon Sep 17 14:15:28 PDT 2001
3,4c3,4
<         22710935 packets sent
<              11564543 data packets (948483097 bytes)
---
>         23311806 packets sent
>              12165046 data packets (1767723069 bytes)
6c6
<              11146389 ack-only packets (10980235 delayed)
---
>              11146757 ack-only packets (10980590 delayed)
10,11c10,11
<         22737918 packets received
<              11385967 acks (for 948550913 bytes)
---
>         22795453 packets received
>              11443047 acks (for 1767790888 bytes)
```

Figure 1.11 Comparing "before" and "after" `netstat` Outputs

---

7.   The effect of UDP socket overflows on NFS performance is discussed in greater detail in Chapter 4.

Using `netstat` and `beforeafter` to troubleshoot a network problem

Although the `diff(1)` procedure does work for locating differences in `netstat` outputs, interpreting `diff` output can be a bit cumbersome. Not only do you have to manually subtract the "after" numbers from the "before" numbers, since the `diff` output removes the subsystem header information lines, you need to carefully confirm which statistics you are interpreting. For example, `netstat` returns "# packets received" under the TCP heading and "# total packets received" under the IP heading. Confusing these two values could lead to incorrect conclusions about the health of your network.

To simplify this procedure of interpreting multiple sets of `netstat` output, HP developed a tool called `beforeafter`. This program takes two `netstat -s` output files and compares them against each other. The output from `beforeafter` looks identical to `netstat -s` output except that the statistics represent only the differences between the "before" and "after" files. The tool is available at: *ftp://ftp.cup.hp.com/dist/networking/tools/beforeafter.tar.gz.*

The procedure for using the `beforeafter` tool is the same as the `diff` method outlined earlier, with the exception of step 6. Instead of using the `diff` command to compare the files, the `beforeafter` tool should be used as follows:

```
# beforeafter netstat.before netstat.after
```

Figure 1.12 contains an example of the `beforeafter` output. Notice the output looks identical to that of "`netstat -s`"; however the statistics reported are not cumulative totals but instead represent the differences between the "before" and "after" files.

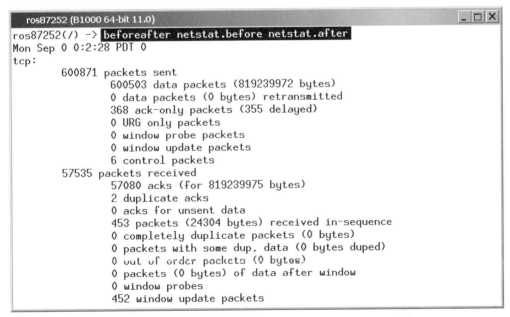

Figure 1.12 `beforeafter` Comparing `netstat -s` Statistics

The `beforeafter` tool even calculates the difference in wall-clock times between the date contained in the "before" and "after" files. Looking at the date line in Figure 1.12 you can see that the "after" file was collected 2 minutes and 28 seconds after the "before" file. The test caused this system to send 600503 packets containing 819239972 bytes of data, and receive 57535 packets containing acknowledgement packets for 819239975 bytes.

Although the `diff` output and the `beforeafter` output reveal the same information, locating and quantifying the key statistics is much easier using the `beforeafter` tool.

1.3.2 `netstat -p <protocol>`

Once you have identified a subset of the `netstat -s` output that is of particular interest, you can limit the statistical output to a single protocol by using the "`-p <protocol>`" syntax. An example is shown in Figure 1.13. Confining the output to a single protocol can greatly simplify the process of identifying specific protocol-related problems compared to analyzing screens full of "`netstat -s`" output.

Figure 1.13 `netstat -p` Output

1.3.3 `netstat -r`

As discussed earlier in the "Analyze Network Layout" section, it is critical to understand the path NFS packets take through the network as they move between the client and server. We saw how utilities such as `traceroute` and "`ping -o`" display the various hops taken by packets going between two network nodes. If the `traceroute` or "`ping -o`" output reveals that packets are not taking the route you expect them to, you should verify the routing tables on both the client and server to make sure they are correct. Ensuring the accuracy of the routing tables is especially important on systems with multiple network interfaces, where outbound packets potentially have several paths to their final destination.

On HP systems, the "`netstat -r`" command is used to display the routing tables. Figure 1.14 shows an example of this. In this example, the "`-n`" (do not resolve IP addresses to hostnames) and "`-v`" (verbose) options were used. Included in the output is the interface name associated with each IP address, as well as the PMTU (Path Maximum Transmission Unit) size for each interface. The MTU information can be very useful in environments where the NFS client and server are on different physical networks and packet fragmentation or translation needs to occur (for example FDDI to Ethernet).

```
atc03 (L2000 64-bit 11i)                                          _ □ ×
atc03(/) -> netstat -rnv
Routing tables
Dest/Netmask              Gateway        Flags  Refs Interface  Pmtu
127.0.0.1/255.255.255.255    127.0.0.1      UH     0   lo0       4136
10.4.64.26/255.255.255.255   10.4.64.26     UH     0   lan0      4136
192.65.5.0/255.255.255.0     192.65.5.43    U      2   lan6      1500
192.65.6.0/255.255.255.0     192.65.6.43    U      2   lan8      1500
10.4.64.0/255.255.248.0      10.4.64.26     U      2   lan0      1500
127.0.0.0/255.0.0.0          127.0.0.1      U      0   lo0          0
default/0.0.0.0              10.4.64.100    UG     0   lan0         0
```

Figure 1.14 `netstat -r` Displaying Network Routing Tables

1.3.4 `netstat -i`

In large customer environments, particularly those where HP's MC/ServiceGuard[8] product is used, it is not uncommon for NFS client and server systems to have multiple network paths to each other for redundancy reasons. In some cases the primary and backup interfaces are not equivalent in terms of their bandwidth capabilities. For example, the systems might use a Gigabit Ethernet interface as their primary connection and have a 100BT interface available as a backup connection. In these environments, sufficient care must be taken when configuring the NFS mount points to ensure that the traffic flows across the faster interface whenever possible. However, even with careful preparation, there is always a possibility that NFS traffic sent between the clients and servers will mistakenly use the slower interface.

A quick and easy way to verify which interface the majority of network traffic is using is to issue the "`netstat -i`" command and examine the inbound and outbound packet counts for all configured interfaces. Figure 1.15 provides an example of this output.

```
atc03 (L2000 64-bit 11i)                                          _ □ ×
atc03(/) -> netstat -in
Name      Mtu Network        Address            Ipkts       Opkts
lan8     1500 192.65.6.0     192.65.6.43     19022175    30668148
lan0     1500 10.4.64.0      10.4.64.26       2432573    58689548
lo0      4136 127.0.0.0      127.0.0.1        6145151     6145151
lan6     1500 192.65.5.0     192.65.5.43        98613       17180
```

Figure 1.15 `netstat -in` Output

By monitoring the inbound and outbound packet rates of the interfaces, you can quickly determine if an unusually high amount of network traffic is using what should be an "idle" or "backup" interface. If this appears to be happening, a network trace can be taken to determine the hostnames of the remote systems that are sending requests to the slower interface.

---

8.   For more information about HP's MC/ServiceGuard product or configuring your servers for Highly Available
     NFS access, visit the HP-UX High Availability web site: *http://hp.com/go/ha*.

1.3.5 `lanadmin(1M)`

As stated earlier, dropped packets on the network can occur if there are problems with the network interface cards, cables, or connectors. While many hardware-based problems can only be detected and identified with external analyzers, HP-UX provides several software-based tools to help monitor the health of the interfaces. The commands available for checking the state of any specific interface card will vary based on interface type (i.e. FDDI, Gigabit Ethernet, etc.). However, the `lanadmin(1M)` utility applies to all network links and it should be queried first.

The `lanadmin` command allows a system administrator to display many useful statistics kept by the LAN driver subsystem, regardless of the interface type. Figure 1.16 shows a sample screen output returned by `lanadmin`.

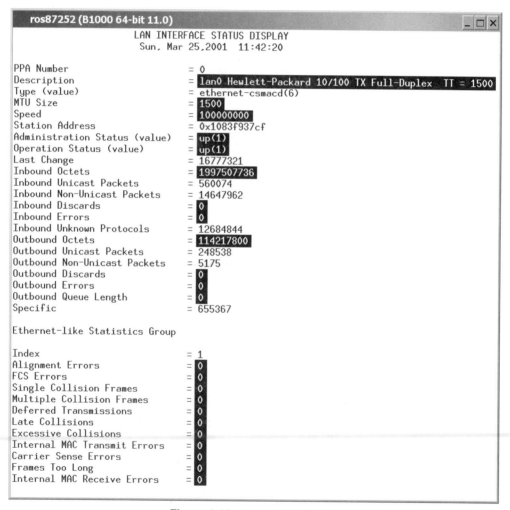

```
ros87252 (B1000 64-bit 11.0)                                              _ □ ×
                         LAN INTERFACE STATUS DISPLAY
                         Sun, Mar 25,2001  11:42:20

PPA Number                        = 0
Description                       = lan0 Hewlett-Packard 10/100 TX Full-Duplex  TT = 1500
Type (value)                      = ethernet-csmacd(6)
MTU Size                          = 1500
Speed                             = 100000000
Station Address                   = 0x1083f937cf
Administration Status (value)     = up(1)
Operation Status (value)          = up(1)
Last Change                       = 16777321
Inbound Octets                    = 1997507736
Inbound Unicast Packets           = 560074
Inbound Non-Unicast Packets       = 14647962
Inbound Discards                  = 0
Inbound Errors                    = 0
Inbound Unknown Protocols         = 12684844
Outbound Octets                   = 114217800
Outbound Unicast Packets          = 248538
Outbound Non-Unicast Packets      = 5175
Outbound Discards                 = 0
Outbound Errors                   = 0
Outbound Queue Length             = 0
Specific                          = 655367

Ethernet-like Statistics Group

Index                             = 1
Alignment Errors                  = 0
FCS Errors                        = 0
Single Collision Frames           = 0
Multiple Collision Frames         = 0
Deferred Transmissions            = 0
Late Collisions                   = 0
Excessive Collisions              = 0
Internal MAC Transmit Errors      = 0
Carrier Sense Errors              = 0
Frames Too Long                   = 0
Internal MAC Receive Errors       = 0
```

Figure 1.16 `lanadmin` Output

By reviewing this information you can learn a great deal about how the queried interface is configured and whether it has been logging any errors at the driver layer. For example, the output shown in Figure 1.16 indicates that this interface card is a 10/100BT card known to the system as device "lan0," the card is enabled and active, it is running at a speed of 100 Mbits/second with an MTU size of 1500, and it is currently configured to run in full-duplex mode. In some cases, this information alone can be enough to determine the cause of a network performance problem (i.e. in the case where LAN interfaces and network switch configurations don't match with regards to speed and duplex settings).

Also available in the `lanadmin` output are various error counts, collision rates, total inbound and outbound packet counts, etc. By monitoring these counters you can, with the assistance of an HP support representative, try to make a qualified determination as to whether a hardware problem exists somewhere in your network. When software-based analysis tools fail to identify the problem, external tools can be used to provide the definitive view of the traffic patterns on the network and to isolate a device that is losing packets.

 KEY IDEA — The Importance of Patching LAN, Transport, and Network Drivers

HP continually strives to improve the quality of HP-UX by distributing software patches containing both defect fixes and functionality enhancements. Many of these fixes and enhancements can significantly improve the performance and behavior of critical system components, such as LAN Common, the Network Transports (TCP, UDP, IP), and the various Network Link Driver subsystems (100BT, 1000BT, FDDI, Token Ring, etc.).

Since NFS relies heavily upon the stability and performance of the network, it is *strongly* recommended that the latest LAN, Transport, and network link driver patches be installed on every HP-UX system in order to take advantage of these improvements. Contact HP support to obtain a current set of patches for your specific operating system. You can also generate a current patch list using the tools available at HP's IT Resource Center: *http://itrc.hp.com*.

For a detailed discussion on the importance of keeping your HP-UX NFS client and server systems patched with current code, refer to Appendix B "Patching Considerations."

Local Filesystem Considerations

The performance of local filesystems, both on the NFS client and server, can have just as big an influence on overall NFS performance as the underlying network. This should come as no surprise since NFS is an acronym for "Network File System." Therefore, when faced with an NFS performance issue, it is a good idea to perform some "sanity checks" on the underlying filesystems involved before launching into a detailed investigation into a specific area of NFS.

This chapter describes a recommended methodology and set of tools available for understanding the physical layout of your filesystems, measuring their throughput capabilities, and a set of recommendations for configuring and maintaining your filesystems. What will not be covered are the numerous available disk and filesystem technologies, such as disk striping, RAID, disk arrays, etc. NFS servers are allowed to export any local filesystems, and it typically performs better with a faster underlying disk subsystem.[1]

2.1 Analyze Filesystem Layout

In some cases the layout of the directory hierarchy and the directory contents on the NFS server can greatly affect performance. In particular, directory reading and traversal speeds can be greatly influenced by the *contents* of the directories being searched.

2.1.1 Number of Files in the Directory

Most applications that reference files and directories will at some point need to obtain the list of files contained in a directory. Some applications retrieve and display directory contents

---

1.   There is a wealth of information about the latest and greatest filesystem technologies available from HP's IT Resource Center: *http://itrc.hp.com*, and HP's online documentation repository: *http://docs.hp.com*.

more frequently than others. For example, most applications that allow you to selectively open files via a menu choice like "File > Open" (including the application used to develop this book) will typically display the contents of the current working directory. As the user moves up or down in the directory hierarchy, the contents of the parent and sub-directories are retrieved in order to build and update the display listing. Figure 2.1 shows a typical "Open File" menu.

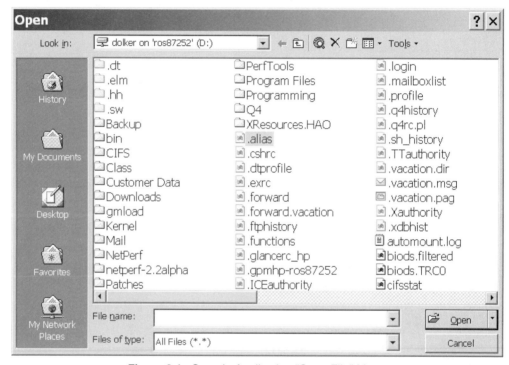

Figure 2.1   Sample Application "Open File" Menu

Reading Directories via NFS   When an application requests the directory contents of an NFS mounted directory, the client will issue either a READDIR or READDIRPLUS request to retrieve this information.[2] If the application requesting the directory contents also requires the attributes associated with each file in order to build its display, the NFS client could potentially issue a LOOKUP request for each file in the directory.[3] In these situations, it is easy to see how a directory containing hundreds, or even thousands, of files could take a long time to process.

---

2.   The difference between READDIR and READDIRPLUS, as well as many other differences between NFS Version 2 and Version 3, are explained in detail in Chapter 9.

3.   This would only be necessary if the client retrieved the original directory contents via the READDIR call, since READDIRPLUS retrieves attribute information automatically.

Even when an application is not requesting the full contents of a directory, the overhead involved in accessing a file in an NFS mounted directory can be significantly affected based on the number of files in the directory, since the server needs to search through the directory contents to identify the file being accessed.

KEY IDEA — Balance Directory Layout and Distribute Busy Directories

Whenever possible, you should try to "balance" the directory hierarchy of your filesystems to achieve a reasonable compromise between the number of directories and the number of files in those directories. At the same time, it is recommended that heavily-accessed directories be distributed across several different filesystems on the server, so that the server can potentially access several of these frequently referenced directories in parallel.

The goals of this exercise are to minimize the number of NFS calls required by the client to retrieve the directory contents, to arrange the files in such a way as to reduce the number of directories searched by a user during a typical operation, and to spread the directory access load across multiple filesystems to avoid overloading a single filesystem. For example, instead of using a single directory containing 20,000 files, create 20 directories with 1000 files each and distribute these 20 directories across multiple physical filesystems.

Some investigation and analysis of file usage patterns may be required to optimally determine which files should be grouped together in each newly created directory.

Certain applications are designed with built-in restrictions on where data files can reside. These restrictions can limit the amount of flexibility a system administrator has to "balance" and distribute the directory hierarchy on an NFS server. Be sure to check with your application provider if you have any concerns about supported directory configurations before re-distributing the files used by an application.

Large Directory Example   Perhaps the best way to appreciate the potential effect of reading large directories over NFS is by examining a real customer-reported example. This example will be referenced throughout the book since it encompasses several factors that can influence NFS performance, including:

- How the number of files residing in a directory can dramatically influence the performance of reading the directory via NFS.
- The influence of kernel parameters such as *ninode* and *ncsize* on NFS performance, and the importance of properly sizing all kernel parameters (discussed in detail in Chapter 12).
- How the design of the buffer cache memory subsystem has been enhanced in HP-UX 11i, and the importance of allocating an appropriate amount of memory to the buffer cache on NFS client and server systems (discussed in detail in Chapter 11).

NFS Performance Example: Reading a Large Directory

Problem: Soon after HP-UX 11.0 shipped, a customer reported that issuing an "ls -l" command in an NFS-mounted directory containing more than 20,000 files took approximately 30 minutes to complete and consumed 98% of the client's CPU resources.

The customer's NFS client system was configured as follows:

- V-Class system with 12GB of physical memory installed
- kernel variable *ninode* set to 2000
- kernel variable *dbc_min_pct* set to 3 (368MB), *dbc_max_pct* set to 10 (1.2GB)

Symptom: After changing the buffer cache configuration to only use 8MB of memory (as opposed to 1.2GB), an "ls -l" command in the same directory completed in 90 seconds.

Question: Why would a simple "ls -l" command issued in a large NFS-mounted directory take so long to complete and consume huge amounts of system resources, and why would the size of the client's buffer cache make such a significant difference?

Answer: When reading an NFS-mounted directory, a *rnode* structure must be allocated for every entry in the directory. The number of rnode entries available on the system can be sized directly via the *ncsize* kernel variable (see Section 12.1.17 "ncsize") or via the *ninode* variable (see Section 12.1.20 "ninode"). Once all of the available rnodes have been used, the system must begin reusing existing rnodes. In order to reuse an rnode, the system must first invalidate all memory pages associated with that rnode from the buffer cache.

The HP-UX 11.0 NFS client kernel does not keep track of which pages in buffer cache are associated with each file, requiring the client to perform a *serial* search of the entire buffer cache looking for pages associated with the existing rnode to invalidate. Fortunately, the buffer cache subsystem was redesigned in HP-UX 11i to keep track of the memory pages associated with NFS files on a per-file basis.

On an NFS client system configured with 2000 rnode entries, whose application is traversing an NFS-mounted directory containing 20,000+ files, the kernel will need to reuse rnodes thousands of times, involving thousands of serial buffer cache searches. With a large buffer cache configured, these serial searches can consume high amounts of CPU resources and take a long time to complete.

Solutions: There are many potential solutions to this problem:

- Reduce the number of files in the NFS-mounted directory.
- Configure a relatively small buffer cache on HP-UX 11.0 NFS clients.
- Configure the *ncsize* or *ninode* kernel variables so that enough rnode structures are allocated to avoid having the client need to frequently reuse them.
- Upgrade to HP-UX 11i where the buffer cache subsystem has been redesigned.

2.1.2 The Use of Symbolic Links in the Directory

As stated in the previous section, one of the goals when designing the directory hierarchy on your NFS server is to minimize the number of NFS calls the client needs to issue when retrieving the contents of frequently accessed directories. With this in mind, it should be pointed out that the use of symbolic links could also negatively affect the overall performance of NFS directory searching and traversal.

Earlier we learned how the NFS client uses either a combination of READDIR and LOOKUP calls or READDIRPLUS calls to retrieve the server's directory contents. If a symbolic link is encountered in the directory, the client needs to make an additional call — READLINK — to resolve the contents of the link. In directories containing few symbolic links, the performance effects of the additional READLINK calls should be negligible; however, in directories containing hundreds of links the effect can be noticeable. While the need for symbolic links is genuine in some situations, their use should be avoided whenever possible.

Symbolic links referencing Automounter-managed filesystems   When symbolic links are used, special care should be taken to ensure that they do not point to files residing in directories managed by an automounter (regardless of whether the legacy automounter or AutoFS is used).[4] While this is a valid configuration, it can dramatically hinder the performance of directory retrieval operations — especially in the case where the automounter must be invoked to mount the target filesystem in order for the symbolic link to be resolved. Again, this is not an invalid configuration, just one to be avoided whenever possible.

2.2   Measure Filesystem Throughput Capabilities

Once the layout of the NFS server's filesystems has been analyzed and optimized wherever possible, the next step in validating your disk subsystems is to measure the throughput of the client's and server's local filesystems. Generally speaking, the faster your underlying disk subsystems are, the better your NFS performance will be.

It is important to measure the local filesystem capabilities of both the client and the server, since both systems are usually involved in NFS activities (i.e. reading from the server's filesystem and writing to the client's filesystem or vice versa). In most cases, the performance of the NFS server's filesystem is far more important to validate, as its performance can affect the throughput of all NFS clients that mount the filesystem. However, if the client's filesystem performance is poor, it too can negatively affect overall NFS throughput.

When assessing the throughput capabilities of a filesystem, an approach similar to the network testing methodology described in Section 1.2 should be used, where NFS is removed from consideration. If a filesystem throughput problem exists on the NFS client or server, the problem should affect any I/O traffic, not just NFS. Therefore, any characterization of the filesystems should be done with tools that do not rely upon NFS, or invoke NFS in any way.

---

4.   The differences between the legacy automounter and AutoFS are explained in Chapter 7.

In addition, the testing utilities should allow the administrator to isolate one type of filesystem I/O at a time. In other words, read throughput should be tested separately from write throughput. Finally, the utilities should not require any filesystem resources while running, as this could affect the results (i.e. don't test filesystem *write* performance with a test that *reads* from a filesystem). Two programs that meet these qualifications are iozone and dd(1).

2.2.1 iozone

iozone is one of the more sophisticated filesystem performance benchmark utilities available. It can perform a wide variety of I/O operations, including: read, re-read, write, re-write, random read, random write, etc. It also has many advanced capabilities, such as testing with different record lengths, locking the target file during reads and writes, unmounting and re-mounting filesystems between tests, etc. It can even generate the test results in Microsoft Excel format to simplify graphing the results. Don Capps, of HP's Technical Computing Division, is one of the authors of iozone.

Figure 2.2 shows a sample output of the iozone utility performing a series of I/O tests against a local VxFS (Veritas File System) filesystem. This output illustrates how a single iozone command can generate over 1600 I/O test results.

```
atc03 (L2000 64-bit 11i)                                                              _ □ ×
atc03(/) -> iozone -a -f /export/testfile -b results.xls
     Iozone: Performance Test of File I/O
             Version $Revision: 3.49 $
             Compiled for 64 bit mode.

     Contributors:William Norcott, Don Capps, Isom Crawford, Kirby Collins
                  Al Slater, Scott Rhine, Mike Wisner, Ken Goss
                  Steve Landherr, Brad Smith, Mark Kelly, Dr. Alain CYR.

     Run began: Thu Mar 29 18:11:04 2001

     Auto Mode
     Time Resolution = 0.000004 seconds.
     Processor cache size set to 1024 Kbytes.
     Processor cache line size set to 32 bytes.
     File stride size set to 17 * record size.
```

KB	reclen	write	rewrite	read	reread	random read	random write	bkwd read	record rewrite	stride read	fwrite	frewrite	fread	freread
64	4	6661	120066	259051	397550	230175	216266	216966	168856	283242	82047	118529	149195	261194
64	8	35146	148823	254991	640316	374270	340341	310788	219898	438460	97871	143492	234395	383083
64	16	35714	146428	318533	659996	552083	524572	378759	289661	592281	90788	140378	257067	474080
64	32	32097	152414	353566	928126	704143	744159	516000	274692	687903	137961	150239	274692	582008
64	64	36384	154209	365604	1049712	770872	186578	347839	101421	552083	106322	143492	156867	447599
128	4	47640	148563	239704	378685	247095	216985	224142	203806	262821	84650	113979	166228	237898
128	8	51780	138521	369943	595383	439977	310649	329020	309217	505898	91628	133062	252975	347889
128	16	51467	137774	358577	603752	586921	606823	428221	406343	649789	122609	140958	274092	426689
128	32	53243	143808	385482	766714	722841	699303	472297	412906	795101	129562	147280	244730	475855
128	64	57605	152749	254474	831426	780083	26919	475855	27158	710877	124745	164119	249044	544923
128	128	56089	153843	405117	991959	883414	194820	490417	119179	482917	118731	147807	143023	467159
256	4	57346	116366	248279	259626	227766	216951	200466	230628	228980	100747	118793	182091	222596
256	8	69114	142695	352598	504999	382697	387321	331174	363644	371058	119288	137119	268353	364632
256	16	73818	141045	373186	538966	555271	551705	415579	502988	668280	109730	140198	290261	423863
256	32	77038	148497	409633	651454	719076	766289	517161	557723	850675	138373	148404	304761	473176
256	64	77718	146962	334163	710982	731320	28011	388442	16558	785345	126289	159398	274985	444388
256	128	82076	161011	439837	828362	897985	27678	556567	33543	780492	153102	165797	259375	494191
256	256	17435	17066	41789	72541	72314	16923	72706	21822	73269	17050	17042	20964	296636
512	4	73299	115862	238470	289761	221647	217505	211143	241054	231879	103186	118271	179207	199067
512	8	91640	144507	332262	425942	362094	374535	280232	405704	379801	132985	144104	262296	319793
512	16	81412	143134	349484	442531	533374	484844	392612	543498	431332	130878	128836	272913	360817
512	32	92319	152881	381793	533838	499040	490436	460021	702314	879855	142144	152653	304576	423840
512	64	95504	156765	402850	576625	745337	36802	470143	14746	937674	143015	157634	292404	350425
512	128	93481	150365	329458	500028	666667	50151	444455	19066	829713	139817	152474	255493	349484
512	256	21199	21769	68412	92385	90476	21756	91576	30430	91231	19034	19248	34015	295279
512	512	18932	19814	69367	85877	86036	19765	85848	22737	85518	19622	19827	21625	143858
1024	4	84314	115939	339083	766666	310820	302574	004240	040000	049069	00759	AAAAAA	AAAAAA	AAAAAA
1024	8	97255	134241	319798	380802	343976	338847	303494	434263	340648	122209	138472	254347	289345
1024	16	101396	137282	345957	372625	470592	449512	366364	633642	433891	127187	128577	277206	323849
1024	32	105425	143739	371144	436315	564813	540946	416689	805021	463983	131959	146036	293668	306953
1024	64	108268	157320	362605	459811	553209	27294	391137	13880	855533	132318	159428	296292	347708
1024	128	112663	156290	379540	350445	499518	33921	462086	16873	880527	124528	152108	252716	296978
1024	256	16670	17048	62580	72102	71593	16889	72015	21833	72031	16930	17019	47674	245978
1024	512	17997	18546	70334	79906	75128	12613	79299	19691	75332	18468	18492	32331	176430
1024	1024	28904	29747	130680	131349	131754	29919	129000	29879	131015	29991	29823	21020	143620
2048	4	50908	136907	223363	233100	183874	165160	192120	244100	188946	96685	133550	176383	180441
2048	8	53578	176231	320003	347887	300465	261962	291359	429438	275895	134286	169537	238999	247016

Figure 2.2 iozone Test Output

Each type of I/O test (i.e. read, write, etc.) is performed using record lengths varying from 4KB to 16MB, and with amounts of data ranging from 64KB to 512MB. Additionally, iozone can be configured to confine its tests to a specific I/O type, as well as to specific record sizes and data amounts, allowing system administrators to tailor the tests to mimic the application they are interested in benchmarking.

The results of iozone tests can easily be imported to Microsoft Excel for charting purposes. Figure 2.3 shows an example of the type of charts that can be generated from iozone data. By analyzing the iozone output, you can determine the throughput capabilities of your filesystem using various record sizes, data sizes, etc.

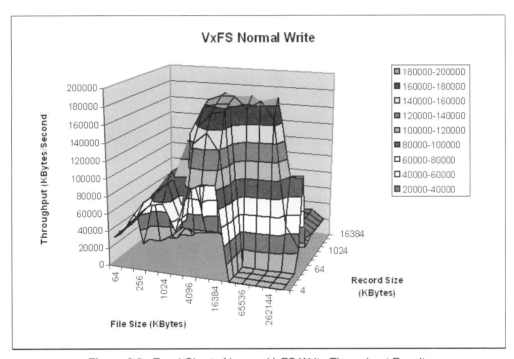

Figure 2.3   Excel Chart of iozone VxFS Write Throughput Results

The best source of iozone information is the dedicated web site: *http://iozone.org*. This site holds the latest iozone source code and documentation, all of which is available at no cost. The users' guide includes a detailed explanation of the available command-line options, sample output charts, and instructions for generating Excel charts using your collected data.[5]

5.   To create Excel charts from your iozone data, iozone must be run with the "-R" option. Once the generated data file is imported into Excel, simply highlight the columns and rows of data associated with the specific I/O test you are interested in charting (including the empty cell in the upper-left-hand corner preceding the data), launch the Chart Wizard tool, select the 3D Surface Graph type, and then label the axes appropriately.

Just as with the networking throughput test results outlined in Section 1.2, iozone test results do not directly correlate to potential NFS throughput numbers — they merely demonstrate the capabilities of the local filesystem.

TIP: The iozone command offers a myriad of command-line options to control the behavior of the tests. Two of the most important iozone options to specify when measuring write throughput are "-c" and "-e." These options instruct iozone to include any wall clock time associated with the *close()* and *flush()* system calls in the test results. Without these options, iozone only calculates how long the *write()* system calls take to complete.

On systems with sufficient buffer cache resources, all *write()* system calls issued by iozone could be satisfied by the buffer cache, causing the write throughput test results to be skewed artificially high. The "-c" and "-e" options force iozone to compute the time required to actually post the test data to the specified filesystem, resulting in a more accurate depiction of the filesystem's throughput capabilities.

2.2.2 dd(1)

The dd(1) command was originally developed to facilitate the duplication of disk drives by transferring their contents to magnetic tape. It has the ability to read from any input device and write to any output device, making it ideal for generating disk I/O requests to specific filesystems. dd allows the administrator to control the record size used for the I/O transactions, which allows it to simulate a wide variety of applications.

As stated earlier, when testing filesystem throughput it is important to use tools that do not require filesystem resources to run, as the added disk overhead may influence the results. When testing filesystem read throughput, dd can be directed to read from the filesystem in question and write to the device file /dev/zero, thereby avoiding any physical disk write requests. Similarly, when measuring the write throughput capabilities of a filesystem, dd can be directed to read from the /dev/zero device file and write to the desired filesystem, thereby eliminating any physical disk read requests during the test.

    Difference Between HP-UX 11.0 and 11i:
The /dev/zero Special File

The /dev/zero special file is delivered with HP-UX 11i; however this file does not exist on HP-UX 11.0 systems. It can be created manually via the following mknod(1M) command:

```
# mknod /dev/zero c 3 4
```

The /dev/zero device file does not exist on HP-UX 11.0 systems; however it can be created via the mknod(1M) command. Once built, reads from /dev/zero always return a buffer full of zeroes. This special device file simulates a file of infinite length, so any application reading from /dev/zero must specify the desired amount of data to read. Writes to /dev/zero are always successful, but any data written is silently discarded.

Figure 2.4 shows an example of using dd to test single-process write performance for a 1GB file. In this test dd is reading from the /dev/zero device in 32KB chunks and writing to a local filesystem.

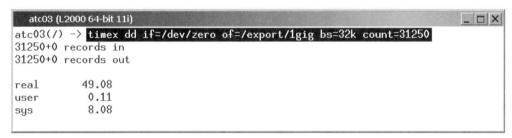

Figure 2.4 dd Measuring Local Filesystem Write Performance

The output in Figure 2.4 shows this 1GB write operation took just over 49 seconds, resulting in a throughput rate of approximately 20.9MB/second. Notice that the "count=" option is needed in this case to tell dd when to stop reading from /dev/zero. Since no physical disk reads are performed during this test, it provides a good estimate of the local filesystem's ability to handle a single-process write request for a 1GB file.

These results do not imply that an NFS client would be able to write a 1GB file to this exported filesystem at this rate, and you certainly should not expect an NFS client to be able to write a 1GB file to this filesystem any faster than this. It is also important to remember that this test only involved a single writing process. If multiple writing processes were used, then the resulting write throughput for this filesystem could have been significantly different.

Figure 2.5 shows a sample dd command where a 1GB file is read from a local filesystem in 32KB chunks and written to the /dev/zero device file.

Figure 2.5 dd Measuring Local Filesystem Read Performance

This test completed in just under 28 seconds, resulting in a read throughput rate of approximately 36.5MB/second. Since no physical disk writes were used, this test provides a good estimate of the local filesystem's capability of handling a single-process read request for a 1GB file.

Again, these results do not imply that an NFS client would be able to read a 1GB file from this exported filesystem at this rate; however you should not expect NFS to be able to perform a similar test any faster than this. It is also important to remember that this test only involved a single reading process. If multiple readers were used then the resulting throughput could have been significantly different.

TIP: When testing filesystem throughput with dd(1), avoid using the "ibs" and "obs" options to specify input and output block sizes. These options force dd(1) to perform internal data conversions, which can dramatically influence the throughput results. Use the "bs" option instead, which forces dd(1) to use the same block size for both input and output files without performing internal data conversions.

2.3 Local Filesystem Recommendations

The recommendations in this section pertain specifically to VxFS filesystems (also known as JFS, meaning Journaled File System) as opposed to High Performance File Systems (HFS).

 KEY IDEA — Always Use VxFS Filesystems on NFS Clients and Servers

HP customers are strongly recommended to use **VxFS** filesystems on NFS clients and servers, as opposed to HFS filesystems.

VxFS filesystems have several advantages over HFS filesystems, many of which are summarized in Table 2.1.

Table 2.1 VxFS Filesystem Advantages over HFS

File System Issue	HFS	VxFS
Maximum Filesystem Size	HFS supports filesystems as large as **128GB** on HP-UX 11.0 and 11i systems.	VxFS supports filesystems as large as **1TB** on 11.0 systems and as large as **2TB** on 11i.[a]
Maximum File Size	HFS supports files as large as **128GB** on HP-UX 11.0 and 11i.	VxFS supports files as large as **1TB** on 11.0 and **2TB** on 11i.[a]

Table 2.1 VxFS Filesystem Advantages over HFS

File System Issue	HFS	VxFS
I/O Performance	The HFS filesystem uses block based allocation schemes which provide adequate random access and latency for small files but limit throughput for larger files. As a result, the HFS filesystem is less than optimal for commercial environments.	VxFS provides the following performance enhancements over HFS filesystems: • extent based allocation • enhanced mount options • data synchronous I/O • caching advisories • explicit file alignment, extent size, and pre-allocation controls • tunable I/O parameters VxFS provides enhanced I/O performance by applying an aggressive I/O clustering policy. I/O clustering is a technique of grouping multiple I/O operations together. The VxFS I/O policies provide more aggressive clustering processes than other filesystems and offer higher I/O throughput when using large files; the resulting performance is comparable to that of raw disk.
Online Administration and Maintenance	HFS filesystems must be taken **offline** (i.e. unmounted) in order to be resized.	With the HP OnLineJFS product, a VxFS filesystem can be defragmented and resized while it remains **online** and accessible to users. Online backups are also available with OnLineJFS.
Buffer Cache Integration	HFS filesystems **do not** keep track of which buffers in the cache are associated with their files. When an HFS file needs to be invalidated from the cache, the entire cache must be searched to locate the pages associated with the file.	VxFS filesystems **do** track their buffer cache memory usage on a per-file basis. This allows the kernel to invalidate a VxFS file from the cache quickly as it knows exactly which memory pages are associated with the file.

Table 2.1 VxFS Filesystem Advantages over HFS

File System Issue	HFS	VxFS
Inode Allocation	If you run out of inodes you have to **rebuild** the filesystem and specify more inodes.	VxFS **dynamically allocates** inodes on the fly as needed.
File System Recovery	The HFS filesystem relies on full structural verification by the fsck(1M) utility as the only means to recover from a system failure. This utility involves a time-consuming process of checking the entire structure, verifying that the filesystem is intact, and correcting any inconsistencies. This fsck process can potentially require **several hours** to complete on a large HFS filesystem.	VxFS provides recovery only **seconds** after a system failure by utilizing a tracking feature called intent logging. This feature records pending changes to the filesystem structure in a circular intent log. During system failure recovery, the VxFS fsck utility performs an intent log replay, which scans the intent log and nullifies or completes filesystem operations that were active when the system failed. The filesystem can then be mounted without completing a full structural check of the entire filesystem.

a.   For a detailed discussion on supported file and filesystem sizes of HFS and VxFS filesystems, refer to
Section 9.1.1 "Maximum Supported File and Filesystem Sizes."

Many of the recommendations described in this section involve modifying the syntax used when initially creating VxFS filesystems. Careful consideration should be used when building your local filesystems to ensure that the optimal options are used, since many of these options cannot be changed once the filesystems are in use.

2.3.1 Use a Block Size of 8KB

The unit of allocation in VxFS is a *block*. There are no fragments smaller than a block because storage is allocated in *extents* that consist of one or more blocks. The smallest block size available is 1KB, which is also the default block size for VxFS filesystems created on filesystems smaller than 8GB. The block size is specified when a filesystem is created; it cannot be changed later.

The recommendation, especially for NFS servers, is to build VxFS filesystems using a block size of 8KB whenever possible. While an 8KB block size may result in wasted space if the filesystem is comprised mainly of very small files, the 8KB block size allows VxFS to perform "block" reads when servicing NFS read requests. These "block" reads employ a more efficient read mechanism which is only used by the kernel when the underlying filesystem extent being read from is 8KB or larger. Since an extent is comprised of one or more blocks, and blocks can be as small as 1KB, the only way to guarantee that an extent will be at least 8KB large is to use a block size of 8KB when building the filesystem. Refer to the mkfs_vxfs(1M) man page for details on specifying block sizes when creating VxFS filesystems.

What block size are my existing filesystems using?   A quick and easy way to determine the block size that was specified when an existing filesystem was built is to use the mkfs(1M) command. When run with the "-m" option, mkfs displays the command-line syntax that was used to build the filesystem in question. Figure 2.6 contains an example of this.

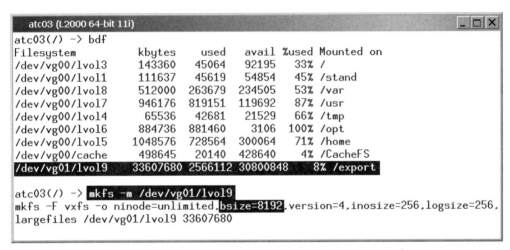

Figure 2.6   mkfs Displaying the Current Filesystem Block Size

This output reveals that /dev/vg01/lvol9, which is the logical volume associated with the /export filesystem, was built using a block size of 8KB ("bsize=8192").

2.3.2   Use VxFS Version 3.3

VxFS version 3.3 offers many new features over previous versions of VxFS, including access control lists (ACLs) for finely-tuned security and improved performance.[6] Version 3.3 introduced many configurable I/O parameters that allow the systems administrator to tune to these filesystems for optimal performance in the OLTP, DSS, and technical computing markets. With appropriate tuning, a VxFS 3.3 filesystem will outperform HFS in every category.

---

6.   For a complete description about the differences between VxFS 3.3 and previous VxFS versions, refer to the *HP OnLineJFS 3.3 Release Notes for HP-UX 11i* and the *HP JFS 3.3 and HP OnLineJFS 3.3 VERITAS File System 3.3 System Administrator's Guide* documents, both of which are available from HP's online documentation repository: *http://docs.hp.com.*

HP- *ux* **11i**   **Difference Between HP-UX 11.0 and 11i:**
                              VxFS Version 3.3 Filesystem Support

HP-UX 11.0 shipped with support for VxFS version **3.1**. In HP-UX 11i, **3.3** became the default version of VxFS filesystems.

VxFS 3.3 is available for systems running HP-UX 11.0. It can be downloaded free of charge from the HP Software Depot web site: *http://software.hp.com*.

2.3.3 Use `vxtunefs(1M)` to Tune VxFS 3.3 Filesystems

VxFS version 3.3 introduced several I/O parameters that allow systems administrators to tailor the behavior of their VxFS filesystems to better meet the needs of a specific application or an underlying storage device. These new parameters are described in Table 2.2.

Table 2.2   Default Values for VxFS 3.3 Tunable Parameters

Variable	Description	Default
read_pref_io	The preferred read request size. The filesystem uses this in conjunction with the *read_nstream* value to determine how much data to read ahead.	**64KB**
read_nstream	The number of parallel read requests of size *read_pref_io* to have outstanding at one time. The filesystem uses the product of *read_nstream* and *read_pref_io* to determine its read ahead size.	**1**
read_unit_io	The less preferred read request size. *This parameter is not currently implemented in HP-UX.*	**N/A**
write_pref_io	The preferred write request size. The filesystem uses this in conjunction with the *write_nstream* value to determine how to do flush behind on writes.	**64KB**
write_nstream	The number of parallel write requests of size *write_pref_io* to have outstanding at one time. The filesystem uses the product of *write_nstream* and *write_pref_io* to determine when to do flush behind on writes.	**1**
write_unit_io	The less preferred write request size. *This parameter is not currently implemented in HP-UX.*	**N/A**

Table 2.2 Default Values for VxFS 3.3 Tunable Parameters

Variable	Description	Default
pref_strength	Indicates to the filesystem how large a performance gain might be made by adhering to the preferred I/O sizes. The higher the value of pref_strength the greater the benefit of issuing correct size I/O requests. *This parameter is not currently implemented in HP-UX.*	**N/A**
buf_breakup_size	Indicates the size where I/O requests will get broken up into multiple operations at the driver level. In general, unless the preferred I/O request indicates a value larger than buf_breakup_size then issuing I/O requests larger than buf_breakup_size can hurt performance. *This parameter is not currently implemented in HP-UX.*	**N/A**
discovered_direct_iosz	Any file I/O requests larger than the *discovered_direct_iosz* are handled as discovered direct I/O. A discovered direct I/O is unbuffered similar to direct I/O, but it does not require a synchronous commit of the inode when the file is extended or blocks are allocated. For larger I/O requests, the CPU time for copying the data into the page cache and the cost of using memory to buffer the I/O data becomes more expensive than the cost of doing the disk I/O. For these I/O requests, using discovered direct I/O is more efficient than regular I/O.	**256KB**
max_direct_iosz	The maximum size of a direct I/O request that will be issued by the filesystem. If a larger I/O request comes in, then it is broken up into *max_direct_iosz* chunks. This parameter defines how much memory an I/O request can lock at once, so it should be set to less than 20 percent of memory.	**1024KB**
max_buf_data_size	The maximum buffer size allocated for file data. The value can either be 8KB or 64KB. Use the larger value for workloads where large reads/writes are performed sequentially. Use the smaller value on workloads where the I/O is random or is done in small chunks.	**8192**

Table 2.2 Default Values for VxFS 3.3 Tunable Parameters

Variable	Description	Default
default_indir_size	On VxFS, files can have up to ten direct extents of variable size stored in the inode. Once these extents are used up, the file must use indirect extents which are a fixed size that is set when the file first uses indirect extents. The filesystem does not use larger indirect extents because it must fail a write and return ENOSPC if there are no extents available that are the indirect extent size. For filesystems containing many large files, the 8KB indirect extent size is too small. The files that get into indirect extents use many smaller extents instead of a few larger ones. By using this parameter, the default indirect extent size can be increased so large that files use fewer larger extents. The tunable *default_indir_size* should be used carefully. If it is set too large, then writes will fail when they are unable to allocate extents of the indirect extent size to a file. In general, the fewer and the larger the files on a filesystem, the larger the *default_indir_size* can be set. This parameter should generally be set to some multiple of the *read_pref_io* parameter.	8KB
max_seqio_extent_size	Increases or decreases the maximum size of an extent. When the filesystem is following its default allocation policy for sequential writes to a file, it allocates an initial extent which is large enough for the first write to the file. When additional extents are allocated, they are progressively larger (the algorithm tries to double the size of the file with each new extent) so each extent can hold several writes' worth of data. This is done to reduce the total number of extents in anticipation of continued sequential writes. When the file stops being written, any unused space is freed for other files to use. Normally this allocation stops increasing the size of extents at 2048 blocks which prevents one file from holding too much unused space. *max_seqio_extent_size* is measured in filesystem blocks.	2048

Table 2.2 Default Values for VxFS 3.3 Tunable Parameters

Variable	Description	Default
qio_cache_enable	Enables or disables the caching of Quick I/O files. *This parameter is not currently implemented in HP-UX.*	N/A
max_diskq	Limits the maximum disk queue generated by a single file. When the filesystem is flushing data for a file and the number of pages being flushed exceeds *max_diskq*, processes will block until the amount of data being flushed decreases. Although this doesn't limit the actual disk queue, it prevents flushing processes from making the system unresponsive.	1MB
initial_extent_size	Changes the default initial extent size measured in blocks. VxFS determines, based on the first write to a new file, the size of the first extent to be allocated to the file. Normally the first extent is the smallest power of 2 that is larger than the size of the first write. If that power of 2 is less than 8K, the first extent allocated is 8K. After the initial extent, the filesystem increases the size of subsequent extents (see *max_seqio_extent_size*) with each allocation. Since most applications write to files using a buffer size of 8K or less, the increasing extents start doubling from a small initial extent. *initial_extent_size* can change the default initial extent size to be larger, so the doubling policy will start from a much larger initial size and the filesystem will not allocate a set of small extents at the start of file. Use this parameter only on filesystems that will have a very large average file size. On these filesystems it will result in fewer extents per file and less fragmentation.	1

Also introduced in version 3.3 is the vxtunefs(1M) command, which is used to tune these new parameters. vxtunefs can be issued interactively or it can operate in conjunction with the configuration file "/etc/vx/tunefstab."[7] When issued with the "-p" option, vxtunefs will display the current values of these I/O parameters for the requested filesystem. An example of this is shown in Figure 2.7.

7.   Refer to the tunefstab(4) man page for more information about configuring VxFS filesystems via the /etc/vx/tunefstab file.

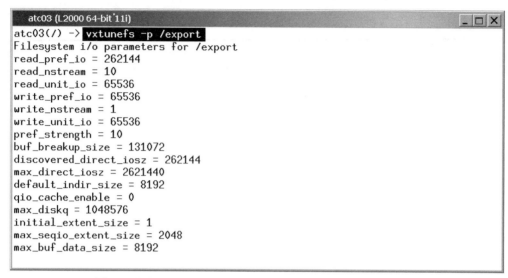

Figure 2.7 vxtunefs Displaying Tunable Parameter Values

The mount_vxfs(1M) command invokes vxtunefs to process the contents of the /etc/vx/tunefstab file at mount time. It is important to note that the mount command will continue even if the vxtunefs call fails or if vxtunefs detects invalid parameters. Also, the parameters in Table 2.2 can still be modified via vxtunefs after the filesystems are mounted.

Recommendations for vxtunefs(1M) Parameter Settings

Just as with most areas of NFS performance tuning, there is no one perfect set of vxtunefs parameters that will work with every application workload or underlying storage subsystem.

Determining the optimal parameter set for a specific VxFS filesystem usually requires some understanding of the disk mechanisms used by the filesystem and how they are configured. For example, are the disks striped? Which RAID level do they use? Are the disks part of an array? In addition, you need to be familiar enough with the applications that will access the filesystem to know what a typical workload generated by these applications looks like. For example, do the applications perform small read and write requests or very large requests? Do they perform sequential I/O or primarily random I/O? All of these factors need to be considered when setting these tunable parameters.

The following excerpt is taken from the *HP OnLineJFS 3.3 VERITAS File System 3.3 System Administrator's Guide*:

> Try to align the parameters to match the geometry of the logical disk as closely as possible. With striping or RAID-5, it is common to set *read_pref_io* to the stripe unit size and *read_nstream* to the number of columns in the stripe. For striping arrays, use the same values for *write_pref_io* and *write_nstream*, but for RAID-5 arrays, set *write_pref_io* to the full stripe size and *write_nstream* to 1.

For an application to do efficient disk I/O, it should issue read requests that are equal to the product of *read_nstream* multiplied by *read_pref_io*. Generally, any multiple or factor of *read_nstream* multiplied by *read_pref_io* should be a good size for performance. For writing, the same rule of thumb applies to the *write_pref_io* and *write_nstream* parameters.

When tuning a filesystem, the best thing to do is try out the tuning parameters under a real life workload. If an application is doing sequential I/O to large files, it should try to issue requests larger than the *discovered_direct_iosz*. This causes the I/O requests to be performed as discovered direct I/O requests, which are unbuffered like direct I/O but do not require synchronous inode updates when extending the file. If the file is larger than can fit in the cache, then using unbuffered I/O avoids throwing useful data out of the cache and it avoids a lot of CPU overhead.

`vxtunefs` Example — Reading a 1GB File Figure 2.8 shows an example of how `vxtunefs(1M)` can be used to improve the performance of a specific type of I/O. In this example, `dd(1)` is used to read two separate 1GB files from a local VxFS filesystem. One file is read using default `vxtunefs` settings and the other is read after adjusting the preferred read request size (*read_pref_io*) and the allowable number of outstanding read requests (*read_nstream*).

Figure 2.8 shows `dd` read the first file in just under 28 seconds, resulting in a throughput of approximately 36.7MB/sec. After increasing the read-ahead allowance via `vxtunefs`, `dd` was able to read the second file in just over 15 seconds, resulting in a throughput of 68MB/sec.

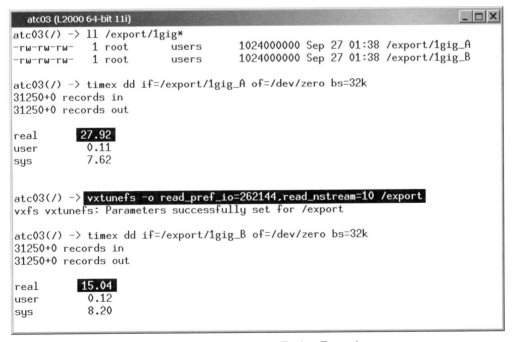

Figure 2.8 `vxtunefs` Tuning Example

This simple example illustrates how `vxtunefs` can dramatically influence the behavior and performance of VxFS 3.3 filesystems, and how changes made with `vxtunefs` take effect immediately. It also shows the importance of understanding what type of I/O your applications are performing in order to properly tune your filesystems to service those I/O requests.

CAE-specific Recommendations   HP has produced a number of `vxtunefs` parameter recommendations for various applications. In the CAE (Computer-Aided Engineering) space, HP has published white papers outlining specific tuning guidelines for applications such as ABAQUS (from HKS Software), NASTRAN and PATRAN (from MSC.Software), and many others. These tuning documents can be downloaded from HP's CAE resource site: *http://hp.com/go/cae*.

SPEC SFS97 Recommendations   SPEC SFS97 is the industry standard test suite used for measuring and comparing performance and throughput capabilities of NFS servers. The benchmark programs are developed by SPEC (Standard Performance Evaluation Corporation) and are made available to any company wishing to publish performance results for their NFS servers. Once a vendor has run a SPEC SFS97 benchmark they are allowed to submit their results to SPEC, along with a detailed description of the hardware configuration they used to achieve the results. Reviewed results are published on SPEC's web site: *http://www.spec.org*.

Part of the information vendors are required to include when they submit their test results to SPEC is a detailed list of the hardware and software used to get the test results. In addition, any kernel parameter changes or filesystem tuning must be disclosed. This allows customers who purchase an NFS server based on the SPEC results to configure their server just as the one used by the vendor during the benchmark, which should allow customers to achieve performance numbers similar to those reported in the test results. Of course, achieving the same results as SPEC SFS97 assumes that the customer's application workload closely resembles the workload generated by the SPEC SFS97 benchmark itself, which is not always the case.

Like most NFS vendors, HP has published several sets of SPEC SFS97 benchmark results. Recently, HP submitted results from a 32-CPU Superdome system running HP-UX 11i. This disclosure includes the `vxtunefs` syntax used to tune the filesystems for this benchmark. Table 2.3 lists the settings disclosed in the benchmark results.

Table 2.3   SPEC SFS `vxtunefs` Values

`vxtunefs(1M)` **Parameter**	**Value**
read_pref_io	8192
read_nstream	1
write_pref_io	8192
write_nstream	1000
max_diskq	104857600

The read and write request sizes (*read_pref_io* and *write_pref_io* respectively) were tuned down from their default value of 64KB to 8KB. The number of outstanding write requests allowed (*write_nstream*) was sized up dramatically from the default of 1 to a value of 1000. The maximum disk queue (*max_diskq*) size was increased substantially as well.

Does this mean that these values would work for *any* NFS server supporting *any* workload? Probably not, but these parameters were found to work best for the workload generated by the SPEC SFS97 benchmark.

2.3.4 Configure the Maximum Sized Intent Log Possible

In the event of a system failure, the VxFS filesystem uses intent logging to guarantee filesystem integrity. The intent log is a circular activity log with a default size of 1024 blocks that records of the intention of the system to update filesystem structures.

VxFS maintains log records in the intent log for all pending changes to the filesystem structure and ensures that the log records are written to disk in advance of the changes to the filesystem. Once the intent log has been written, the transaction's other updates to the filesystem can be written in any order. In the event of a system failure, the pending changes to the filesystem are either nullified or completed by the fsck(1M) utility.

The intent log size is specified when a filesystem is created and cannot be subsequently changed. When building the VxFS filesystems on your NFS server, the maximum intent log size (16MB) should be used, as this allows the largest number of requests to be pending in the log file before any intent log maintenance is required by the kernel. With larger intent log sizes, recovery time is proportionately longer and the filesystem may consume more system resources (such as memory) during normal operation.

 KEY IDEA — Use the Maximum Intent Log Size when Building VxFS Filesystems

When building the VxFS filesystems on your NFS server, the maximum intent log size (16MB) should be used, as this allows the largest number of requests to be pending in the log file before any intent log maintenance is required by the kernel.

The intent log size is a calculated value determined by multiplying the mkfs(1M) *logsize* parameter with the *bsize* parameter (i.e. *logsize* * *bsize*).

For example, if you are building your filesystem with a block size of 8KB then you should specify a *logsize* of 2048 (8KB * 2048 = 16MB). If you are using a block size of 1KB then a *logsize* of 16384 should be used (1KB * 16384 = 16MB).

The size of the intent log can only be specified when the filesystem is created. It cannot be increased or decreased afterwards.

How big is the intent log on the existing filesystems?   A quick and easy way to determine the size of the intent log for an existing filesystem is to issue the mkfs(1M) command with the "-m" option and calculate the size of the intent log by multiplying the *bsize* and *logsize* values of the filesystem you are interested in. An example of this mkfs output is included in Figure 2.9. In this example, the "/export" filesystem was built with a *bsize* of 8KB and a *logsize* of 256, resulting in a 2MB intent log.

2.3.5 Use *delaylog* and *tmplog* Options when Appropriate

One final tuning consideration specific to the VxFS intent log is controlling how aggressively the kernel records transactions to the intent log before committing the actual filesystem changes to disk. HP provides several VxFS-specific mount options for controlling the behavior and performance of the intent log mechanism. Two of the most commonly used options are *delaylog* and *tmplog* (also known as *nolog*).

```
atc03 (L2000 64-bit 11i)                                                    _ □ X
atc03(/) -> bdf
Filesystem              kbytes      used    avail  %used Mounted on
/dev/vg00/lvol3         143360     45064    92195    33% /
/dev/vg00/lvol1         111637     45619    54854    45% /stand
/dev/vg00/lvol8         512000    263679   234505    53% /var
/dev/vg00/lvol7         946176    819151   119692    87% /usr
/dev/vg00/lvol4          65536     42681    21529    66% /tmp
/dev/vg00/lvol6         884736    881460     3106   100% /opt
/dev/vg00/lvol5        1048576    728564   300064    71% /home
/dev/vg00/cache         498645     20140   428640     4% /CacheFS
/dev/vg01/lvol9       33607680   2566112 30800848     8% /export

atc03(/) -> mkfs -m /dev/vg01/lvol9
mkfs -F vxfs -o ninode=unlimited,bsize=8192,version=4,inosize=256,logsize=256,
largefiles /dev/vg01/lvol9 33607680
```

Figure 2.9 mkfs Displaying the *bsize* and *logsize* Values

The default logging method is *log*. In log mode, any system call that results in a change to a filesystem structure, or metadata (such as *mkdir()*, *create()*, *rename()*, etc.), will block until the transaction has been recorded in the intent log. While this provides complete protection against metadata loss in the event of a system failure, operating in *log* mode can be very detrimental to filesystem performance, especially for workloads that involve frequent metadata changes.

In *delaylog* mode, some system calls return before the intent log is written. This typically results in a performance improvement of 15 to 20 percent over *log* mode. When servicing metadata intensive workloads, *delaylog* has been shown to improve performance by more than 100% over *log* mode. Although some metadata changes are not guaranteed until a short time after the system call returns (when the intent log is written), *delaylog* most closely approximates traditional UNIX semantics and guarantees for correctness in case of system failures. This is the recommended logging method for all data-critical filesystems, as it provides the best compromise between data integrity and filesystem performance.

In *tmplog* mode, intent logging is almost always delayed. This greatly improves performance, even over *delaylog*, but filesystem changes may be lost if the system crashes. This mode is only suggested for temporary or "scratch" filesystems where data loss is an acceptable risk.[8]

2.3.6 Monitor Fragmentation and Defragment Filesystems

VxFS filesystems can get fragmented with heavy use over time. I/O performance can be severely affected on badly fragmented volumes resulting from slow access times (via the *open()* and *close()* systems calls) and slow write performance, especially in cases where existing files need to be expanded, when the kernel must search for available extents of sufficient size. It is therefore important to monitor the fragmentation level of your exported filesystems and periodically defragment them via the `fsadm(1M)` command.

`fsadm` is capable of reorganizing both disk *extents* and *directories*. Extent reorganization typically provides a much bigger improvement in performance than directory reorganization, but both are needed for optimal filesystem performance. `fsadm` is able to *report* on the fragmentation levels of extents and directories without actually performing the defragmentation, which can help in formulating a good defragmentation strategy for your filesystems.

Figure 2.10 shows an example of `fsadm` performing an extent defragmentation on `/var`. By specifying both the "`-e`" and "`-E`" options, `fsadm` not only performs the defragmentation but displays fragmentation statistics both before and after the operation so that you can measure the effectiveness of the defragmentation. By comparing the "before" and "after" statistics in Figure 2.10 you can see how `fsadm` was able to substantially increase the number of extents containing 64 or more blocks (82.42% vs. 62.85%), and it was successful at shrinking the percentage of free space contained in extents smaller than 8 blocks (0.16% vs. 2.23%).[9]

It is recommended that a defragmentation schedule be created for your NFS servers to reduce the risk of your critical exported filesystems becoming fragmented. The easiest way to ensure that directory and extent fragmentation does not become a problem is to schedule regular `fsadm` runs from `cron(1M)`. Periodic defragmentation checks should be performed anywhere from weekly to monthly, depending upon the utilization of your filesystems.

---

8   For more information about the available VxFS mount options refer to the mount_vxfs(1M) man page and the
     HP OnLineJFS 3.3 VERITAS File System 3.3 System Administrator's Guide available at HP's online documentation repository: *http://docs.hp.com*.

9.   For more information about defragmenting VxFS filesystems and directories or interpreting fsadm output, refer
     to the fsadm_vxfs(1M) man page.

```
atc03 (L2000 64-bit 11i)                                        _ □ X
atc03(/) -> fsadm -F vxfs -E -e /var
  Extent Fragmentation Report
          Total    Average      Average    Total
          Files    File Blks    # Extents  Free Blks
          6057     42           8          249348
  blocks used for indirects: 1048
  % Free blocks in extents smaller than 64 blks: 8.93
  % Free blocks in extents smaller than  8 blks: 2.23
  % blks allocated to extents 64 blks or larger: 62.85
  Free Extents By Size
            1:     2294            2:     1077          4:      281
            8:      218           16:      339         32:      298
           64:      210          128:       11        256:       19
          512:       13         1024:       10       2048:        3
         4096:        3         8192:        3      16384:        1
        32768:        4        65536:        0     131072:        0
       262144:        0       524288:        0    1048576:        0
      2097152:        0      4194304:        0    8388608:        0
     16777216:        0     33554432:        0   67108864:        0
    134217728:        0    268435456:        0  536870912:        0
   1073741824:        0   2147483648:        0

  Extent Fragmentation Report
          Total    Average      Average    Total
          Files    File Blks    # Extents  Free Blks
          6057     42           1          249341
  blocks used for indirects: 16
  % Free blocks in extents smaller than 64 blks: 2.44
  % Free blocks in extents smaller than  8 blks: 0.16
  % blks allocated to extents 64 blks or larger: 82.42
  Free Extents By Size
            1:       65            2:       54          4:       58
            8:      111           16:      109         32:       95
           64:      131          128:       85        256:       63
          512:       42         1024:       22       2048:       12
         4096:        2         8192:        2      16384:        1
        32768:        3        65536:        0     131072:        0
       262144:        0       524288:        0    1048576:        0
      2097152:        0      4194304:        0    8388608:        0
     16777216:        0     33554432:        0   67108864:        0
    134217728:        0    268435456:        0  536870912:        0
   1073741824:        0   2147483648:        0
```

Figure 2.10   fsadm Performing an Extent Defragmentation

2.3.7 Monitor Filesystem Utilization via bdf(1M) and df(1M)

In general, VxFS filesystems perform best when the percentage of free space does not shrink below 10 percent. Once filesystems grow beyond 90% utilized, the number of free extents are few and they can quickly become fragmented. Once this occurs, the fsadm command will have a difficult time defragmenting these extents because of the limited remaining contiguous space.

It is therefore important to monitor the utilization rate of critical filesystems, in particular those filesystems residing on NFS servers that are exported for read/write access. The bdf(1M) and df(1M) commands may be used for this purpose. Figure 2.11 shows an example of the bdf command reporting on filesystem space utilization and inode utilization.

```
atc03 (L2000 64-bit 11i)                                              _ □ X
atc03(/) -> bdf -i -t vxfs
Filesystem           kbytes     used    avail %used   iused   ifree %iuse Mounted on
/dev/vg00/lvol3      143360    45147    92117   33%    2169   24551    8% /
/dev/vg00/lvol8      512000   262793   235336   53%    8450   62298   12% /var
/dev/vg00/lvol7      946176   819158   119685   87%   29324   31752   48% /usr
/dev/vg00/lvol4       65536    42665    21543   66%     139    5717    2% /tmp
/dev/vg00/lvol6      884736   881460     3106  100%   16503     817   95% /opt
/dev/vg00/lvol5     1048576   728564   300064   71%    7984   80000    9% /home
/dev/vg01/lvol9    33607680  2566112 30800848    8%    1339  970021    0% /export
```

Figure 2.11 bdf Reporting Disk Space and Inode Utilization

The df command has many features that are not available with bdf. It can report filesystem statistics similar to bdf (as shown in Figure 2.12), or it can perform advanced functions like displaying the entire statvfs(2) structure for a filesystem.[10]

```
atc03 (L2000 64-bit 11i)                                              _ □ X
atc03(/) -> df -F vxfs -k -P
Filesystem           1024-blocks    Used  Available Capacity Mounted on
/dev/vg01/lvol9        33366960  2566112 30800848      8%    /export
/dev/vg00/lvol5         1028628   728572   300056     71%    /home
/dev/vg00/lvol6          884566   881460     3106    100%    /opt
/dev/vg00/lvol4           64208    42665    21543     67%    /tmp
/dev/vg00/lvol7          938843   819162   119681     88%    /usr
/dev/vg00/lvol8          498129   262798   235331     53%    /var
/dev/vg00/lvol3          137266    45179    92087     33%    /
```

Figure 2.12 df -P Output

Any filesystems that are nearing or have exceeded 90% of their configured disk space capacity should be examined for files that can be removed or relocated to a filesystem with more available space. VxFS filesystems may also be expanded, either via the fsadm_vxfs(1M) command or via sam(1M).[11]

---

10.   Refer to the bdf(1M) and df_vxfs(1M) man pages for descriptions of the available command-line options.

11.   Refer to the fsadm_vxfs(1M) man page or the *HP OnLineJFS 3.3 VERITAS File System 3.3 System Administrator's Guide* for a description of online filesystem expansion.

KEY IDEA — The Importance of Patching VxFS Kernel and Commands

HP continually strives to improve the quality of HP-UX by distributing software patches containing both defect fixes and functionality enhancements. Many of these fixes and enhancements can significantly improve the performance and behavior of critical system components, such as the VxFS filesystem.

Since NFS relies heavily upon the stability and performance of the underlying filesystems, it is *strongly* recommended that the latest VxFS kernel and user-space commands patches be installed on every HP-UX system in order to take advantage of these improvements. Contact HP support to obtain a current set of patches for your specific operating system. You can also generate a current patch list using the tools available at HP's IT Resource Center: *http://itrc.hp.com*.

For a detailed discussion on the importance of keeping your HP-UX NFS client and server systems patched with current code, refer to Appendix B "Patching Considerations."

biod Daemons

The biods (asynchronous block I/O daemons) are the primary client-side NFS daemons. Their sole purpose is to try to increase the performance of remote file access by providing read-ahead and write-behind semantics on the NFS client. Although they are implemented as user-space processes, they spend the majority of their time running in the kernel. In most cases, but not all, they can dramatically improve NFS read and write performance. However, NFS clients are not *required* to run biod daemons in order to issue NFS read and write requests.

Determining the appropriate number of biod processes to run on a specific NFS client, like most every other performance related issue, is not easily defined and usually falls into the category of "it depends." Some clients will perform best with 4 biod daemons while others work better with 16. Still other clients perform best when no biod daemons are running. Rarely will an HP-UX NFS client, particularly an 11.0 client, perform optimally with a large number of biods, for reasons that will be explained.

This chapter describes how the biod daemons work in both the read and write scenarios. It explains why running a large number of biods does not necessarily result in better performance, and why in some cases running no biods could result in better performance or more desirable behavior. It also discusses the various factors involved in selecting the appropriate number of biod daemons to run on any given client. Finally, it describes the tools and methods available for troubleshooting biod-related problems.

3.1 How Do the biods Work?

In order to make an informed decision about the optimal number of biod daemons for a particular NFS client to run, some basic understanding of the way biods work is required.

HP-UX 11i   **Difference Between HP-UX 11.0 and 11i:**
                     The Default Number of biods Started

The default number of biod daemons launched on HP-UX systems at boot prior to 11i is **4**. Starting at 11i, the default number was increased to **16**.

3.1.1 What Types of NFS Requests Do the biods Handle?

NFS clients perform many types of I/O operations, including READ (read from a remote file), WRITE (write to a remote file), GETATTR (retrieve the current attributes of a remote file or directory), SETATTR (modify the attributes of a remote file or directory), LOOKUP (locate a specific file within a specific NFS directory), READDIRPLUS (retrieve the contents, including attribute information, of a remote directory), etc.

The only NFS requests that involve the biod daemons are READ and WRITE requests. All other NFS request types are processed directly by the application running on the client that generated the NFS traffic. In other words, if a user on an NFS client issues the ls(1) command to read the contents of an NFS mounted directory, any NFS requests generated as a result of this command will be handled by the ls thread itself. For example, a root user on the NFS client "ros87252" issues the ls command in an NFS mounted directory. Using GlancePlus, the thread ID of the ls command is identified as "2158" (see the "TID" column in Figure 3.1).

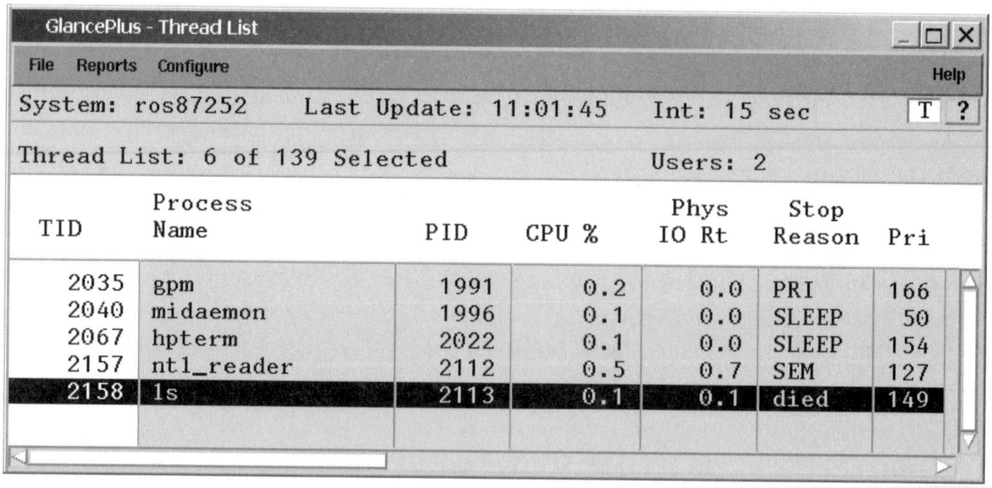

TID	Process Name	PID	CPU %	Phys IO Rt	Stop Reason	Pri
2035	gpm	1991	0.2	0.0	PRI	166
2040	midaemon	1996	0.1	0.0	SLEEP	50
2067	hpterm	2022	0.1	0.0	SLEEP	154
2157	ntl_reader	2112	0.5	0.7	SEM	127
2158	ls	2113	0.1	0.1	died	149

GlancePlus - Thread List

File   Reports   Configure   Help

System: ros87252   Last Update: 11:01:45   Int: 15 sec   T ?

Thread List: 6 of 139 Selected   Users: 2

Figure 3.1   GlancePlus Thread List Screen

A network trace collected while the ls command was run shows the NFS client sending a READDIRPLUS request to the server to obtain the directory contents. The formatted trace output (see Figure 3.2) confirms thread "2158" is issuing the READDIRPLUS call.

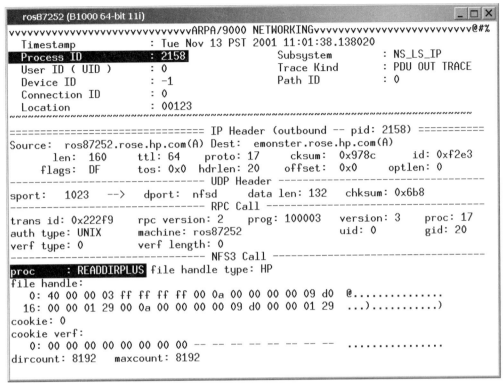

Figure 3.2 `nettl` Trace of `ls` Issued on an NFS Client

KEY IDEA — Identifying Thread IDs in Formatted `nettl(1M)` Traces

When analyzing `nettl(1M)` traces that have been formatted with `netfmt(1M)`, it is important to note that the field labeled "Process ID" in the header section of each packet is actually the identification number of the *kernel thread* that generated the network packet, not that of the *process*. This field is incorrectly labeled by `netfmt`.

Only *asynchronous* I/O requests are off-loaded by the biods The biods are only invoked by the kernel when applications are performing asynchronous I/O to NFS-mounted files. Asynchronous I/O semantics is the default behavior on HP-UX but can be overridden at file open time. If an application opens a file with the `O_SYNC`, `O_DSYNC`, or `O_RSYNC` flags (requesting synchronous I/O semantics), the biods will not be invoked during any read or write I/O requests for the file.

3.1.2 How Many biods Are Activated when Requests Arrive?

Any biod daemons that are not currently servicing a request will sleep in the kernel at a single location called "`async_bufhead`" waiting for new requests to be put into the biod work queue. Until somewhat recently, whenever a new request was added to the queue, all idle biod daemons would be activated simultaneously — even if only a single biod process was needed to service the new request. The remaining biod processes would realize there was nothing for them to do and go back to sleep. As you might imagine, this process of waking all idle biod processes whenever a new request arrived and then putting most of them back to sleep caused NFS performance to suffer, especially when there were many biods configured on the client.

In HP-UX 11.0 and 11i the biod processes are awoken one at a time when new requests arrive, thus eliminating the performance degradation associated with waking all daemons and putting them back to sleep. This enhancement provided better NFS client performance in 11.0 and 11i over earlier releases of HP-UX.

3.1.3 How Do biods Work in the WRITE Case?

When an application writes data asynchronously to an NFS file, the client will post the data to the local buffer cache. Once the buffer cache data has been written, *if biod daemons are not enabled*, the application will generate an NFS write request in its own process context to push the data to the server. The application will block waiting for the NFS write request to complete before continuing.

If biod daemons are enabled, the client application will not make any NFS write calls on its own process context. Instead, the writing process will post its data to the local buffer cache and an NFS write request will be generated by a biod. The writing process will not block during the actual *write()* system call waiting for the data to be written to the server. As long as sufficient free space exists in the client's buffer cache, the *write()* system call will complete as soon as the data is posted to the client's cache. This allows the application to continue writing as quickly as it can, letting the biods pull the data from the cache and send it to the server. While the writing process will not block when writing to the cache, it will eventually block — when the file being written to is flushed, synced, or closed — until all data has been sent to the server. Also, if buffer cache resources are exhausted, then the writing process must block and wait for the biods to drain the cache and free up buffer cache memory.

Therefore, the goal of the biods in the NFS *write* case is to keep the client's buffer cache sufficiently drained, so that when a writing process needs to *flush()*, *sync()*, *fclose()*, or *fflush()* a file it would only need to block for a short time while any remaining data in the cache is posted to the server. Keeping the client's buffer cache drained also allows applications to continuously write data to the cache without having to block while buffer cache resources are made available.

KEY IDEA — The biod's Influence on Client-side Buffer Cache Memory Consumption

When biods are running, the NFS client is only allowed to consume **25%** of the available buffer cache resources to hold data associated with NFS asynchronous write requests. For example, if an NFS client system dedicates 400MB of physical memory for buffer cache, only 100MB of that space can be used to hold NFS asynchronous write data.

This limitation is enforced to stop the NFS client from potentially consuming all available buffer cache resources with NFS asynchronous write data. Remember that writing processes will not block when writing NFS data to the buffer cache while biods are running. If this 25% cache limitation were not enforced, a single NFS writing process could potentially consume all available buffer cache memory, resulting in poor system performance or even system hangs.

Another important reason for this safeguard is to avoid deadlock situations. One potential deadlock case is when two systems NFS-mount filesystems from each other and simultaneously write huge amounts of data to each other's filesystems. If the NFS client code were allowed to consume buffer cache memory without bounds, both systems could potentially get into a deadlock. This is because the NFS server code on each system would not have the buffer cache resources they need to process the inbound `WRITE` requests from the other system. Another deadlock scenario is the case where a system mounts a local filesystem to itself via a loopback NFS mount and then writes a huge file to the loopback NFS filesystem. In this case the local NFS client processes could starve the local NFS server processes by consuming all buffer cache resources.

This 25% buffer cache restriction is only enforced when biods are running. When biods are not present, each writing process will send NFS `WRITE` requests in its own process context and block until the data is sent to the server, thus eliminating the potential for any one writing process to consume all buffer cache memory.

Will a writing process send its own NFS requests if the biods are busy?

We just learned that NFS client applications will block if they are writing data across an NFS mounted filesystem and the client's buffer cache resources are exhausted. What about the case where buffer cache resources are available but all of the biod daemons are busy servicing requests? Will a writing process block waiting for the biods to service its requests or will it begin sending NFS write calls on its own behalf?

While some might argue that allowing the writing process to send its own requests in addition to the biods would provide higher overall client throughput, testing has revealed that this is not the case for HP-UX 11.0 and 11i clients — particularly when writing sequential data to an NFS server that is exporting VxFS filesystems. In this scenario it is preferable to have the writing process block and wait for the biods to service the write requests, which is exactly what the 11.0 and 11i clients do.

The VxFS filesystem is traditionally tuned to perform very well with sequential writes; however, performance degrades comparatively in the random write case. If a process performing sequential writes on an NFS client were allowed to send write calls on its own behalf when the biod daemons were busy, then there is the strong possibility that the NFS server would treat the sequential writes effectively as random writes. Consider the following scenario:

- A server exports a VxFS filesystem for NFS clients to access.
- A client has biod daemons running and has 400MB of memory dedicated to buffer cache.
- An application on the client needs to write 300MB of data to a file in the NFS directory.
- The client begins performing asynchronous sequential writes to an NFS file.
- Since HP-UX allows NFS clients to consume a maximum of 25% of buffer cache for asynchronous writes, the client can write up to 100MB of data to buffer cache before it must wait for these buffers to be flushed and made available for use.
- While the client is writing data to the cache, the biod daemons are furiously working to drain the buffer cache and get the data to the server.
- At some point, the writing process finds it can no longer write to buffer cache (because it has reached the 25% cache limit) and all biod daemons are busy servicing requests.
- The next I/O request will be handled within the process context of the writing application, and may be sent to the server *before* the previous requests, which are still waiting in the biod queues to be serviced.

Let us assume that the client hits this case after writing 150MB of the target file into buffer cache. At this point, the NFS server has received 50MB of data from the client's biod daemons while the other 100MB is still sitting in the client's buffer cache waiting to be sent. If the writing process on the client was allowed to send an NFS write call on its own behalf it would send a call with a starting offset of 151MB, since the application has already written 150MB of data to the cache to this point. This would cause the NFS server to receive the sequential write requests out of order, as illustrated in Figure 3.3.

This example shows the NFS server receiving write requests for offset 49MB and 50MB from the biod daemons, followed by a request from the writing application at offset 151MB, followed by two more requests from biods, etc. This illustrates that if the writing process were allowed to send its own requests while the biods were busy, the server would receive the sequential write requests out of sequence, effectively causing the sequential write from the client to become a random write on the server.

The example in Figure 3.3 is not meant to imply that each write request contains 1MB of data. The offset values in the example are merely used to illustrate the point that the NFS server is receiving the write requests in non-sequential order. As stated earlier, if the server is writing to a VxFS filesystem the performance would suffer dramatically compared to a true sequential write. By forcing the writing process to block until the biod daemons have drained buffer cache enough to continue writing, the data is sent to the server in order and the server writes the data sequentially to the underlying VxFS filesystem.

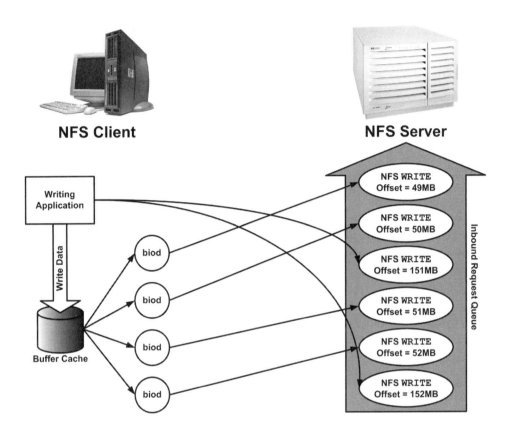

Figure 3.3 Why Writing Processes Block when biods Are Busy

3.1.4 How Do biods Work in the READ Case?

When the client needs to read data from an NFS mounted file, the client will first check its local buffer cache to see if the block of data is already present in cache. If it is, the read is satisfied without generating an NFS request. If the data is not present, an NFS READ call will be made to retrieve this data. If *no* biod daemons are running, the process requesting the data will generate the NFS READ calls in its own process context, just as NFS requests other than READ and WRITE are handled (see example in earlier Section 3.1.1).

If biod daemons *are* running, the application process will send two initial read requests in its own process context. If these two initial read requests are sequential (i.e. the starting offset of the second read request is the same as the ending offset of the first request), and more data is requested by the application, then the kernel will put the reading process to sleep and trigger a number of read-ahead requests via the biods.

Figure 3.4 shows an example of an application reading a file across an NFS mounted filesystem using the cat(1) command.

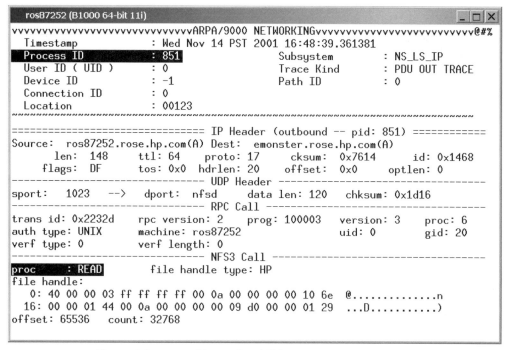

Figure 3.4 `nettl` Trace of an NFS `READ` Handled by a biod

Since `cat` reads the entire remote file sequentially, the first two NFS read requests will be performed by the `cat` process and all subsequent read requests will be handled by the biods. The formatted trace in Figure 3.4 lists the ID of the thread making this read request as "851." The GlancePlus "Thread List" screen (Figure 3.5) confirms that thread 851 is indeed one of the running biod daemons.

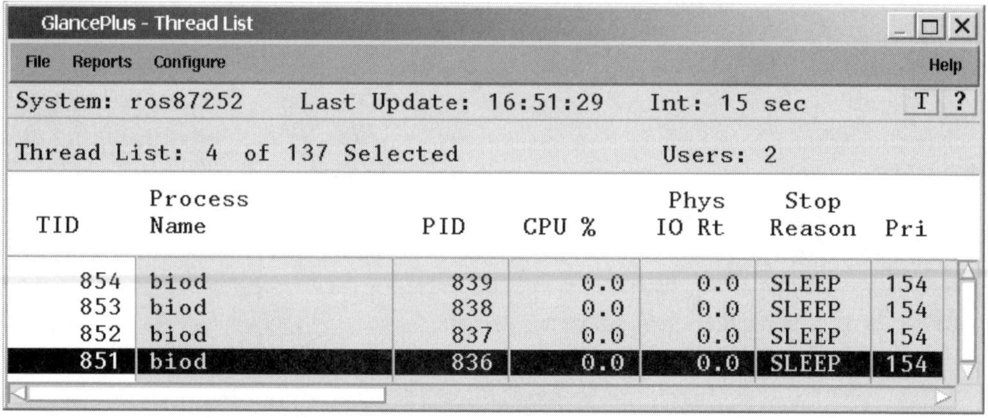

Figure 3.5 GlancePlus Thread List Displaying Running biods

Once the biod daemons retrieve the requested data from the NFS server, they place the data in the client's buffer cache and the sleeping process is awoken and allowed to access it. The biods will continue performing sequential read requests on behalf of the client application until the application stops requesting data from this location in the file. Therefore, the goal of the biod daemons in the read case is to keep the client's buffer cache populated with the data that the client needs and avoid having client applications block waiting for data from the NFS server.

Will a reading process send its own NFS requests if the biods are busy?
We've just learned that when a client application begins reading an NFS file it sends the initial two READ calls on its own behalf before the kernel invokes the biods. What happens if all the biods are busy servicing requests? Will the client application begin sending READ calls on its own behalf again? Until recently, the answer was "no" — the application would block waiting for biods to perform the READ calls. This behavior can lead to serious performance issues on NFS clients that have both reading and writing processes running simultaneously.

When biods are running, reading applications will block and wait for biods to retrieve data from the NFS server and place it in the client's buffer cache for the application to access. At the same time, writing processes are allowed to continuously post their data directly to the client's buffer cache without blocking (assuming buffer cache resources are available). The end result is that asynchronous write requests are enqueued in buffer cache much faster than asynchronous read requests, thus monopolizing the biods and causing starvation for the reading processes.

 KEY IDEA — NFS Read Behavior when All biods Are Busy Servicing Requests

HP offers customers the ability to configure their NFS clients so that reading processes can send NFS READ calls on their own behalf when all biods are busy, thus improving NFS read performance on busy clients. This new functionality is delivered in patch PHNE_24034 (for 11.0) and PHNE_24035 (for 11i). Since all HP NFS patches are cumulative, any patch superseding these patches will also contain this feature.

This feature is disabled by default and must be manually enabled on any client system wishing to take advantage of the new NFS READ semantics. To enable this feature the systems administrator should issue the following commands:

```
# echo 'async_read_avoidance_enabled?W 0d1' | adb -w /stand/vmunix /dev/kmem
# echo 'async_read_avoidance_enabled/W 0d1' | adb -w /stand/vmunix /dev/kmem
```

Two separate adb commands are used in this case to modify both the on-disk kernel file (?W syntax) and kernel memory (/W syntax). This allows the NFS READ semantics change to take effect immediately and remain in effect even if the client system is rebooted. This parameter will be reset to 0 (i.e. disabled) if the kernel is re-built, either manually (via mk_kernel(1M)) or by installing a kernel patch. This should be kept in mind when installing kernel patches on a system where *async_read_avoidance_enabled* is modified.

3.2   Why Not Just Launch Hundreds of biods?

Based on the biod benefits described in Section 3.1, you might conclude that the more biod daemons running the better your NFS client will perform, so why not just launch 200 biod daemons and be done with it? Unfortunately, HP-UX 11.0 NFS clients typically perform poorly with a large number of biods running. The primary reason for this poor performance is that the NFS client's *read()* and *write()* paths use the global filesystem semaphore to protect critical data structures and I/O operations. The filesystem semaphore is one of the only remaining "empire semaphores" (i.e. locks that govern an entire subsystem). This semaphore is typically acquired when performing operations that manipulate critical data structures in the virtual filesystem layer (VFS), which require that all filesystem operations on the system be temporarily suspended to ensure data integrity, particularly in multi-processor systems. Since the VFS layer resides logically above the filesystem layers such as NFS, VxFS, and HFS, acquiring the filesystem semaphore effectively locks out all other filesystem activity on the system.

This means that whenever a biod daemon processes a READ or a WRITE request it must acquire the filesystem semaphore, which effectively locks out all other filesystem related operations on the system. When a large number of biod daemons are run on a client system, the overhead of managing the acquiring and releasing of the filesystem semaphore becomes detrimental to NFS and overall system performance.

This issue only affects client-side NFS performance as it causes the client to be unable to send requests to the server as quickly as it otherwise would if it didn't have to acquire this global semaphore. HP recognized this shortcoming in the 11.0 NFS implementation and spent considerable time and effort redesigning the client-side NFS code for the 11i release to avoid the use of the filesystem semaphore wherever possible.

 Difference Between HP-UX 11.0 and 11i: Dependence on the Filesystem Semaphore

Dependence on the filesystem semaphore has been greatly reduced in HP-UX 11i. The 11i NFS client code uses locks of finer granularity (i.e. on smaller filesystem objects, which are held for shorter durations) to achieve higher parallelism.

This means an 11i client could *potentially* run more biod processes and generate higher client throughput because it is not experiencing the overhead of acquiring and releasing the global filesystem semaphore.

3.3   When Might an NFS Client *Not* Benefit from biods?

In Section 3.1 we learned that NFS clients are not required to run biods to perform NFS read and write requests. In certain situations, running with biods provides little or no benefit to an NFS client, and can even result in lower throughput than running without biods.

3.3.1 Applications Performing Synchronous I/O

Biods are only invoked when applications perform asynchronous I/O to NFS-mounted files. In most cases, biods provide a significant performance boost since the majority of today's applications issue primarily asynchronous *read()* and *write()* requests. However, if your NFS client applications only perform *synchronous* I/O, then biods will offer no benefit.

3.3.2 Reading or Writing to a Very Busy or Down NFS Server

Most NFS clients mount filesystems simultaneously from many different servers. Over time, it is not uncommon for one of these NFS servers to become very busy, suffer from a network outage, or fail. When this happens, the applications running on the NFS client can still attempt to access files on this unavailable server. If biods are running during a server outage, the potential exists for all of the biods to become blocked trying to read from or write to files residing on the non-responsive NFS server. These biods will hang waiting for the server to respond.

As explained earlier in Section 3.1, when biod daemons are present any application that is reading from or writing to an NFS server will block expecting the biod daemons to service its requests. If all the biods are hung waiting for an unresponsive server, all NFS client reads and writes to all NFS servers — *even those servers that are available and responding* — can potentially hang. If biod daemons are not running then each client-side process will generate NFS read and write requests on its own behalf. The end result is that those applications attempting to access files on the unavailable server will hang as expected, but any applications accessing files residing on available NFS servers will not be affected.

3.3.3 Applications Reading Data Non-sequentially

We learned earlier that biods perform read-ahead requests on behalf of those processes reading from NFS-mounted files. Their goal is to keep the client's buffer cache populated with data that the reading application will want, thereby avoiding having the application block and wait for the data to be retrieved from the server. Keep in mind that the biods request *sequential* blocks of file data from the server. While this sequential pre-fetching definitely helps the performance of applications that read sequentially, if an NFS client application is performing predominantly non-sequential reads, the data pre-fetched by the biods will most likely be unwanted by the application, resulting in wasted system overhead.

Not all non-sequential reads will trigger the biod's read-ahead mechanism. In fact, purely random reading will most likely not generate biod involvement due to the design of the read-ahead algorithm. The current algorithm is very simple: if the starting offset of the current read request is equal to the ending offset in the previous request then it assumes the client process is performing sequential reads and the biods begin performing read-ahead operations. In the purely non-sequential read case, where each read request made by the application is for a different non-sequential location in the file, there should be no read-ahead requests performed by the biods.

Most applications do not perform purely random or purely sequential reads, so if some sequential reading is occurring followed by non-sequential reads there is still the potential for wasted overhead from unnecessary read-ahead requests. The overhead caused by having the biods pre-fetch sequential data when it is not needed by applications can, in some cases, result in worse performance than if no biods are present. Only by testing with and without biods can you determine whether your applications benefit from the biods' read-ahead semantics or not.

3.3.4 Applications Writing to Locked NFS-Mounted Files

Many of today's multi-user applications use file locks to synchronize access to shared resources. When an application on a client system locks an NFS-mounted file, any read or write requests made to this file will be performed *synchronously*. In effect, buffer cache and biod daemons are disabled for that file when a lock is present, so no benefit is gained by running biod daemons in this case. This is done to ensure data integrity in a multi-client environment.

 KEY IDEA — Client Behavior when Writing to Locked NFS-Mounted Files

HP recognized that disabling buffer cache and the biod daemons for locked NFS-mounted files, while guaranteeing data integrity, caused application performance to suffer tremendously. HP now offers customers the ability to keep buffer cache and biods enabled when locking NFS files.

This new functionality is delivered in patch PHNE_24034 (for 11.0 systems) and PHNE_24035 (for 11i systems). Since all HP NFS patches are cumulative, any patch that supersedes these patches will also contain this feature.

This feature is disabled by default and must be manually enabled on any NFS client system wishing to take advantage of the new lock semantics. To enable this feature the systems administrator should issue the following commands:

```
# echo 'nfs_new_lock_code?W 0d1' | adb -w /stand/vmunix /dev/kmem
# echo 'nfs_new_lock_code/W 0d1' | adb -w /stand/vmunix /dev/kmem
```

Two separate adb commands are used in this case to modify both the on-disk kernel file (?W syntax) and kernel memory (/W syntax). This allows the NFS file lock semantics change to take effect immediately and remain in effect even if the client system is rebooted. This parameter will be reset to 0 (i.e. disabled) if the kernel is re-built, either manually (via mk_kernel(1M)) or by installing a kernel patch. This should be kept in mind when installing kernel patches on a system where *nfs_new_lock_code* is intentionally modified.

It is important to note that even when the required patches are installed and the new locking behavior is enabled, only those NFS files that have locks placed on *the entire file* will take advantage of buffer cache and biods. NFS files that have only partial locks present (i.e. only a portion of the file is locked) will continue to use the original mechanism where biods and buffer cache are disabled.

3.3.5 Many Processes Simultaneously Reading or Writing

When biods are running, any process issuing read or write requests to an NFS mounted file will block to allow the biods to perform the I/O on their behalf. It therefore stands to reason that the maximum number of *simultaneous* I/O operations an NFS client with biods running can perform is roughly equal to the number of running biods. (The number of operations is *approximately* the same as the number of biods because reading processes can make NFS READ calls on their own behalf in certain circumstances, even with biods running.)

If the number of processes on an NFS client that are simultaneously issuing asynchronous I/O requests to NFS files is greater than the number of configured biods, it is possible that the client would experience higher throughput if no biod daemons were running. For example, if a client runs 4 biods and has 25 processes trying to simultaneously read from or write to NFS-mounted files, these 25 processes will block to let the 4 biods service their requests. If there were no biods running, each of the 25 processes would send NFS requests on its own behalf, potentially resulting in higher throughput.

3.4 How Many biods Should Your NFS Client Run?

Unfortunately, there is no one right answer for every NFS client. Setting the number of biods too low can result in poor read performance if too few read-ahead requests are occurring to keep the client's buffer cache populated. Write performance can also degrade if there are not enough biods running to keep the client's buffer cache drained, forcing writing processes to block while the biods work to empty the cache. Starting too many biods, especially on HP-UX 11.0 clients, can result in poor NFS performance because of filesystem semaphore contention.

When trying to achieve the best possible NFS client throughput, *the goal is to maximize the number of simultaneous read or write requests the client is capable of making.* This will either be achieved by tuning the number of biods appropriately for the specific client system or by disabling the biods entirely. The best course of action is to start a reasonable number of biods and then experiment with raising and lowering the number of daemons until the optimal application performance is identified.

 KEY IDEA — The Recommended Number of biods to Run on HP-UX NFS Clients

A good starting point for the number of biods is **16**. This number has shown to be large enough to allow a reasonable number of simultaneous requests but small enough to keep HP-UX 11.0 clients from paying the performance overhead of acquiring and releasing the filesystem semaphore during each request. Even though filesystem semaphore contention has been reduced in HP-UX 11i, **16** biods remains the recommended starting value on 11i.

The number of biods started at system boot time is configurable via the "NUM_NFSIOD" parameter in the /etc/rc.config.d/nfsconf file.

Remember, your mileage will vary, so it is important to experiment with different numbers of biod daemons, using production applications and load whenever possible. The optimal number of daemons may vary on a per-client basis depending upon the hardware configuration of the client (i.e. number of CPUs, physical memory, network interfaces, etc.), the number of users who share the client system, and the applications running on the client. Also, don't be afraid to experiment with disabling the biods. You may find that your NFS client performance and behavior improves without them.

3.5 Troubleshooting the biod Daemons

Most biod-related problems manifest themselves as NFS client panics, application hangs, or poor application performance. Since the biods primarily operate in the kernel, these problems usually require kernel-space troubleshooting tools and techniques to identify the root cause. However, network traces and the nfsstat(1M) command can be a used as a first-pass means of trying to determine whether the NFS client or server is causing a performance problem.

3.5.1 NFS Client System Panic

Analyzing HP-UX system dumps is a very complex and involved process, which is typically performed only by experienced HP support personnel or lab engineers. If your NFS client experiences a system panic, your best course of action is to save the system memory dump and contact HP support requesting that your memory dump be analyzed. However, there are some initial steps that can be performed to help HP support more quickly identify if the panic was triggered by one of the running biod daemons.

HP-UX 11.0 and 11i system panics are typically analyzed using the Q4 tool. Q4 is a very sophisticated and powerful debugger for HP-UX kernel crash dumps. It supports all HP-UX systems running Release 10.0 or later on PA-RISC platforms. Q4 can also be used to analyze live systems to examine kernel data structures, processes and threads, and system resources.

Listed below is a step-by-step set of instructions for using Q4 to obtain the stack trace of the process that caused the panic to occur. The <u>underlined</u> steps are the commands you type.

1. Log into the system as root and cd into the directory where the memory dump resides:

```
# cd /var/adm/crash
# ll -d crash*
drwxr-xr-x   2 root     root       1024 Feb 10 2000 crash.0
```

   In this case there is only one dump and it is located in the crash.0 directory.

```
# cd crash.0
```

2. Prepare the kernel found in the dump directory with the q4pxdb command:

```
# /usr/contrib/bin/q4pxdb ./vmunix
```

3. Launch q4:

```
# /usr/contrib/bin/q4 .
```

4. Obtain the stack trace from the process that generated the panic:

```
q4> trace event 0
    stack trace for event 0
    crash event was a panic
    panic+0x10
    report_trap_or_int_and_panic+0x8c
    b_single_word_loop+0x0
    lan6_bld_outbound_DMA_chain+0x210
    lan6_fragment_xmit_pkt+0x54
    lan6_if_resolved_output+0xb8
    unicast_ippkt+0x884
    arp_resolve+0x100
    lanc_if_output+0x50
    ip_output+0x7d4
    udp_output+0x1d4
    ku_sendto_mbuf+0x90
    clntkudp_callit+0x390
    rfscall+0x7e0
    nfswrite+0xd4
    do_bio+0x26c
    async_daemon+0x37c
    syscall+0x1f4
    $syscallrtn+0x0
```

You can identify a panic as being triggered by a biod process by examining the stack trace and looking for the **"async_daemon"** procedure, as illustrated in the above sample trace output. Most times, there will also be a procedure in the stack beginning with "nfs," such as "nfswrite," "nfsread," etc. In the above example, we can determine that the biod process was servicing an NFS write call, since "**nfswrite**" is part of the stack trace.

It is important to keep in mind that just because a biod triggered the panic, that does not imply that a defect exists in the biod code. In most cases, the biod process is simply an innocent victim of a problem located in the network transport code, the network driver code, the virtual memory subsystem, etc. However, by using the simple steps outlined earlier, you can locate several potential keywords to use when searching the online customer-viewable databases available from the IT Resource Center: *http://itrc.hp.com*.

Again, in order to determine the root cause of any system panic, the best course of action is to save the crash dump and contact HP support, requesting that the dump be analyzed.

3.5.2 NFS Client Application Hangs

NFS-based client application hangs can be caused by any number of reasons: resource limitations, non-responding NFS servers, etc. These hangs can also occur if the biods are blocked for some reason. Since the biods run in kernel space, when they block for any reason, the only way to determine what they are waiting on is to use Q4 to obtain their stack traces.

However, before diving into kernel stack debugging, some less complicated methods can be used to determine if the biods are active. A network trace can be collected and searched for any NFS requests originating from the biods, and the nfsstat(1M) command can be used to see if the client is performing any NFS read or write calls.

Look for biod requests in a network trace   One of the first steps you can take to see if the biods are generating requests is to collect a network trace on the NFS client system via the nettl(1M) command. If the trace shows any outbound NFS read or write calls issued by the biods then you can be certain that at least some of the biods are not hung.

Here are the steps for collecting a network trace and examining it for biod traffic. The underlined steps are the commands you type.

1. Use a tool such as GlancePlus to determine the TID (Thread ID) numbers for the running biod daemons. Figure 3.6 shows an example of the GlancePlus "Thread List" screen, displaying only the running biod daemons sorted by their TID fields.

```
GlancePlus - Thread List                                          _ |□| x|
File   Reports   Configure                                            Help
System: ros87252      Last Update: 16:53:26    Int: 15 sec        | T | ? |

Thread List: 4 of 107 Selected                     Users: 1

          Process                              Phys    Stop
  TID     Name                PID    CPU %     IO Rt   Reason   Pri

    806   biod                788     0.0       0.0    OTHER    154
    805   biod                787     0.0       0.0    OTHER    154
    804   biod                786     0.0       0.0    OTHER    154
    803   biod                785     0.0       0.0    OTHER    154
```

Figure 3.6   GlancePlus Thread List Displaying biod Threads

2. Start a nettl trace, collecting only outbound traffic as it passes through the IP layer. Log the output to a file named "biods." nettl will automatically append an extension of ".TRC0" on HP-UX 11.0 systems or ".TRC000" on HP-UX 11i systems:

   # /etc/nettl -tn pduout -e ns_ls_ip -f biods

3. Attempt to generate some NFS traffic on the same NFS-mounted filesystem the application is using. In this example, we assume the NFS filesystem is called "/nfs_mount":

   # cp localfile /nfs_mount/nfsfile

4. Stop the trace:

   # /etc/nettl -tf -e ns_ls_ip

5. Format the trace via `netfmt(1M)` re-directing the output to a file called "`biods.out`."

   `# /etc/netfmt -1N biods.TRC0 > biods.out`

6. Search the formatted trace for any outbound NFS write calls whose thread ids match those of the biods. Figure 3.7 contains an example of a formatted NFS write request.

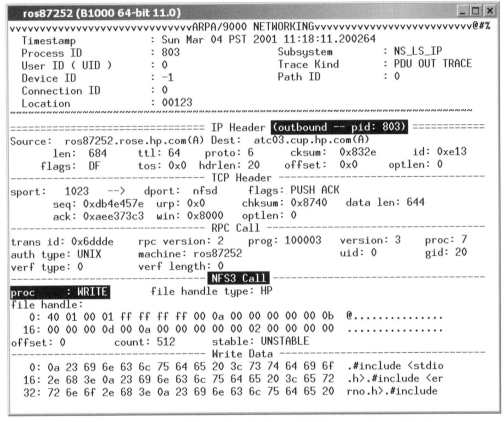

```
 ros87252 (B1000 64-bit 11.0)                                              _ □ ✕
vvvvvvvvvvvvvvvvvvvvvvvvvvvvvvvvvvARPA/9000 NETWORKINGvvvvvvvvvvvvvvvvvvvvvvvvvvv@#%
  Timestamp          : Sun Mar 04 PST 2001 11:18:11.200264
  Process ID         : 803              Subsystem     : NS_LS_IP
  User ID ( UID )    : 0                Trace Kind    : PDU OUT TRACE
  Device ID          : -1               Path ID       : 0
  Connection ID      : 0
  Location           : 00123
~~~~~~~~~~~~~~~~~~~~~~~~~~~~~~~~~~~~~~~~~~~~~~~~~~~~~~~~~~~~~~~~~~~~~~~~~~~~~~~~~~~~~~~~
================================ IP Header (outbound -- pid: 803) ============
Source:  ros87252.rose.hp.com(A) Dest:  atc03.cup.hp.com(A)
       len:  684     ttl: 64     proto: 6      cksum:  0x832e     id: 0xe13
     flags:  DF       tos: 0x0   hdrlen: 20    offset:  0x0     optlen: 0
------------------------------- TCP Header --------------------------------
sport:   1023    -->  dport:  nfsd     flags: PUSH ACK
       seq: 0xdb4e457e  urp: 0x0      chksum: 0x8740   data len: 644
       ack: 0xaee373c3  win: 0x8000    optlen: 0
------------------------------- RPC Call ----------------------------------
trans id: 0x6ddde    rpc version: 2   prog: 100003   version: 3   proc: 7
auth type: UNIX      machine: ros87252              uid: 0        gid: 20
verf type: 0         verf length: 0
------------------------------- NFS3 Call ---------------------------------
proc    : WRITE        file handle type: HP
file handle:
   0: 40 01 00 01 ff ff ff ff 00 0a 00 00 00 00 00 0b  @..............
  16: 00 00 00 0d 00 0a 00 00 00 00 00 02 00 00 00 00  ..............
offset: 0        count: 512      stable: UNSTABLE
------------------------------- Write Data --------------------------------
   0: 0a 23 69 6e 63 6c 75 64 65 20 3c 73 74 64 69 6f  .#include <stdio
  16: 2e 68 3e 0a 23 69 6e 63 6c 75 64 65 20 3c 65 72  .h>.#include <er
  32: 72 6e 6f 2e 68 3e 0a 23 69 6e 63 6c 75 64 65 20  rno.h>.#include
```

Figure 3.7 `nettl` Trace of an Outbound NFS `WRITE` from a biod

This trace output shows thread 803 sending an outbound NFS write call. GlancePlus identified thread 803 as being one of the biod threads (refer back to Figure 3.6). This proves that at least some of the biods are servicing requests, and thus are not blocked in the kernel.

Monitor `nfsstat(1M)` output to see if NFS client requests are occurring

Another non-intrusive method of determining whether biod activity is occurring is to use `nfsstat(1M)`. The `nfsstat` command retrieves a variety of statistical data maintained by the HP-UX kernel regarding the NFS and RPC (Remote Procedure Call) sub-systems. It displays this information in an easy-to-read format, allowing a systems administrator to quickly determine the number and type of NFS requests that have occurred on the system.

The following two figures (Figure 3.8 and Figure 3.9) show successive runs of the "nfsstat -cn" command taken 30 seconds apart. The "-cn" options tell nfsstat to limit the output to only the client-side NFS statistics. Comparing the output in Figure 3.8 and Figure 3.9 you can see a significant difference in the number of NFS Version 3 write calls. This is more evidence that the biods are not blocked in the kernel and there must be another reason for the non-responsive application.

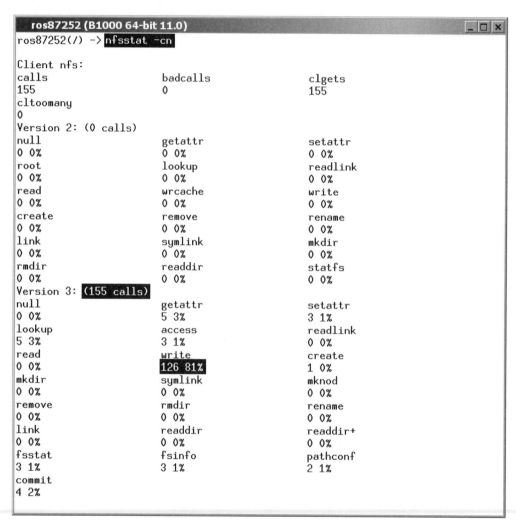

Figure 3.8 Sample Initial nfsstat Output

nfsstat can also be used to re-initialize the kernel's counters to zero (via the "-z" option), which is very useful when trying to determine which NFS client requests, if any, are sent during a specific test. Also, since clients are able to mount both NFS Version 2 and Version 3 filesystems, be sure to compare both "Version 2" and "Version 3" counters in the output.

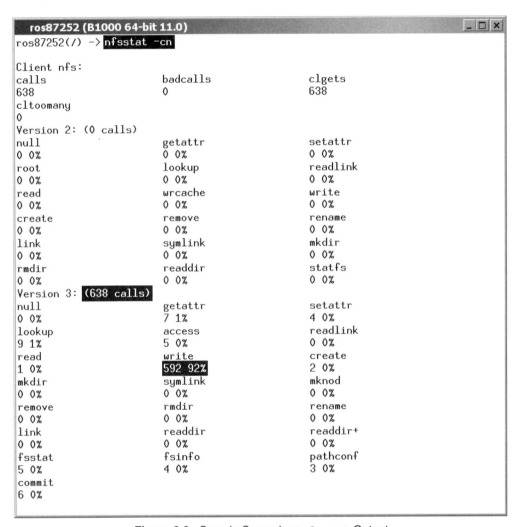

Figure 3.9 Sample Secondary `nfsstat` Output

Examining the biod daemons on the live system   If the network trace data and `nfsstat` output show no biod activity and you still believe your application is hanging as a result of the biods being blocked, the next thing to try is examining the running biods on the live system. Since the biods run in kernel space, if they become blocked for any reason, the only way to determine what they are waiting on is to use a kernel debugger such as Q4 to obtain the biods' stack traces.

The procedure for examining the biod daemons on a live system is described in detail below. The <u>underlined</u> steps are the commands you type.

1. Log into the system and make a backup copy of the running kernel:
   ```
   # cp /stand/vmunix /tmp/vmunix
   ```

2. Prepare the backup kernel with the q4pxdb command:
   ```
   # /usr/contrib/bin/q4pxdb /tmp/vmunix
   ```

3. Launch q4 specifying the backup kernel and /dev/mem
   ```
   # q4 /tmp/vmunix /dev/mem
   ```

4. Load the list of system processes. The command used to perform this task differs slightly between HP-UX 11.0 and 11i due to the redesign of the process table in 11i.
   ```
   11.0 q4> load struct proc from proc max nproc
   11i  q4> load struct proc from proc_list max nproc next p_factp
   ```

5. Find the list of biods by printing the process ID and the ASCII string label of all processes. Use grep(1) to filter out only those processes whose p_comm field is "biod."
   ```
   q4> print p_pid p_comm | grep biod
           786     "biod"
           787     "biod"
           788     "biod"
           785     "biod"
   ```

6. Keep only the biod processes:
   ```
   q4> keep p_pid>=785&&p_pid<=788
   kept 4 of 1024 struct proc's, discarded 1020
   ```

7. Print out the stack traces of all of the biod daemons:
   ```
   q4> trace pile
   stack trace for process at 0x0'01029640 (pid 786), thread at
   0x0'011174a8 (tid 804)
   process was not running on any processor
   _sleep+0x50c
   async_daemon+0x298
   coerce_scall_args+0xcc
   syscall+0x200
   $syscallrtn+0x0

   stack trace for process at 0x0'01029a00 (pid 787), thread at
   0x0'011176b0 (tid 805)
   process was not running on any processor
   _sleep+0x50c
   async_daemon+0x298
   coerce_scall_args+0xcc
   syscall+0x200
   $syscallrtn+0x0
   ```

```
stack trace for process at 0x0'01029dc0 (pid 788), thread at
0x0'011178b8 (tid 806)
```
process was not running on any processor
_sleep+0x50c
async_daemon+0x298
```
coerce_scall_args+0xcc
syscall+0x200
$syscallrtn+0x0
```

```
stack trace for process at 0x0'0102a540 (pid 785), thread at
0x0'01117cc8 (tid 803)
```
process was not running on any processor
_sleep+0x50c
async_daemon+0x298
```
coerce_scall_args+0xcc
syscall+0x200
$syscallrtn+0x0
```

As discussed earlier in Section 3.5.1 "NFS Client System Panic," the biod processes will always have "**async_daemon**" in their stack trace. Looking at the above trace output, we see that all four daemons have identical stacks and all four are calling "_sleep" directly from the "async_daemon" function. This indicates that all four of the biods are idle, waiting for new requests to arrive. The output shows that none of the processes were running on a CPU, which is expected if the daemons are idle.

If the biods are processing requests when you collect the stack trace data then you should be able to distinguish the type of request (i.e. nfsread, nfswrite) by examining the output. The information contained in the stack traces may not be immediately understandable to most people, but this data could help an HP support engineer determine whether the biods are blocked, and if so, why. The non-idle stack trace data could also provide a number of good keyword candidates to use when searching for known NFS client hang problems via HP's IT Resource Center web site: *http://itrc.hp.com.*

In some cases, Q4 may be unable to obtain a viable stack trace of the running threads. In that event, your best course of action is open a support call with HP. The support engineer will most likely request that you initiate a TOC (Transfer of Control) of the system, effectively forcing your system to write the contents of its memory to disk and reboot. The resulting memory dump would then need to be analyzed by HP support.

3.5.3 Poor NFS Application Performance

In some cases, the problem is not that an NFS application hangs completely, but rather performs poorly. These types of problems are usually the most difficult to resolve because the slow performance could be influenced by so many factors, including: a slow server, slow networks, slow disks, lack of memory, lack of buffer cache, higher priority processes consuming system resources, etc.

While these problems can be elusive, there are many tools available to help narrow down the list of potential candidates. A `nettl` trace can be examined to determine if there are delays in the outbound NFS requests sent by the client or delays in the inbound replies from the server. The `nfsstat` command can show whether the client is experiencing NFS retransmissions and timeouts, which can dramatically influence an application's performance. There are also tools available from HP Support, such as `tusc`, that can help determine what system calls the NFS application is making during the performance slowdown. Finally, there are kernel profiling tools available, such as kgmon, which can reveal what the NFS client's kernel is spending its time doing. All of this information, when analyzed by an HP Support Engineer, can help establish the root cause of the performance problem.

Look for delays or retransmissions in a network trace   We learned in the previous section how a `nettl` trace can be used to determine if the biod processes are generating any outbound requests. A similar procedure can be used to collect a set of network traces for use in troubleshooting an NFS application that is performing poorly. The only difference from the procedure outlined in Section 3.5.2 is that a network trace should be collected on *both* the NFS client and the server systems while the application slowness is observed.

 KEY IDEA — Collect Network Traces on Both NFS Client and Server Systems

When troubleshooting an NFS performance problem via network traces, it is strongly recommended that traces be collected **on both the client and server** systems so that any discrepancies (i.e. delays, requests that get no replies, retransmitted requests, etc.) can be verified from both systems' perspective.

For example, if the client-side trace shows that an NFS request was successfully sent to the server but no reply was received, the server's trace should be consulted to verify whether the client's request ever arrived intact on the server. If the server's trace shows that the request never arrived, it would indicate that the request was dropped in transit somewhere in the network, and the network should therefore become the focus of your investigation. However, if the server-side trace confirms that the server received the request but did not reply, it would indicate that a potential problem exists on the server system itself. In this situation, the server system should be investigated further.

Alternately, if a server-side trace shows that the server received a request and successfully sent a reply, but the client's trace does not show the reply being received, it would indicate that the reply packet was most likely dropped by the network before arriving on the client.

Without *both* client-side and server-side traces to confirm and validate your findings, incorrect conclusions could be reached and valuable time could be wasted troubleshooting the wrong component of your NFS environment.

Sample NFS call and reply packets are included in Figure 3.10 and Figure 3.11. These two figures have several key fields highlighted which are frequently referenced during network trace analysis, including:

1. **Timestamps** — used for calculating delays occurring between outbound requests and inbound replies, delays between successive outbound requests, and retransmitted requests

2. **Inbound** vs. **Outbound** — whether the packet is being sent or received by the system

3. **Call** vs. **Reply** — indicates whether the client is sending a Call or receiving a Reply

4. **Procedure Type** — the type of NFS operation in the packet (i.e. READ, WRITE, etc.)

5. **Transaction ID** — unique identifier for the specific NFS request and its associated reply

6. **Procedure Status** — indicates if an error occurred while the server processed the request (contained in reply packets only — see Figure 3.11)

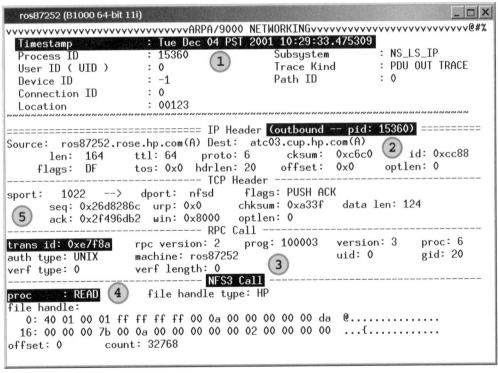

Figure 3.10 `nettl` Trace of an Outbound NFS READ Call

By referencing these fields in the trace we can identify this packet as an outbound READ request that was sent at 10:29:33.475309 on December 4th, 2001 with a transaction ID of 0xe7f8a. We can also identify the packet in Figure 3.11 as the reply to the earlier READ request because the reply has the transaction IDs in both packets match. We can further conclude that the READ call completed successfully (status: OK). Finally, by subtracting the timestamp in the outbound request packet from the timestamp in the inbound reply, we know that this request/reply sequence took only 0.007468 seconds to complete.

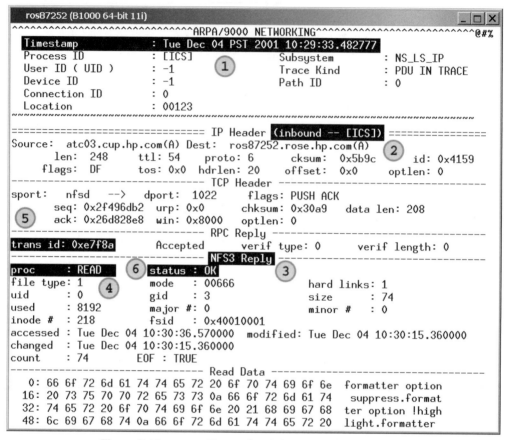

Figure 3.11 nettl Trace of an Inbound NFS READ Reply

Using these same key fields, you can search the formatted client and server traces you collected for several possible scenarios, including:

1. Delays occurring between the time the client receives a reply to an existing request and the time the client sends a new request.

2. Delays occurring between an outbound request and the inbound reply from the server.

3. Replies from the server taking too long to arrive, causing the client to re-send the request.

4. Outbound requests that receive no reply from the server.

5. NFS replies indicating that an error condition occurred on the server while processing the request (i.e. a reply status other than "0," "OK," or "SUCCESS").

Spotting delays in a trace can be a very difficult process, since it involves identifying matching call and reply packets by matching their transaction IDs and computing the duration of the call/reply sequence by subtracting the "call" timestamp from the "reply" timestamp. However, this information can be very useful in determining whether the cause of the application slowdown is the NFS server, the client (either the system or the application), or the network.

Also, on busy networks a `nettl` trace can capture large amounts of data very quickly, causing the size of formatted trace files to become unwieldy to search. Care should be taken to capture as tight a sample of data surrounding the problem as possible.

KEY IDEA — Collecting `nettl(1M)` Traces on Fast Network Links

Due to architectural limitations, the `nettl` trace utility is not always able to keep up with today's faster links. It is not uncommon for formatted traces collected on Gigabit EtherNet links to contain many `nettl` warning messages indicating the number of packets that could not be collected.

It is therefore very important to configure `nettl` to use the largest buffer sizes available (via the "`-tracemax`" and "`-size`" options) when collecting data on fast networks. You can also instruct nettl to capture only a small portion of each packet (via the "`-m`" option), thereby limiting the total amount of data collected. Refer to `nettl(1M)` man page for more information.

In some situations it may be necessary to use hardware-based network tracing tools, such as network sniffers or LAN Analyzers, to collect the data needed to accurately troubleshoot an NFS performance problem.

If the collected traces show that the server is responding quickly to requests but the NFS client seems to be pausing between requests, this would indicate that either the client system or the client application is the cause of the slow performance, and they should be the focus of further investigation via tools such as `tusc` (described later in this section). If noticeable delays are detected between the client's outbound requests and the server's inbound replies it would indicate that the server and/or the network are busy. If the server's replies are taking so long to arrive that the client is forced to retransmit requests, it would indicate that either the server is extremely busy or the network is dropping packets. Retransmitted requests can be found by searching the trace for multiple outbound requests with matching transaction ID numbers.

This again points out the importance of having both a client and server trace to validate your assumptions. The client trace may indicate a delay, but without the server trace to compare against there is no way of knowing whether the delay is induced by the server or the network.

Monitor `nfsstat(1M)` output for potential performance problems We saw earlier how the `nfsstat(1M)` command can be used to determine whether outbound NFS calls are being sent. This tool can also display a wealth of information about how the NFS subsystem and the underlying RPC subsystem are behaving on the client.

Figure 3.12 shows an example of "`nfsstat -cr`" output. The "`-cr`" options instruct `nfsstat(1M)` to only display the client-side RPC statistics. A description of each of these statistic is included in Table 3.1.

```
gmnfsb31 (J6000 64-bit 11i)                                        _ □ ✕
gmnfsb31(/) -> nfsstat -cr

Client rpc:
Connection oriented:
calls                   badcalls                badxids
1865049                 10                      10
timeouts                newcreds                badverfs
0                       0                       0
timers                  cantconn                nomem
0                       0                       0
interrupts
10
Connectionless oriented:
calls                   badcalls                retrans
1314088                 0                       13
badxids                 timeouts                waits
8                       13                      0
newcreds                badverfs                timers
0                       0                       4
toobig                  nomem                   cantsend
0                       0                       0
bufulocks
0
```

Figure 3.12 `nfsstat` Displaying Client-side RPC Statistics

The NFS client system used in the above example is running HP-UX 11i, which supports both NFS/UDP and NFS/TCP. Since both UDP and TCP transport protocols are supported, the HP-UX kernel maintains separate sets of counters for each transport protocol, allowing `nfsstat` to display separate statistics associated with NFS/TCP traffic (Connection oriented) and NFS/UDP traffic (Connectionless oriented). On HP-UX 11.0 clients that have installed NFS patches containing the NFS/TCP functionality and enabled NFS/TCP support, both sets of statistics will be displayed. On HP-UX 11.0 clients that do not have NFS/TCP support enabled, only the NFS/UDP (Connectionless oriented) statistics will be displayed.

For more information about enabling NFS/TCP on HP-UX 11.0 systems refer to Chapter 10 "NFS/UDP vs. NFS/TCP."

Table 3.1 Definitions for `nfsstat` Client-side RPC Statistics

Variable	Transport	Description
calls	Connectionless or Connection-oriented	The total number of RPC calls sent across the specific transport
badcalls	Connectionless or Connection-oriented	The total number of calls rejected by the RPC layer
badxids	Connectionless or Connection-oriented	The number of times a reply from a server was received which did not correspond to any outstanding call
timeouts	Connectionless or Connection-oriented	The number of times a call timed out while waiting for a reply from the server
newcreds	Connectionless or Connection-oriented	The number of times authentication information had to be refreshed
badverfs	Connectionless or Connection-oriented	The number of times the call failed due to a bad verifier in the response
timers	Connectionless or Connection-oriented	The number of times the calculated time-out value was greater than or equal to the minimum specified time out value for a call
cantconn	Connection-oriented	The number of times the call failed due to a failure to make a connection to the server
nomem	Connectionless or Connection-oriented	The number of times the call failed due to a failure to allocate memory
interrupts	Connection-oriented	The number of times the call was interrupted by a signal before completing
retrans	Connectionless	The number of times a call had to be retransmitted due to a timeout while waiting for a reply from the server
waits	Connectionless	Reserved for future use
toobig	Connectionless	Reserved for future use
cantsend	Connectionless	The number of times a client was unable to send an RPC request over a connectionless transport when it tried to do so
bufulocks	Connectionless	Reserved for future use

Many of the same statistics are kept for both UDP and TCP protocols. Each protocol maintains several transport-specific counters as well. Once you understand what these counters indicate, you can use this information to make an informed decision about the likely cause of an NFS performance problem. Here are two examples to illustrate how these statistics can be used.

Scenario 1   If the connectionless statistic "badxids" is roughly the same as the "timeouts" counter it typically indicates that the NFS server is slow in responding to requests. Here's how this scenario would develop:

1. The client sends a request with a unique transaction ID and waits a calculated period of time for the server to reply using the same transaction ID.
2. The client does not receive a reply in the calculated time period and it retransmits the request using the same transaction ID. This causes the "timeouts" counter to increment.
3. The server receives both the original request and the retransmitted request and replies to both using the same transaction ID.
4. The client receives both replies from the server. The first reply satisfies the client's outstanding request. The second reply causes the client to increment its "badxids" counter because the client no longer has a request waiting for a reply with this transaction ID.

Scenario 2   If the connectionless "retrans" and "timeouts" rates were an order of magnitude larger than the "badxids" count, it typically indicates that packet loss is occurring somewhere in the environment because the client must not be receiving replies to every outbound request and retransmission it sends.

In other words, if every single request and reply were to successfully traverse the network then the client should receive a reply for every request it sends — including any retransmitted requests. We learned in Scenario 1 that when a client receives multiple replies with the same transaction ID it will increment its "badxids" counter. Since this counter is not incrementing with the same frequency as the "timeouts" counter, the inference is that some requests or replies are being dropped before arriving on the client or server.

TIP: Connection-oriented NFS filesystems use the built-in TCP/IP retransmission and timeout mechanism to determine when to re-send requests. It is therefore uncommon to see many connection-oriented "timeouts" logged, unless the *timeo* mount option is specified on the NFS/TCP mount point. *Specifying the "timeo" option on an NFS/TCP mount is not recommended.*

For more information about the UDP and TCP retransmission mechanisms and the *timeo* mount option, refer to Sections 10.3 "Managing Retransmissions and Timeouts" and 10.3.6 "How Does the timeo Mount Option Affect UDP and TCP?"

Use `tusc(1)` to look for delays during system call When troubleshooting slow NFS-based applications, it can sometimes be very useful to understand exactly where in the application's source code a delay is occurring. In the case where a network trace shows that your NFS server is responding quickly to requests but the client seems to be pausing in between sending new requests, it would be extremely helpful to know which system calls your application is making in order to help identify the possible cause of these delays.

For example, is the application making a system call like `gethostbyname(3N)` in order to resolve a remote hostname? If so, this could indicate a problem with the hostname resolution mechanisms your environment uses, such as NIS, NIS+, DNS, or LDAP. Is your application pausing while attempting to perform I/O to an NFS filesystem by executing a `read(2)`, `write(2)`, or `mmap(2)` call? Knowing exactly where the application is experiencing a slowdown can be instrumental in determining which subsystems to investigate.

This type of application-specific information can be collected using several different methods, some more intrusive and time-consuming than others. The program can be examined with a debugger, although attaching to a running process and trying to collect stack traces can dramatically change the timing of an application's execution. Also, there is no guarantee that if you attach to the program and take a snapshot that the application will still be sitting in the code where it experienced a delay. Another way to collect this information would be to rewrite the application and add instrumentation in the form of debug logging. This method is very time-consuming and it assumes you have source code access and a build environment for the application. Also, without knowing where to begin instrumenting in the application there is no guarantee that you will add the debug logging statements in the appropriate location to find the delay.

The least intrusive method of determining where an application is seeing a delay is to use a system call tracing facility to monitor the progress of the program while it executes. The tracing utility can log the various system calls made by the application along with their elapsed time. This information, in the hands of someone familiar with the application source code, can be used to pinpoint the location in the application source code where the delay is occurring.

While HP-UX does not distribute a system call tracing facility with their operating systems, several of these utilities have been developed for HP-UX. The most commonly used system call tracer on HP-UX is `tusc(1)`, which stands for "Trace UNIX System Calls." `tusc` was developed by Chris Bertin of the HP Open Systems Lab. Chris also maintains the program, adding new features and porting to new operating system platforms as needed.

The latest version of the `tusc` utility can be obtained from: *ftp://ftp.cup.hp.com/dist/networking/misc/tusc.shar* or from the "Software Porting and Archive Centre for HP-UX" web site: *http://hpux.cs.utah.edu*. The `tusc` shell archive package includes the `tusc` utility itself, a man page explaining the extensive command-line options available, and a "`truss`" symbolic link, which allows `tusc` to emulate the Solaris™ `truss(1)` utility.

`tusc` can be run on the same command-line as the application experiencing the problem, or it can attach to a currently running instance of the application. Figure 3.13 shows an example of running the "`ls`" command with `tusc` and a portion of the collected output.

```
ros87252 (B1000 64-bit 11i)                                              _ □ X
ros87252(/) -> tusc -T %T -o ls.tusc.output ls
.ICEauthority    .sh_history     dev              net              usr
.TTauthority     .sw             etc              nfs_mount        var
.Xauthority      CacheFS         home             opt
.dt              bin             lib              sbin
.dtprofile       cache           lost+found       stand
.profile         core            ls.tusc.output   tmp

ros87252(/) -> head -15 ls.tusc.output
12:41:36 execve("/usr/bin/ls", 0x7f7f0400, 0x7f7f0408) ... = 0 [32-bit]
12:41:36 utssys(0x7f7f24d0, 0, 0) ..................... = 0
12:41:36 open("/usr/lib/dld.sl", O_RDONLY, 01734) ........ = 4
12:41:36 read(4, "02\v010e0512@ \0\0\0\0\0\0\0\0\0"..., 128) = 128
12:41:36 lseek(4, 128, SEEK_SET) ......................... = 128
12:41:36 read(4, "10\0\004\0\0\0( \001a194\0\0\0\0"..., 48) = 48
12:41:36 mmap(NULL, 106900, PROT_READ|PROT_EXEC, MAP_SHARED|MAP_SHLIB, 4, 0x7000
) = 0xc0010000
12:41:36 mmap(NULL, 13000, PROT_READ|PROT_WRITE|PROT_EXEC, MAP_PRIVATE|MAP_SHLIB
, 4, 0x22000) = 0x7b050000
12:41:36 close(4) ........................................ = 0
12:41:36 getuid() ........................................ = 0 (0)
12:41:36 getuid() ........................................ = 0 (0)
12:41:36 getgid() ........................................ = 20 (20)
12:41:36 getgid() ........................................ = 20 (20)
12:41:36 mmap(NULL, 8192, PROT_READ|PROT_WRITE|PROT_EXEC, MAP_PRIVATE|MAP_ANONYM
OUS, -1, NULL) = 0x7b04e000
12:41:36 sysconf(_SC_CPU_VERSION) ........................ = 532
```

Figure 3.13 tusc Output Collected from the ls Command

This sample output illustrates how even a relatively simple command like "ls" required over 100 system calls to complete, including opening shared libraries, seeking to specific locations in the library, reading the library, memory-mapping data, retrieving user ID numbers, etc.

Since tusc was launched with the "-T %T" option, each entry in the log file contains a timestamp showing when the system call was made. By reviewing this timestamp information, it may be possible to identify where the unexpected application delays occur. Dozens of other tusc command-line options are available for doing such things as following forked processes, displaying the arguments passed to the exec(2) system call, counting the number of system calls issued by the application, etc.[1]

While the data in the tusc output file may not seem easily understandable, in the hands of a knowledgeable systems administrator or application developer it can provide critical insight into where in the NFS environment the performance problem resides.

---

1.   Refer to the tusc(1) man page included in the downloadable shell archive package for details on the available command-line options and their syntax.

Use kernel profiling utilities to interrogate the client's kernel behavior

When other data collection methods have been exhausted and there is still no clear evidence of where the performance problem lies, it can sometimes be useful to collect kernel profiling data on the NFS client. The goal of any kernel profiling effort is to identify which functions the kernel is spending the majority of its time executing. Knowing where the kernel is dedicating its resources can provide a great deal of insight into deciding which subsystem to investigate.

The most commonly used kernel-profiling tool available for HP-UX systems is kgmon. This tool has been used on numerous occasions to help HP labs locate bottlenecks in our kernel.

WARNING!   **WARNING!**   **WARNING!**

Profiling a live kernel can be a very risky proposition. It should never be performed on a production system unless there is absolutely no way to reproduce the same performance behavior in a test environment.

Many precautions need to be taken before even attempting this procedure on a test system, such as configuring the kernel with sufficient equivalently mapped memory. Unexpected results can occur during any profiling effort, including system panics. For this reason, HP does not ship kgmon or any other kernel profiling tools with HP-UX, nor does HP officially support using kgmon on customer systems. However, when used with caution (preferably in a test environment) by knowledgeable HP support engineers, kernel profiling data can be extremely useful in better understanding an elusive performance issue.

WARNING!   **WARNING!**   **WARNING!**

A good example of how kgmon was used to isolate the source of an NFS client bottleneck occurred when HP investigated an issue where the "ls" command, issued on an HP-UX 11.0 client, took an excessive amount of time to return the contents of an NFS-mounted directory containing thousands of files. A detailed explanation of this problem and the identified solutions are included in the box labeled "NFS Performance Example: Reading a Large Directory" in Section 2.1.1. Figure 3.14 shows an example of the kgmon output collected during such a test.

```
ros87252 (B1000 64-bit 11.0)                                          _ □ x
%time  cumsecs  seconds   calls   msec/call  name
 49.7    46.39    46.39                       idle
 30.5    74.83    28.44                       binvalfree
 13.0    86.97    12.14                       psema_spin_n
  3.0    89.77     2.80                       bflush1
  0.7    90.38     0.61                       pdc_call
  0.6    90.95     0.57                       tflush
  0.4    91.33     0.38                       find_thread_other_spu
```

Figure 3.14 kgmon Output Collected on HP-UX 11.0 NFS Client

The output reveals that the NFS client was spending the majority of its non-idle time in the "binvalfree" routine, which is one of the primary buffer cache management functions. While this information might be meaningless to someone who does not have access to HP-UX kernel source code, it was a critical piece of data that helped HP labs understand the root cause of the problem and design a solution.

 KEY IDEA — The Importance of Patching the NFS Client Kernel and Commands

HP continually strives to improve the quality of HP-UX by distributing software patches containing both defect fixes and functionality enhancements. Many of these fixes and enhancements can significantly improve the performance and behavior of critical system components, such as the NFS client kernel and commands code.

It is *strongly* recommended that the latest NFS patches be installed on every HP-UX system in order to take advantage of these improvements. Contact HP support to obtain a current set of patches for your specific operating system. You can also generate a current patch list using the tools available at HP's IT Resource Center: *http://itrc.hp.com*.

For a detailed discussion on the importance of keeping your HP-UX NFS client and server systems patched with current code, refer to Appendix B "Patching Considerations."

nfsd Daemons and Threads

The nfsd daemons and threads are the primary NFS server-side workhorses. They are responsible for handling the majority of all NFS server requests with the exception of MOUNT[1] requests and file locking[2] requests. HP-UX 11.0 and 11i servers use *nfsd* daemons to service NFS/UDP requests and kernel threads, spawned by a special nfsd daemon called *nfsktcpd*, to service NFS/TCP requests. Unlike the biods on NFS clients, these daemons and threads must be running on a system for it to serve NFS filesystems.

Identifying the optimal number of NFS/UDP nfsd daemons and NFS/TCP kernel threads to run on a given system is key to achieving optimal NFS performance. While one server will perform best with 64 daemons and threads, another may need over 100 to perform at its peak. Although the UDP daemons and TCP threads perform similar functions (i.e. they both service NFS requests for clients, albeit on different network transports), they are managed quite differently by the server's kernel. Understanding these differences can be helpful when trying to determine the proper balance of UDP daemons and TCP threads for your NFS server.

This chapter begins by describing the various daemon and thread components that HP-UX 11.0 and 11i servers use to process NFS requests. This is followed by a high-level overview of how the server's kernel allocates and distributes the UDP-based nfsds and how the threads used to handle NFS/TCP requests are managed. It then offers recommendations for identifying the optimal number of UDP nfsd daemons and TCP kernel threads for your NFS server to run. Finally, it describes the tools and techniques available for troubleshooting nfsd problems.

1. MOUNT requests are handled by the rpc.mountd daemon, which is described in Chapter 5.

2. NFS file lock requests are handled by the rpc.lockd and rpc.statd daemons, which are described in Chapter 6.

HP-~~UX~~11i   Difference Between HP-UX 11.0 and 11i:
                        The Default Number of UDP nfsds Started

The default number of UDP nfsd daemons launched on HP-UX systems prior to 11i is **4**.
Starting at 11i, the default number was increased to **16**.

4.1 What Are the Various "nfsd" Daemons and Threads?

Prior to HP-UX 11.0, the only daemon used to service inbound NFS requests was *nfsd*.
This daemon only serviced NFS/UDP filesystems since NFS/TCP was not supported prior to
11.0. In fact, NFS/TCP was not supported on HP-UX 11.0 when it originally shipped. Support
for this technology was added via NFS patches in March 2000.[3]

When HP Labs developed its NFS/TCP solution, they decided to use pools of kernel
threads to service NFS/TCP requests as opposed to the traditional nfsd daemons. A quick look at
the list of threads[4] running on an HP-UX 11.0 or 11i NFS server, such as the list in Figure 4.1,
reveals that several daemons and threads are now used to service NFS requests, including
multiple nfsds, multiple nfsktcpd threads, and a single nfskd process.

GlancePlus - Thread List							_ □ ×
File Reports Configure							Help
System: ros87252 Last Update: 18:29:28 Int: 15 sec							T ?
Thread List: 10 of 112 Selected				Users: 1			
TID	Process Name	PID	PPID	CPU %	Phys IO Rt	Stop Reason	Pri
18529	nfsktcpd	18274	0	0.2	4.4	SYSTM	152
18523	nfsktcpd	18274	0	0.2	4.4	SYSTM	152
18340	nfsktcpd	18274	0	0.0	4.4	OTHER	152
18306	nfsktcpd	18274	0	0.0	4.4	NFS	153
1840	nfsd	1820	1813	0.0	0.0	OTHER	154
1836	nfsd	1816	1813	0.0	0.0	OTHER	154
1834	nfsd	1814	1813	0.0	0.0	OTHER	154
1833	nfsd	1813	1	0.0	0.0	OTHER	154
1829	nfsd	1809	1	0.0	0.0	SLEEP	154
767	nfskd	748	0	0.0	0.0	OTHER	152

Figure 4.1 GlancePlus Thread List Displaying NFS Server Threads

3.   For a complete discussion of NFS/TCP and how it differs from NFS/UDP, refer to Chapter 10.

4.   GlancePlus must be configured to list "threads" instead of "processes" or the nfsktcpd threads will not be listed.

4.1.1 nfsd

As stated earlier, *nfsds* have traditionally been used on HP-UX systems to service NFS requests that arrive on the server via the UDP transport. Until HP-UX added support for NFS/TCP, these were the only daemons used to service NFS requests. Although implemented as a user-space daemon, the nfsd spends the majority of its time working in the kernel. Today, these daemons are still used to process NFS/UDP requests on HP-UX 11.0 and 11i servers; however nfsds also plays a critical role in delivering NFS/TCP functionality — connection management. On NFS/TCP-enabled servers[5] one additional nfsd is launched whose sole responsibility is to establish TCP connections with NFS clients upon request and tear down idle connections.[6]

How can I tell which nfsd is managing NFS/TCP connections? The nfsd process used for managing NFS/TCP connections is distinguishable from the NFS/UDP nfsds by the fact that it will always have a parent process ID (PPID) of 1 and it will never have any child processes associated with it (i.e. its PID is not listed as the PPID of any other process). Looking at the GlancePlus output in Figure 4.2, you will notice this system has five nfsds running — only one of which has a PPID of 1 and no child processes — PID 1809.

```
┌─────────────────────────────────────────────────────────────────────────┐
│  GlancePlus - Thread List                                    _│□│×│      │
├─────────────────────────────────────────────────────────────────────────┤
│  File   Reports   Configure                                      Help     │
├─────────────────────────────────────────────────────────────────────────┤
│  System: ros87252    Last Update: 18:29:28    Int: 15 sec       │T│ ?│   │
├─────────────────────────────────────────────────────────────────────────┤
│  Thread List: 10 of 112 Selected                     Users: 1            │
└─────────────────────────────────────────────────────────────────────────┘
```

TID	Process Name	PID	PPID	CPU %	Phys IO Rt	Stop Reason	Pri
18529	nfsktcpd	18274	0	0.2	4.4	SYSTM	152
18523	nfsktcpd	18274	0	0.2	4.4	SYSTM	152
18340	nfsktcpd	18274	0	0.0	4.4	OTHER	152
18306	nfsktcpd	18274	0	0.0	4.4	NFS	153
1840	nfsd	1820	1813	0.0	0.0	OTHER	154
1836	nfsd	1816	1813	0.0	0.0	OTHER	154
1834	nfsd	1814	1813	0.0	0.0	OTHER	154
1833	nfsd	1813	1	0.0	0.0	OTHER	154
1829	nfsd	1809	1	0.0	0.0	SLEEP	154
767	nfskd	748	0	0.0	0.0	OTHER	152

Figure 4.2 Identifying the nfsd Managing TCP Connections

---

5. NFS/TCP is enabled by default on all 11i systems. NFS/TCP must be manually enabled on HP-UX 11.0 systems. Refer to Chapter 10 "NFS/UDP vs. NFS/TCP" for a set of step-by-step instructions to enable NFS/TCP on HP-UX 11.0 systems.

6. For a complete description of how NFS/TCP connections are managed, refer to Section 10.2 "Connection Management."

4.1.2 nfsktcpd

As stated earlier, HP decided to use pools of kernel threads to service NFS/TCP requests instead of user-space nfsds. These threads are all associated under a single process called *nfsktcpd*. This process is dynamically created by the server's kernel the first time an NFS/TCP request is received by the server. Since the process is created in the kernel, as opposed to being created by a user-space process, the parent process ID will be "0" and the process cannot be killed. In addition, all of the individual threads associated with this process are also named *nfsktcpd*.

The GlancePlus thread list in Figure 4.3 shows this system is currently running 4 nfsktcpd threads whose TIDs are 18306, 18340, 18523, and 18529.

```
GlancePlus - Thread List                                              _ □ ×

File   Reports   Configure                                                Help

System: ros87252      Last Update: 18:29:28     Int: 15 sec          T   ?

Thread List: 10 of 112 Selected                        Users: 1

          Process                                    Phys    Stop
   TID    Name              PID     PPID   CPU %     IO Rt   Reason  Pri

   18529  nfsktcpd          18274      0     0.2       4.4   SYSTM   152
   18523  nfsktcpd          18274      0     0.2       4.4   SYSTM   152
   18340  nfsktcpd          18274      0     0.0       4.4   OTHER   152
   18306  nfsktcpd          18274      0     0.0       4.4   NFS     153
    1840  nfsd               1820   1813     0.0       0.0   OTHER   154
    1836  nfsd               1816   1813     0.0       0.0   OTHER   154
    1834  nfsd               1814   1813     0.0       0.0   OTHER   154
    1833  nfsd               1813      1     0.0       0.0   OTHER   154
    1829  nfsd               1809      1     0.0       0.0   SLEEP   154
     767  nfskd               748      0     0.0       0.0   OTHER   152
```

Figure 4.3 nfsktcpd Threads Used to Service NFS/TCP Requests

4.1.3 nfskd

The *nfskd* daemon currently serves no useful purpose on HP-UX 11.0 or 11i systems. It was originally intended to be a UDP-equivalent of the *nfsktcpd* daemon — a single process where NFS/UDP kernel threads would associate themselves. HP has not yet implemented server-side NFS/UDP kernel thread support — NFS/UDP requests are serviced by the nfsd daemons — so the nfskd daemon remains idle.[7] Like nfsktcpd, nfskd is dynamically created by the kernel, which means it will always have a PPID of "0" and it cannot be killed.

---

7.   Currently nfskd is started merely as a placeholder in the event that NFS/UDP kernel threads functionality is added in a future release of HP-UX.

4.2 NFS Server UDP Daemon Management

When trying to determine the optimal number of UDP nfsds for a given server, it is helpful to have some basic understanding of how these daemons process inbound requests. With this information, a systems administrator can better determine when a different number of nfsds may be needed on an NFS server to achieve optimal performance.

4.2.1 Influences of a Streams-based Network Transport

Prior to 11.0, HP-UX used a sockets-based network transport implementation. By adopting a Streams-based network transport in HP-UX 11.0, several performance gains were realized.

Decreased likelihood of UDP socket overflows   The nfsd daemons use a well-known port number to receive requests from clients — 2049. With the sockets-based transport used prior to HP-UX 11.0, only a single UDP socket was used to receive all NFS requests from the clients. The nfsds worked to pull requests from the socket buffer quickly enough to keep the socket from running out of memory. When too few nfsds were running to keep up with demand, the socket memory on port 2049 would eventually be exhausted and overflows would result. When overflows occur, inbound requests are dropped without ever being queued on the server's socket, forcing NFS clients to retransmit their requests.

With the release of version 11.0, HP-UX switched to a Streams-based network transport. While this did not change the fact that all NFS clients still sent their requests to the server's port 2049, having a Streams-based implementation allowed HP to use techniques like stream "cloning" and increased stream head buffer capacities to decrease the likelihood of overflows occurring. Both of these techniques are discussed in greater detail below.

Even with the Streams-based transport used by HP-UX 11.0 and 11i, UDP overflows can still occur, and thus remain a consideration when determining the appropriate number of UDP daemons to run on a given NFS server.[8]

Each CPU has a separate stream head (stream "cloning")   One of the techniques used to increase NFS server efficiency on HP-UX 11.0 and 11i is stream "cloning." This is where the single stream associated with UDP port 2049 is replicated on a per-CPU basis, thus providing multiple queues for inbound requests. By allowing each CPU its own streams instance on which to receive requests, the likelihood of overflowing port 2049 is greatly diminished.

In addition, a new kernel module was introduced called "*nfsm*" and pushed directly onto the stream stack. This module allows the nfsds to interact directly with kernel, avoiding process context switches occurring between the stream head and the nfsd. Figure 4.4 shows an example of how this cloned stream mechanism would work on a 2-CPU server. A separate stream head is allocated for each CPU, and each stream head has a "dedicated" pool of nfsd daemons associated with it. The concept of multiple nfsd pools is discussed in more detail in Section 4.2.2.

---

8.   UDP socket overflow detection is explained in detail in the troubleshooting Section 4.5.3.

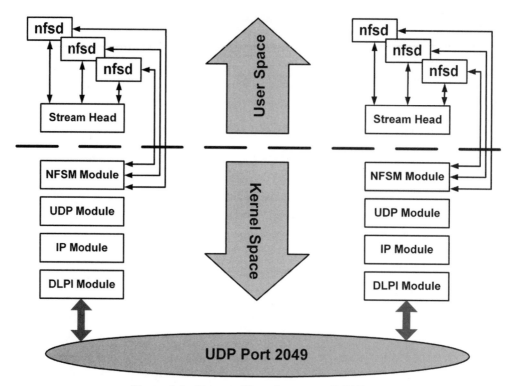

Figure 4.4   Streams Cloned on a per-CPU Basis

Streams receive buffer size is calculated by the number of nfsds running

Prior to HP-UX 11.0, a single UDP socket was used to receive all inbound NFS requests. This socket had a buffer size of 256KB, which had a tendency to fill up rather quickly if the server was being bombarded with large requests (especially WRITE requests, which could contain up to 32KB of data per request) and not enough nfsds were running to keep the socket drained.

We just learned how HP-UX 11.0 and 11i implement separate stream heads for each CPU, and each stream head has its own receive buffer. The *minimum* size for this buffer is 65,536 bytes (64KB) and the *maximum* size is 524,288 bytes (512KB). The buffer size increases by 8KB for each new nfsd launched. This means that at least 64 nfsds must be running in order for the kernel to allocate the maximum allowable buffer space for each stream head (i.e. 64 daemons * 8192 bytes = 512KB). If more than 64 daemons are launched the buffer size will remain at 512KB. If 8 or fewer nfsds are started the high-water mark will be set to 64KB.

The maximum size of the stream head buffer is calculated at nfsd start time and reported in the /var/adm/syslog.log file, as shown in Figure 4.5. The system in this example is starting 6 nfsd daemons. Since this number is less than 8, the minimum sized stream head buffer (65,536 bytes) is used.

```
┌──────────────────────────────────────────────────────────────────────────────┐
│  atc03 (L2000 64-bit 11i)                                              _ □ X   │
├──────────────────────────────────────────────────────────────────────────────┤
│ atc03(/) -> tail -15 /var/adm/syslog/syslog.log                               │
│ Jan 20 16:33:14 atc03 /usr/sbin/nfsd[8406]: Setting STREAMS-HEAD high water value to 65536. (1)│
│ Jan 20 16:33:15 atc03 /usr/sbin/nfsd[8408]: nfsd do_one mpctl succeeded: ncpus = 2. (2)│
│ Jan 20 16:33:15 atc03 /usr/sbin/nfsd[8408]: nfsd do_one pmap 2 (3)            │
│ Jan 20 16:33:15 atc03 /usr/sbin/nfsd[8408]: nfsd do_one pmap 3 (3)           │
│ Jan 20 16:33:15 atc03 /usr/sbin/nfsd[8408]: Number of NFS server daemons increased to 6 in order│
│ to cover all processors.                                                  (4) │
│ Jan 20 16:33:15 atc03 /usr/sbin/nfsd[8408]: nfsd do_one bind 1 (5)           │
│ Jan 20 16:33:15 atc03 /usr/sbin/nfsd[8409]: nfsd do_one bind 0               │
│ Jan 20 16:33:15 atc03 /usr/sbin/nfsd[8409]: Return from t_optmgmt(XTI_DISTRIBUTE) 0│
│ Jan 20 16:33:15 atc03 /usr/sbin/nfsd[8408]: Return from t_optmgmt(XTI_DISTRIBUTE) 0│
│ Jan 20 16:33:15 atc03 /usr/sbin/nfsd[8411]: nfsd 1 0  sock 4                │
│ Jan 20 16:33:15 atc03 /usr/sbin/nfsd[8410]: nfsd 0 0  sock 4                │
│ Jan 20 16:33:15 atc03 /usr/sbin/nfsd[8409]: nfsd 0 2  sock 4                │
│ Jan 20 16:33:15 atc03 /usr/sbin/nfsd[8412]: nfsd 0 1  sock 4 (6)            │
│ Jan 20 16:33:15 atc03 /usr/sbin/nfsd[8413]: nfsd 1 1  sock 4                │
│ Jan 20 16:33:15 atc03 /usr/sbin/nfsd[8408]: nfsd 1 2  sock 4                │
└──────────────────────────────────────────────────────────────────────────────┘
```

Figure 4.5 Sample `syslog.log` File Showing nfsd Startup

This example also shows several other steps the kernel performs at nfsd start time:

1. The maximum stream head buffer size is calculated (in this example the size is 65536).
2. The number of CPUs in the system is determined (in this example there are 2 CPUs).
3. The nfsds register support for NFS Version 2 and Version 3 with `rpcbind(1M)`.[9]
4. The total number of nfsds is increased, if needed, to allocate an equal number of daemons to each CPU pool (explained in Section 4.2.2).
5. The stream head is replicated once for each CPU in the system.
6. As the nfsds are launched, each daemon is assigned to a per-CPU pool (see Section 4.2.2).

4.2.2 nfsds Are Allocated to per-CPU Pools and Can "Task Steal"

When the UDP nfsds are started on the NFS server, the kernel creates separate pools for these daemons associated with each of the CPUs in the system and then begins allocating daemons to these pools. In other words, on an 8-CPU system there will be 8 separate pools of nfsd daemons — each associated with a different processor. Each CPU will therefore have its own "dedicated" set of nfsd daemons that will always attempt to service requests on that CPU.

By coercing the nfsds to continuously process requests on the same CPU, the daemons have a much higher chance of utilizing the CPU's memory caches effectively since any cached information about the files being accessed by the nfsds will likely be found in the CPU's cache — thereby increasing overall CPU efficiency and nfsd performance. If the nfsds were constantly switching upon which CPU they were executed, the likelihood of them finding the information they need in the CPU's caches would be greatly diminished.

The daemons are assigned to their respective per-CPU pools via a method called "processor affinity." The affinity mode used by NFS is "advisory," meaning that the nfsds *can* execute

---

9.   Refer to the rpcbind(1M) man page for more information about rpcbind.

on a CPU other than the one they were originally bound to. In other words, when a processor is ready to choose another nfsd to execute, if the highest priority nfsd process is bound to a different processor, that nfsd will execute on the selecting processor rather than waiting for the specified processor to which it was bound.[10]

For example, if CPU-1 is available and none of the nfsds in its pool are ready to execute, CPU-1 will search the system for an nfsd that has the highest process priority and is ready to run (i.e. has all of the resources it needs to execute). If that nfsd is bound to a different CPU which is currently busy (CPU-2 for instance), then CPU-1 will "steal" the waiting nfsd and execute it rather than force it to wait for CPU-2. This process is known as "task stealing." Although task stealing defeats the benefits of processor affinity (i.e. CPU cache utilization), it does contribute to overall NFS performance by allowing waiting nfsds to execute when the CPU they were bound to is temporarily busy.

The nfsds can "steal" tasks from other CPU queues   Just as the nfsds associated with a busy CPU can be "stolen" by an available CPU, nfsds associated with one CPU can "steal" requests from another CPU's queue. When an nfsd finishes processing the request it is currently working on, it checks the queue associated with the CPU it has affinity with to see if any new requests have arrived. If new requests are waiting it will take the next request off the queue and process it.

If no new requests are waiting in its CPU's queue, it will check the queues of the other CPUs to see if any requests are pending in their queues. If it finds a request waiting in the queue of another CPU it will "steal" the request and process it. If no requests were waiting in the queues of the other CPUs on the system, it will make one final check at its own CPU's queue just to make sure a new request hasn't arrived while it was checking the queues of the other CPUs. If no new requests are waiting on any queues the daemon will go to sleep and wait for new requests to arrive.

How does the server decide which queue to use for an inbound request?

Since the kernel creates multiple queues on the server to process inbound requests (on systems with multiple CPUs configured), when a new NFS request arrives the server needs to determine the appropriate queue in which to place the request. Ideally the kernel would like to spread the workload evenly to all the CPUs on the server, but at the same time fully utilize each CPU's data cache by assigning all the requests for the same file to the same CPU. While there is no way to guarantee that this will always happen (for reasons that will be explained shortly), the algorithm used by the NFS server's kernel attempts to do exactly that.

---

10.   Refer to the mpctl(2) man page for more information about processor affinity.

The server uses three values when determining the appropriate queue to place a specific inbound NFS request:

1. The IP address of the NFS client that sent the request
2. The port number the NFS client used when sending the request
3. The number of CPUs in the NFS server system

The number of CPUs in the system will typically remain constant while the server is booted.[11] By using both the NFS client's IP address and the port number the client used when sending the request in the kernel algorithm, the server attempts to put all requests from a specific NFS client *application* to the same CPU's queue. By doing so, the hope is that a given NFS client application (which will typically send multiple requests using the same port number) will be serviced by a pool of nfsds sharing a single CPU — thereby attempting to maximize the cache hit rate of that CPU.

Also, by including the client's sending port number in the calculation, the kernel ensures that *all* requests from the same IP address are *not* sent to the same CPU queue. In other words, if a single NFS client sends two requests they will both typically contain the same sending IP address;[12] however, each request could very easily be sent from a different port on the client. Since the client's port number is used in the calculation, there is a strong likelihood that the two inbound requests from the same client will be placed in different CPU queues on the server. Thus the server is able to distribute the client workload to multiple CPUs — even when all the workload originates from a single NFS client.

While the server always attempts to place inbound requests into their appropriate queues, there is no guarantee that the request will eventually be executed by the CPU the request was queued for. Remember that both the nfsds and the CPUs can "task steal" — the nfsds can "steal" requests from CPU queues other than the CPU it has affinity with, and available CPUs can "steal" waiting nfsds (i.e. nfsds that have all their necessary resources and are ready to run) from other CPUs and execute them. For these reasons, it is not often that you will find many idle nfsd daemons on a busy NFS server.

Each pool is allocated an equal number of nfsds   The kernel ensures that each CPU pool is allocated an equal number of nfsds at start time. If the number of nfsds requested (either on the `/usr/sbin/nfsd` command line or via the `/etc.rc.config.d/nfsconf` file) is not evenly divisible by the number of CPUs, the kernel will automatically increase the number of daemons to the next whole number that is evenly divisible by the number of CPUs.

---

11.   HP does offer a product that allows spare CPUs to be installed in a server system and activated on the fly, without requiring a system reboot. This product is called Instant Capacity on Demand (iCOD). For more information about iCOD, visit: *http://hp.com/go/icod*.

12.   The NFS client could have multiple IP interfaces, but for this example we will assume a single interface is used by the client when sending all requests.

An example of this nfsd distribution mechanism in shown in Figure 4.5. Item #6 in Figure 4.5 consists of the following 6 lines:

```
Jan 20 16:33:15 atc03 /usr/sbin/nfsd[8411]: nfsd 1 0 sock 4
Jan 20 16:33:15 atc03 /usr/sbin/nfsd[8410]: nfsd 0 0 sock 4
Jan 20 16:33:15 atc03 /usr/sbin/nfsd[8409]: nfsd 0 2 sock 4
Jan 20 16:33:15 atc03 /usr/sbin/nfsd[8412]: nfsd 0 1 sock 4
Jan 20 16:33:15 atc03 /usr/sbin/nfsd[8413]: nfsd 1 1 sock 4
Jan 20 16:33:15 atc03 /usr/sbin/nfsd[8408]: nfsd 1 2 sock 4
```

Each of these lines contains the process ID of the nfsd being started (contained in the [] brackets), followed by the CPU pool the nfsd is being assigned to (in this case either '0' or '1' since there are only 2 CPUs in the system), followed by the total number of daemons already assigned to the queue at the time the daemon was added. For example, the first line in the above example shows the nfsd with process ID 8411 is assigned to CPU-1 and it was the first daemon to be allocated to this pool (i.e. there were zero daemons in the pool when it was added). The last line above shows the nfsd with process ID 8408 is assigned to CPU-1 and it is the third daemon allocated (i.e. there were already two daemons in the queue when this one was added).

 KEY IDEA — Why Are More nfsds Running than I Requested?

Question: I attempted to start 100 nfsds on my HP-UX 11.0 NFS server by issuing the "/usr/sbin/nfsd 100" command, but according to the ps(1) command 105 nfsd daemons are running. Why?

System Configuration: The customer's NFS server is an N-Class system with 8 CPUs installed. NFS/TCP support is enabled on the system.

Answer: There are three factors that determine the number of UDP nfsd daemons that get launched on any given HP-UX 11.0 or 11i server:

- The number of daemons requested
- The number of CPUs in the server system
- Whether NFS/TCP is enabled on the server

In this example, the kernel creates 8 nfsd pools (one per CPU) and begins allocating daemons to these pools. It determines that the requested number of nfsds is not evenly divisible into the 8 pools (100 daemons / 8 CPUs = 12.5). The kernel continues launching daemons until an equal number of daemons is allocated to each pool. In this case, it launches 13 daemons per pool for a total of 104. Since NFS/TCP is enabled on this server, an additional nfsd is launched to handle the TCP connection management functions, resulting in a grand total of **105** nfsds.

4.2.3 How Many nfsds Are Activated when Requests Arrive?

Just as with the client-side biod daemons, HP-UX servers used to wake all nfsds when a new request arrived on the server — even if only a single nfsd was needed to service the request. A single nfsd would process the request and the remaining nfsds would realize there was nothing for them to do and go back to sleep. This process of waking all the idle nfsds and putting them back to sleep wasted valuable CPU cycles on overhead.

The HP-UX 11.0 and 11i nfsds are designed to activate only the number of daemons or threads required to handle the inbound workload. This allows NFS servers to run larger numbers of nfsd daemons and threads without paying a performance penalty associated with waking all daemons and putting them back to sleep.

4.3 NFS Server TCP Thread Management

Moving to a kernel thread model for NFS/TCP offered several benefits over the user-space daemon approach. The design decisions made by HP labs when implementing the NFS/TCP thread allocation mechanism were made to provide good performance and behavior in most NFS environments. However, there are certain situations where the default values selected by HP could result in sub-optimal performance for NFS/TCP filesystems. Fortunately, most of these default values can be overridden by tuning the kernel appropriately.

This section will describe some of the benefits we gained by moving to a kernel thread design. It will then describe the default values selected by HP labs for NFS/TCP thread management, and some of the NFS environments where these default values may be an issue. Finally, it will explain how these default values may be changed via kernel tuning.

4.3.1 Benefits of Adopting a Kernel Thread Model for NFS/TCP

HP gained numerous benefits by adopting a kernel thread model for their NFS/TCP implementation.

NFS/TCP threads are launched and killed dynamically When a client mounts an NFS filesystem via TCP from an HP-UX server, the server launches several threads in anticipation of incoming NFS requests. As requests begin arriving, the server launches more threads to handle the request load. This will continue until the server launches the maximum number of threads, which is 10 by default, allowed for the connection. Once the request load decreases on the TCP connection, the server begins destroying unneeded threads. This dynamic launching and killing of threads helps the server save valuable system resources by limiting the number of active threads to only those that are needed to meet the current demand from the clients.

Threads are associated with a specific TCP connection Each NFS/TCP connection is allocated its own dedicated pool of threads to service requests that arrive on that connection. These threads cannot be used to process inbound requests for other clients on other connections. This means that one client cannot consume all of the server's available NFS/TCP threads, effectively starving other client connections from getting their requests processed.

Threads consume fewer resources than processes   All of the NFS/TCP kernel threads launched by the server are associated with the single nfsktcpd process. This allows the threads to occupy a single entry in the system's process table. By comparison, each individual UDP nfsd daemon consumes an entry in the process table. While this difference may not be significant when only a few UDP nfsds are used, in environments where hundreds of nfsd processes are launched the resource difference can be noticeable.

Brings HP's NFS offering closer to other NFS vendors' implementations   Many vendors have been using a kernel-threaded version of NFS for some time. While HP's current implementation of NFS only uses kernel threads on the server — and only when servicing NFS/TCP requests, it is a positive step towards bringing our implementation in line with our competitors. Future plans include replacing the NFS client-side biod daemons with kernel threads, as well as potentially replacing the server's NFS/UDP nfsds with kernel threads.

4.3.2   Default Values Used for NFS/TCP Thread Allocation

When designing the new NFS/TCP kernel thread implementation for 11.0 and 11i, HP tried to select default values for thread allocation that would allow HP-UX servers to perform well in most NFS environments without requiring additional tuning.

The *server* allocates 10 threads to each NFS/TCP connection   As stated earlier, each NFS/TCP connection is allocated its own dedicated pool of kernel threads to service requests. This design helps ensure that no one client can monopolize the server's resources. By default, HP-UX 11.0 and 11i NFS servers allocate up to 10 threads for each client connection. Since the server dynamically creates and destroys threads as needed, there is no guarantee that all 10 threads will be running for each connection at any given time.

NFS *clients* open a single TCP connection to each server they mount from   By default, when an HP-UX 11.0 or 11i client begins mounting NFS/TCP filesystems, it opens a single TCP connection with each server — regardless of the number of filesystems it eventually mounts from each server. In other words, if a client were to mount ten filesystems from the same server, it would multiplex requests for all ten filesystems across a single TCP connection.

Potential performance issue using the default NFS/TCP values   In most NFS environments, where large NFS servers are supporting many comparatively smaller NFS client systems, the single TCP connection and 10 threads per connection defaults should not be an issue. However, in the case where large multi-processor clients are mounting many NFS/TCP filesystems from a single server and multiplexing huge numbers of requests across that connection, these defaults could introduce a performance problem.

Compare this behavior with a UDP environment — where the client is not restricted to a single connection (since UDP is a "connectionless" protocol), and where the server can be configured to run as many UDP nfsd daemons as it needs to handle the client's requests — and you can see where this single TCP connection/10 threads paradigm could lead to sub-optimal performance for some clients.

Fortunately, both the number of TCP connections opened by NFS clients and the number of NFS/TCP kernel threads allocated to each connection are configurable on HP-UX systems.

4.3.3 Changing Client TCP Behavior via *clnt_max_conns*

The kernel variable on HP-UX 11.0 and 11i NFS clients that defines the number of TCP connections opened to each NFS server is *clnt_max_conns*. By default, this variable is set to 1, allowing clients to open only a single connection to each NFS server, regardless of how many NFS filesystems the client mounts from the server.

The *clnt_max_conns* variable is undocumented and is not currently configurable via the normal supported methods (i.e. `sam(1M)` or `kmtune(1M)`). The only way to change this parameter is via the `adb(1)` command.

 KEY IDEA — Modifying the Undocumented
_clnt_max_conns_ Kernel Parameter

A great deal of care should be taken when increasing *clnt_max_conns* because it affects the number of NFS/TCP connections opened by HP-UX NFS clients to *every NFS server* — not just HP-UX servers. In addition, changing this parameter will directly affect the number of NFS/TCP kernel threads launched by HP-UX NFS servers. Unless the server's kernel is tuned appropriately to handle these extra threads — specifically by adjusting *nkthread*, *max_thread_proc*, and *ncallout* — unexpected results can occur.[a]

WARNING — Modifying the _clnt_max_conns_ variable from its default value of "1" is not currently supported by HP. Use the following procedure at your own risk.

To allow an HP-UX client to establish more than one NFS/TCP connection with each server, the systems administrator should issue the following commands on the NFS *client*:

```
# echo 'clnt_max_conns?W 0d2' | adb -w /stand/vmunix /dev/kmem
# echo 'clnt_max_conns/W 0d2' | adb -w /stand/vmunix /dev/kmem
```

In the above example, the "0d2" parameter instructs the client to open 2 connections per server. A value of "0d3" would specify 3 connections, and so on. A value of "0d1" would return the client to the default behavior of opening a single connection.

Two separate `adb` commands are used in this case to modify both the on-disk kernel file (?W syntax) and kernel memory (/W syntax). This allows the NFS/TCP connection semantics change to take effect immediately and remain in effect even if the client system is rebooted. This parameter will be reset to 1 if the kernel is re-built, either manually (via `mk_kernel(1M)`) or by installing a kernel patch. This should be kept in mind when installing kernel patches on a system where *clnt_max_conns* is intentionally modified.

---

a.   For a complete discussion on tuning the HP-UX kernel parameters that influence NFS, refer to Chapter 12.

4.3.4 Changing Server TCP Thread Pool Size via *maxthreads*

The kernel variable on HP-UX 11.0 and 11i NFS servers that defines the maximum number of threads allowed per NFS/TCP connection is *maxthreads*. By default, this variable is set to 10, allowing the server to allocate up to 10 threads per client connection, regardless of how many NFS filesystems the client mounts from the server.

The *maxthreads* variable is undocumented and is not currently configurable via the normal supported methods. The only way to change this parameter is via the adb(1) command.

 KEY IDEA — Modifying the Undocumented
**   *maxthreads* Kernel Parameter**

A great deal of care should be taken when increasing the *maxthreads* parameter because it affects the number of kernel threads allowed for *every NFS/TCP connection*, not just connections opened by HP-UX clients. In addition, changing this parameter can dramatically affect the total number of threads running on the server system. Unless the server's kernel is tuned appropriately to handle these extra threads — specifically by adjusting *nkthread*, *max_thread_proc*, and *ncallout* — unexpected results can occur.[a]

WARNING — Modifying the *maxthreads* variable from its default value of "10" is not currently supported by HP. Use the following procedure at your own risk.

To allow an HP-UX server to launch more than 10 kernel threads per NFS/TCP connection, the systems administrator should issue the following commands on the NFS *server*.

```
# echo 'maxthreads?W 0d20' | adb -w /stand/vmunix /dev/kmem
# echo 'maxthreads/W 0d20' | adb -w /stand/vmunix /dev/kmem
```

In the above example, the "0d20" parameter instructs the server to allow up to 20 threads per connection. A value of "0d30" would allow 30 threads, and so on. A value of "0d10" would return the server to the default 10 threads per connection.

Two separate adb commands are used in this case to modify both the on-disk kernel file (?W syntax) and kernel memory (/W syntax). This allows the NFS/TCP kernel thread semantics change to take effect immediately; however, it will have no effect on existing connections, as the thread pool limit is set when the connection is established. Only NFS/TCP connections established after the above commands are issued will use the new thread limit. The new settings will remain in effect even if the server system is rebooted.

This parameter will be reset to 10 if the kernel is re-built, either manually (via mk_kernel(1M)) or by installing a kernel patch. This should be kept in mind when installing kernel patches on a system where *maxthreads* is intentionally modified.

---

a.   For a complete discussion on tuning the HP-UX kernel parameters that influence NFS, refer to Chapter 12.

4.3.5 The Relationship between *clnt_max_conns* and *maxthreads*

It is very important to understand the relationship between the *maxthreads* parameter and the *clnt_max_conns* parameter. If *clnt_max_conns* has been increased above the default value of 1 on your NFS client systems, these clients will establish multiple TCP connections with the server when they mount NFS filesystems. Based on the load generated by these clients, this could result in the server launching more than 10 threads to service requests for each client. In this case, modifying *maxthreads* may not be necessary.

Similarly, if *maxthreads* has been increased above the default value of 10 on your NFS server, then increasing *clnt_max_conns* on your clients could have a significant effect on the total number of NFS/TCP kernel threads launched by the server. If the NFS server's kernel has not been tuned appropriately to handle these extra threads — specifically by adjusting *nkthread*, *max_thread_proc*, and *ncallout* — unexpected results could occur.

In a production environment, modifying *clnt_max_conns* should only be done in situations where the single NFS/TCP connection behavior appears to be causing a performance bottleneck. Likewise, *maxthreads* should only be modified in situations where the server's 10-thread limit seems to be yielding sub-optimal performance. Before changing either of these parameters in your production environment, extensive performance testing should be conducted using non-production systems to ensure that the desired results are achieved.

4.4 How Many nfsds Should Your NFS Server Run?

Just as with sizing the biod daemons on an NFS client, there is no magic number of nfsd daemons and threads that will provide optimal throughput on every server. However, unlike the biods, there is no real performance penalty incurred for running too many nfsds. Since the daemons are activated individually as needed to process new requests, the only resources consumed by a large number of nfsds are entries in the kernel process table and memory resources used by the processes themselves. That being the case, it is usually better to err on the high side when sizing nfsds to ensure that enough daemons are running to handle your client workload.

The best course of action is to choose a reasonable starting point for the number of nfsds and then experiment with raising and lowering the number of daemons until the optimal performance is identified. This number will typically vary on a per-server basis depending upon the hardware configuration of the server (i.e. number of CPUs, physical memory, network interfaces, etc.), the number of clients accessing the server simultaneously, etc.

Many schools of thought exist regarding the best way to select an appropriate number of nfsds to run on a given system. One of the most common nfsd sizing "rules of thumb" is to run two nfsds for every physical disk installed on the server. In practice, with today's disk arrays and virtual memory subsystems, there is little correlation between nfsds and disks. If the server has adequate buffer cache memory available, the file data being requested may already be in memory and not require a physical disk access. Likewise, if the server has an adequately sized memory-resident inode table, any inode data being requested may also be in memory and not require a disk access.

UDP nfsd Recommendation   We learned in Section 4.2.1 how the server's kernel calculates the size of the memory buffer used to receive inbound NFS/UDP requests based on the number of nfsd launched. The kernel will only allocate the maximum receive buffer memory (512KB) if 64 or more nfsds are running. With this in mind, it makes sense for most NFS servers to start at least 64 nfsds to ensure that the maximum receive buffer memory is allocated, thus reducing the likelihood of experiencing UDP socket overflows on port 2049.

We also learned (in Section 4.2.2) how the kernel assigns the UDP-based nfsd daemons to separate pools on a per-CPU basis. Therefore, a more practical approach is to size the nfsds based on the number of CPUs in the system. A reasonable starting point for most NFS servers is to multiply the number of CPUs by 8, thus allocating 8 daemons per pool.

Taken together, these two recommendations imply that a server with 8 or fewer CPUs should start with 64 nfsds. A server with more than 8 CPUs should start 8 nfsds for each CPU in the system (i.e. a server with 16 CPUs would start 128 nfsds).

 KEY IDEA   — Recommended Number of UDP nfsds to Run on HP-UX NFS Servers

A good starting point for the number of UDP nfsds is either **64** or **(8 * number of CPUs)** — whichever is *greater.*

The number of UDP nfsds started at system boot time is configurable via the "NUM_NFSD" variable in the /etc/rc.config.d/nfsconf file.

Your mileage will vary, so it is important to experiment with different numbers of nfsd daemons in order to achieve optimal performance for your specific server. Also, remember that modifying the NUM_NFSD variable in the /etc/rc.config.d/nfsconf file only controls the number of nfsds used to service NFS/UDP filesystems. It has no affect on the number of kernel threads launched by the server to process TCP requests.

TCP nfsktcpd Recommendation   We learned in Section 4.3.4 how the kernel allocates a maximum of 10 nfsktcpd threads for each NFS/TCP connection by default. We also learned in Section 4.3.3 that HP-UX NFS/TCP clients only open a single TCP connection to each NFS server, regardless of how many NFS/TCP filesystems are mounted from a server. These default settings have been tested by HP and shown to perform well in most environments.

Currently, there is no *supported* method of changing either the client-side single-TCP-connection behavior or the server-side 10-thread limit; however, there are two unsupported kernel variables that control these features — *clnt_max_conns* and *maxthreads*. Modifying these variables is not currently supported by HP, therefore the recommendation is to leave them set to their default values initially.

**KEY IDEA — NFS/TCP Kernel Thread Recommen-
dations for HP-UX NFS Servers**

The default NFS/TCP settings (i.e. the client opening a single TCP connection to each server and the server allocating 10 threads per connection) have been tested by HP and shown to work well in most NFS environments.

Since modifying the kernel variables that control these settings (*clnt_max_conns* and *maxthreads*) is not currently supported by HP, the recommendation is to leave them set to their default values.

In NFS environments where very fast, multi-processor client systems are mounting many NFS/TCP filesystems and multiplexing large numbers of requests across a single TCP connection, these default settings could yield sub-optimal performance. Before changing *clnt_max_conns* on production NFS clients or changing *maxthreads* on production NFS servers, thorough testing should be performed in a non-production environment if possible. Only after testing confirms an improvement in NFS/TCP performance should these parameters be changed on production systems.

It is also important to remember that changing the *clnt_max_conns* parameter on an HP-UX client will influence how it operates with all NFS/TCP servers — not just HP-UX servers. Similarly, modifying *maxthreads* on an HP-UX server will affect how the server treats all NFS/TCP clients, not just HP-UX clients. Finally, remember that altering these parameters can directly influence the total number of threads managed by the server, so it is important to ensure that the server's kernel is properly tuned to correctly deal with these additional threads — specifically, the *nkthread*, *max_thread_proc*, and *ncallout* parameters need to be sized properly.[13]

4.5 Troubleshooting the nfsd Daemons and Threads

Most nfsd-related problems manifest themselves as NFS server panics, application hangs, or poor application performance. Since the nfsds primarily operate in the kernel, these problems usually require kernel-space troubleshooting tools and techniques to identify the root cause. However, the `rpcinfo(1M)` command, collecting network traces via `nettl(1M)`, and the `nfsstat(1M)` command can be a used as a first-pass means of trying to determine whether the NFS client or server is causing a performance problem.

4.5.1 NFS Server System Panic

Analyzing HP-UX system dumps is a very complex and involved process, which is typically performed only by experienced HP support personnel or lab engineers. If your NFS server

---

13.   For a complete discussion on tuning the HP-UX kernel parameters that influence NFS, refer to Chapter 12.

experiences a system panic, your best course of action is to contact HP support and request that the memory dump be analyzed. However, there are some initial steps that can be performed to help HP support more quickly determine if the panic was triggered by one of the nfsds.

HP-UX 11.0 and 11i system panics are typically analyzed using the Q4 tool. Q4 is a very sophisticated and powerful debugger for HP-UX kernel crash dumps. It supports all HP-UX systems running Release 10.0 or later on PA-RISC platforms. Q4 can also be used to analyze live systems to examine kernel data structures, processes and threads, and system resources.

Listed below is a step-by-step set of instructions for using Q4 to obtain the stack trace of the process that caused the panic to occur. The underlined steps are the commands you type.

1. Log into the system as root and `cd` into the directory where the memory dump resides:
   ```
   # cd /var/adm/crash
   # ll -d crash*
   drwxr-xr-x    2 root      root        1024 Feb 13 2000 crash.0
   ```
   In this case there is only one dump and it is located in the `crash.0` directory.
   ```
   # cd crash.0
   ```

2. Prepare the kernel found in the dump directory with the `q4pxdb` command:
   ```
   # /usr/contrib/bin/q4pxdb ./vmunix
   ```

3. Launch q4:
   ```
   # /usr/contrib/bin/q4 .
   ```

4. Obtain the stack trace from the process that generated the panic:
   ```
   q4> trace event 0
      stack trace for event 0
      crash event was a panic
      panic+0x14
      report_trap_or_int_and_panic+0x80
      trap+0xe10
      nokgdb+0x8
      svc_clts_krecv+0x84
      svc_getreq+0x8c
      svc_run+0x1e0
      nfsexp_svc+0x1d4
      nfs_stub_svc+0xa4
      coerce_scall_args+0xcc
      syscall+0x5cc
      $syscallrtn+0x0
   ```

You can identify a panic as being triggered by an NFS/UDP nfsd by examining the stack trace and looking for the "**nfs_stub_svc**" procedure, as illustrated in the above trace output. An NFS/TCP kernel thread will either have "**nfs_stub_svc**" or "**tcp_svc_run**" in its stack.

It is important to keep in mind that just because an nfsd process triggered the panic, that does not imply that a defect exists in the NFS server code. In most cases, the nfsd process is simply an innocent victim of a problem located in the network transport code, the network driver code, the virtual memory subsystem, the underlying local filesystem code, etc. However, by using these simple steps outlined earlier, you can locate several potential keywords to use when searching the online customer-viewable databases available from HP's IT Resource Center web site: *http://itrc.hp.com*.

Again, in order to determine the root cause of any system panic, the best course of action is to save the crash dump and contact HP support, requesting that the dump be analyzed.

4.5.2 NFS Application Hangs

NFS-based application hangs can be caused by any number of reasons: resource limitations, network outages, non-responding NFS servers, etc. These hangs can also occur if the nfsd daemons or threads become non-responsive or blocked for some reason. Since the nfsds run in kernel space, if they become blocked the only way to determine what they are waiting on is to use Q4 to obtain their stack traces. Instructions for collecting nfsd stack trace information are outlined later in this section.

However, before diving into kernel stack debugging, some less complicated methods can be used to determine if the biods are active. The `rpcinfo(1M)` command can be used to "ping" the daemons and threads to make sure they are responding to requests. A network trace can be collected via `nettl(1M)` and searched for any NFS replies sent by the nfsds, and the `nfsstat(1M)` command can be used to see if the server is processing any NFS requests.

Use the `rpcinfo(1M)` command to "ping" the nfsds   One of the quickest and most non-intrusive methods of determining whether the nfsds are responding is to use the `rpcinfo(1M)` command. This command has many features,[14] one of which is the ability to send a request to the NULL procedure of any local or remote RPC-based program. Sending a NULL procedure request should always result in the RPC program responding with an empty NULL reply. While this doesn't reveal anything about the functionality of the RPC program, it does confirm whether the program is "alive" and responding to requests. This is sometimes referred to as "pinging" the RPC program.

When testing the NFS server's daemons and threads responsiveness, rpcinfo can be issued on either the client or server system. The recommendation is to test the nfsds from the NFS client, as this will also verify the network connection between the two systems. Figure 4.6 shows an example of the `rpcinfo` command issued on NFS client ros87252.rose.hp.com testing the UDP-based nfsd daemons on remote server atc03.cup.hp.com.

---

14.   Refer to the rpcinfo(1M) man page for a complete list of features and available command-line syntax.

```
ros87252 (B1000 64-bit 11.0)                                    _ □ ×
ros87252(/) -> rpcinfo -T udp atc03.cup.hp.com nfs
program 100003 version 2 ready and waiting
program 100003 version 3 ready and waiting
```

Figure 4.6 `rpcinfo` "pinging" the UDP nfsds

The "ready and waiting" response in this output shows that the UDP-based nfsds are successfully responding to both NFS Version 2 and Version 3 requests. Figure 4.7 shows the same
client testing the NFS/TCP kernel threads and getting a similar response. Since these rpcinfo
commands were issued on the NFS client during these tests, the results also verify that RPC
requests were able to successfully traverse the network separating these systems.

```
ros87252 (B1000 64-bit 11.0)                                    _ □ ×
ros87252(/) -> rpcinfo -T tcp atc03.cup.hp.com nfs
program 100003 version 2 ready and waiting
program 100003 version 3 ready and waiting
```

Figure 4.7 `rpcinfo` "pinging" NFS/TCP Threads

If, however, the rpcinfo commands returned an error, such as the "Timed out" status
shown in Figure 4.8, it would be a strong indication that either the nfsds are unable to service
inbound requests, or RPC packets are not able to successfully traverse the network separating
the client and server.

```
ros87252 (B1000 64-bit 11i)                                     _ □ ×
ros87252(/) -> rpcinfo -T udp atc03.cup.hp.com nfs
rpcinfo: RPC: Timed out
program 100003 version 0 is not available
```

Figure 4.8 `rpcinfo` Returning an Error During nfsd "ping" Test

The network component can be eliminated from consideration by issuing the same rpcinfo
command on the NFS server system directly. If rpcinfo returns the same error when issued
against the local daemons on the NFS server, then the daemons are very likely blocked and
unable to process new requests. This inability to service requests could be a temporary phenomenon, and additional corroborating data should be collected using the procedures outlined in the
remainder of this section before any definitive conclusions can be reached.

Look for NFS reply packets in a network trace Another method of determining
whether nfsds are responding to requests is to collect a network trace on the NFS server via the
`nettl(1M)` command. If the trace shows any outbound NFS replies then you can be certain
that at least some of the nfsds are responding to requests and are thus not blocked in the kernel.

Here are the steps for collecting a network trace and examining it for NFS reply traffic. The <u>underlined</u> steps are the commands you type.

1. Start a `nettl` trace, collecting only outbound traffic as it passes through the IP layer. Log the output to a file named "nfsds." `nettl` will automatically append an extension of ".TRC0" on HP-UX 11.0 systems or ".TRC000" on HP-UX 11i systems:

   # <u>/etc/nettl -tn pduout -e ns_ls_ip -f nfsds</u>

2. On the client, attempt to generate some NFS traffic on the same filesystem the application is using. In this example, we assume the NFS filesystem is called "/nfs_mount":

   # <u>cp localfile /nfs_mount/nfsfile</u>

3. Stop the trace:

   # <u>/etc/nettl -tf -e ns_ls_ip</u>

4. Format the trace via the `netfmt(1M)` command. In this example we assume an HP-UX 11.0 client is used, which explains the ".TRC0" extension appended to the trace filename:

   # <u>/etc/netfmt -lN nfsds.TRC0 > nfsds.formatted</u>

5. Search the formatted trace for any outbound NFS packets using a port number of 2049 (or "nfsd"), which is the well-known port number for nfsd.

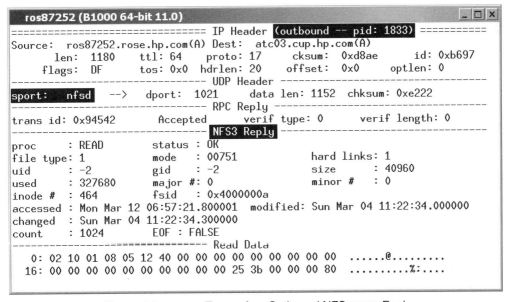

Figure 4.9 `nettl` Trace of an Outbound NFS READ Reply

The trace output in Figure 4.9 shows the NFS server sending a reply to a READ request via thread ID 1833. Looking back at the list of threads in Figure 4.1, we find that thread 1833 is one of the nfsds serving NFS/UDP mounts. This network trace data proves that the nfsds, or at least the one servicing this request, are not blocked in the kernel.

Monitor nfsstat(1M) output to see if the server is processing requests

Another non-intrusive method of determining whether nfsd activity is occurring is to use nfsstat(1M). The nfsstat command retrieves a variety of statistical data maintained by the HP-UX kernel regarding the NFS and RPC (Remote Procedure Call) sub-systems. It displays this information in an easy-to-read format, allowing a systems administrator to quickly determine the number and type of NFS requests that have been processed by the server.

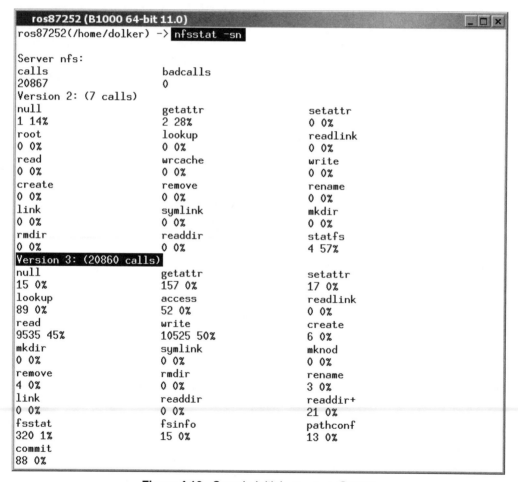

Figure 4.10 Sample Initial nfsstat Output

Figure 4.10 and Figure 4.11 show successive "nfsstat -sn" commands taken 30 seconds apart. The "-sn" options tell nfsstat to display the server-side NFS statistics only.

Comparing the output in Figure 4.10 and Figure 4.11 you can see a difference in the total number of NFS Version 3 calls (20860 vs. 21513). This is more evidence that the nfsds are not blocked in the kernel and there must be another reason for the non-responsive application.

nfsstat can also be used to re-initialize the kernel's counters to zero (via the "-z" option), which is very useful when trying to determine which requests, if any, the server processed during a specific test. Also, since HP-UX servers are able to service both NFS Version 2 and Version 3 filesystems simultaneously, be sure to compare both "Version 2" and "Version 3" counters in the output.

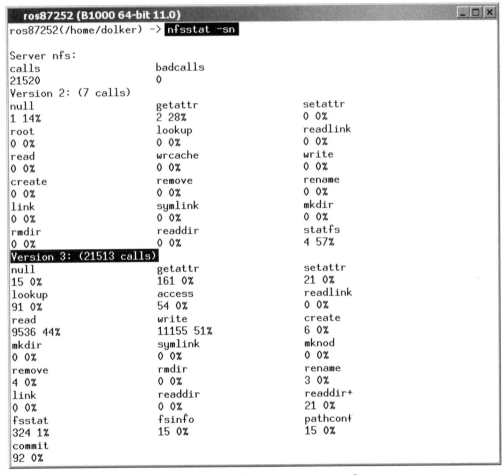

Figure 4.11 Sample Secondary nfsstat Output

Examine the nfsd daemons and threads on a live system If the network trace data and `nfsstat` output show no nfsd activity and you still believe your application is hanging as a result of the nfsds being blocked, the next thing to try is examining the running nfsd daemons and threads on the live system. Since the nfsds run in kernel space, if they become blocked the only way to determine what they are waiting on is to use a kernel debugger such as Q4 to obtain their stack traces. The procedures for examining both the UDP-based nfsd daemons and the TCP-based nfsktcpd kernel threads on a live system are detailed below. The <u>underlined</u> steps are the commands you type.

1. Log into the system and make a backup copy of the running kernel:
   # <u>cp /stand/vmunix /tmp/vmunix</u>

2. Prepare the backup kernel with the `q4pxdb` command:
   # <u>/usr/contrib/bin/q4pxdb /tmp/vmunix</u>

3. Launch q4 specifying the backup kernel and `/dev/mem`:
   # <u>q4 /tmp/vmunix /dev/mem</u>

4. Load the list of system processes. The command used to perform this task differs slightly between HP-UX 11.0 and 11i due to the redesign of the process table in 11i:
   11.0 q4> <u>load struct proc from proc max nproc</u>
   11i q4> <u>load struct proc from proc_list max nproc next p_factp</u>

5. Find the list of nfsd processes by printing the process ID, the parent process ID, and the ASCII string label of all the system processes. Use the `grep(1)` command to filter out only those processes whose "p_comm" field contains the string "nfs":
   ```
   q4> print p_pid p_ppid p_comm | grep nfs
       1809          1 "nfsd"
       1814       1813 "nfsd"
       1820       1813 "nfsd"
       1813          1 "nfsd"
       1816       1813 "nfsd"
      18274          0 "nfsktcpd"
   ```

   Looking at the above output, process 1813 is the parent process for processes 1814, 1816, and 1820. These four daemons service the NFS/UDP mount points. Process 1809 is the nfsd used for managing the NFS/TCP connections (since its parent process ID is 1 and it has no child processes), and process 18274 is the nfsktcpd process where all NFS/TCP kernel threads are associated.

6. Initially examine the NFS/UDP nfsd processes by selecting process 1813 and any processes whose PPID is 1813:
   ```
   q4> keep p_pid==1813 || p_ppid==1813
   kept 4 of 1024 struct proc's, discarded 1019
   ```

7. Print out the stack traces of all of the NFS/UDP nfsd daemons:

```
q4> trace pile
    stack trace for process at 0x0'013be600 (pid 1814),
    thread at 0x0'014ab3d8 (tid 1834)
    process was not running on any processor
    _sleep_one+0x278
    svc_run+0x398
    nfsexp_svc+0x4d4
    nfs_stub_svc+0xa4
    coerce_scall_args+0xcc
    syscall+0x200
    $syscallrtn+0x0

    stack trace for process at 0x0'013be9c0 (pid 1820),
    thread at 0x0'014ab5e0 (tid 1840)
    process was not running on any processor
    _sleep_one+0x278
    svc_run+0x398
    nfsexp_svc+0x4d4
    nfs_stub_svc+0xa4
    coerce_scall_args+0xcc
    syscall+0x200
    $syscallrtn+0x0

    stack trace for process at 0x0'013c0b80 (pid 1813),
    thread at 0x0'014ac828 (tid 1833)
    process was not running on any processor
    _sleep_one+0x278
    svc_run+0x398
    nfsexp_svc+0x4d4
    nfs_stub_svc+0xa4
    coerce_scall_args+0xcc
    syscall+0x200
    $syscallrtn+0x0

    stack trace for process at 0x0'013c2980 (pid 1816),
    thread at 0x0'014ad868 (tid 1836)
    process was not running on any processor
    _sleep_one+0x278
    svc_run+0x398
    nfsexp_svc+0x4d4
    nfs_stub_svc+0xa4
    coerce_scall_args+0xcc
    syscall+0x200
    $syscallrtn+0x0
```

Looking at the above stack traces, it appears all four NFS/UDP daemons are idle. Each stack is identical, where "**_sleep_one**" is called from the main server routine "svc_run." This indicates that all four UDP nfsd daemons are sleeping, waiting for requests to arrive. Now it is time to examine the TCP-based kernel threads.

8. We need to reload the list of system processes again so that we can examine the NFS/TCP threads. Again, the Q4 syntax varies between HP-UX 11.0 and 11i:

   11.0 q4> <u>load struct proc from proc max nproc</u>
   11i q4> <u>load struct proc from proc_list max nproc next p_factp</u>

9. This time we keep only the NFS/TCP processes we identified earlier — 1809 and 18274:

   q4> <u>keep p_pid==1809 || p_pid==18274</u>
   kept 2 of 1024 struct proc's, discarded 1022

10. Print out the stack traces of all of the TCP nfsd threads:

   q4> <u>trace pile</u>
   ```
       stack trace for process at 0x0'013ba280 (pid 1809),
       thread at 0x0'014a8d40 (tid 1829)
       process was not running on any processor
       sleep+0x50c
       poll+0x1b8
       syscall+0x480
       $syscallrtn+0x0
   ```

   The NFS/TCP nfsd (pid 1809) appears idle, as it is sleeping in the "**poll**" routine. This normally indicates the daemon is waiting for an inbound connection request.

   ```
       stack trace for process at 0x0'013c7fc0 (pid 18274),
       thread at 0x0'014b0720 (tid 18306)
       process was not running on any processor
       _sleep+0x7b4
       hpnfs_delay+0x54
       tcpd_proc_create+0x14c
       tcpd_thread_create+0x5c
       tcp_xprt_register+0x3c
       tcp_tli_kcreate+0x218
       tcp_svc+0x84
       nfstcp_svc+0x50
       nfs_stub_svc+0x25c
       coerce_scall_args+0xcc
       syscall+0x480
       $syscallrtn+0x0

       stack trace for process at 0x0'013c7fc0 (pid 18274),
       thread at 0x0'014b1350 (tid 19830)
       process was not running on any processor
       _sleep_one+0x520
   ```

```
ksleep_one+0x194
hp_cv_timedwait+0x68
tcp_svc_run+0x268
kthread_daemon_startup+0x24
kthread_daemon_startup+0x0
```

stack trace for process at 0x0'013c7fc0 (**pid 18274**),
thread at 0x0'014af6e0 (tid 19835)
process was not running on any processor

```
swtch+0xd0
thread_exit+0x29c
thread_process_suspend+0x78
kthread_daemon_exit+0xcc
svc_thread_exit+0xf4
tcp_svc_run+0x29c
kthread_daemon_startup+0x24
kthread_daemon_startup+0x0
```

stack trace for process at 0x0'013c7fc0 (**pid 18274**),
thread at 0x0'014aecb8 (tid 19837)
process was not running on any processor

```
_sleep_one+0x520
ksleep_one+0x194
hp_cv_timedwait+0x68
tcp_svc_run+0x268
kthread_daemon_startup+0x24
kthread_daemon_startup+0x0
```

stack trace for process at 0x0'013c7fc0 (**pid 18274**),
thread at 0x0'014af8e8 (tid 19838)
process was not running on any processor

```
_sleep_one+0x520
ksleep_one+0x194
hp_cv_timedwait+0x68
tcp_svc_run+0x268
kthread_daemon_startup+0x24
kthread_daemon_startup+0x0
```

stack trace for process at 0x0'013c7fc0 (**pid 18274**),
thread at 0x0'014afaf0 (tid 19839)
process was not running on any processor

```
_sleep_one+0x520
ksleep_one+0x194
hp_cv_timedwait+0x68
tcp_svc_run+0x268
kthread_daemon_startup+0x24
kthread_daemon_startup+0x0
```

The NFS/TCP process nfsktcpd (pid 18274) currently has six kernel threads associated with it. Threads 19830, 19837, 19838, and 19839 all have identical stack traces. Each of their stacks shows the thread calling "`_sleep_one`," indicating that they are idle and waiting to service a new request. Thread 18306 appears to be in the process of starting a new NFS/TCP thread since it is calling "`tcpd_thread_create`," while thread 19835 appears to be in the process of exiting, as it is calling "`thread_exit`." This illustrates how the kernel will launch and kill threads as needed to handle the incoming NFS/TCP workload.

The output shows that none of the nfsd processes or threads were running on a CPU, which makes sense since they appear to be idle. However, if the nfsd daemons were processing requests when the stack trace data was collected you may be able to distinguish the type of request by examining the stack trace.

The information contained in these stack traces may not be immediately understandable to most people, but this data could help an HP support engineer determine whether the nfsd daemons or threads are blocked, and if so, why. The non-idle stack trace data could also provide a number of good keyword candidates to use when searching for known NFS server hang problems via HP's IT Resource Center: *http://itrc.hp.com*.

In some cases, Q4 may be unable to obtain a viable stack trace of the running daemons and threads. In that event, your best course of action is open a support call with HP. The support engineer will most likely request that you initiate a TOC (Transfer of Control) of the system, effectively forcing your system to write the contents of its memory to disk and reboot. The resulting memory dump would then need to be analyzed by qualified HP support personnel.

4.5.3 Poor NFS Application Performance

In some cases, the problem is not that an NFS application hangs completely, but rather performs poorly. These types of problems are some of the most difficult to resolve because the slow performance could be influenced by so many factors, including a slow server, slow networks, slow disks, lack of memory, lack of buffer cache, etc.

While these problems can be elusive, there are many tools available to help narrow down the list of potential candidates. A set of network traces can be used to determine if the client system is sending retransmitted requests because the NFS server is not responding to requests in a timely fashion. The `nfsstat(1M)` command can show whether the server is logging NFS or RPC errors or receiving duplicate requests from the clients. The `netstat(1)` and `ndd(1M)` commands can be used to see if UDP socket overflows are occurring, possibly indicating that too few UDP-based nfsds are running. The `/var/adm/syslog/syslog.log` file can be examined for warning messages indicating that NFS/TCP kernel thread resources are exhausted, indicating that certain kernel parameters may need to be adjusted. Finally, there are kernel profiling tools available, such as kgmon, which can reveal what the NFS server's kernel is spending time doing. All of this information can help establish the root cause of the performance problem.

Look for delays or retransmissions in a network trace   We learned in the previous section how a `nettl` trace can be used to determine if the nfsd daemons or nfsktcpd kernel threads are generating any outbound replies. A similar procedure can be used to collect a set of network traces for use in troubleshooting an NFS application that is performing poorly. The only difference from the procedure outlined in Section 4.5.2 is that a network trace should be collected on *both* the NFS client and the server systems while the application slowness is observed.

 KEY IDEA — Collect Network Traces on Both NFS Client and Server Systems

When troubleshooting an NFS performance problem via network traces, it is strongly recommended that traces be collected **on both the client and server** systems so that any discrepancies (i.e. delays, requests that get no replies, retransmitted requests, etc.) can be verified from both systems' perspective.

For example, if the client-side trace shows that an NFS request was successfully sent to the server but no reply was received, the server's trace should be consulted to verify whether the client's request ever arrived intact on the server. If the server's trace shows that the request never arrived, it would indicate that the request was dropped in transit somewhere in the network. If the server-side trace confirms that the request was received but the server didn't reply, it would indicate a potential problem on the server system itself. If the server's trace shows that the server received the request and successfully sent a reply, but the client's trace does not show the reply being received, it would indicate that the reply was dropped by the network before arriving on the client.

Without *both* client-side and server-side traces to confirm and validate your findings, incorrect conclusions could be reached.

Sample NFS call and reply packets are included in Figure 4.12 and Figure 4.13. These two figures have several key fields highlighted which are frequently referenced during network trace analysis, including:

1. **Timestamps** — used for calculating delays occurring between outbound requests and inbound replies, delays between successive outbound requests, and retransmitted requests
2. **Inbound** vs. **Outbound** — whether the packet is being sent or received by the system
3. **Call** vs. **Reply** — indicates whether the client is sending a Call or receiving a Reply
4. **Procedure Type** — the type of NFS operation in the packet (i.e. READ, WRITE, etc.)
5. **Transaction ID** — unique identifier for the specific NFS request and its associated reply
6. **Procedure Status** — indicates if an error occurred while the server processed the request (contained in reply packets only — see Figure 4.13)

By referencing these fields in the sample trace we can identify this packet as an outbound READ request that was sent at 10:29:33.475309 on December 4th, 2001 with a transaction ID of 0xe7f8a. We can also identify the packet in Figure 4.13 as the reply to the earlier READ request because the transaction IDs in both packets match. We can further conclude that the READ call completed successfully (status: OK). Finally, by subtracting the timestamp in the outbound request packet from the timestamp in the inbound reply, we know that this request/reply sequence took only 0.007468 seconds to complete.

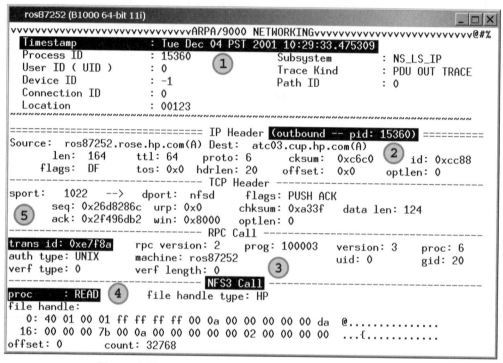

Figure 4.12 nettl Trace of an Outbound NFS READ Call

Using these same key fields, you can search formatted client and server traces for several possible scenarios, including:

1. Delays occurring between the time the client receives a reply to an existing request and the time the client sends a new request.
2. Delays occurring between an outbound request and the inbound reply from the server.
3. Replies from the server taking too long to arrive, causing the client to re-send the request.
4. Outbound requests that receive no reply from the server.
5. NFS replies indicating that an error condition occurred on the server while processing the request (i.e. a reply status other than "0," "OK," or "SUCCESS").

Spotting delays in a trace can be a very difficult process since it involves identifying matching call and reply packets by matching their transaction IDs, and computing the duration of the call/reply sequence by subtracting the "call" timestamp from the "reply" timestamp. However, this information can be very useful in determining whether the cause of the application slowdown is the NFS server, the client (either the system or the application), or the network.

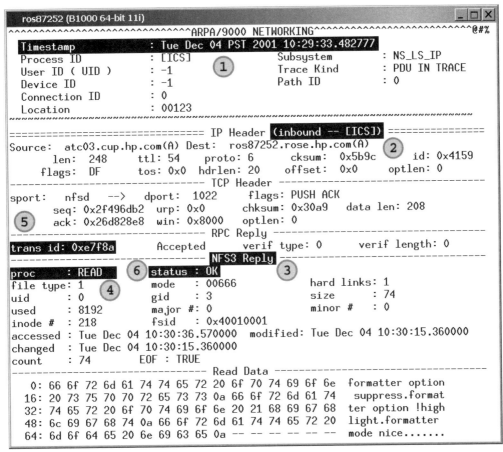

Figure 4.13 `nettl` Trace of an Inbound NFS `READ` Reply

Also, on busy networks a `nettl` trace can capture large amounts of data very quickly, causing the size of formatted trace files to become unwieldy to search. Care should be taken to capture as tight a sample of data surrounding the problem as possible.

If the collected traces show that the server is responding quickly to requests but the NFS client seems to be pausing between requests, this would indicate that either the client system or the client application is the cause of the slow performance, and they should be the focus of further investigation via tools such as `tusc` (described earlier in Section 3.5.3).

If noticeable delays are detected between the client's outbound requests and the server's inbound replies it would indicates that the server and/or the network are busy. If the server's replies are taking so long to arrive that the client is forced to retransmit requests, this would indicate that either the server is busy or the network is dropping packets. Retransmitted requests can be found by searching the trace for multiple outbound requests with the same transaction ID.

This again points out the importance of having both a client and server trace to validate assumptions with. The client trace may indicate a delay, but without the server trace to compare against there is no way of knowing whether the delay is induced by the server or the network. If both the client and server traces confirm that the server is not replying to requests at all then it points to the NFS server being the culprit and should therefore be the focus of the investigation.

KEY IDEA — Collecting nettl(1M) Traces on Fast Network Links

Due to architectural limitations, the nettl trace utility is not always able to keep up with today's faster links. It is not uncommon for formatted traces collected on Gigabit EtherNet links to contain many nettl warning messages indicating the number of packets that could not be collected.

It is therefore very important to configure nettl to use the largest buffer sizes available (via the "-tracemax" and "-size" options) when collecting data on fast networks. You can also instruct nettl to capture only a small portion of each packet (via the "-m" option), thereby limiting the total amount of data collected. Refer to nettl(1M) man page for more information.

In some situations it may be necessary to use hardware-based network tracing tools, such as network sniffers or LAN Analyzers, to collect the data needed to accurately troubleshoot an NFS performance problem.

Monitor nfsstat output for potential performance problems   We saw earlier how the nfsstat(1M) command can be used to determine whether the server is receiving and processing inbound NFS requests. This tool can also display a wealth of information about how the NFS subsystem and the underlying RPC subsystem are behaving on the server.

Figure 4.14 shows an example of the "nfsstat -sr" command. The "-sr" options instruct nfsstat to only display the server-side RPC statistics. A description of each statistic is included in Table 4.1. Since HP-UX 11i supports both NFS/UDP (Connectionless-oriented) and NFS/TCP (Connection-oriented), both protocols' statistics are returned. On HP-UX 11.0 servers that have NFS/TCP enabled,[15] both sets of statistics would be displayed. On HP-UX 11.0 servers that do not have NFS/TCP enabled, only the UDP (Connectionless) statistics are displayed.

---

15.   For more information on enabling NFS/TCP on HP-UX 11.0 systems, refer to Chapter 10.

Once you understand what these various counters indicate and how they relate to each other, you can use the information returned by "`nfsstat -sr`" to make informed decisions about the possible causes of your performance problem.

```
┌────────────────────────────────────────────────────────────────────────┐
│ atc03 (L2000 64-bit 11i)                                    _ □ x        │
│ atc03(/) -> nfsstat -sr                                                  │
│                                                                          │
│ Server rpc:                                                              │
│ Connection oriented:                                                     │
│ calls               badcalls              nullrecv                       │
│ 1618417             0                     0                              │
│ badlen              xdrcall               dupchecks                      │
│ 0                   0                     877623                         │
│ dupreqs                                                                  │
│ 0                                                                        │
│ Connectionless oriented:                                                 │
│ calls               badcalls              nullrecv                       │
│ 1354533             0                     0                              │
│ badlen              xdrcall               dupchecks                      │
│ 0                   0                     695339                         │
│ dupreqs                                                                  │
│ 19                                                                       │
└────────────────────────────────────────────────────────────────────────┘
```

Figure 4.14 `nfsstat` Displaying Server-side RPC Statistics

For example, if the server is logging a high number of "badcalls," this could indicate that one or more NFS clients are sending in malformed requests — either of an invalid length, which would cause the "badlen" counter to increment, or requests that cannot be decoded at the XDR (External Data Representation) layer, causing "xdrcall" to increment. This usually indicates that a hardware problem exists, which is causing the NFS packets to get corrupted.

Table 4.1 Definitions for `nfsstat` Server-side RPC Statistics

Variable	Transport	Description
calls	Connectionless or Connection-oriented	The total number of RPC calls received across the specific network transport (i.e. UDP or TCP)
badcalls	Connectionless or Connection-oriented	The total number of calls rejected by the RPC layer (the sum of "badlen" and "xdrcall" as defined below)
nullrecv	Connectionless or Connection-oriented	The number of times an RPC call was not available even though it was believed to have been received

Table 4.1 Definitions for `nfsstat` Server-side RPC Statistics

Variable	Transport	Description
badlen	Connectionless or Connection-oriented	The number of RPC calls received with a length shorter than that allowed for valid RPC calls
xdrcall	Connectionless or Connection-oriented	The number of RPC calls whose header could not be decoded by XDR
dupchecks	Connectionless or Connection-oriented	The number of RPC calls that were looked up in the duplicate request cache
dupreqs	Connectionless or Connection-oriented	The number of RPC calls that were found to be duplicates in the duplicate request cache

The "dupchecks" and "dupreqs" counters indicate the utilization rate of the NFS server's *duplicate request cache*. Before using these counters to decide if an NFS problem exists, a general understanding of the design and intention of the duplicate request cache is required.

The Duplicate Request Cache

The duplicate request cache is used by NFS servers to keep track of recent *non-idempotent* requests. A request is considered *non-idempotent* if executing the request would cause the contents of the NFS server's on-disk data to be modified. Examples of non-idempotent requests are: WRITE, CREATE, MKDIR, REMOVE, RMDIR, and SETATTR. These requests should only be executed by the server once in order to avoid data corruption.

The cache stores the original completion status of non-idempotent requests along with their transaction IDs. If a duplicate copy of a request is received and a matching transaction ID is found in the cache, then the original completion status is returned to the client and the duplicate request is not executed.

Why is a duplicate request cache needed?

The server needs to employ a duplicate request cache because of the "stateless" nature of the NFS protocol, and because NFS is allowed to run over unreliable network transports. The "stateless" design of NFS allows the server to treat each individual request sent by a client as a stand-alone entity.

The server does not keep track of which NFS clients are reading from or writing to which files on the server, nor does it care. It merely takes each request as it comes in and executes it. However, certain request types should not be allowed to execute more than once or data corruption can occur. This would be less of a concern if NFS requests and replies were always sent on reliable network transports that not only guaranteed packet delivery, but also guaranteed that packets would arrive in the order they were sent. This is not the case with UDP, which does not incorporate a reliable delivery mechanism, nor does it guarantee to deliver packets in sequence.

Even a connection oriented network transport like TCP does not eliminate the need for a duplicate request cache. Retransmissions can still occur on NFS/TCP-mounted filesystems for a variety of reasons, such as a busy NFS server, a network outage, or configuring a small timeout value for the mount point (via the *timeo* mount option).

What could happen if the server did not use a duplicate request cache?

If the NFS server did not use a duplicate request cache then data loss could occur when NFS packets are lost or delayed. An example is shown in Figure 4.15.

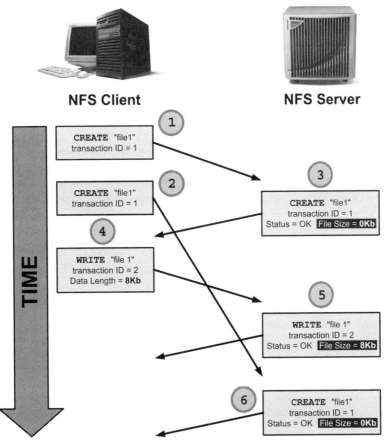

Figure 4.15 Why NFS Servers Need a Duplicate Request Cache

In this example, the following sequence of events occurs:

1. The NFS client sends a CREATE request to create a new file called "file1." This request uses a transaction ID of "1."
2. For whatever reason (i.e. network latency, busy NFS server, etc.), the client does not receive a response in the time period it expected. It retransmits the CREATE request using the same transaction ID as the original request — "1."
3. The NFS server receives the initial CREATE request and it creates an empty file called "file1." The server sends a reply to the client using the same transaction ID as the client used in the CREATE request — "1."
4. The client receives the server's reply to the original CREATE request. It sends a WRITE request containing 8Kb of data and using a transaction ID of "2."
5. The server receives the WRITE request and posts the data to the file. It sends a WRITE reply using the same transaction ID as the WRITE request — "2."
6. The server receives the retransmitted CREATE call sent by the client in step 2. It executes the request and effectively destroys the data written in step 5.

This simple example illustrates the need for the duplicate request cache to maintain data integrity. If the NFS server in the above example had used a duplicate request cache it would have identified the second CREATE call as a duplicate, sent back the status from the original request, and discarded the duplicate thus leaving the 8Kb of data written in step 5 intact.

With this understanding we can now return to the "dupchecks" and "dupreqs" counters. The "dupchecks" counter increments every time a non-idempotent request is processed by the server. It is not uncommon for this value to be very high, as this would indicate that the server is processing a large number of non-idempotent requests such as WRITE and CREATE requests.

The "dupreqs" counter increments when a non-idempotent request is received and the server finds a matching entry in its duplicate request cache. This usually indicates that one or more NFS clients are sending retransmitted requests. This could be a sign that the server is not responding to requests in a timely fashion, resulting in the client having to re-send its requests.

Look for socket overflows on UDP port 2049   Another potential cause of poor NFS performance for those applications that use NFS/UDP-mounted filesystems is if an insufficient number of UDP-based nfsds are running to efficiently handle the inbound request load. When too few daemons are running, the potential exists for the UDP port associated with the nfsds (2049) to reach its capacity and eventually overflow, causing inbound NFS requests to be dropped and forcing the clients to retransmit them. In this situation, starting more UDP nfsds would likely help to keep the UDP port 2049 sufficiently drained, thus allowing new requests to be enqueued rather than discarded.

The quickest way to check for UDP socket overflows on a system-wide basis is to use the netstat(1) command with the "-p udp" options, such as the example in Figure 4.16.

```
atc01 (L2000 64-bit 11.0)                                                    _ □ X
atc01(/) -> netstat -p udp
udp:
        0 incomplete headers
        0 bad checksums
      120 socket overflows
```

Figure 4.16 netstat -p Displaying UDP Socket Overflows

In this example we find this system has experienced 120 UDP socket overflows. This represents the total number of socket overflows that have occurred since the time the system was booted. In other words, these 120 socket overflows could have occurred ten per month over a twelve month period, or they could have happened during a temporary traffic spike three weeks ago. It is therefore important to monitor this statistic to see if it continues to increase over time. It is also important to understand that this counter represents socket overflows for *all UDP sockets on the system* — not just the sockets used by NFS. There is no way to know from this netstat data which UDP socket(s) experienced these overflow conditions.

HP recognized the importance of being able to accurately identify the overflowing UDP sockets in order to identify which applications are affected by the overflows. Without knowing for certain which socket is overflowing there is little hope of determining the underlying cause and correcting the situation. HP responded by enhancing the ndd(1M) utility to display overflow information on a per-UDP-socket basis.

ndd is a very powerful utility used to examine, and in some cases modify, the various networking components on HP-UX systems. The list of tunable parameters that can be inspected varies based on the network protocol being queried. In other words, the list of UDP-based parameters will differ significantly from the list of TCP parameters. The total number of viewable parameters is well over 100.[16]

One of the UDP-specific parameters that can be queried is "ip_udp_status." This variable displays information about all currently open UDP sockets on the system. It has been enhanced to include socket overflow information on a per-socket basis. An example showing the specific ndd syntax and sample output is included in Figure 4.17.

A new column called "overflows" was added to the "ip_udp_status" output. This column displays the number of times a socket overflow was experienced on the current open connection. Each entry in the displayed table contains "laddr" and "faddr" fields showing the local and remote IP addresses respectively. Each entry also has a "lport" and "fport" field indicating the local and foreign (remote) port numbers associated with the UDP socket.

---

16.   Refer to the ndd(1M) man page for a description of the available command-line options.

```
atc01 (L2000 64-bit 11.0)                                                          _ □ ×
atc01(/) -> ndd -get /dev/udp ip_udp_status
UDP ipc           hidx lport fport laddr           faddr           flags    overflows  dist head
0000000041a28e68 0001 0801  0000 000.000.000.000 000.000.000.000 60900000 0000000000 0002 00000000451ed8d8
0000000041ac3468 0001 0801  0000 000.000.000.000 000.000.000.000 60900000 0000000001 0000 0000000000000000
000000004ad3ca68 0002 0202  0000 000.000.000.000 000.000.000.000 20800000 0000000000 0000 0000000000000000
000000004be92a68 0006 0206  0000 000.000.000.000 000.000.000.000 a0800000 0000000000 0000 0000000000000000
000000004be8b468 0007 0007  0000 000.000.000.000 000.000.000.000 a0800000 0000000000 0000 0000000000000000
000000004be79468 0009 0009  0000 000.000.000.000 000.000.000.000 a0800000 0000000000 0000 0000000000000000
000000004bacd468 000b c00b  0000 000.000.000.000 000.000.000.000 20800000 0000000000 0000 0000000000000000
000000004be83a68 000d c00d  0000 000.000.000.000 000.000.000.000 20800000 0000000000 0000 0000000000000000
000000004beb7668 000d 000d  0000 000.000.000.000 000.000.000.000 a0800000 0000000000 0000 0000000000000000
000000004be91268 000f c00f  0000 000.000.000.000 000.000.000.000 20800000 0000000000 0000 0000000000000000
000000004ad40a68 0010 c010  0000 000.000.000.000 000.000.000.000 20800000 0000000000 0000 0000000000000000
000000004be90e68 0011 c011  0000 000.000.000.000 000.000.000.000 20800000 0000000000 0000 0000000000000000
000000004beb7068 0013 0013  0000 000.000.000.000 000.000.000.000 a0800000 0000000000 0000 0000000000000000
000000004b88ee68 0014 c014  0000 000.000.000.000 000.000.000.000 20800000 0000000000 0000 0000000000000000
0000000041972668 001d c01d  0000 000.000.000.000 000.000.000.000 20800000 0000000000 0000 0000000000000000
0000000418aa868 002b 042b   0000 000.000.000.000 000.000.000.000 a0800000 0000000000 0000 0000000000000000
0000000041a64a68 002c 042c  0000 000.000.000.000 000.000.000.000 20800000 0000000000 0000 0000000000000000
000000004beb9468 0044 0044  0000 000.000.000.000 000.000.000.000 20800000 0000000000 0000 0000000000000000
000000004ad53a68 0045 0045  0000 000.000.000.000 000.000.000.000 a0800000 0000000000 0000 0000000000000000
000000004bec8068 0049 0849  0000 000.000.000.000 000.000.000.000 20800000 0000000000 0000 0000000000000000
000000004abd3068 006f 006f  0000 000.000.000.000 000.000.000.000 20800000 0000000000 0000 0000000000000000
0000000041748c68 0073 c873  0000 000.000.000.000 000.000.000.000 20800000 0000000000 0000 0000000000000000
0000000419d4e68 0087 0087   0000 000.000.000.000 000.000.000.000 20800000 0000000000 0000 0000000000000000
000000004be91a68 00a1 00a1  0000 000.000.000.000 000.000.000.000 20800000 0000000000 0000 0000000000000000
000000004bf3be68 00b1 00b1  0000 000.000.000.000 000.000.000.000 20800000 0000000000 0000 0000000000000000
0000000418aa068 00b6 14b6   0000 000.000.000.000 000.000.000.000 a0800000 0000000000 0000 0000000000000000
```

Figure 4.17 ndd Displaying Open UDP Sockets and Overflows

In this example only a single currently open UDP socket has experienced a socket over-flow — the second entry in the list with a hexadecimal local port number of 0x0801. Converting 0x0801 to decimal we find the local port number is 2049, which means that the UDP nfsds have experienced a single socket overflow.

HP-ux 11i   Difference Between HP-UX 11.0 and 11i:
Enhanced ndd(1M) ip_udp_status Output

The ndd(1M) variable "ip_udp_status" has been modified on HP-UX 11.0 systems to include socket overflow information on a per-UDP-socket basis. This enhancement was added in patch PHNE_23456. This patch, or a patch that supersedes PHNE_23456, must be installed to take advantage of this feature on 11.0 systems.

The ndd version that shipped with HP-UX 11i includes support for the enhanced "ip_udp_status" variable, so no 11i patch is needed to take advantage of this feature.

Since no other currently open UDP sockets show any overflows, the conclusion is that the remaining 119 socket overflows reported by "netstat -p udp" (see Figure 4.16) occurred on UDP sockets that are no longer active. This again illustrates the importance of monitoring the system over a period of time and looking for repeated occurrences of socket overflows before concluding that the overflows are caused by the nfsds.

If the `ndd` output had shown other UDP sockets experiencing overflows, your best course of action would be to determine which application uses that UDP socket and then try to understand why the overflows are occurring. Once you learn why an applications socket is overflowing you may be able to make adjustments to the system to stop these overflows from occurring.

Typically the affected application is identified by converting the local port address (reported by `ndd` in the "`lport`" column) to its decimal equivalent and then determining which application is using the port. The most common place to begin looking for a matching port number is the service name data base file "`/etc/services`."[17] This file contains a listing of the "well-known" applications and their assigned port numbers. As this is an ASCII file, it can easily be searched for any decimal port number. An example is included in Figure 4.18.

```
ros87252 (B1000 64-bit 11i)                                              _ □ ✕
ros87252(/) -> grep 2049 /etc/services
nfsd           2049/udp                    # NFS remote file system
nfsd           2049/tcp                    # NFS remote file system
```

Figure 4.18   Search `/etc/services` for Well-known Ports

If the port number is not listed in the `/etc/services` file you can try examining the output from "`rpcinfo -p`" (a partial listing is included in Figure 4.19) to see if the port experiencing the overflows matches any of the port numbers associated with the running RPC programs that have registered with the `rpcbind(1M)` daemon.

```
ros87252 (B1000 64-bit 11i)                                              _ □ ✕
ros87252(/) -> rpcinfo -p
   program vers proto    port   service
    100000    4   tcp     111   rpcbind
    100000    3   tcp     111   rpcbind
    100000    2   tcp     111   rpcbind
    100000    4   udp     111   rpcbind
    100000    3   udp     111   rpcbind
    100000    2   udp     111   rpcbind
    100024    1   tcp   49152   status
    100024    1   udp   49153   status
    100021    1   tcp   49153   nlockmgr
    100021    1   udp   49156   nlockmgr
    100021    3   tcp   49154   nlockmgr
    100021    3   udp   49157   nlockmgr
    100021    4   tcp   49155   nlockmgr
    100021    4   udp   49158   nlockmgr
```

Figure 4.19   `rpcinfo` Displaying Ports Used by RPC Programs

17.   If NIS is used in your environment, the "services" NIS map should be checked via the ypcat(1) command. If NIS+ is used, the "services" table should be checked via the niscat(1) command.

If you are still not able to determine which application is using the overflowing port, your best bet is to use a third party utility, such as the `lsof(8)` command, to get this information. `lsof` was written by Victor A. Abell of Purdue University. It is a very powerful utility capable of listing information about the files opened by processes running on UNIX systems. There are literally dozens of command-line options available for `lsof`. The latest version of the source code, pre-compiled binaries for various flavors of UNIX, and the current `lsof` man page are available for download from: *ftp://vic.cc.purdue.edu/pub/tools/unix/lsof*.

An example of how `lsof` output can be used to map a UDP port with a running application is shown in Figure 4.20. For this exercise, the `lsof` output was filtered via the `grep(1)` command to only display the active UDP sockets. This allows us to quickly identify which applications are using which specific UDP ports. If, for example, the ndd output in Figure 4.17 had shown that port 135 was overflowing ("lport" of 0x0087), we could use the `lsof` output to ascertain that this port is in use by the `dced(1M)` daemon.

```
ros87252 (B1000 64-bit 11i)                                              _ □ X
ros87252(/)  -> lsof -P | grep -E 'COMMAND|UDP'
COMMAND    PID    USER    FD    TYPE    DEVICE      SIZE/OFF   NODE NAME
syslogd    622    root    5u    inet    0x40d65040       0t0   UDP *:514 (Idle)
inetd      980    root    4u    inet    0x41246840       0t0   UDP *:49162 (Idle)
inetd      980    root    7u    inet    0x40d654c0       0t0   UDP *:67 (Idle)
inetd      980    root   11u    inet    0x40d65ac0       0t0   UDP *:518 (Idle)
inetd      980    root   15u    inet    0x4121d200       0t0   UDP *:13 (Idle)
inetd      980    root   18u    inet    0x4121d680       0t0   UDP *:7 (Idle)
inetd      980    root   20u    inet    0x4121d980       0t0   UDP *:9 (Idle)
inetd      980    root   22u    inet    0x4121dc80       0t0   UDP *:19 (Idle)
bootpd    1160    root    0u    inet    0x40d654c0       0t0   UDP *:67 (Idle)
bootpd    1160    root    1u    inet    0x40d654c0       0t0   UDP *:67 (Idle)
bootpd    1160    root    2u    inet    0x40d654c0       0t0   UDP *:67 (Idle)
dced      1399    root    7u    inet    0x412d2580       0t0   UDP *:135 (Idle)
swagentd  1651    root   12u    inet    0x41373ac0       0t0   UDP *:2121 (Idle)
nmbd      1717    root    5u    inet    0x41499080       0t0   UDP *:137 (Idle)
nmbd      1717    root    6u    inet    0x41499200       0t0   UDP *:138 (Idle)
```

Figure 4.20 `lsof` Output Filtered to Show Active UDP Sockets

Look for errors associated with NFS/TCP thread exhaustion Soon after HP delivered support for NFS/TCP on HP-UX 11.0 and 11i, a critical defect was discovered that caused NFS servers to stop servicing NFS/TCP requests when a specific condition was reached on the server. If the number of threads associated with the nfsktcpd process reached the value defined by the kernel variable *max_thread_proc* (which specifies the maximum number of threads a given process may own), the server will stop responding to NFS/TCP requests, causing any client applications accessing this server via NFS/TCP to hang.

Fortunately, this defect was quickly isolated and resolved. The fix was included in patch PHNE_22642 for 11.0 systems and PHNE_23502 for 11i systems. It is highly recommended that these patches, or patches that supersede them, be installed on any HP-UX NFS/TCP server.

Even with current patches installed, it is still possible for a server's nfsktcpd process to eventually reach the *max_thread_proc* limit of threads. If this happens on a patched NFS server, an error similar to "`vmunix: WARNING: tcpd_thread_create: thread_create failed: 11`" will be appended to the system's "`/var/adm/syslog/syslog.log`" file, indicating that the nfsktcpd process was not able to create a new kernel thread when it needed to. With the appropriate patches installed, this warning message will be returned but NFS/TCP will not stop servicing requests.

If your NFS server is logging these "`tcpd_thread_create`" warning messages in the `syslog.log` file, it is an indication that one or more kernel variables may need to be adjusted. The most likely reasons a new thread could not created are that the nfsktcpd daemon has reached the limit of allowable threads per process, in which case the *max_thread_proc* variable should be increased, or the server has reached the system-wide maximum number of threads, in which case the *nkthread* variable will need to be adjusted. For a detailed description of these kernel variables, how to increase them, and a list of other variables that might need to be adjusted when changes are made to *nkthread* and *max_thread_proc*, refer to Chapter 12 "Kernel Parameters."

Use kernel-profiling utilities to interrogate the server's kernel behavior

When other data collection methods have been exhausted and there is still no clear evidence of where the performance problem lies, it can sometimes be useful to collect kernel-profiling data on the NFS server. The goal of any kernel profiling effort is to identify which functions the kernel is spending the majority of its time running. Knowing where the kernel is dedicating its resources can provide a great deal of insight into deciding which subsystem needs to be investigated. The most commonly used kernel-profiling tool on HP-UX systems is *kgmon*.

WARNING!   **WARNING!**   **WARNING!**

Profiling a live kernel can be a very risky proposition. It should never be performed on a production system unless there is absolutely no way to reproduce the same performance behavior in a test environment.

Many precautions need to be taken before even attempting this procedure on a test system, such as configuring the kernel with sufficient equivalently mapped memory. Unexpected results can occur during any profiling effort, including system panics.

For this reason, HP does not ship kgmon or any other kernel profiling tools with HP-UX, nor does HP officially support using kgmon on customer systems. However, when used with caution (preferably in a test environment) by knowledgeable HP support engineers, kernel profiling data can be extremely useful in better understanding an elusive performance issue.

WARNING!   **WARNING!**   **WARNING!**

A good example of how kgmon was used to isolate the source of an NFS server bottleneck was when HP was investigating an issue where mounting or unmounting a VxFS filesystem on the server took an excessive amount of time. The problem only occurred after issuing a command such as "find /" on the server prior to issuing the mount(1M) or umount(1M) command. Figure 4.21 shows an example of the kgmon output collected during such a test.

```
hpnec07 (dolkersu) - /home/dolker                                      _ □ x
%time cumsecs seconds    calls   msec/call name
 86.7   91.44   91.44                       dnlc_purge
 10.6  102.58   11.14                       idle
  0.2  102.75    0.17                       clock_int
  0.1  102.89    0.14                       pgcopy
  0.1  103.02    0.13                       syscall
  0.1  103.13    0.11                       rwip
  0.1  103.22    0.10                       dnlc_rm
  0.1  103.31    0.08                       $fdc_one_page
  0.1  103.39    0.08                       getblk1
  0.1  103.45    0.07                       per_spu_hardclock
  0.1  103.52    0.06                       bmap
  0.1  103.58    0.06                       brelse
```

Figure 4.21   kgmon Output Collected while Mounting a Filesystem

This sample kgmon output reveals that the NFS server was spending the majority of its time in the dnlc_purge() routine, which is one of the primary functions of the Directory Name Lookup Cache. While this information might be meaningless to someone who does not have access to HP-UX kernel source code, it was a critical piece of data that helped HP labs understand the root cause of the problem and design a solution.

 KEY IDEA — The Importance of Patching the NFS Server Kernel and Commands

HP continually strives to improve the quality of HP-UX by distributing software patches containing both defect fixes and functionality enhancements. Many of these fixes and enhancements can significantly improve the performance and behavior of critical system components, such as the NFS server kernel and commands code.

It is *strongly* recommended that the latest NFS patches be installed on every HP-UX system in order to take advantage of these improvements. Contact HP support to obtain a current set of patches for your specific operating system. You can also generate a current patch list using the tools available at HP's IT Resource Center: *http://itrc.hp.com*.

For a detailed discussion on the importance of keeping your HP-UX NFS client and server systems patched with current code, refer to Appendix B "Patching Considerations."

rpc.mountd

Before an NFS client can begin accessing files on an NFS server, it first needs to mount the desired remote filesystem. This involves contacting the server and requesting permission to access the exported filesystem. Once the server confirms that the client is allowed to access the filesystem in question, it returns the filehandle for the root of the exported filesystem. These MOUNT requests are not handled by the NFS protocol directly. Instead, a separate MOUNT protocol was designed to run on the NFS server and process these inquiries. On HP-UX systems, the MOUNT protocol is implemented via the *rpc.mountd* daemon.

rpc.mountd (also known as mountd) is an RPC-based daemon that processes filesystem mount requests. It consults the /etc/xtab[1] file to determine which directories are available to which client systems. It also attempts to keep track of which NFS clients have mounted which exported filesystems at any given time.

Many times the rpc.mountd daemon is overlooked when troubleshooting NFS server problems. In fact, it is not uncommon for rpc.mountd-related problems to be misdiagnosed as client-side problems because the only external symptom may be an NFS client application hanging while attempting to access an NFS mount point.

This chapter begins by describing the various services provided by the rpc.mountd daemon. This is followed by a discussion of the factors in your NFS environment that can adversely affect the performance of rpc.mountd. Special attention is given to the subject of host-name resolution and its influence on rpc.mountd behavior and performance. Finally, this chapter outlines the tools and techniques available for troubleshooting rpc.mountd-related problems.

---

1.   Refer to the exports(4) man page for information about the contents of the /etc/xtab file.

5.1   What Services Does rpc.mountd Provide?

rpc.mountd is often overlooked during troubleshooting efforts. Although it only performs a few functions, many of them are essential for proper NFS operation.

5.1.1   Process MOUNT Requests

Servicing MOUNT requests is the single most important function performed by rpc.mountd. It is also the most time consuming and resource intensive operation, and is therefore the operation most sensitive to external factors in the NFS environment, such as hostname resolution problems. Processing a MOUNT request on the server involves several steps:

1. Confirm the identity of the NFS client sending the request by resolving the IP address in the packet header to a hostname via the resolution mechanism(s) used by the server.
2. Extract the pathname of the desired filesystem from the MOUNT request.
3. Examine the /etc/xtab file to see if the requested filesystem is exported for access.
4. Compare the hostname returned from the hostname resolution server against any access lists configured for the exported filesystem.
5. If the client is allowed to mount the filesystem, rpc.mountd adds an entry to the /etc/rmtab file indicating which NFS client has mounted the requested filesystem, and returns the filehandle for the root of the exported filesystem to the client.
6. If the client is denied access to the requested filesystem, then return an error to the client.

As you can see, there are many steps involved in servicing a simple MOUNT request. Since there is only a single rpc.mountd daemon running on each server, and since every NFS client needs to contact the rpc.mountd daemon before it can begin accessing the NFS filesystem exported by the server, it is critical that rpc.mountd service MOUNT requests as quickly and efficiently as possible. This is especially true in environments where an automounter is used by the clients, since automounters tend to send multiple MOUNT and UNMOUNT requests in succession, thereby exacerbating any rpc.mountd problem.

5.1.2   Process UMOUNT Requests

Unlike the MOUNT case, processing UMOUNT requests is not really a critical task since the only purpose it serves is to update the /etc/rmtab file on the server. However, rpc.mountd goes through many of the same steps when processing a UMOUNT request, including:

1. Confirm the identity of the NFS client sending the request by resolving the IP address in the packet header to a hostname via the resolution mechanism(s) used by the server.
2. Extract the pathname of the desired filesystem from the UMOUNT request.
3. Search the /etc/rmtab file for an entry matching the hostname of the client and the exported filesystem being unmounted; once found, "deactivate" the entry by changing the first character of the entry to a "#."

What is the /etc/rmtab file used for?   The /etc/rmtab file contains a record of all NFS clients that have mounted remote filesystems from the server. Whenever an NFS mount is processed by rpc.mountd, an entry is made in the server's rmtab file indicating which remote client mounted which exported filesystem. A umount from the client "deactivates" the entry from the rmtab file by changing the first character of the entry to a "#."

This file is only read by rpc.mountd during startup. Once running, rpc.mountd keeps an in-memory copy of the rmtab table to handle requests such as "showmount -a." See Figure 5.1 for an example of "showmount -a" output.

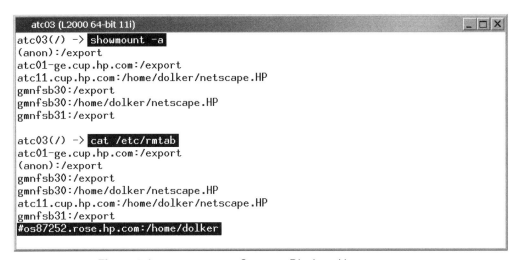

Figure 5.1   /etc/rmtab Contents Displayed by showmount

In this example, the /etc/rmtab file contains seven entries; six of which are "active" — meaning they represent current NFS mounts from clients, and one "deactivated" entry (#os87252.rose.hp.com:/home/dolker) — indicating that rpc.mountd processed a request from client "ros87252.rose.hp.com"[2] to unmount the "/home/dolker" filesystem.

Unfortunately, the majority of the information in this sample /etc/rmtab file is inaccurate. All of the client systems that supposedly have existing NFS mounted filesystems from this server (gmnfsb30, gmnfsb31, and atc11) were rebooted and none of them have re-mounted these filesystems. Since the clients were rebooted without first issuing unmount requests for these filesystems, the server's rpc.mountd was never notified that these clients were no longer using these filesystems, and thus never updated the server's /etc/rmtab file.

The only way that the /etc/rmtab file contents could remain accurate is if every client that mounted NFS filesystems from a server issued corresponding umount requests for each

---

2.   This unmount request could have originated from a client other than "ros87252," since we don't know for certain that the first character of the hostname was an "r" before being replaced by a "#" character.

filesystem before it is shutdown. In most NFS environments this is simply not a realistic expectation. There are several real-world factors that can cause the contents of /etc/rmtab to become inaccurate, including: NFS clients crashing unexpectedly, NFS client systems being disconnected from one network subnet and re-deployed in a different part of the country, PC clients (running Windows or Linux) mounting filesystems and then rebooting, etc. In other words, in most environments the /etc/rmtab file contents are notoriously inaccurate and should therefore be considered suspect.

5.1.3 Report which NFS Clients Have Filesystems Mounted

As stated in the previous section, rpc.mountd attempts to keep an accurate table of those NFS clients that have mounted filesystems from the server. The /etc/rmtab file is the on-disk version of the table maintained in memory by rpc.mountd. The in-memory table is reported when rpc.mountd receives a DUMP request. This is normally done via the "showmount -a" command. Refer to Figure 5.1 for an example. Again, this information is highly suspect and should not be used to make any performance-related decisions about the NFS server.

5.1.4 Provides a List of Exported Filesystems

Another important function of rpc.mountd is reporting which filesystems are currently exported by the server. rpc.mountd returns this information in response to an EXPORT request, which is used by two NFS components: the showmount(1M) command and the automounter.

showmount(1M)   The showmount command, when issued with the "-e" option, displays the server's exported filesystems along with their associated access lists — even when issued from a remote NFS client. This information can be very useful in cases where an NFS mount fails with an unexpected "Permission denied" error and you wish to verify how the filesystems are exported without accessing the server. Figure 5.2 contains an example of an NFS client in Cupertino, CA issuing a "showmount -e" command to display the list of filesystems exported by a server in Roseville, CA.

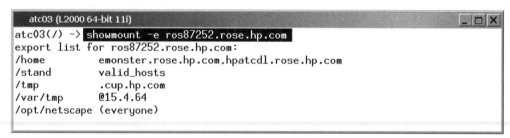

Figure 5.2 Sample showmount -e Output

This output reveals that this NFS server is exporting five different filesystems, and each filesystem is exported using a different access list. Again, this information can be very helpful in understanding whether a failing NFS mount was denied because of the way the filesystem is currently exported on the server.

automount   Both automounters supported by HP-UX (i.e. the legacy automounter and the newer AutoFS product[3]) support a special map type called the "-hosts" map. This map provides an easy way to configure an NFS client to automatically mount all exported filesystems from an NFS server — at least all filesystems that the client has permission to mount.

By default, the -hosts map syntax is: "/net -hosts -nosuid,soft."[4] With the automounter configured to use this map, a reference to the path "/net/<server name>" will force the client to send `MOUNT` requests to the specified server for all exported filesystems.

How does the automounter know which filesystems are available to mount? It determines this by sending an `EXPORT` request to the server's rpc.mountd, causing the daemon to return the list of exported filesystems to the client. The automounter then simply issues `MOUNT` requests for each filesystem. Those filesystems that the client is allowed to access will be mounted, and those filesystems whose access list restricts the client from mounting will not be mounted.

5.2   What Factors Influence rpc.mountd Performance?

There is very little that can be done to "tune" the performance of rpc.mountd *directly.* rpc.mountd runs as a user-space process (as opposed to being implemented in the kernel), which means there are no kernel tunable parameters available to influence the behavior of rpc.mountd. Also, rpc.mountd is a single-threaded process, and only one instance of the daemon may run at a time, which means there is no way to achieve any parallelism with rpc.mountd.

This does not mean there is no way to influence the behavior and performance of rpc.mountd. In fact, there are several factors that can dramatically affect how quickly rpc.mountd responds to requests. The primary influence on rpc.mountd performance is the speed and accuracy of the hostname resolution mechanism(s) used by the NFS server. The contents of the `/etc/rmtab` file can, in some cases, induce a delay when rpc.mountd is first started, affecting rpc.mountd's ability to begin servicing requests quickly. Finally, the syntax used when exporting filesystems via the `exportfs(1M)` command can dramatically affect how much work rpc.mountd performs when servicing `MOUNT` requests.

5.2.1   Hostname Resolution

Hostname resolution is the mapping of a computer's hostname to its network address (typically an IP address) and vice versa. These mapping services are used extensively during NFS filesystem mounting, both on the client and the server. The NFS `mount(1M)` command on the client system must resolve the IP address of the server in order to send the `MOUNT` request. The

---

3.   The legacy automounter and newer AutoFS products are described in detail in Chapter 7.

4.   This is the default syntax used by HP-UX 11.0 and 11i systems. Other vendors may use different map options.

server's rpc.mountd daemon contacts the hostname resolution server to verify the identity of the client sending the MOUNT request, and again when validating the client's rights to access the requested filesystem. It is therefore critical to rpc.mountd performance that the hostname resolution mechanism(s) used by your NFS servers respond to hostname or IP address queries accurately and quickly.

 KEY IDEA — The Importance of Hostname Resolution on rpc.mountd Performance

The vast majority of all customer-reported rpc.mountd problems turn out to be related in one way or another to **hostname resolution**. Since rpc.mountd is a single-threaded daemon, if it must block waiting for a hostname resolution server to respond to a hostname or IP address query, the daemon will be unable to respond to (or will be slow in processing) incoming requests.

It is therefore critical to familiarize yourself with, and verify the performance and accuracy of, the hostname resolution mechanisms used in your NFS environment.

Familiarize yourself with the resolution methods used by your server   Several different hostname resolution mechanisms are available on HP-UX systems, including:

• DNS — Domain Name System
• NIS — Network Information Service
• NIS+ — Network Information Name Service Plus
• LDAP — Light weight Directory Access Protocol
• /etc/hosts — hostname file

It is important to familiarize yourself with the hostname resolution method(s) used in your environment, as this will allow you to make an informed decision about where to begin troubleshooting when a hostname resolution issue arises. The quickest way to verify which resolution service(s) your environment uses is to examine the contents of the Name Services Switch configuration file — /etc/nsswitch.conf. The "hosts" entry defines the hostname resolution scheme(s) used for the system, the order in which the various mechanisms are referenced during a hostname or IP address query, and the circumstances under which each source will be tried.

Figure 5.3 shows a sample /etc/nsswitch.conf file on an HP-UX 11i system. In this example, the "hosts" entry instructs this system to initially query DNS for hostname or IP address information. If the lookup fails because the DNS tables do not contain the requested data, then the lookup will return a failure. If the DNS query fails because DNS is not configured on the system, then NIS will be checked. Like DNS, if the requested information is not found in the NIS hosts map, then the lookup will return a failure. Only when both DNS and NIS are not properly configured will the local /etc/hosts file be consulted. Neither NIS+ nor LDAP are being used by this system for hostname resolution.

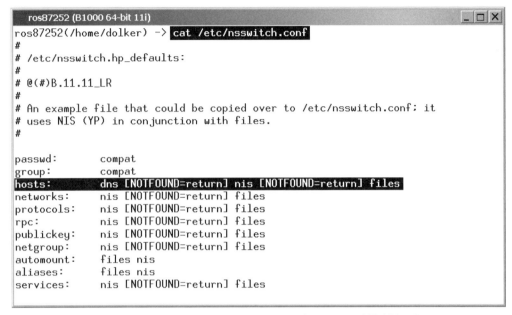

```
ros87252 (B1000 64-bit 11i)                                    _ □ X
ros87252(/home/dolker) -> cat /etc/nsswitch.conf
#
# /etc/nsswitch.hp_defaults:
#
# @(#)B.11.11_LR
#
# An example file that could be copied over to /etc/nsswitch.conf; it
# uses NIS (YP) in conjunction with files.
#

passwd:          compat
group:           compat
hosts:           dns [NOTFOUND=return] nis [NOTFOUND=return] files
networks:        nis [NOTFOUND=return] files
protocols:       nis [NOTFOUND=return] files
rpc:             nis [NOTFOUND=return] files
publickey:       nis [NOTFOUND=return] files
netgroup:        nis [NOTFOUND=return] files
automount:       files nis
aliases:         files nis
services:        nis [NOTFOUND=return] files
```

Figure 5.3 Default nsswitch.conf Settings on HP-UX 11i

When a hostname resolution problem occurs, the /etc/nsswitch.conf file contents may not tell you conclusively which subsystem is causing the problem. However, it will tell you which mechanisms should be checked and in which order. For example, if system ros87252 experienced a hostname resolution problem, the /etc/nsswitch.conf file shown in Figure 5.3 would suggest to the systems administrator that the health of DNS should be checked first. If DNS is not configured on the system, then NIS should be investigated. If the system is not a member of an NIS domain, then the /etc/hosts file should be analyzed.

Be sure to check the /etc/nsswitch.conf file on both your NFS client and server systems, as each system can use a different resolution scheme.

TIP: HP-UX does not include an nsswitch.conf file by default; however, HP-UX does provide several "template" files, such as "nsswitch.conf.files" and "nsswitch.conf.hp_defaults," each containing examples of different hostname resolution schemes. These templates can be used as the basis for designing an nsswitch.conf file for your system. On HP-UX clients and servers that do not have an nsswitch.conf file configured, the system will use the hostname resolution behavior outlined in the "nsswitch.conf.hp_defaults" file.

For more information about configuring name services via the `/etc/nsswitch.conf` file, see the `nsswitch.conf(4)` man page.

5.2.2 The Size of the `/etc/rmtab` File

As explained in Section 5.1.2, the `/etc/rmtab` file is used by rpc.mountd in an attempt to track which NFS clients have mounted which exported filesystems. rpc.mountd reads this file at start time and keeps a copy in memory while running. Over time, this file can grow to be quite large, especially if the server is exporting many filesystems to a large number of clients. Customers have reported seeing `/etc/rmtab` files containing upwards of 30,000 records. An `rmtab` file of this size can delay rpc.mountd's ability to begin servicing requests for several seconds, or even minutes.

 KEY IDEA — The Influence of the `/etc/rmtab` File on rpc.mountd Behavior

Since the data contained in `/etc/rmtab` is usually inaccurate (for reasons explained in Section 5.1.2), it is recommended that this file be monitored and periodically removed and re-built on the NFS server. As rpc.mountd uses and maintains `/etc/rmtab` while it is running, **rpc.mountd must be stopped before the `rmtab` file is removed**. This procedure should therefore only be performed during scheduled maintenance periods.

To safely remove the `/etc/rmtab` file on an NFS server, log into your server as a root user and issue the following commands:

```
# kill $(ps -e | grep rpc.mountd | awk '{print $1}')
# rm /etc/rmtab
# /usr/sbin/rpc.mountd
```

When rpc.mountd is re-started after the `rmtab` file has been removed, rpc.mountd will create an empty `rmtab` file and begin adding new entries as needed.

5.2.3 Access List Syntax Used when Exporting Filesystems

Before a filesystem can be successfully mounted by an NFS client, it must first be exported on the server via the `exportfs(1M)` command. Each filesystem exported on the server has an associated access list that delineates which client machines are allowed to access the filesystem. The access list syntax can take on a number of different formats, as we saw earlier in the "`showmount -e`" output in Figure 5.2. If we examine the `/etc/exports` file on the server used in the earlier "`showmount -e`" example, we can see exactly how these access lists are constructed (see Figure 5.4).

```
┌─────────────────────────────────────────────────────────────────────┐
│  ros87252 (B1000 64-bit 11i)                                _ □ X    │
├─────────────────────────────────────────────────────────────────────┤
│ ros87252(/) -> cat /etc/exports                                      │
│ /home              -access=emonster.rose.hp.com:hpatcdl.rose.hp.com  │
│ /stand             -access=valid_hosts                               │
│ /tmp               -access=.cup.hp.com                               │
│ /var/tmp           -access=@15.4.64                                  │
│ /opt/netscape                                                        │
└─────────────────────────────────────────────────────────────────────┘
```

Figure 5.4 /etc/exports Displaying Access List Formats

This exports file contains five filesystems, each using a different access list format:

- /home uses *client hostnames* to restrict access
- /stand uses a *netgroup* to determine which clients may access it
- /tmp uses a *DNS domain name* to restrict access
- /var/tmp is secured via a *subnet address*
- /opt/netscape has an *empty* access list

The syntax used when exporting a filesystem can directly influence the amount of work required by rpc.mountd to process a MOUNT request for that filesystem.

Client Hostname   Individual hostnames of NFS clients may be listed in a colon separated list. If DNS is the hostname resolution mechanism used by the server, then each hostname listed should be represented using its fully-qualified domain name (FQDN). An example of a fully-qualified domain name is "client.rose.hp.com." HP-UX does not currently *require* all hostnames in an access list to be fully-qualified;[5] however, HP strongly recommends that all hosts be fully-qualified in order to avoid unnecessary gethostbyname(3N) calls.

One of the first things rpc.mountd does when processing a MOUNT request is retrieve the FQDN of the client issuing the MOUNT request. It does this by extracting the IP address of the client from the MOUNT request packet and resolving that address to its FQDN. rpc.mountd uses this FQDN when comparing against any hostnames in an access list.

When rpc.mountd encounters a hostname in the access list that is not fully-qualified, it assumes that a conclusive match cannot be made by comparing hostname text strings, and thus changes to an IP address comparison algorithm. rpc.mountd calls gethostbyname(3N) to retrieve all IP addresses associated with the hostname in the access list and then performs an IP address comparison against the IP address of the client that issued the MOUNT request.

This IP address comparison mechanism is far more expensive in terms of CPU, network, and hostname resolution overhead compared to a simple hostname string comparison. It also makes rpc.mountd more susceptible to any hostname resolution problems in the environment. It is therefore highly recommended that all hostnames in an access list use the FQDN syntax.

---

5.   HP will likely change this requirement of using FQDN syntax in access lists in a future HP-UX release.

KEY IDEA — The Influence of Access List Syntax on rpc.mountd Performance

HP strongly recommends that all client hostnames included in an access list use their fully-qualified domain name format, thus allowing rpc.mountd to avoid making `gethostbyname(3N)` calls to resolve the client's IP addresses.

Netgroups   A netgroup defines a network-wide group of hostnames and/or user names, which can be used when securing exported filesystems or during permission checking for remote logins and remote shells.[6] Netgroups may be stored locally in the `/etc/netgroup` file or may be distributed via NIS. Individual members of a netgroup are commonly referred to as "triplets" because they may contain up to three fields:

```
(hostname, username, domainname)
```

When netgroups are used in access lists for exporting filesystems, only the "hostname" portion of the triplet is examined. A netgroup member may also be the name of another netgroup, thus allowing netgroups to nest any number of levels deep. Consider the following sample netgroup entries:

```
valid_hosts    engineering
engineering    hardware software (host3, mikey, hp)
hardware       (hardwhost1, chm, hp)    (hardwhost2, dae, hp)
software       (softwhost1, jad, hp)    (softwhost2, dds, hp)
```

In this example the netgroup "valid_hosts" references a second netgroup entry called "engineering." The engineering netgroup consists of two additional netgroups ("hardware" and "software") as well as a triplet containing the hostname "host3." The "hardware" and "software" netgroups each contain two triplets, which specify additional hostnames.

Looking back at the `/stand` example from Figure 5.4, the list of NFS clients allowed to mount the filesystem is determined by evaluating the netgroup "valid_hosts." Using the sample netgroup entries shown above, rpc.mountd may need to traverse through several levels of netgroups to locate the matching entry to complete a `MOUNT` request for `/stand`. If these netgroup entries were managed by NIS, rpc.mountd would need to issue many NIS requests to retrieve this information, exposing rpc.mountd to any NIS performance problems in the environment.

It is therefore recommended that when using netgroups in your access lists, to carefully construct the netgroup entries to minimize the number of internal nesting levels. Also, if NIS is used to manage your netgroups, ensure that your NIS environment has the spare bandwidth needed to adequately handle these netgroup lookups.

6.   For a detailed explanation of netgroup syntax, refer to the netgroup(4) man page.

DNS Domain Name   A DNS domain name may be used to allow every NFS client in the specified domain access to an exported filesystem. Any entry in the access list beginning with a "." character is assumed to be a DNS domain name. In Figure 5.4, the /tmp filesystem is exported to allow any NFS client in the ".cup.hp.com" DNS domain access.

From an rpc.mountd perspective, this is a very low overhead method of exporting filesystems, since all rpc.mountd needs to do is compare the domain portion of the client's fully-qualified hostname against the DNS domain in the access list. rpc.mountd already retrieves the NFS client's fully-qualified hostname at the beginning of processing every MOUNT request, so there is very little additional overhead associated with obtaining the domain portion.

If your DNS namespace is partitioned in such a way as to group all valid NFS clients for a given exported filesystem into a single sub-domain (for instance *marketing*.hp.com, or *support*.hp.com), then exporting via the DNS domain name is an ideal solution.

Subnet Address   Like the DNS domain name syntax, a subnet address may be used to allow every NFS client in the specified subnet to mount an exported filesystem. Any entry in the access list beginning with a "@" character is assumed to be a subnet address. The /var/tmp filesystem in Figure 5.4 may be mounted by any NFS client residing in the "15.4.64" subnet.

This is another relatively low overhead method of exporting filesystems, since rpc.mountd merely converts the client's IP address (which it extracted from the MOUNT packet at the start of processing the request) to its subnet address and compares this to the subnet in the access list.

If your network topology is designed such that all valid NFS clients for a given exported filesystem reside in a single subnet, then exporting via the subnet address is an ideal solution.

Empty   If no access list is defined, then *any* NFS client may mount the filesystem. This is the easiest syntax for rpc.mountd to process since there is nothing to compare against. Of course, allowing every NFS client to have mount access may not be desirable.

   Difference Between HP-UX 11.0 and 11i:
Supported Access List Syntax

When HP-UX 11.0 originally shipped, the access list syntax only supported a limited number of configurations: hostnames and netgroups. Support for the DNS Domain syntax and the Subnet Address syntax were added in patch PHNE_18221.

HP-UX 11i shipped with support for all current access list formats.

For more information about exporting filesystems and specifying access lists, refer to the exportfs(1M) man page.

5.3 Troubleshooting rpc.mountd

The most common symptom of a slow or non-responsive rpc.mountd is a hung mount request. This can often be mistaken for a problem on the NFS client — especially when the client is running automount or AutoFS. If rpc.mountd is not responding to a mount request issued by an automounter, a common reaction is to blame the NFS client and begin collecting debug information from the automount or AutoFS daemon. In these cases, the automounter log file will usually show a long delay occurring during the mount attempt, at which point additional data is needed to understand the root cause of the delay.

When troubleshooting an rpc.mountd related issue, the most important piece of information HP support will typically request is a debug rpc.mountd log file taken while the problem is reproduced. The log file data should at least confirm whether rpc.mountd is receiving requests and attempting to process them. It could also potentially reveal the reason rpc.mountd is blocked. In some cases, a network trace is also needed to fully understand the root cause of rpc.mountd's non-responsiveness.

However, before collecting and analyzing debug log files or network traces, other steps should be taken to verify whether rpc.mountd is able to respond to simple requests. Also, any hostname resolution mechanism(s) used by the NFS server should be checked to ensure that they are responding quickly with accurate information.

5.3.1 Use `rpcinfo(1M)` to "ping" rpc.mountd

One of the quickest and least intrusive methods of determining whether the rpc.mountd process is responding is to use the `rpcinfo(1M)` command to "ping" the running daemon.

The `rpcinfo` command can be issued on either the NFS client or server. The recommendation is to test rpc.mountd from the client, as this will also verify whether RPC packets can traverse the network separating the client and server systems. The syntax to use for this test is: "rpcinfo -T <transport> <system name> mount." This `rpcinfo` syntax will tests all registered versions of the MOUNT protocol. Figure 5.5 shows an `rpcinfo` command issued on NFS client "ros87252" testing the rpc.mountd daemon on server "atc03.cup.hp.com" via UDP.

```
ros87252 (B1000 64-bit 11.0)                                          _ □ ×
ros87252(/) -> rpcinfo -T udp atc03.cup.hp.com mount
program 100005 version 1 ready and waiting
rpcinfo: RPC: Program/version mismatch; low version = 1, high version = 3
program 100005 version 2 is not available
program 100005 version 3 ready and waiting
```

Figure 5.5 `rpcinfo` "pinging" rpc.mountd via UDP

This output shows rpc.mountd is responding to Version 1 and Version 3 requests. It also shows that rpc.mountd did not reply to the Version 2 request. This is the expected output since HP's implementation of rpc.mountd does not support Version 2 of the MOUNT protocol — it currently only supports Versions 1 and 3. This can be verified by issuing the `rpcinfo` command with the "`-p`" option, as shown in Figure 5.6.

```
ros87252 (B1000 64-bit 11.0)                                    _ □ ×
ros87252(/) -> rpcinfo -p atc03.cup.hp.com | grep -E 'mount|proto'
  program vers proto   port  service
   100005   1   udp  49383  mountd
   100005   3   udp  49383  mountd
   100005   1   tcp  49200  mountd
   100005   3   tcp  49200  mountd
```

Figure 5.6 `rpcinfo -p` Output

This output shows HP's rpc.mountd supports Versions 1 and 3 of the MOUNT protocol, and that rpc.mountd can accept requests via either the UDP or TCP transports. Figure 5.7 shows the same client testing rpc.mountd on the same server via TCP and getting similar results.

```
ros87252 (B1000 64-bit 11.0)                                    _ □ ×
ros87252(/) -> rpcinfo -T tcp atc03.cup.hp.com mount
program 100005 version 1 ready and waiting
rpcinfo: RPC: Program/version mismatch; low version = 1, high version = 3
program 100005 version 2 is not available
program 100005 version 3 ready and waiting
```

Figure 5.7 `rpcinfo` "pinging" rpc.mountd via TCP

As these `rpcinfo` commands were issued on the NFS client, these tests confirm that RPC packets are able to successfully traverse the network separating this client and server.

5.3.2 Verify that Hostname Servers Respond Quickly

As described earlier, HP-UX supports many different directory service back-ends for hostname resolution data — DNS, NIS, NIS+, LDAP, and `/etc/hosts`. Each of these repositories has different amounts of overhead associated with retrieving hostname data from them. Any latency involved in retrieving this information can negatively affect the performance of applications that rely on hostname or IP address information, including NFS. It is therefore important to ensure that your hostname resolution servers respond quickly to queries.

HP provides several utilities that can be used to test the performance of your hostname resolution servers. Two of the most common programs are `nslookup(1)` and `nsquery(1)`.

`nslookup(1)` `nslookup` was developed at the University of Berkeley as a means to query DNS servers. It has since been extended to follow the configured name resolution policy obtained from the name services switch configuration file `/etc/nsswitch.conf`. Figure 5.8 shows an example of using `nslookup` and `timex(1)` to time a DNS query.

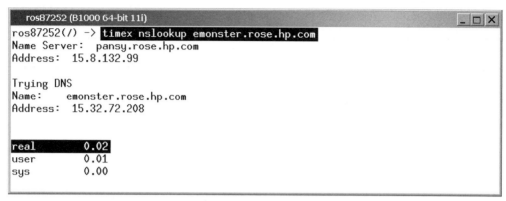

Figure 5.8 `nslookup` Measuring the Responsiveness of DNS

In this example, `nslookup` successfully retrieved the requested information from the DNS server in .02 seconds, thus confirming that the configured DNS name server is responding quickly to requests.

`nslookup` can retrieve hostname or network address information from DNS, NIS, or the local `/etc/hosts` file. Currently it cannot be used to query NIS+ or LDAP. If the "hosts" entry in `/etc/nsswitch.conf` specifies either "nisplus" or "ldap" these sources will be ignored.

For more information about using `nslookup`, refer to the `nslookup(1)` man page.

nsquery(1)   nsquery was developed by HP as a general purpose utility for querying name server repositories. It has many capabilities that `nslookup` does not, including:

- Support for NIS+
- Support for LDAP
- Queries for passwd or group information

Figure 5.9 shows an example of using `nsquery` to resolve a hostname to its IP address. In this example an LDAP name server is queried.

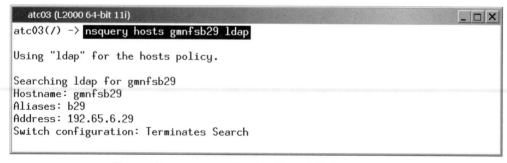

Figure 5.9 `nsquery` Used to Query LDAP Repository

When used in conjunction with the `timex(1)` command, `nsquery` can be an effective tool for gauging the responsiveness of a hostname server, as shown in Figure 5.10. Just as we saw with `nslookup` earlier, the DNS server resolved the specified hostname in .02 seconds.

Like `nslookup`, `nsquery` follows the lookup policies specified in the `/etc/nsswitch.conf` file. The "hosts" policy is used when resolving hostnames or IP addresses, the "passwd" policy is used when looking up user names or UID numbers, and the "group" policy is referenced when resolving group names or GID numbers.

For more information about using `nsquery` refer to the `nsquery(1)` man page.

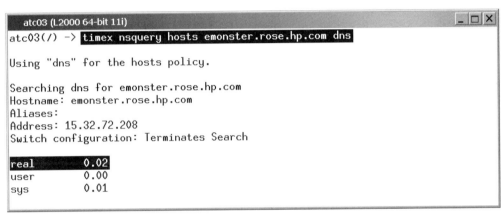

Figure 5.10 `nsquery` Measuring Name Server Responsiveness

5.3.3 Verify the Accuracy of Hostname Resolution Data

Even when the hostname resolution servers are responding quickly to requests, if they return inaccurate or inconsistent data, or if they do not contain the requested information, then the results can be very detrimental to rpc.mountd behavior and performance. It is therefore important to verify that your repository servers contain up-to-date information for all the NFS client and server systems in your environment. This includes making sure that all network interfaces of multi-homed clients and servers (i.e. those systems with more than one network interface) are properly represented in the name server repository. This also involves ensuring that any virtual IP addresses used by HP's MC/ServiceGuard product are assigned valid hostnames, and that these hostnames are included in the name server's databases.

The `netstat(1)` command was previously described in detail in Section 1.3 "Network Troubleshooting Tools." When used with the "`-in`" options, `netstat` displays all of the configured interfaces on a given system, including any virtual IP addresses added by MC/ServiceGuard. The IP address information returned by `netstat` can be compared against the hostname or IP address queries performed with the `nslookup(1)` and `nsquery(1)` commands, allowing the systems administrator to verify the accuracy of the information returned by the hostname servers.

Figure 5.11 shows an example of issuing the "netstat -in" command on a multi-homed NFS server running MC/ServiceGuard. Notice that the "netstat -in" output includes information for all local interfaces: those configured with valid IP addresses (lan3, lan2, lan9, lan0), those interfaces that are currently down (lan11, lan10), the loopback interface (lo0), and the virtual interfaces configured as part of MC/ServiceGuard (lan9:1, lan3:1). These IP addresses should be validated by querying the hostname servers with nslookup or nsquery to ensure that the repositories are accurate.

```
nfsd-c52 (N4000 64-bit 11.0)                                              _ □ ✕
nfsd-c52(/) -> netstat -in
Name          Mtu Network           Address            Ipkts        Opkts
lan11*        1500 none             none                   0            0
lan3          1500 192.65.6.0       192.65.6.52        26735        26859
lan10*        1500 none             none                   0            0
lan2          1500 100.100.100.0    100.100.100.5     101501       201791
lan9:1        1500 192.65.5.0       192.65.5.152         577            0
lan9          1500 192.65.5.0       192.65.5.52          553          843
lan0          1500 15.4.64.0        15.4.64.17        227445       228218
lo0           4136 127.0.0.0        127.0.0.1         277008       277008
lan3:1        1500 192.65.6.0       192.65.6.152           0            0
```

Figure 5.11 netstat Displaying Local IP Addresses

It is also important to configure your NFS clients and servers to use the same hostname repository servers whenever possible. This will ensure that both clients and servers have access to the same hostname and IP address information, thereby decreasing the likelihood of encountering an IP address conflict, resulting in unexpected NFS behavior.

5.3.4 Collect a Debug-level rpc.mountd Log File

The rpc.mountd daemon that ships with HP-UX has the ability to enable and disable debug-level logging without having to be shutdown and restarted. This feature allows the system administrator to easily toggle logging on, reproduce the objectionable behavior, and toggle logging back off — thereby producing a log file that only contains the relevant data. Many of the other NFS-related daemons on HP-UX share this capability as well.

To enable or disable debug-level logging by rpc.mountd, simply send the running processes a SIGUSR2 signal. This is done via the kill(1) command. Below are the steps for collecting a debug rpc.mountd log file. The underlined steps are the commands you type.

1. Determine the process ID used by rpc.mountd via the ps command:

   ```
   # ps -e | grep rpc.mountd
    1801 ?              0:00 rpc.mountd
   ```

2. Toggle debug logging ON by sending rpc.mountd a SIGUSR2 via the kill command:

   ```
   # kill -SIGUSR2 1801
   ```

3. Reproduce the undesirable behavior.

4. Toggle debug logging OFF by sending the daemon another SIGUSR2 signal:

   `# kill -SIGUSR2 1801`

The default location of the debug rpc.mountd log file is "`/var/adm/mountd.log`." A sample screen shot of the debug log file is included in Figure 5.12.

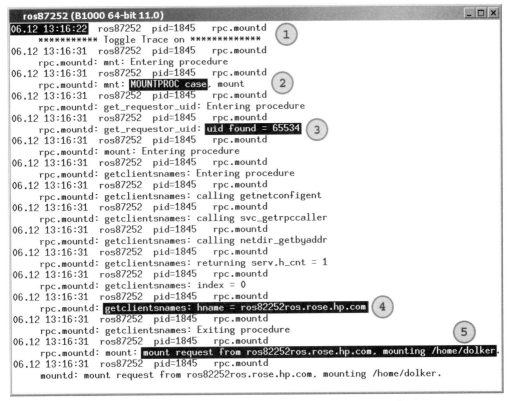

Figure 5.12 Debug rpc.mountd Log Entries During a MOUNT Request

The information collected in the debug rpc.mountd log file may not be intuitively obvious to interpret. However, in the hands of a trained HP support engineer this data can be instrumental in determining the cause of a rpc.mountd problem. For example, the sample output in Figure 5.12 shows:

1. Debug logging was enabled on June 12th at 1:16:22 PM.

2. The rpc.mountd received a MOUNT request at 1:16:31 PM.

3. The UID of the user on the NFS client requesting the MOUNT is 65534.

4. The NFS client sending the request is "ros82252.rose.hp.com."

5. The filesystem requested by the client is "`/home/dolker`."

Again, the format and syntax of the log file does not lend itself to easy interpretation. However, the debug log file contains a wealth of information about the types and frequency of requests sent to rpc.mountd. Also, since every entry in the log file is time stamped, any long delays that occur during the processing of a request should be visible.

5.3.5 Collect a Network Trace of the Mounting Problem

In addition to the debug log file information, a network trace should be taken of any NFS filesystem mounting problem. The trace can quickly reveal if the NFS server is at least receiving mount requests. Here are the steps for collecting and examining a `nettl(1M)` trace for rpc.mountd traffic. The <u>underlined</u> steps are the commands you type.

1. Start a `nettl(1M)` trace on the server. The trace will collect both inbound and outbound traffic as it passes through the IP layer. Log the output of the trace to the file "mountd." The resulting trace filenames will have an extension of ".TRC0" (HP-UX 11.0) or ".TRC000" (HP-UX 11i) appended automatically by the `nettl` command:

   # <u>/etc/nettl -tn pduin pduout -e ns_ls_ip -f mountd</u>

2. Reproduce the NFS filesystem mounting issue on the NFS client.
3. Stop the `nettl(1M)` trace:

   # <u>/etc/nettl -tf -e ns_ls_ip</u>

4. Format the trace via the `netfmt(1M)` command. In this example we assume HP-UX 11.0 systems are used, which explains the ".TRC0" extension appended to the trace filename:

   # <u>/etc/netfmt -lN mountd.TRC0 > mountd.formatted</u>

5. Search the formatted traces for any NFS mount requests.

The `nettl` output in Figure 5.13 shows the NFS server "atc03.cup.hp.com" receiving a `MOUNT` request from client "ros87252.rose.hp.com" for filesystem "/export." It also shows the server sending back a reply with a status of 0 (OK). We also know that the reply packet in the trace is in response to the "/export" `MOUNT` request because the transaction id in both packets (0x3aa846c0) match. This indicates that the rpc.mountd daemon is responding to requests.

If the trace had not shown a reply packet from the server, then the trace would need to be examined more closely. One possible thing to check is if the trace shows the server sending a name services lookup request (i.e. DNS, NIS, NIS+) in an attempt to resolve the IP address of the client who sent the `MOUNT` request. If the trace does show a hostname query being sent, the reply should be in the trace as well.

Since the entries in the formatted trace are time stamped, you can determine how long the name server is taking to respond, thus determining if an underlying name services issue is causing rpc.mountd to block. If the trace shows a name services request but no reply, that is fairly conclusive evidence that an underlying hostname resolution issue is stopping rpc.mountd from responding.

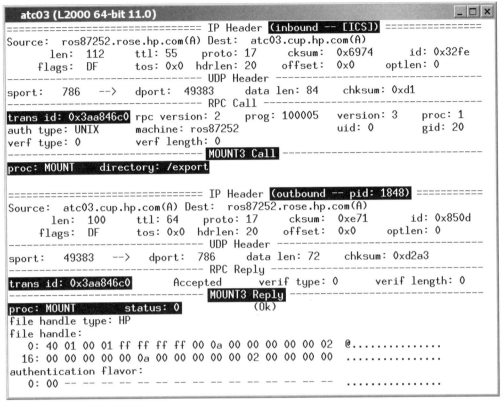

Figure 5.13 `nettl` Trace of MOUNT Request and Reply Packets

 KEY IDEA — The Importance of Patching the NFS Server rpc.mountd Code

HP continually strives to improve the quality of HP-UX by distributing software patches containing both defect fixes and functionality enhancements. Many of these fixes and enhancements can significantly improve the performance and behavior of critical system components, such as the rpc.mountd code.

It is *strongly* recommended that the latest NFS patches be installed on every HP-UX system in order to take advantage of these improvements. Contact HP support to obtain a current set of patches for your specific operating system. You can also generate a current patch list using the tools available at HP's IT Resource Center: *http://itrc.hp.com*.

For a detailed discussion on the importance of keeping your HP-UX NFS client and server systems patched with current code, refer to Appendix B "Patching Considerations."

CHAPTER 6

rpc.lockd and rpc.statd

T he NFS protocol is commonly referred to as a "stateless" protocol because the NFS server maintains no state information about the clients. Every request from a client is processed independently. This behavior allows an NFS client to gracefully recover from an NFS server crash, as it will simply re-send its requests to the server until it gets a response.[1] Since the server does not maintain any state information about the client, after a reboot it simply starts servicing inbound requests as if nothing happened.

This design works fine, except when it comes to NFS file locking. In the file locking case, both the client and the server need to maintain some state information — the client needs to keep track of the files it is currently locking with all servers, and the server needs to monitor which files are locked by the clients.

In order to manage this "state" information on top of a "stateless" protocol, a new mechanism was created to manage NFS file locks — the Network Lock Manager protocol. On HP-UX systems, the NLM protocol is implemented via the *rpc.lockd* daemon. A second protocol — the Network Status Monitor protocol — was created to work in conjunction with NLM and manage the task of recovering file locks after a system failure. HP-UX implements the NSM protocol via the *rpc.statd* daemon.

Many of today's complex NFS-based applications, such as CAD and CAE programs, rely heavily on file locking semantics in order to preserve data integrity in multi-user environments. In these environments, file locking problems can manifest themselves in any number of ways, ranging from poor application performance to application hangs, or even data corruption. It is therefore important to ensure that rpc.lockd and rpc.statd are working correctly on your systems.

---

1.   Assuming the *hard* NFS mount option is used.

Before discussing the ways you can tune your systems for optimal rpc.lockd and rpc.statd performance, some understanding of how these daemons work together to provide file-locking semantics is in order.

This chapter begins by describing how these daemons process NFS file lock requests, and how they recover locks after server failures. It also explains why many file lock hangs occur and how to avoid them. Also included is some useful information explaining how to tell which systems are participating in NFS file locking. This is followed by a discussion of the factors that can adversely affect the performance of rpc.lockd and rpc.statd. Finally, a troubleshooting section describes the recommended tools to use and procedures to follow when investigating NFS file locking issues.

6.1   How Do rpc.lockd and rpc.statd Handle NFS Lock Requests?

In most cases, there is a rpc.lockd and rpc.statd process running on both the NFS client and server.[2] Both client and server maintain a queue of the locks being held. The client's queue contains references to any locks the client's applications are currently holding against all NFS-mounted filesystems. In the server's case, its queue contains reference to all locks being held against its local files from all clients. It is very important that these queues be kept in sync. In other words, both client and server must agree about which process on which client owns a specific lock on a specific file. If the queues become out of sync, data corruption could occur if multiple clients think they have exclusive access to the same lock. For this reason, accurate communication between the client's and server's rpc.lockd and rpc.statd daemons is critical.

6.1.1   Communication Flow for the Initial NFS Lock Request

Figure 6.1 shows the communication flow between the rpc.lockd and rpc.statd processes on both the client and server during the initial lock request (i.e. the first lock request sent between a specific client and server). The steps involved in servicing this request are as follows:

1. An application on the client uses either the `lockf(2)` or `fcntl(2)` system call requesting to lock a file. This lock request is sent to the local kernel for processing.
2. The kernel examines the pathname of the file to be locked and resolves to an NFS rnode,[3] indicating the file resides on a remote system. The kernel forwards the lock request to the local rpc.lockd daemon.
3. Since this is the first time this client is performing an NFS file lock, the client's rpc.lockd contacts the local rpc.statd informing it that the client is about to begin locking NFS files. It asks the local rpc.statd to add this client to the list of systems rpc.statd is monitoring. rpc.statd does this by creating a file in the `/var/statmon/sm` directory on the client.

2.   Most PC-NFS implementations do not include a Network Status Monitor component.

3.   An rnode is the NFS equivalent of an inode.

The contents of this file and the name of this file are identical — they both contain either the name of the system or the IP address of the system being monitored, which in this case is the NFS client.

4. The client rpc.statd replies to the local rpc.lockd that it has successfully added the client to its list of monitored systems.

5. The client's rpc.lockd sends a request to the NFS server's rpcbind daemon to obtain the port number that the server's rpc.lockd is listening on for requests.

6. The server rpcbind daemon replies to the client rpc.lockd, telling it on which port the server's rpc.lockd is accepting requests.

7. The client rpc.lockd sends the lock request to the server rpc.lockd.

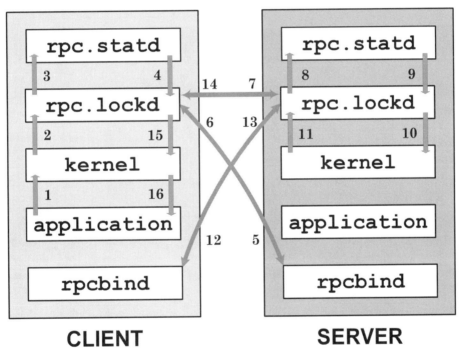

Figure 6.1   rpc.lockd and rpc.statd Flow During Initial Lock Request

8. Since this is the first time this NFS server has received a lock request from this client, the server's rpc.lockd contacts its local rpc.statd asking it to begin monitoring the client. rpc.statd again does this by creating a file in the /var/statmon/sm directory on the server. The contents of this file and the name of this file are identical — they both contain the name of the system or the IP address of the system being monitored, which in this case is the client.

9. The server's rpc.statd replies to its local rpc.lockd that it has added the NFS client to its list of monitored systems.

10. The server's rpc.lockd forwards the lock request to the server's kernel.

11. The kernel on the server performs the lock request and replies to the server's rpc.lockd with the status (i.e. did the lock succeed or fail).

12. The server's rpc.lockd sends a request to the client's rpcbind daemon requesting the port number on which the client's rpc.lockd is accepting requests.

13. The client's rpcbind daemon replies to the server's rpc.lockd with the port number on which the client's rpc.lockd is accepting requests.

14. The server's rpc.lockd sends the results of the lock request to the client's rpc.lockd.

15. The client's rpc.lockd forwards these results back to the client's kernel.

16. The client's kernel forwards the lock results back to the requesting application.

6.1.2 Communication Flow for Subsequent NFS Lock Requests

After the initial lock, the communication flow between the two systems is a bit less involved. From the procedure outlined in Section 6.1.1, only steps 1, 2, 7, 10, 11, 14, 15, and 16 are needed. In other words, after the initial request rpc.lockd does not need to contact rpc.statd on either system. Also, once rpc.lockd has retrieved the port number information for the remote rpc.lockd process it caches this information and only retrieves it from rpcbind again under certain error conditions.

6.2 How Do rpc.lockd and rpc.statd Perform Lock Recovery?

Lock recovery involves a new communication step — labeled 17 in Figure 6.2. This arrow signifies the communication that takes place in the event of a "change in state." A state change refers to an event that causes rpc.lockd and rpc.statd to be restarted, either due to the client or server rebooting, rpc.lockd and rpc.statd being killed and re-started manually, or if the daemons are killed and re-started as part of an MC/ServiceGuard[4] NFS package failover event. In these situations, rpc.statd is instrumental in notifying remote systems that a state change occurred on the local system. When the remote system receives this notification, depending upon whether it is a client or server, it knows that it must take some form of corrective action.

If the NFS client is the system experiencing the state change, then its rpc.statd notifies the rpc.statd process on every NFS server with which the client was performing file locking, letting the servers know they should discard any locks they are currently holding for this client. This communication needs to occur because once a client system reboots, all processes on the client that were holding NFS file locks are destroyed. The NFS server should therefore release these locks to allow other NFS clients to acquire them.

---

4.   NFS file locks are currently not maintained following an MC/ServiceGuard NFS package failover. This feature will be added to HP's Highly Available NFS product in a future HA/NFS release.

If the NFS server experiences the change in state, any locks it was holding prior to the state change are gone. However, any NFS clients that were holding locks against files on the server still believe they have valid locks. It is the responsibility of the NFS server's rpc.statd daemon to contact the rpc.statd process on all NFS clients who have issued file lock requests with the server and inform them that any locks they were holding with the server are gone, and they now have very little time to reclaim their locks before the server will begin allowing other processes to acquire them.

The amount of time the server will wait for clients to reacquire their locks after a failure is known as the "grace period," which defaults to 50 seconds on HP-UX systems.[5] During the grace period, the NFS server will only accept "reclaim" requests. A reclaim is a special request used by a client to reclaim a lock that was held prior to the server's state change. The server does not accept non-reclaim requests during the grace period, as it wants to allow clients the opportunity to reclaim any locks they were holding prior to the state change. If a client does not reclaim its locks during the grace period, the server is free to allow another process to claim the lock.

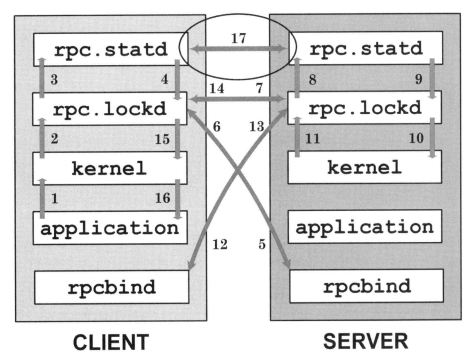

Figure 6.2   rpc.lockd and rpc.statd Flow During Lock Recovery

5.   The grace period timer is configurable via the rpc.lockd "-g <seconds>" option. This option may be specified manually on the rpc.lockd command-line, or you can configure rpc.lockd to always start with a customized grace period timer by adding the "-g" option to the LOCKD_OPTIONS line in the /etc/rc.config.d/nfsconf file.

6.2.1 How Does the rpc.statd Notification Process Work?

Following a state change on either an NFS client or server, the rpc.statd daemon will go through a recovery process to try to notify remote systems that a change in state has occurred. This recovery process includes the following steps:

1. rpc.statd moves all of the files residing in the `/var/statmon/sm` directory into the backup directory — `/var/statmon/sm.bak`. Remember that rpc.statd created these files during their initial lock attempts (refer to steps 3 and 8 in Figure 6.1).

2. One by one, the local rpc.statd opens each `/var/statmon/sm.bak` file and attempts to contact the rpc.statd on the remote system whose hostname matches the name of the file.

3. If rpc.statd is successful in contacting the remote rpc.statd, the file is removed from the `sm.bak` directory. On the system receiving the notification, the rpc.statd will contact its local rpc.lockd and explain that it received a crash notification. If the receiving system is an NFS client, it knows that it needs to try to reclaim any locks it was holding with the server that notified it. If the receiving system is an NFS server, it knows that it should release any locks it is holding for the client that sent the notification.

4. In either case, the receiving system knows that it must discard any UDP and TCP port information it had cached about this remote system. This will force the receiving system to contact the sending system's rpcbind daemon to retrieve the new UDP and TCP port numbers where rpc.lockd and rpc.statd are now listening for requests. This discarding of cached port numbers is an important step, since the remote rpc.lockd and rpc.statd are likely listening on different ports than before the state change.

5. If rpc.statd is unable to notify the remote rpc.statd (because the remote system is down, the hostname of the remote system cannot be resolved, the remote system's rpc.statd is not running, etc.), the file will remain in the `/var/statmon/sm.bak` directory.

6. Once the entire list of `/var/statmon/sm.bak` files has been processed, any remaining files in this directory indicate those systems that rpc.statd was unable to notify. rpc.statd will continually attempt to notify these systems every 15 seconds until it is successful.

 KEY IDEA — The Significance of the Files in `/var/statmon/sm.bak`

Any files residing in the `/var/statmon/sm.bak` directory indicate that rpc.statd was not able to make contact with the rpc.statd daemon running on the remote system associated with the `sm.bak` file. rpc.statd will continuously attempt to contact these systems every 15 seconds until a connection with the remote rpc.statd is established.

6.3 Examining NFS File Locks

Many times, when an NFS locking problem occurs on one client, it can hinder the performance or behavior of many clients. For example, if multiple clients run the same database application, and one client experiences a problem while holding an exclusive NFS lock on a frequently used record in the database, any clients that need to acquire this lock will hang waiting for the client holding the lock to relinquish it. In these cases, the quickest way to determine which client is holding the critical lock may be to examine the NFS file locks on your server.

6.3.1 Which Systems Have Been Locking NFS Files?

We learned earlier that rpc.statd keeps track of those remote systems that are performing NFS file locking with the local system by creating unique files in the /var/statmon/sm directory. This means that at any time you can see which NFS clients have sent lock requests to the local system (if the local system is acting as a server), or which NFS servers the local system has sent lock requests to (if the local system is a client), by looking at the contents of the /var/statmon/sm directory. The hostnames of the remote systems being monitored will match the names of the files in /var/statmon/sm.

Figure 6.3 contains an example of the /var/statmon/sm directory contents on a typical NFS server. In this example, rpc.statd is currently monitoring three systems: "ros87252" (the local system), "emonster," and "atc03.cup.hp.com."

```
ros87252 (B1000 64-bit 11i)                                              _ □ X
ros87252(/) -> ll /var/statmon/sm
total 6
--w-------   1 root      root            17 Feb  6 21:04 atc03.cup.hp.com
--w-------   1 root      root             9 Feb  6 21:02 emonster
--w-------   1 root      root             9 Feb  6 21:02 ros87252
```

Figure 6.3 Sample Contents of /var/statmon/sm Directory

One thing to keep in mind about the files in the /var/statmon/sm directory is that they represent all systems that have performed file locking with the local system since rpc.statd was started. In other words, these files are not removed when file locks are removed, so there is no way to tell from looking at the /var/statmon/sm directory which systems are currently holding file locks with the local system. The files in this directory are only removed during the file lock recovery period that occurs when rpc.statd is restarted.

The only way to know for certain which remote systems are holding locks against local files at any given time is to enable debug rpc.lockd logging and examine the log file. This procedure is outlined in the next section.

6.3.2 Which NFS Files Are Currently Locked?

rpc.lockd keeps track of the files that are currently locked, and those files that are waiting to be locked, by maintaining three separate queues:

- **Granted** Queue — contains current *granted* NFS file locks
- **Blocked** Queue — contains locks that could not be granted because another process owns the lock (i.e. they are *blocked* waiting for the current lock owner to release the lock)
- **Message** Queue — holds requests that have been sent to a remote system but have not yet received a reply (i.e. they are waiting for a *message* from the remote system)

The current state of these queues and their contents can be displayed by enabling debug rpc.lockd logging and examining the log file. Debug logging can be toggled on and off by sending the running rpc.lockd daemon a SIGUSR2 signal via the `kill(1)` command. The default location of the debug log file is `/var/adm/rpc.lockd.log`.

Figure 6.4 shows a small portion of a sample rpc.lockd log file displaying the current state of the three queues. In this example, the granted queue contains a single lock, while the message queue and blocked queues are empty. Looking at the lock entry, we can identify the name of the server by looking for the string "svr=." In this case, the locked file resides on server "emonster." Now the issue becomes how to interpret the lock entry to know which file is being locked.

```
ros87252 (B1000 64-bit 11i)                                          _ □ X
02.06 23:38:10  ros87252  pid=979     rpc.lockd
    LOCKD QUEUES:
*****  granted reclocks  *****
(400a8e70), oh=ros872522490, svr=emonster,
  fh=40000004ffffffff000a0000000000330000000000a00000000000200000000,
  op=6, range=[0, 2199023255552], client=ros87252, cookie=53c48d96
***** no entry in msg queue *****
***** no blocked reclocks ****
```

Figure 6.4 Sample `rpc.lockd.log` Data Showing Lock Queues

One of the most important steps in identifying the locked file is knowing how to interpret the *filehandle* in the lock request (this is the string beginning with "fh=" in Figure 6.4).

What is a filehandle? A filehandle is a reference to a file or directory residing on an NFS server. All NFS operations use filehandles to identify the file or directory to which the operation applies. Filehandles are opaque to the client — meaning that the content of the filehandle means nothing to the client. The server creates filehandles and only the server can interpret the contents. The NFS client should make no attempt to interpret the filehandle; it merely uses the filehandle when it needs to reference a specific file or directory. The server uses the contents of the filehandle to determine exactly to which file the client operation is referring.

KEY IDEA — Interpreting HP-UX NFS Filehandles

Using the sample lock entry from Figure 6.4, the 32-byte HP-UX NFS filehandle is:

40000004ffffffff000a0000**00000033**00000000000a00000000000200000000

Every portion of the above filehandle will not be discussed, as there are only two critical components of the filehandle that must be interpreted to locate the file on the server.

- Bytes 1-4 identify the major and minor numbers of the block device file for the server's exported filesystem in which the file resides.

In this example, we need to examine the exported filesystems on NFS server "emonster" looking for one whose major number is **0x40** (decimal **64**) and minor number is **0x000004** (decimal **4**). The exportfs(1M) command tells us which filesystems are exported:

```
emonster(/) -> exportfs
/data
/stand
```

The bdf(1M) command shows us which device files are used by these filesystems:

```
emonster(/) -> bdf /data /stand
Filesystem            kbytes      used     avail %used Mounted on
/dev/vg00/lvol4     3948544   450603 3279379    12% /data
/dev/vg00/lvol1       83733    35386   39973    47% /stand
```

The ls(1) command shows the major and minor numbers of the device files in question:

```
emonster(/) -> ls -l /dev/vg00/lvol1 /dev/vg00/lvol4
brw-r-----   1 root sys 64 0x000001 Sep 24 21:36 /dev/vg00/lvol1
brw-r-----   1 root sys 64 0x000004 Nov 16 2000 /dev/vg00/lvol4
```

The **/dev/vg00/lvol4** device file has a major number of 64 and a minor number of 4, so we now know that **/data** is the exported filesystem where the file resides.

- Bytes 13-16 refer to the inode number of the file on the server.

Now that we know which filesystem the target file resides in, we can use the find(1) command to locate the file by searching for a file whose inode is **0x00000033** (decimal **51**):

```
emonster(/) -> find /data -inum 51
/data/TESTFILE
```

The above filehandle maps to the file "**/data/TESTFILE**" on the NFS server.

The structure and contents of NFS filehandles are implementation-specific, meaning each NFS vendor may store whatever information they require in the filehandle to allow their server to uniquely identify individual files or directories. An AIX or Solaris™ filehandle could look substantially different than an HP-UX filehandle.[6] This freedom to determine the contents of the filehandle should not lead to inter-operability issues because the NFS client makes no attempt to interpret the filehandle contents, nor does it base any decisions upon the filehandle contents.

Filehandles can also differ based on the version of the NFS protocol used. NFS Version 2 specified a 32-byte filehandle, while Version 3 allows larger filehandles to be used if needed. When HP implemented NFS Version 3, the NFS lab attempted to minimize the differences between the PV3 filehandle and the existing PV2 filehandle. HP's PV3 filehandle is 36 bytes in length — the first 4 bytes are a length field that always contains a value of 0x0020 (the hexadecimal equivalent of 32) indicating that the remainder of the filehandle is 32 bytes long. The last 32 bytes of the Version 3 filehandle are identical to the Version 2 filehandle.

6.3.3 Which NFS Clients Are Locking Files on the Server?

The NFS client associated with a given NFS file lock can also be identified by examining the rpc.lockd debug log file. Each lock entry contains a string similar to "client=," indicating which NFS client requested the specific lock. In the NFS file lock shown in Figure 6.5 the NFS client holding the granted lock is "ros87252."

```
 ros87252 (B1000 64-bit 11i)                                              _ □ ×
02.06 23:38:10   ros87252   pid=979      rpc.lockd
    LOCKD QUEUES:
***** granted reclocks *****
(400a8e70), oh=ros872522490, svr=emonster,
  fh=40000004ffffffff000a00000000003300000000000a00000000000200000000,
  op=6, range=[0, 2199023255552], client=ros87252, cookie=53c48d96
*****no entry in msg queue *****
***** no blocked reclocks ****
```

Figure 6.5 NFS File Lock Entry Showing Client and Owner Handle

6.3.4 Which Client-side Process Is Holding the Lock?

Most NFS clients, including HP-UX clients, include a field in their lock requests called an "owner handle." On HP-UX systems, the owner handle is the concatenation of the NFS client hostname and the process ID of the client application requesting the lock. It is discernible in the lock entries by the string "oh=." Looking at Figure 6.5, the owner handle in this lock request is "ros872522490." Since we already know the hostname of the NFS client is "ros87252," we can

---

6.   Any information in this book, such as examples or figures depicting filehandle contents, pertains to HP's 11.X NFS implementation only. Other vendors' filehandles are likely constructed differently from those of HP-UX.

quickly determine the process ID of the application holding this lock by stripping off the client's hostname from the owner handle string, leaving us with a process ID of 2490. This information can be extremely valuable in situations where a single rogue client process is holding a critical file lock and blocking other application processes waiting for this lock.

6.4   Avoiding NFS File Lock Hangs in Your Environment

The most common complaints from customers regarding rpc.lockd and rpc.statd involve hanging file locks. These problems usually manifest themselves as application hangs (i.e. Korn Shell login hangs, e-mail program hangs, etc.) because the application is unable to obtain the file lock it needs to continue working. While some lock hangs are normal (i.e. another process is holding the lock your application is asking for), many are not. Here are some precautions you can take to avoid lock hangs in your environment.

6.4.1   Make Sure Hostname Resolution Data Is Accurate

Looking at the earlier discussions about file lock processing and lock recovery, it is clear that rpc.lockd and rpc.statd are *heavily* dependent upon hostname resolution. It is therefore important to verify that the sources providing hostname and IP address data (i.e. /etc/hosts, DNS, NIS, NIS+, or LDAP) return accurate and consistent information.

 KEY IDEA   —   The Importance of·Hostname Resolution to rpc.lockd and rpc.statd

The vast majority of all customer-reported NFS file locking problems turn out to be related in one way or another to **hostname resolution**. Since rpc.lockd and rpc.statd are a single-threaded daemons, if either of them must block waiting for a hostname resolution server to respond to a hostname or IP address query, the daemon will be unable to respond to (or will be slow in processing) incoming requests.

It is therefore critical to familiarize yourself with, and verify the performance and accuracy of, the hostname resolution mechanisms used in your NFS environment.

6.4.2   DNS Name Space Considerations

When an NFS client sends a lock request to the server, one piece of information included in the request is the hostname of the client. The server uses this hostname information to determine where to send the reply to the lock request. If the server is unable to resolve the IP address of the client based on the client's hostname, then the lock request will hang, as the server cannot send the reply correctly.

Even if the server's DNS tables are accurate, the potential still exists for lock requests to fail when the NFS client and server reside in different DNS domains. The reason for this is that the NFS client does not send its fully-qualified domain name (FQDN) in the lock request, it sends the information returned by the `gethostname(2)` call, which is the same name displayed by the `hostname(1)` command.

For example, let us say an NFS client in Roseville, California named "bart.rose.hp.com" mounts an NFS filesystem from a server located in Cupertino, California called "homer.cup.hp.com." When an application on client "bart" attempts to lock a file in the NFS-mounted filesystem, the client will only send the hostname "bart" in the lock request, as opposed to the FQDN version "bart.rose.hp.com." If the NFS server's DNS subsystem is not configured to resolve IP addresses for the "rose.hp.com" portion of the name space, the server could fail to correctly resolve the client's IP address, resulting in a failed lock. Alternately, if there is a system in the "cup.hp.com" portion of the name space with the hostname "bart," the server could mistakenly send the lock reply to "bart.*cup*.hp.com" instead of "bart.*rose*.hp.com," again resulting in a failed lock.

There are several precautions you can take to avoid this situation.

Use unique hostnames for NFS clients and servers   Rather than using names that would be commonly found in different parts of the DNS name space like "client1" and "server1," assign unique hostnames to systems. This will help avoid the situation where the NFS server incorrectly sends a lock reply to a system in a different portion of the DNS name space, simply because it has the same hostname as the NFS client that requested the lock.

Configure the NFS server to resolve the client's portion of the name space

When the NFS server receives a lock request from a client in a different part of the DNS name space, it needs to be able to resolve the client's portion of the name space to get the correct IP address. Using the earlier example, NFS server "homer.cup.hp.com" needs to be able to resolve IP addresses for the "rose.hp.com" portion of the name space in order to send a lock reply to "bart.rose.hp.com." Usually this is done by adding or modifying the "search" tag in the `/etc/resolv.conf` file on the NFS server. Refer to the `resolver(4)` man page for more information on modifying the `/etc/resolv.conf` file.

Configure the client's hostname using its FQDN   As stated earlier, the NFS client includes its hostname in every lock request. Ordinarily this hostname is not the FQDN of the client because by default most system administrators configure the hostname of their systems using only the first portion of the FQDN. Consider the NFS client in Figure 6.6. This system's FQDN is "client1.rose.hp.com," but the name returned by the `hostname(1)` command is "client1." It is this short version of the hostname that is sent in NFS file lock requests.

If the NFS client were configured such that the `hostname(1)` command returned the FQDN, then the client would send this fully-qualified name in its NFS file lock requests. This would allow the NFS server to resolve the FQDN of the client and ensure that it sends the lock reply to the correct system. For more information on configuring the hostname of the client, refer to the `hostname(1)` man page.

Figure 6.6 `hostname` Output vs. Fully-Qualified Domain Name

6.4.3 Remove Corrupted `/var/statmon/sm.bak` Files

The `/var/statmon/sm.bak` directory contains monitor files associated with remote systems, which at one time performed file locking with the local system, and which rpc.statd has been unable to contact following a change in state. In rare occasions, customers have reported finding a corrupted `/var/statmon/sm.bak` file — i.e. the contents of the file does not match the name of the file. A corrupted `sm.bak` file can have a very disruptive effect on rpc.statd's behavior, resulting in poor lock performance, lock hangs, or even rpc.statd dying. It is therefore recommended to periodically monitor the contents of this directory, as shown in Figure 6.7.

```
ros87252 (B1000 64-bit 11i)                                          _ □ ×
ros87252(/) -> ll /var/statmon/sm.bak
total 4
--w-------   1 root       users          17 Feb  8 14:43 atc03.cup.hp.com
--w-------   1 root       users           9 Feb  8 14:43 emonster

ros87252(/) -> cat /var/statmon/sm.bak/atc03.cup.hp.com
atc03.cup.hp.com

ros87252(/) -> cat /var/statmon/sm.bak/emonster
emonster
```

Figure 6.7 Verifying `/var/statmon/sm.bak` Directory Entries

In this example, the `/var/statmon/sm.bak` directory contains two files: "emonster" and "atc03.cup.hp.com." This indicates that the local rpc.statd daemon has been unable to notify these remote systems following a state change on the local system. The contents of these files match the names of the files, so they are not corrupted.

If corrupted files are found, they should be removed during the next scheduled maintenance window. In order to clean out these files you must first stop both rpc.statd and rpc.lockd, remove the files, then re-start the daemons.

KEY IDEA   —   Precautions when Killing and Restarting rpc.lockd and rpc.statd

rpc.statd should always be stopped before rpc.lockd, and rpc.statd should always be started before rpc.lockd. Since stopping and re-starting the daemons constitutes a change of state, this procedure should only be done during a maintenance window so that normal production file locking will not be affected.

6.4.4 Do Not Remove `/var/statmon/sm` Entries

A common practice among system administrators, when troubleshooting NFS file locking problems, is to kill rpc.statd and rpc.lockd, remove the contents of the `/var/statmon/sm` and `/var/statmon/sm.bak` directories, and restart the daemons. The idea is that by clearing out the monitor directories and restarting the daemons you can clear up a hung NFS file lock.

While this procedure might appear successful in some situations, the lock hang is rarely cleared up as a result of removing the `/var/statmon/sm` contents, but rather the stopping and restarting of the daemons.[7] In fact, clearing the `/var/statmon/sm` contents on only one system (either client or server), as opposed to clearing out this directory on both systems, can actually *cause* file lock hangs to occur. The reason for this is that by clearing out the `/var/statmon/sm` directory, you are effectively breaking the rpc.statd notification mechanism. When rpc.statd is restarted after these entries have been removed it will not notify any remote system of the fact that the local system has experienced a state change. This can result in undesirable consequences, including:

• If the local system is a *client*, then it will not notify any of the servers that it had been locking with of the fact that it has experienced a state change. This means that these servers could be holding locks in their queues that no process will be able to acquire because the server believes these locks are still owned by processes on the client that has restarted. Since the client did not send a crash notification message to the servers, these locks will remain in the server's queues and the client and server queues will be out of sync. Any attempts by clients to acquire these locks will be denied by the server.

• If the local system is a *server*, then it will not notify any of the clients that have been sending lock requests of the fact that it has experienced a state change. This means that these clients could be holding locks in their queues that they believe are still valid locks on the server, while the server's queue is empty. This again is a situation where the client and server queues are out of sync and data corruption could result.

---

7.   To understand why stopping and restarting the rpc.lockd and rpc.statd daemons can resolve hung file locks, see Section 6.5 "Why Would Restarting the Daemons Clear a Lock Hang?"

Another side effect of stopping and restarting the daemons is that when the new daemons start they will be listening on different UDP and TCP ports than the old daemons were. The daemons will register these new port numbers with the rpcbind daemon. However, by not notifying the remote systems of the fact that the daemons have been restarted, these remote systems will continue to send lock requests and replies to the old port numbers which they cached back when the old daemons were running. The end result again is hanging lock requests because the lock replies are sent to obsolete port numbers that the new daemons are not listening on.

NFS Performance Example: Korn Shell Login Hangs

Problem: One of the most frequently reported NFS file locking problems is the "Korn Shell login hang." This is where the NFS client system is configured as follows:

- A user's home directory is mounted from an NFS server
- The user's login shell is the Korn Shell (`/usr/bin/ksh`)

Symptom: When the user attempts to log into the client their login process hangs

Reason: The Korn Shell keeps a running history of the commands issued by each user and logs them to a file in the user's home directory called ".`sh_history`." At login time, the Korn Shell attempts to lock this history file. Since the user's home directory is NFS-mounted, locking this file relies on the ability of the client's and server's rpc.lockd and rpc.statd daemons to communicate correctly.

Solutions: There are several possible solutions to this problem:

- Configure the Korn Shell to log to a ".`sh_history`" file residing in a local filesystem on the client. This is via the "HISTFILE" environment variable.
- Use a shell other than the Korn Shell.
- Troubleshoot the underlying NFS file locking problem and determine why the client and server rpc.lockd daemons are unable to communicate successfully.

6.4.5 Use the "`-c`" Option in Heterogeneous Environments

There is a known incompatibility between HP's NLM implementation and the industry-standard NLM protocol used by other NFS vendors like Sun Microsystems. A problem can occur when an HP client has mounted a filesystem from a Solaris™ server, sent several lock requests, and then attempts to cancel an outstanding lock request that has not yet been granted by the server. The server does in fact cancel the lock and sends back a reply indicating that the lock was canceled. The problem occurs because the HP client misinterprets the reply as a failure on the server's part to cancel the lock, and it re-issues the same cancel request again. The two systems can eventually end up sending the same cancel requests and replies over and over again.

HP could not simply change the way we interpreted the reply to all cancel requests or we would make our systems stop working properly with other HP systems (i.e. a patched HP client and an unpatched HP server would have the same problem as the existing HP client and Solaris™ server). Instead, HP chose to implement the solution by adding a "-c" command-line option to the rpc.lockd daemon to be used when HP clients reside in an NFS environment with Solaris™ systems. Starting rpc.lockd with the "-c" option allows rpc.lockd to correctly interpret the reply of a cancel request from a Solaris™ server.

 KEY IDEA — rpc.lockd and the "-c" Option

It is recommended that rpc.lockd be started with the "-c" option on any HP-UX NFS system that needs to perform file locking with a Solaris™ system, or any other UNIX system running an NFS implementation based on the Solaris™ code.

However, if you enable the rpc.lockd "-c" option on one HP NFS system, you must enable this option on **all** HP systems in the environment or you run the risk of making your HP clients stop working correctly with HP servers. In other words, an HP client running rpc.lockd with the "-c" option may fail to lock correctly with an HP server running rpc.lockd without the "-c" option.

To force rpc.lockd to use the "-c" option when it is started at system boot time, modify the "LOCKD_OPTIONS" line in the /etc/rc.config.d/nfsconf file to include this option (i.e. LOCKD_OPTIONS="-c").

6.5 Why Would Restarting the Daemons Clear a Lock Hang?

There are many situations where hanging NFS file locks can be cleared by simply killing and restarting the rpc.lockd and rpc.statd daemons.

6.5.1 Hostname Resolution Policy Has Changed

Customers sometimes decide to migrate their hostname resolution data from one repository to another. As an example, a customer might choose to migrate their hostnames and IP addresses from the /etc/hosts file to a DNS server, or from NIS to NIS+ — the point being that hostname data that was once available from one source is no longer available. As part of this migration, the customer needs to update the "hosts" entry of their /etc/nsswitch.conf file to reflect the new location of the data.

Unfortunately, most daemons, rpc.lockd and rpc.statd included, read the /etc/nsswitch.conf file at initialization time only. The hostname resolution policy is cached by the daemons and used for the duration of their process life. This means that if the resolution policy changes (i.e. "files" to "dns"), any daemons that cached the old information will have to be stopped and restarted in order to recognize the new configuration. Until that time, they will continue to reference the old data source, which will no longer contain the necessary hostname and IP address information. This results in NFS file lock hangs, which are cleared up by stopping and restarting the rpc.lockd and rpc.statd processes.

6.5.2 Kernel *nflocks* Resource Is Exhausted

NFS file locks require some kernel resources to function properly. If these resources are limited or exhausted it can result in file lock hangs. The primary kernel resource associated with NFS file locks is the *nflocks*[8] variable. This variable defines the size of the system-wide kernel lock table, which dictates the maximum number of file locks that can exist on a system at any given time. In dynamic environments, where more and more NFS clients are added to existing servers, it is not uncommon for the server's kernel lock table resources to eventually get exhausted. When this happens, the server will be unable to service any new lock requests and NFS client applications that require file locking services will hang as a result.

Any entries in the kernel's lock table associated with the rpc.lockd daemon are released when this daemon is killed and restarted. So, while stopping and starting the daemon can provide some temporary relief in this situation, eventually the lock table will fill again if corrective action is not taken. The current size and utilization of the kernel lock table, and other critical system resources, can be monitored via GlancePlus. If *nflocks* utilization is nearing the upper limit of its configured value, this table should be increased during the next available maintenance window.

6.5.3 Obsolete UDP and TCP Port Information Is Cached

We learned earlier how one of the steps that occurs during file lock recovery is that the system receiving a crash notification message will discard any cached UDP and TCP port information associated with the rpc.lockd daemon on the recovering system. This forces the system receiving the crash notification to contact the recovering system's rpcbind daemon and retrieve the new port numbers where rpc.lockd and rpc.statd are now listening for requests.

We also learned how a common practice among system administrators is to stop rpc.lockd and rpc.statd, remove the /var/statmon/sm directory contents, and then restart the daemons. In this situation the remote system (client or server) will not realize that the local system experienced a state change and they will continue to send requests or replies to the cached obsolete port numbers. This results in lock hangs.

By stopping and restarting rpc.lockd and rpc.statd on both systems, this effectively destroys the cached port information both systems were holding. The result is that the next lock request after the daemons are restarted will force both systems to obtain current port information from each other's rpcbind daemons, allowing rpc.lockd communication to function again.

---

8.   For information about sizing the *nflocks* kernel variable, refer to Section 12.1.19 "nflocks."

6.6 Ensuring Optimal NFS File Locking Performance

There is no way to *directly* tune the performance of the rpc.lockd and rpc.statd daemons. However, there are many precautions you can take to ensure that your NFS environment is configured to provide optimal NFS file locking performance.

6.6.1 Ensure Hostname Resolution Is Performing Correctly

Even when NFS file locking is functionally working, hostname resolution still plays a key role in rpc.lockd and rpc.statd performance. There are several places in the rpc.lockd and rpc.statd source code where the gethostbyname(3N) routine is called to retrieve the IP address of the remote system. If hostname resolution performance is poor, then NFS file locking performance will suffer as a result. The nslookup(1) or nsquery(1) tools can be used to verify the performance of your hostname repositories.[9]

6.6.2 Remove Obsolete /var/statmon/sm.bak Files

Back in Section 6.2.1, we learned that rpc.statd is responsible for notifying remote systems following a change of state. rpc.statd keeps track of which remote systems it needs to contact by referencing the files in the /var/statmon/sm.bak directory. During NFS lock recovery, if rpc.statd is unable to notify a system associated with an sm.bak file, this file remains in the sm.bak directory and rpc.statd will continue to attempt to notify this remote host every 15 seconds until it is successful in notifying the remote rpc.statd daemon.

In environments where the NFS clients are changing frequently (i.e. new clients are added, old clients being removed, IP addresses change, systems migrating from UNIX to NT, etc.) this can become a problem for NFS servers. There have been reported cases where an NFS server's rpc.statd daemon is spending 90% of its time trying to notify NFS clients that do not exist any longer, are powered down for extended periods of time, have changed operating systems, etc.

If rpc.statd is spending all its time trying to contact these non-existent or dead clients, it will either be unable to handle new monitor requests for legitimate NFS clients, or it will take a long time to process these requests. In either case, NFS file lock performance can suffer. It is therefore important to periodically monitor the contents of the /var/statmon/sm.bak directory on your NFS servers. If sm.bak files associated with obsolete clients are found, then they should be removed during the next scheduled maintenance window.

6.7 Troubleshooting rpc.lockd and rpc.statd

The most common customer-visible symptoms seen when rpc.lockd or rpc.statd experience a problem are NFS application hangs, or application failures caused by a failing lock attempt. In these cases, one of the first pieces of information HP support will request is a debug rpc.lockd and rpc.statd log file taken while the problem is reproduced. By analyzing the log file,

---

9.   These tools, and their use, are described in more detail in Section 5.3.2.

the sequence of events that lead up to the problem can be determined. This data is also instrumental in helping HP support duplicate the problem internally.

However, before collecting and analyzing debug log files and network traces, a simple test can be performed to verify that rpc.lockd and rpc.statd are at least responding to RPC requests.

6.7.1 Use `rpcinfo(1M)` to "ping" rpc.lockd and rpc.statd

One of the easiest and least intrusive methods of determining whether rpc.lockd and rpc.statd are responding is to use `rpcinfo(1M)` to "ping" the running daemons.[10] `rpcinfo` can be issued on either the NFS client or server. The recommendation is to test the servers's rpc.lockd and rpc.statd from the client and the client's daemons from the server, as this will also verify whether RPC packets can traverse the network separating the client and server systems.

The syntax to use for these tests are: "`rpcinfo -T <transport> <system name> nlockmgr`" and "`rpcinfo -T <transport> <system name> status`." These commands test all registered versions of the NLM and NSM protocols. Figure 6.8 shows the rpcinfo commands issued on NFS client "ros87252" testing the rpc.lockd and rpc.statd daemons on remote server "atc03.cup.hp.com" via UDP.

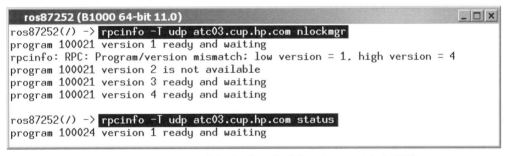

Figure 6.8 `rpcinfo` "pinging" rpc.lockd and rpc.statd via UDP

This output shows that the remote rpc.lockd is responding to Version 1, Version 3, and Version 4 requests via UDP. It also shows that rpc.lockd did not reply to the Version 2 request. This is the expected output, since HP's rpc.lockd does not support Version 2 of the NLM protocol — it currently only supports Versions 1, 3, and 4. This test also confirms that RPC requests are able to successfully traverse the network separating this client and server.

6.7.2 Collect Debug-level rpc.lockd and rpc.statd Log Files

Both HP's rpc.lockd and rpc.statd daemons have the ability to enable and disable debug-level logging without having to be shutdown and restarted. This feature allows the system administrator to easily toggle logging on, reproduce a problem, and toggle logging back off —

---

10.   Refer to the rpcinfo(1M) man page for a complete description of the program's features and syntax.

thereby producing a log file that only contains the data relevant to the problem. To enable or disable debug-level logging by either rpc.lockd or rpc.statd, simply send the running processes a SIGUSR2 signal via the `kill(1)` command. Below are the steps for collecting a debug rpc.lockd and rpc.statd log file. The <u>underlined</u> steps are the commands you type.

1. Determine the process IDs used by rpc.lockd and rpc.statd via the `ps(1)` command. In this example, rpc.lockd has a process ID of 651 and rpc.statd's process ID is 657:

```
# ps -e | grep -E 'rpc.lockd|rpc.statd'
   651 ?           0:00 rpc.statd
   657 ?           0:00 rpc.lockd
```

2. Toggle debug logging ON by sending the rpc.lockd and rpc.statd daemons a SIGUSR2 signal via the `kill(1)` command:

```
# kill -SIGUSR2 651 657
```

3. Reproduce the undesirable behavior.

4. Toggle debug logging OFF by sending the daemons another SIGUSR2 signal:

```
# kill -SIGUSR2 651 657
```

By default, the rpc.lockd and rpc.statd log files are created in the "`/var/adm`" directory and are named "`rpc.lockd.log`" and "`rpc.statd.log`" respectively. Sample rpc.lockd log file data is included in Figure 6.9 and sample rpc.statd log file data is shown in Figure 6.10.

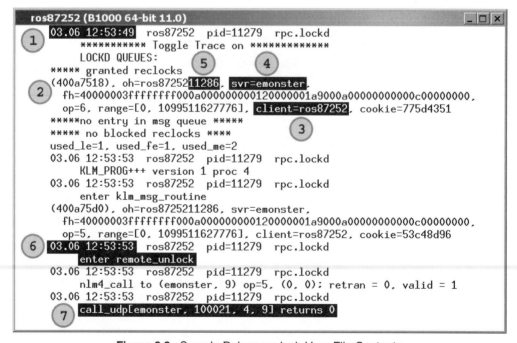

Figure 6.9 Sample Debug rpc.lockd Log File Contents

The format and syntax of the rpc.lockd log file contents may not lend themselves to easy interpretation; however, the log file contains a wealth of information about the state of rpc.lockd at any given time, as well as a history of the lock requests that have occurred since debug logging was enabled. This debug logging information, in conjunction with a network trace collected during the same time period (discussed further in the next section), will usually reveal the underlying cause of most NFS file locking problems.

For example, the log file output in Figure 6.9 shows:

1. Debug logging was enabled on March 6th at 12:53:49 PM.

2. At the time logging was started, the rpc.lockd daemon had a single lock in its granted queue, indicating that one process is holding a remote file lock.

3. The NFS client holding the lock is "ros87252."

4. The NFS server holding the lock is "emonster."

5. The process ID of the application on the client holding the lock is 11286.

6. At 12:53:53 PM, process 11286 on client "ros87252" sent an UNLOCK request to server "emonster" to remove the lock currently in the granted queue.

7. The UNLOCK request was sent successfully to the server.

This information can be indispensable for troubleshooting rpc.lockd issues. For more information on interpreting the NFS file lock entries contained in a debug rpc.lockd log file, refer to Section 6.3 "Examining NFS File Locks."

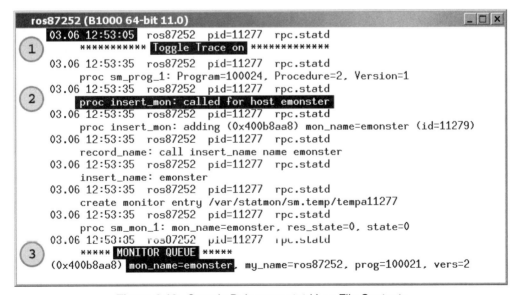

Figure 6.10 Sample Debug rpc.statd Log File Contents

As with the rpc.lockd log file example earlier, the rpc.statd log file contains a good deal of useful information, provided you know how to interpret it. For example, Figure 6.10 shows:

1. Debug logging was enabled on March 6th at 12:53:05 PM.
2. At 12:53:35 PM, rpc.statd received a request to monitor the remote system "emonster."
3. As of 12:53:35 PM, system "emonster" was successfully added to rpc.statd's MONITOR QUEUE, indicating that rpc.statd is now monitoring this system for any state changes.

Again, the significance of the rpc.statd log file contents may not be immediately obvious to someone without internal knowledge of rpc.statd. However, in the right hands, the debug information can provide invaluable insight into understanding the sequence of events leading up to a rpc.statd problem. Also, since the individual entries in both the rpc.lockd and rpc.statd debug log file are time stamped, this log file data can also be used in cases where NFS file locking is working, but performing poorly.

6.7.3 Collect a Network Trace of the File Locking Problem

In addition to the debug log file information, a network trace should be taken of any NFS file-locking problem. The trace can quickly reveal if the NFS client is at least sending lock requests to the server. Since the NFS server could be causing the problem by sending the lock replies to the wrong client, it is important to capture a network trace on both the client and the server of the same duplication effort. By comparing these traces against each other you can hopefully determine if the locking problem resides on the client or the server.

Here are the steps for collecting and examining a `nettl(1M)` trace for rpc.lockd traffic. The underlined steps are the commands you type.

1. Start a `nettl(1M)` trace on both the client and the server. On the client, log the output of the trace to the file "client" and on the server log to the file "server." The resulting trace filenames will have an extension of ".TRC0" (HP-UX 11.0) or ".TRC000" (HP-UX 11i) appended automatically by the `nettl` command:

   ```
   Client> /etc/nettl -tn pduin pduout -e ns_ls_ip -f client
   Server> /etc/nettl -tn pduin pduout -e ns_ls_ip -f server
   ```

2. Reproduce the file locking issue on the NFS client.
3. Stop the `nettl(1M)` traces on both systems:

   ```
   Client> /etc/nettl -tf -e ns_ls_ip
   Server> /etc/nettl -tf -e ns_ls_ip
   ```

4. Format the traces via the `netfmt(1M)` command. In this example we assume HP-UX 11.0 systems are used, which explains the ".TRC0" appended to the trace file names:

   ```
   Client> /etc/netfmt -1N client.TRC0 > client.formatted
   Server> /etc/netfmt -1N server.TRC0 > server.formatted
   ```

5. Search the formatted traces for any NFS lock requests.

Figure 6.11 shows an example of formatted nettl(1M) trace packets of a client's outbound NFS lock request followed by the server's reply. In this trace output, client "ros87252" sends a lock request (LOCK_MSG) to server "emonster." The server sends back a reply (LOCK_RES) with a status of "GRANTED," indicating that this lock completed successfully.

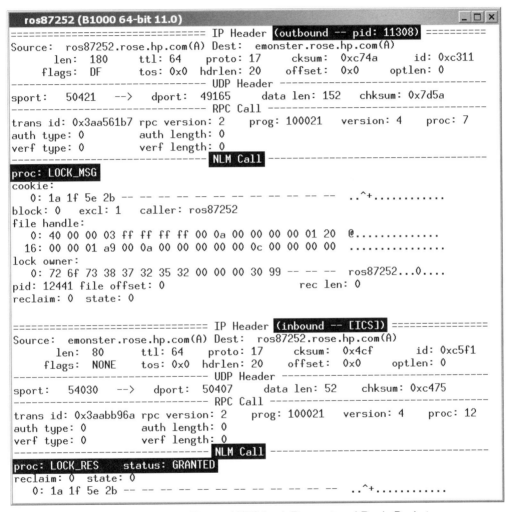

Figure 6.11 nettl Trace of NFS Lock Request and Reply Packets

If the client-side trace had not included a reply packet from the server, then the server-side trace would need to be examined. By looking at the server trace you can confirm whether the server ever received the lock request and whether it tried to reply. If the server-side trace shows that a reply was sent, you can confirm whether it was sent to the client's correct IP address and to the port number currently used by the client's rpc.lockd daemon.

This network trace information, in conjunction with the collected debug rpc.lockd and rpc.statd log file data described in Section 6.7.2, is instrumental in determining why NFS file locking is not behaving or performing as desired in your environment.

KEY IDEA — The Importance of Patching the rpc.lockd and rpc.statd Code

HP continually strives to improve the quality of HP-UX by distributing software patches containing both defect fixes and functionality enhancements. Many of these fixes and enhancements can significantly improve the performance and behavior of critical system components, such as the rpc.lockd and rpc.statd code.

It is *strongly* recommended that the latest NFS patches be installed on every HP-UX system in order to take advantage of these improvements. Contact HP support to obtain a current set of patches for your specific operating system. You can also generate a current patch list using the tools available at HP's IT Resource Center: *http://itrc.hp.com*.

For a detailed discussion on the importance of keeping your HP-UX NFS client and server systems patched with current code, refer to Appendix B "Patching Considerations."

## CHAPTER 7

Automount and AutoFS

Automounters are used to automatically mount filesystems when they are needed and unmount filesystems when they are idle. They have existed on HP-UX systems for more than a decade. The original *automount* daemon first arrived on HP-UX systems in December 1991 as part of the 8.07 release. The newer protocol — *AutoFS* — (implemented via the *automountd* daemon and *automount* command) first became available in April 1997 as part of the HP-UX 10.20 ACE 2.0 Networking Bundle. While AutoFS was not originally included in HP-UX 11.0, AutoFS support was added to 11.0 in August 1998. Unlike most NFS vendors,[1] HP currently allows its customers to run either the legacy automounter or AutoFS on HP-UX systems.[2]

Customers typically choose to use an automounter in order to ease their NFS client filesystem administration tasks, especially in large NFS installations. The decision of whether or not to use these products is best made by a knowledgeable systems administrator who is familiar with the needs of the NFS environment. For those administrators who decide to use an automounter, there are several performance issues to consider.

This chapter explains how the legacy automounter differs from the newer AutoFS protocol in terms of functionality and performance. Also described are the many configuration-related factors that can influence the performance of both automounters. This is followed by a discussion on which automounter is a better fit for your NFS environment. Finally, a troubleshooting section is included that describes the methodology and tools used to investigate most automount and AutoFS problems.

---

1.   Most NFS vendors have discontinued support of the legacy automounter and only support the AutoFS protocol.

2.   HP will likely discontinue support of the legacy automounter in a future OS release.

HP-~~UX~~11i   **Difference Between HP-UX 11.0 and 11i: AutoFS Support**

When HP-UX 11.0 originally shipped, the only automounter supported was the legacy automount product. Support for AutoFS was added in August 1998.

11i shipped with support for both automount and AutoFS.

7.1   Performance Differences between Automount and AutoFS

There are many differences between the legacy automounter and the AutoFS protocol. While both products perform the same basic functions (i.e. automatically mounting and unmounting filesystems) they do so in very different ways. This section outlines their many differences (summarized in Table 7.1) that can directly influence NFS performance.[3]

Table 7.1   Performance Differences between Automount and AutoFS

Feature	Automount	AutoFS
Supported Filesystem Types	NFS	NFS, CacheFS, CDFS, LOFS
Supported NFS Protocol Versions	2	2, 3
Supported NFS Network Transports	UDP	UDP, TCP
Multi-Thread Support	Single Threaded	Multi-Threaded
Busy Filesystem Detection	NO	YES
Mounting via alternate IP address	Loopback NFS mount	LOFS mount
Mounted filesystem location	Mounts to a holding directory and re-directs requests with symbolic links	Mounts filesystems in place
Implementation Type	Pseudo NFS server	Legitimate Filesystem
Forcibly Stopping the Automounter	Never use "kill -9"	"kill -9" may be used if necessary
Modifying automount map contents	Must be restarted for changes to take effect	Changes take effect immediately

3.   This section is not intended to be an exhaustive list of *every* difference between these products, but rather a description of those differences that directly influence NFS performance. For additional information about the differences between automount and AutoFS, refer to the automount(1M) man page or the *Installing and Administering NFS Services* manual, available online at *http://docs.hp.com*.

7.1.1 Supported Filesystem Types

Automount   The legacy automounter was developed as a tool to help systems administrators manage their NFS filesystems. It was never intended to manage filesystem types other than NFS. At that time, Version 3 of the NFS protocol had not yet been developed, and the only supported network transport for NFS traffic was UDP. Thus, the automounter was designed to issue only NFS Version 2 mount requests that use the UDP transport. Automount uses the now obsolete `vfsmount(2)` system call, which is neither NFS PV3 nor TCP aware.

AutoFS   The development team who worked to design the replacement for automount (which eventually became the AutoFS protocol), saw the value of being able to automatically manage filesystem types other than NFS. Also, with the introduction of the NFS Version 3 protocol, and the need to support networking transports other than UDP, the designers worked to remove the restrictions imposed by the legacy automounter and allow it to support newer filesystem and networking technologies as they become available.

AutoFS uses the `mount(2)` system call, which is capable of issuing mount requests for any filesystem type, including: NFS, CacheFS, CDFS, LOFS, and even other AutoFS filesystems. This architecture allows AutoFS to support all available versions of the NFS protocol, as well as both the UDP and TCP network transports.

7.1.2 Multi-Thread Support

Automount   The original automounter daemon is single-threaded. While servicing a mount request for one process, other processes requiring AutoFS to mount a filesystem must wait until the existing mount request is complete.

AutoFS   HP's AutoFS implementation is multi-threaded, which allows it to perform certain operations in parallel. However, HP's current implementation of AutoFS uses locking mechanisms to serialize requests through many critical code functions, thus minimizing the potential parallelism of multiple threads.[4] Enhanced thread support will be added to AutoFS in a future OS release.

7.1.3 Detecting Busy Filesystems

Automount   One of the primary functions automount and AutoFS perform is unmounting filesystems which are not in use. The legacy automounter makes no attempt to keep track of which filesystems are in use at any given time. In other words, it knows which

---

4.   As of HP-UX 11.0 and 11i, HP's AutoFS implementation is based on the ONC 1.2 code provided by Sun Microsystems. This version of AutoFS does gain some benefits from the multi-thread design; however certain portions of the code still require single thread semantics. The newer version of AutoFS, based on the ONC 2.3 version of Solaris™ code, uses different locking schemes in critical code functions, which allows it to more fully utilize threads and gain substantially greater parallelism. HP will be releasing a newer AutoFS version, based on the Solaris™ ONC 2.3 code, in an upcoming OS release.

filesystems are currently mounted, but not which ones users or applications are actively refer-encing. The only criterion automount uses to decide which filesystems to unmount is a simple timer, which is set to 5 minutes by default.

In certain situations, this inability to track busy filesystems can lead to a serious performance problem because, while an unmount attempt against a busy filesystem will fail (with a "Device busy" error), the mere act of attempting to unmount the NFS filesystem causes the kernel to search the client's buffer cache and page cache[5] for any memory pages associated with this filesystem and invalidate them.[6]

 KEY IDEA — A Side Effect of Unmounting Busy NFS Filesystems

One of the steps performed by the HP-UX kernel while processing an NFS filesystem unmount request is to search the client's buffer cache and page cache[5] for any memory pages associated with the filesystem being unmounted. If the kernel finds any such pages it invalidates them. This step is done in order to accurately determine if the filesystem being unmounted is still in use by any client processes, and should therefore remain mounted. In other words, these memory pages are invalidated *regardless* of whether the NFS filesystem is successfully unmounted or not.

As you might imagine, this behavior can lead to a serious performance prob-lem for applications running on the client that are actively using the NFS filesystem being unmounted. Although the filesystem will remain mounted if it is busy, all buffer cache and page cache memory buffers used by applications referencing this filesystem are invalidated. In other words, any memory buffers associated with application binaries that were executed across this NFS mount point will be removed from the page cache, forcing the client to re-acquire these pages from the server. Also, any data pages read across this NFS mount point will be removed from the buffer cache, forcing the client to get this data from the server again.

Note: This phenomenon occurs even when NFS filesystems are unmounted manually via the `umount(1M)` command — it is not limited to automounter-managed filesystems. However, since the automounters frequently issue unmount requests, it is much more common for NFS clients managing their NFS filesystems via an automounter to experience this performance problem.

---

5. The HP-UX buffer cache and page cache mechanisms are described in detail in Section 11.1.1 "How Does Buffer Cache Differ from the Page Cache?"

6. This issue is of invalidating buffer cache pages, and the performance ramifications of doing so, are explained in further detail in Section 7.2.4 "Default Unmount Timer and Its Effect on Client Caching."

AutoFS   AutoFS is designed to keep track of which filesystems are actively being used by client processes. It accomplishes this by maintaining a "last-reference timer" for the filesystems it manages, and it updates this timer whenever the filesystem is accessed. This feature stops AutoFS from issuing unmount requests for filesystems until they have been *idle* for the specified timeout value (5 minutes by default). The end result is that these filesystems are less likely to have their buffer cache and page cache memory buffers invalidated by AutoFS while these buffers are still needed by a client application.

HP's current version of AutoFS only maintains these last-reference timers for filesystems configured via *direct* maps. Any filesystems managed by "indirect" maps or "hierarchical" maps (which are a special form of an indirect map) are not assigned last-reference timers, and are thus subject to the default 5-minute unmount timer.[7] This "last-reference timer" feature will be expanded to include all AutoFS-managed filesystems in a future OS release.

7.1.4 Mounting Filesystems via an Alternate IP Address

Automounters are typically run on client systems to mount remote NFS filesystems. Many customers also choose to run automounters on their NFS servers, and often they will configure a common set of automount maps, distributed via a service such as NIS, so that every system in the environment (client or server) uses the same pathname hierarchy to access a given file set.

Depending upon how the NFS server is configured, and how the automount maps are configured, this type of setup can result in very poor file access performance for processes running on the NFS server that are accessing local files through automount-managed mount points. In certain situations, using an automounter in this way may even cause MC/ServiceGuard to be unable to migrate exported filesystems properly during a failover event.[8]

Automount   When the legacy automounter is run on an NFS server and one of the automount map entries references a filesystem that is exported by the local system, when a process accesses the pathname associated with this map entry the automounter will do one of two things:

* If the NFS server hostname in the automount map entry *matches* the text string returned by the `hostname(1)` command, then automount will recognize this filesystem as residing on the local system and will create a symbolic link between the exported filesystem and the pathname in the automount map.

---

7.   As of HP-UX 11.0 and 11i, HP's AutoFS implementation is based on the ONC 1.2 code provided by Sun Microsystems. This version of AutoFS only maintains last-reference timers for *direct* maps. The newer version of AutoFS, based on the ONC 2.3 version of Solaris™ code, maintains last-reference timers for all AutoFS-managed filesystems, which helps deter AutoFS from attempting to unmount busy filesystems. HP will be releasing a newer AutoFS version, based on the Solaris™ ONC 2.3 code, in an upcoming OS release.

8.   For more information about HP's MC/ServiceGuard product or configuring your servers for Highly Available NFS access, visit the HP-UX High Availability web site: *http://hp.com/go/ha*.

• If the NFS server hostname in the automount map entry *does not match* the text string returned by the `hostname(1)` command, then automount will not realize this filesystem is actually exported on the local system and will create a loopback NFS mount between the exported filesystem and the pathname in the automount map.

Consider the NFS server configuration shown in the example in Figure 7.1.

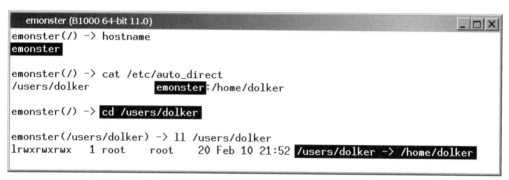

Figure 7.1   Automount Creating a Symlink to a Local Filesystem

In this example, the NFS server is configured with the hostname "emonster." The `/etc/auto_direct` map contains an entry requesting that the "`/users/dolker`" pathname be managed by the automounter, and that any reference to this pathname result in the "`/home/dolker`" filesystem from server "emonster" be made available in this location.

When a user on system "emonster" accesses the "`/users/dolker`" path, automount recognizes the requested path as a local filesystem because the server name in the map entry matches the text string returned by the `hostname(1)` command. Automount creates a symbolic link between the local "`/home/dolker`" filesystem and the requested path "`/users/dolker`." This typically does not create a performance problem, as there is very little overhead involved with reading from or writing to a local file via a symbolic link.

Now, consider the NFS server configuration shown in Figure 7.2. In this example the NFS server is configured as follows:

1. The server's hostname is "atc03."
2. There are 2 LAN interfaces in the system.
3. The local IP address 192.65.6.43 maps to the hostname "atc03-ge2."
4. The `/etc/auto_direct` map contains an entry requesting the "`/nfs_mount`" pathname be managed by the automounter, and that any reference to this pathname result in the "`/tmp`" filesystem from server "atc03-ge2" be made available in this location.
5. When a user process on system "atc03" references the `/nfs_mount` path, automounter does not recognize that the requested filesystem actually resides on the local system (because the name of the server "atc03-ge2" does not match the value returned by the

`hostname(1)` command — "atc03"), and the automounter creates a *loopback NFS mount* to map the requested referenced pathname "`/nfs_mount`" to the local "`/tmp`" directory.

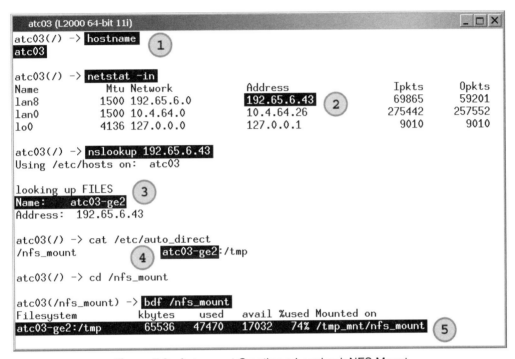

Figure 7.2 Automount Creating a Loopback NFS Mount

Why is this important? Because the performance of accessing local files through a loopback NFS mount can be *significantly* slower than accessing these files directly, via a symbolic link, or via an LOFS mount. Figure 7.3 shows an example of writing to a local filesystem via a loopback NFS mount and then performing the same operation to the local filesystem directly.

This simple example shows how writing a 15MB file through the loopback NFS mount created by the legacy automounter took over 22 seconds to complete, while creating the same file directly in the `/tmp` directory completes in less than one second. Why is there such a significant performance difference between writing to a loopback NFS mount point created by the legacy automounter vs. writing directly to the local filesystem? Several reasons:

• Any file access operations through the loopback NFS mount point will traverse the entire NFS client-side and server-side code stacks, including invoking the biods and nfsds to service the requests.

• Any NFS mount created by the legacy automounter will use the NFS Version 2 protocol, which limits read and write requests to a maximum size of *8KB*.

• NFS Version 2 mount points use *synchronous* NFS write semantics unless the filesystem is explicitly exported with the *async* option.[9]

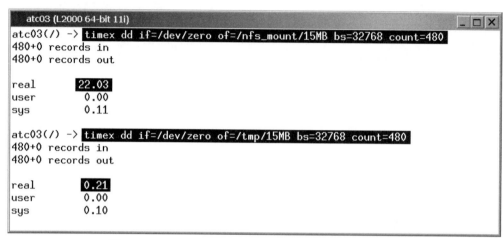

Figure 7.3 Loopback NFS Write Performance Example

When compared against the speed of writing to the local filesystem directly, it is clear that using a loopback NFS mount is a very inefficient method of accessing local files.

AutoFS When AutoFS is used in the scenarios detailed in Figure 7.1 and Figure 7.2, AutoFS will not create a symbolic link or a loopback NFS mount. Instead, AutoFS will create LOFS (Loopback Filesystem) mounts between the exported filesystems and the requested pathnames in the automount maps — even when mounting via a server hostname that does not match the text string returned by the hostname(1) command on the server.

AutoFS accomplishes this feat by building a list of all local IP interfaces on the system, including any relocatable IP addresses used by MC/ServiceGuard. When AutoFS receives a request to mount a filesystem, it compares the IP address of the server with the local address list to determine if the filesystem actually resides on the local system. It is important to note that AutoFS only builds the list of local interfaces at the time AutoFS starts. Any interfaces added to the system after AutoFS is running will not be in this list, and so any mount attempts using these newly added interfaces will cause AutoFS to create a loopback NFS mount.

Figure 7.4 shows another example of creating a 15MB file to a local filesystem — this time via an LOFS mount created by AutoFS. The same NFS server was used as in the previous examples shown in Figure 7.2 and Figure 7.3. The only configuration change made to the server system was to run AutoFS in place of the legacy automounter. This output shows AutoFS

9. For more information about exporting NFS Version 2 filesystems with the *async* option, see Section 9.1.2 "Safe Asynchronous Writing."

creating an LOFS mount point when a user process references the "/nfs_mount" directory — even though the automount map entry specifies an NFS server name that does not match the configured local hostname. The performance seen writing to this LOFS filesystem is comparable to creating the file directly in the local filesystem (as shown in Figure 7.3 earlier).

 KEY IDEA — Recommendations when Using AutoFS with MC/ServiceGuard

Problem: When AutoFS is run on NFS servers participating in a Highly Available NFS cluster (via MC/ServiceGuard), this behavior of building a local IP interface list can, in certain cases, render ServiceGuard unable to migrate an NFS package during a failover event.

Cause: HA/NFS uses relocatable IP addresses that migrate from a primary NFS server to an adoptive node during a failover event. If AutoFS is started on an HA/NFS server *after* ServiceGuard is running, these relocatable IP addresses will be included in AutoFS' list of local IP interfaces. Any AutoFS map entries referencing these relocatable addresses will cause AutoFS to create LOFS mounts to the exported local filesystems.

It is these LOFS mounts that can wreak havoc with ServiceGuard because HA/NFS makes no attempt to unmount LOFS filesystems prior to a package migration. Any AutoFS-managed LOFS mounts that are holding resources in the exported filesystems when ServiceGuard tries to initiate a package failover may render ServiceGuard unable to successfully unmount the local filesystems and migrate them to the adoptive node.

Solutions: There are three potential solutions to this problem:

1. **Make sure AutoFS is running on the NFS server *before* HA/NFS is started.** This will allow AutoFS to generate its list of local IP addresses *before* the relocatable addresses are added to the system. When AutoFS receives a request to mount a filesystem from the relocatable IP address, it will not recognize this as a local filesystem and it will create a loopback NFS mount. Then, if a package failover occurs, the exported filesystem will migrate to the adoptive server, and filesystem that began as a loopback NFS mount will become a regular NFS mount.

2. **Run the legacy automounter on HA/NFS server systems.** The legacy automounter does not have this feature of generating a list of local interfaces at start time. It is therefore unable to distinguish automount map entries referencing the relocatable IP addresses used by ServiceGuard as local exported filesystems, and thus it will create loopback NFS mounts for these filesystems.

3. **Configure the HA/NFS server as a dedicated NFS server.** This would involve migrating all user applications off of the HA/NFS servers so that there is no need to run either automount or AutoFS on these systems.

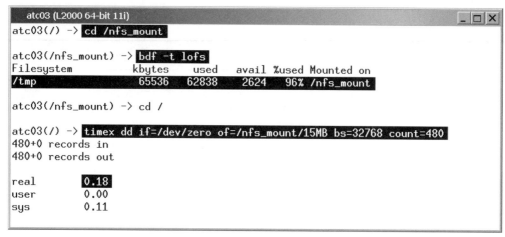

Figure 7.4 LOFS Write Performance Example

7.1.5 Mounted Filesystem Location

Automount   The legacy automounter does not mount filesystems directly into the location specified in the automount map. Instead, it creates a holding directory called "/tmp_mnt" (by default), where it performs the actual NFS mounts. It then creates a symbolic link from the real NFS mount point under the /tmp_mnt directory to the desired location in the automount map entry. Figure 7.5 shows an example of this behavior.

In this example, the /etc/auto_direct map contains an entry requesting that the "/tmp" filesystem on server "atc01" be made available when the "/nfs_mount" directory is referenced. The bdf(1M) output shows how automounter performed the requested NFS mount from server atc01, but it mounted the remote filesystem to the local "/tmp_mnt/nfs_mount" directory rather than the requested path "/nfs_mount." Automount then created a symbolic link from the real NFS mount to the requested location, as shown by the ll(1) output.

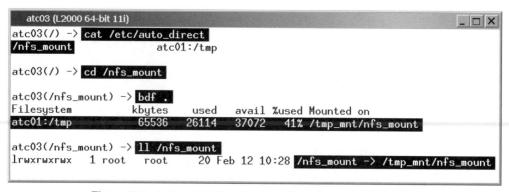

Figure 7.5 Automount Mounting and Creating a Symbolic Link

This mechanism of using symbolic links pointing to mounted filesystems can lead to confusing or conflicting output from commands that use the getwd(3C) routine. If a process invokes getwd(3C) while in an automounted filesystem, it will obtain the pathname of the real NFS directory ("/tmp_mnt/nfs_mount" in this example). If this "/tmp_mnt" path is cached and used sometime later, there is no guarantee that the filesystem will still be mounted, as automounter could have unmounted the filesystem if it was idle. The automounter cannot detect references to empty mount points unless they are made through the automounter's mount point ("/nfs_mount" in this example).

This behavior can lead to problems for programs that cache directory path information, such as the at(1) command. This command is used to launch scripts at scheduled times. at(1) records the current directory where the scheduled script resides so that it can later cd(1) into the directory to execute the script at the desired time. If the script resides in an automount-managed directory, and that directory is not mounted when at(1) tries to launch the script, it will fail.

These symbolic links can also cause confusion for customers who are not expecting to see the "/tmp_mnt" string appear as a prefix to their current directory. Depending upon the shell run by the user, the pwd(1) command will return the symbolic link path ("/nfs_mount") or the real NFS mount path containing the "/tmp_mnt" prefix. Figure 7.6 shows an example of how the three most popular UNIX shells (i.e. Korn, Posix, and C) deal with symbolic linked directory pathnames.

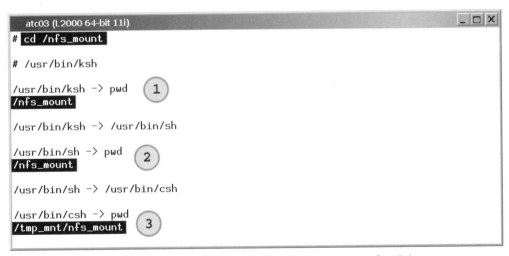

Figure 7.6 How Various Shells Deal with Automount Symlinks

As you can see, items 1 and 2 show that the Korn and Posix shells return the directory pathname of the symbolic link, while the C shell (item 3) returns the pathname of the actual NFS mounted directory. This difference in behavior can lead to problems for shell scripts that depend on directory pathname information to execute properly.

In addition to the shell confusion caused by symbolically linked directory pathnames, a *potential* performance issue can also result from automount's extensive use of symbolic links.

Whenever an application references an automount-managed directory pathname (such as "/nfs_mount" in the earlier examples), the kernel invokes the automount daemon to re-direct the application's request to the real NFS mount point ("/tmp_mnt/nfs_mount" in the earlier examples). Depending upon how NFS client applications reference automount-managed pathnames, the amount of overhead added by the automounter to resolve symbolic links on the applications's behalf can be trivial or significant.

A good example of how the way in which an application references an automounted directory can influence the application's performance is shown in Figure 7.7. In this example, the ls(1) command is issued two times against an automount-managed directory containing over 25,000 files — once where ls uses the full pathname of the automount directory, and once after the cd(1) command is used to position the shell inside the automount directory.

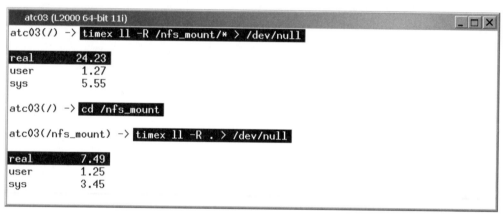

Figure 7.7 Example of Automounter Symbolic Link Overhead

The initial ll(1) command specified a pathname of "/nfs_mount/*," which causes the command to resolve each of the 25,000 files in the automount-managed directory via its full pathname (i.e. /nfs_mount/file1, /nfs_mount/file2, etc.). Using ll in this manner causes the kernel to invoke the automount daemon once for each file in the directory — over 25,000 times — to resolve the "/nfs_mount" symbolic link to the actual NFS mount residing at "/tmp_mnt/nfs_mount." Figure 7.8 contains a small portion of a debug automount log file collected while the initial ll command was running.[10] This log file data shows the automounter servicing a few of the 25,000+ READLINK calls it performed during the initial ll command.

10.   To learn more about the debug logging facility of automount and AutoFS, refer to Section 7.4.1.

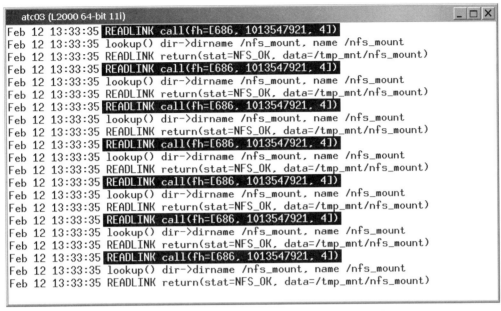

Figure 7.8 Debug Automount Log Entries of `READLINK` Requests

The second `ll` command shown in Figure 7.7 did not invoke the automounter at all. The command was launched while the user resided in the automount-managed directory, and the `ll` command did not cross any other automount-managed pathnames while resolving the files in the `/nfs_mount` directory.

Not only did the first `ll` command take over three times longer to complete than the second, it tied up the single-threaded automount daemon for nearly the entire 24.23 seconds it ran, because the automounter was forced to resolve 25,000 symbolic link requests for this single `ll` command. This is a significant amount of automounter overhead for a single command to consume. If many client applications are referencing automounted filesystems in this manner, the automount daemon can spend the majority of its time servicing symbolic link requests. It is therefore important to understand how your NFS client applications reference automount-managed pathnames to ensure that they are using automounter resources as efficiently as possible.

AutoFS   AutoFS mounts filesystems directly into the location specified in the automounter map. This avoids the `getwd(3C)` confusion associated with the symbolic links used by the legacy automounter, and it eliminates any overhead associated with resolving symbolic links as part of managing NFS filesystems.

7.1.6 Automount Pseudo-NFS Server vs. AutoFS Filesystem

Automount   The automounter is implemented as a user-space daemon process that runs on the NFS client and emulates a remote NFS server. Automount puts placeholders in the VFS

(Virtual Filesystem) layer of the kernel for the mount points it manages. This is why an automount entry in the `/etc/mnttab` file (see Figure 7.9) looks syntactically like an `mnttab` entry for a typical NFS-mounted filesystem.

Figure 7.9 `/etc/mnttab` File Showing an Automount Entry

This automount entry reveals that the pseudo-NFS server is managing the "`/nfs_mount`" filesystem, and the automount daemon is running with a process ID of 6059. When any process on the client system references the `/nfs_mount` directory path, the kernel will invoke the automount daemon. This pseudo-NFS server behavior is the reason the kernel displays an "`NFS server not responding`" message when the automount daemon is not responding quickly:

```
NFS server (pid687@/nfs_mount) not responding still trying
```

While automount does perform the functions of an NFS server on the local system, it does not actually intercept the `READ` and `WRITE` calls destined for the NFS filesystems it manages. However, this does not mean that automounter stops intercepting NFS requests after it has successfully mounted a filesystem. Since applications running on the NFS client typically expect to access files via the requested path, which in the case of automounted filesystems is a symbolic link, it is the job of the automounter to redirect these pathname requests to the location of the real NFS mount point. It does this by processing `LOOKUP` calls destined for the requested path and redirecting these `LOOKUP` requests to the real file locations.

For example, using the same automount map entries shown earlier in Figure 7.5:

```
/nfs_mount              atc01:/tmp
```

If a process on the client wished to write to the file "`/nfs_mount/file1`," it will begin by resolving the path to this file. Upon reaching the "`/nfs_mount`" portion of the path, the kernel recognizes this as a filesystem managed by the automounter. Since automount masquerades as a pseudo-NFS server, the kernel sends an NFS `LOOKUP` call to the automount daemon (thinking it is a remote NFS server) requesting information about the "`/nfs_mount`" filesystem. Automount resolves the symbolic link residing at "`/nfs_mount`" and sends a `LOOKUP` reply, redirecting the kernel to the real NFS-mounted directory pathname "`/tmp_mnt/nfs_mount`."

The kernel examines this "/tmp_mnt/nfs_mount" path and recognizes this as the real NFS mount point serviced by system "atc01." It sends a new LOOKUP request to the remote NFS server. Server "atc01" returns a LOOKUP reply with the information for this remote filesystem. The kernel returns the remote pathname information to the writing application and normal NFS traffic ensues. At this point, any NFS READ or WRITE calls go directly to the remote NFS server, bypassing the automounter.

As you can see, the automounter stays involved in servicing pathname lookup requests even after it has mounted remote filesystems. Usually the overhead added by the automounter is minimal. However, since the automounter is a single-threaded process that performs filesystem mounts as needed, unmounts idle filesystems, and redirects symbolic link pathname LOOKUP requests, it can add noticeable delays when the client's automounter use becomes heavy.

AutoFS   AutoFS is implemented as a true filesystem, just like HFS, VxFS, CDFS, etc. Since AutoFS does not masquerade as a pseudo-NFS server, it does not try to intercept client requests for mounted filesystems, and thus adds no overhead when applications access currently mounted filesystems.

7.1.7 Forcibly Stopping the Automounter

Automount   Since automount is implemented as a user-space daemon which puts placeholders in the VFS layer, if you kill the automount process with a -9 (SIGKILL) the daemon will forcibly exit without first removing the VFS placeholders from the kernel. At this point, any access to any automount-managed filesystem will hang, as the kernel views these entries as belonging to a dead NFS server. Any attempt to start a new automount process to manage the hung automounted filesystems will also hang because the new daemon will be listening on a different port number and using a different process ID than the previous automounter. The new daemon will also be unable to overlay the entries placed in the VFS layer by the previous invocation of automount.

At this point your only recourse is to reboot the NFS client system in order to remove these stale VFS placeholders. While this issue is not directly related to NFS performance, rebooting NFS clients can cause a serious disruption to most production environment.

AutoFS   The portions of AutoFS that manage the VFS layer entries are in the kernel, which makes it "safe"[11] to stop the user-space automountd daemon with a SIGKILL if necessary. This will not cause the currently mounted NFS filesystems to become non-responsive, nor will it impede your ability to start a new automountd process to resume managing the AutoFS directories.

---

11.   Killing the automountd daemon with a -9 (SIGKILL) should only be used when attempts to stop the automountd via a standard kill command (SIGTERM) are unsuccessful.

7.1.8 Modifying Map Contents

Automount   Once the legacy automounter has been started, any changes made to the master map or any direct maps will be ignored until the automounter is stopped and restarted. As explained in the previous section, killing and restarting the automounter can sometimes be a risky proposition.

AutoFS   AutoFS has the ability to re-read the contents of all maps while running, simply by issuing the "/usr/sbin/automount" command. Any changes in the maps take effect immediately. While this feature does not necessarily affect NFS performance, it does eliminate potential downtime in the environment.

7.2 Automounter Performance Considerations

If you do decide to use either the legacy automounter or AutoFS in your NFS environment, there are several ways to ensure that these products perform efficiently.

7.2.1 Replicated Servers in Maps

Both automounters allow an administrator to configure multiple NFS servers for a given mount point. This feature is designed to increase the availability of a filesystem and provide load balancing among several servers. Below is a sample map entry with a replicated server list:

```
man -ro alpha,bravo,charlie,delta:/usr/share/man
```

In this example, there are four systems configured to serve the "/usr/share/man" filesystem: "alpha," "bravo," "charlie," and "delta."[12] This feature is primarily used to manage read-only filesystems, as the same directory contents are expected to reside on all configured servers. Manual pages are an ideal candidate for this type of map entry since they typically reside on all NFS servers and they are not modified by the clients.

If you plan to use this feature, be certain to list only NFS servers that are present in the environment and that contain the filesystem referenced in the map entry. Listing NFS servers that are not present in the network (i.e. servers that have been decommissioned, moved to different company locations, no longer serve NFS filesystems, etc.) or active NFS servers that do not export the specified filesystem will force the automounter to waste a large amount of time trying to locate an appropriate server to satisfy the mount request.

7.2.2 Environment Variables Referenced in Maps

Another feature common to both the legacy automounter and AutoFS is the ability to specify environment variables as part of the command-line options used when starting the automounters (via the "-D" option) and then referencing those variables in the maps.[12] The

---

12.   For a complete description of this feature, refer to the automount(1M) man page.

automounter resolves the environment variables to their ASCII string equivalents, substitutes them into the automount map entry, and then attempts the mount request for the resulting filesystem name. Here is an example of a map entry specifying the "OSREL" variable:

```
/nfs_mount              emonster:/data/$OSREL
```

When the automounter running on an HP-UX 11i client encountered this map entry, it would formulate the following mount request:

```
emonster:/data/B.11.11 /nfs_mount
```

The same map automount entry processed by an HP-UX 11.0 NFS client would result in the following NFS mount request:

```
emonster:/data/B.11.00 /nfs_mount
```

This feature allows NFS clients of different architectures and operating system releases to share a common set of automount maps, thus easing the burden on the systems administrator. Just as with replicated servers feature described earlier, this environment variable feature requires a good deal of planning and coordination to ensure that the pathnames resolved via these environment variables actually exist on the target NFS servers, and thus avoid having the automounter waste time requesting filesystems that are not present on the server.

7.2.3 Hierarchical Mount Points in Maps

A hierarchical map entry is one that defines multiple filesystems that are to be mounted and unmounted as a group. An example of this type of map entry is the special "-hosts" entry, which instructs the automounter to mount all exported filesystems from a given NFS server into a hierarchical structure on the client. The default "-hosts" map entry looks like this:

```
/net -hosts -nosuid,soft
```

With this map entry in place, when a user references a path such as "/net/emonster," the automounter will contact NFS server "emonster" and ask for a list of all the filesystems it is currently exporting. Once the server responds with the list of filesystems,[13] the automounter begins sending MOUNT requests to the server for each filesystem in the list. Those filesystems that the client is allowed to mount (i.e. the client system is a member of the access list configured for the exported filesystem) are mounted beneath the "/tmp_mnt/net/emonster/" directory, and symbolic links are created referencing the path configured in the automount map — i.e. "/net/emonster/<path>."

Once the permitted filesystems are mounted, the automounter manages these filesystems as a single unit. When the default unmount timer expires, the automounter attempts to unmount all filesystems in the hierarchy. If any one filesystem in the hierarchy is in use and cannot be

---

13.   Refer to Section 5.1.4 in the "rpc.mountd" chapter for more information about how the automounter retrieves the list of exported filesystems from the NFS server.

unmounted, all filesystems in the group that were successfully unmounted must be re-mounted in order to preserve the hierarchy. Consider the following example:

- Server "emonster" exports five filesystems: `/data`, `/home`, `/stand`, `/opt`, and `/tmp`.
- NFS client "ros87252" is running AutoFS with the "-hosts" map.
- A user on the client issues the following command: "`cd /net/emonster/opt`."
- The automounter contacts server "emonster" and requests a list of exported filesystems, and then sends mount requests for each filesystem in the list.
- The automounter successfully mounts all five filesystems.

What happens when the unmount timer expires 5 minutes later? Figure 7.10 contains a portion of a debug AutoFS log file collected during this event.

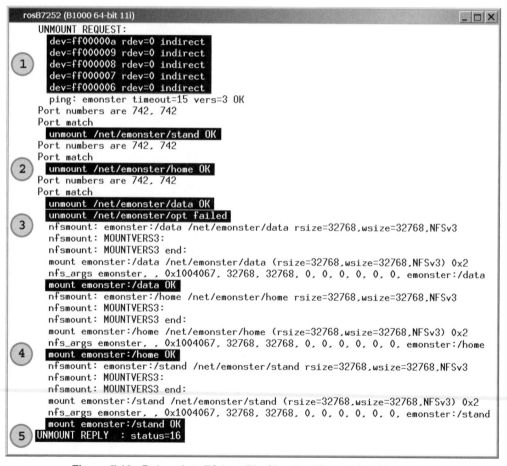

Figure 7.10 Debug AutoFS Log File Showing Hierarchical Unmounts

Figure 7.10 reveals that the automounter performed the following steps:

1. AutoFS received five simultaneous unmount requests from the kernel, which is expected since there are five filesystems in this hierarchy.
2. AutoFS was able to successfully unmount "/net/emonster/stand," "/net/emonster/home," and "/net/emonster/data."
3. When AutoFS tried to unmount "/net/emonster/opt" the unmount attempt failed, which is expected since the user's shell that issued the "cd" command is holding this filesystem busy.
4. AutoFS must now re-mount the three filesystems it just finished unmounting.
5. AutoFS returns an error of EBUSY (status=16) to the kernel indicating it was not able to unmount the entire hierarchy successfully.

So, while the "-hosts" map entry provides an easy way of configuring NFS clients to mount all exported filesystems from your servers, it can induce a tremendous amount of overhead both to the automounter on the client and to the rpc.mountd daemon on the NFS server.

This example shows how a process requesting access to a single filesystem resource (i.e. /net/emonster/opt) caused AutoFS to mount five filesystems. When the unmount timer expired, AutoFS performed four unmount operations (three successful attempts and one failed attempt) only to have to re-mount the three filesystems it unmounted. Each of these mount and unmount requests requires the services of the NFS server's rpc.mountd daemon.

In a large NFS environment, where many NFS clients use hierarchical maps, both the client's automounter and the server's mountd can become heavily burdened. It is therefore recommended that the use of hierarchical maps be avoided whenever possible.

7.2.4 Default Unmount Timer and Its Effect on Client Caching

By default, automount and AutoFS attempt to unmount idle filesystems every 5 minutes. In most NFS environments this default value is much too small. Today's client applications typically use NFS filesystems for hours or even days at a time, rather than minutes. This 5 minute default unmount timer not only keeps the automounters busy trying to unmount filesystems (and in the case of hierarchical mount points, re-mount filesystems that were just successfully unmounted), it also increases the burden on the NFS server's rpc.mountd daemon since rpc.mountd is involved in every NFS filesystem mount and unmount request.

An even more important reason to consider configuring the automounter to use a large unmount timer was discussed back in Section 7.1.3. To recap, when attempting to unmount an NFS filesystem, the kernel will invalidate all buffer cache and page cache[14] memory buffers associated with the filesystem — *regardless of whether the unmount attempt is successful or not.*

---

14. The HP-UX buffer cache and page cache mechanisms are described in detail in Section 11.1.1 "How Does Buffer Cache Differ from the Page Cache?"

This means that any memory buffers associated with executable binaries and libraries that were loaded via the NFS filesystem will be discarded from the client's page cache, and any application data retrieved across the NFS mount point will be invalidated from the client's buffer cache — even if the unmount attempt fails because the filesystem is currently in use.

The effect of this behavior can be dramatic, particularly for those NFS clients that run large applications across automounted filesystems.

NFS Performance Example: Automount Unmount Timer

Problem: A customer reported experiencing very good performance when initially launching a large CAE application and loading a large data file on an HP-UX 11.0 client. After a period of time, the customer noticed the application performance degrade significantly.

Configuration: Both the CAE application and data files reside in an automount-managed filesystem. The customer uses "indirect" maps and the default 5 minute unmount timer.

Question: Why does the application performance degrade over time?

Answer: The request to launch the CAE application triggers the automounter to mount the necessary NFS filesystem and application loading begins. This customer's application requires just over three minutes to load, after which the user loads a data file across the same mount point, which takes 45 seconds to complete. At this point performance is very good because the memory pages associated with the application binaries are stored in the client's page cache and the data file memory pages are stored in the client's buffer cache.

Five minutes after the NFS filesystem was originally mounted, the automounter attempts to unmount this filesystem. The unmount attempt fails because the filesystem is still in use by the CAE application; however all memory pages in the client's buffer cache associated with the data file are now gone. The memory pages in the page cache associated with the application binaries are also invalidated, which forces the client to retrieve these pages from the NFS server in order to continue running. These memory pages are once again stored in the client's caches. Five minutes later the whole process repeats when the automounter tries to unmount this filesystem again.

Solutions: There are several possible solutions to this problem:

- Manually mount the NFS filesystem, as this will avoid unwanted unmount attempts.
- Use AutoFS and "direct" maps. As described in Section 7.1.3, AutoFS maintains a "last reference" timer any filesystems configured via direct-style maps. This stops AutoFS from attempting to unmount NFS filesystems until they have been *idle* for 5 minutes.
- Increase the unmount timer via the "`-tl`" (automount) or "`-t`" option (AutoFS).[a]

---

a. For more information about configuring a longer unmount timer via the "-tl" automount option or the "-t" AutoFS option, refer to the automount(1M) man page.

The appropriate value for the unmount timer is largely dependent upon the client's usage patterns for the filesystems the automounter manages. In one environment, a timeout value of 8 hours would be appropriate, while in another environment a value of 30 minutes may work better. A knowledgeable system administrator should make this determination based upon the specific needs of the NFS client's applications.

7.2.5 NFS Mount Options Used in the Master Map

NFS mount options may be specified in any automount map entry. If these mount options are included in a filesystem-specific entry within an indirect or direct map, then these options affect only that specific mount point. If the mount options are specified in the *master* map as part of a direct or indirect map definition, then these options affect *every* mount point within the subordinate direct or indirect map.

Consider the following direct map entry:

```
/nfs_mount       -ro,soft          emonster:/tmp
```

In this example, the *ro* and *soft* options only affect the behavior of the /nfs_mount filesystem. Other entries within this direct map are not affected by these options.

Now consider the following master map entry:

```
/-      auto_direct      -noac,nointr
```

In this example, the *noac* and *nointr* NFS mount options would be applied to every entry within the auto_direct map. While modifying the master map in this manner provides a convenient method of forcing all entries within an underlying direct or indirect map to use the same mount options, some care should be taken to ensure that the NFS mount options specified in the master map are really appropriate for every underlying map entry to use.

For example, the *noac* mount option is used to disable client-side attribute caching for an NFS-mounted filesystem.[15] While a client application may require this behavior on a specific mount point, disabling attribute caching on all NFS filesystems can have a very negative effect on NFS performance. In this situation, the specific entry within the direct or indirect map for the mount point requiring the *noac* option should be modified, rather than the master map entry for the direct or indirect map itself.

7.3 Should You Use Automount or AutoFS?

As stated at the beginning of the chapter, automounters are not used to increase client performance, but rather to ease client filesystem administration. The decision to use an automounter should be made by a systems administrator who is familiar with the needs of the client environment. If you decide that an automounter makes sense for your NFS environment, the question becomes "should I use the legacy automounter or the newer AutoFS?"

---

15.   Refer to Section A.4 in Appendix A for more information about the *noac* NFS mount option.

KEY IDEA — The Recommended Automounter

Given the long list of performance and functionality differences between the legacy automounter and AutoFS described in Section 7.1, there is really only one environment where the legacy automounter holds an advantage over AutoFS: on NFS server systems participating in a Highly Available NFS Cluster. For more details on why the legacy automounter is safer to use in this situation, refer to the Section 7.1.4 "Mounting Filesystems via an Alternate IP Address."

Since AutoFS includes all of the functionality of the legacy automounter and adds several new features that can greatly enhance NFS performance (i.e. support for NFS PV3, NFS/TCP, CacheFS, last reference timers, etc.) most NFS environments that require an automounter will likely benefit from using **AutoFS**.

The parameters that govern which automounter (if any) is started at system boot time are "AUTOMOUNT" and "AUTOFS," located in the `/etc/rc.config.d/nfsconf` file. The various combinations of these parameters, and their resulting behavior, are as follows:

AUTOMOUNT=1, AUTOFS=1 — **AutoFS** is started
AUTOMOUNT=1, AUTOFS=0 — **Legacy Automounter** is started (**HP-UX Default**)
AUTOMOUNT=0, AUTOFS=1 — **NO Automounter** is started
AUTOMOUNT=0, AUTOFS=0 — **NO Automounter** is started

7.4 Troubleshooting Automount and AutoFS

When automount or AutoFS experience a problem, the customer-visible symptoms can range anywhere from NFS client application hangs to disappearing mount points. In most cases, the most important piece of information HP support will request is a debug automounter log file collected while the problem is reproduced. In analyzing the log file, the goal is to piece together the sequence of events that lead up to the problem. This data is instrumental in helping HP support understand, possibly duplicate, and resolve the problem.

7.4.1 Collect a Debug-level Automounter Log File

Both HP's legacy automount daemon and AutoFS daemon (automountd) have the ability to enable and disable debug-level logging without having to be shutdown and restarted. This feature allows the system administrator to easily toggle logging on, reproduce a problem, and toggle logging back off — thereby producing a log file that only contains the data relevant to the problem. To enable or disable debug-level logging by either automount or automountd, simply send the running processes a SIGUSR2 signal via the `kill(1)` command.

Below are the steps for collecting a debug automounter log file. The <u>underlined</u> steps are the commands you type.

1. Determine which automounter is running by issuing the `ps(1)` command listed below. In this example, the automountd (AutoFS) daemon is running with a process ID of 813.

   ```
   # ps -e | grep automount
   813 ?           0:00 automountd
   ```

2. Toggle debug logging ON by sending the running daemon a SIGUSR2 signal via the `kill(1)` command:

   ```
   # kill -SIGUSR2 813
   ```

3. Reproduce the undesirable behavior.

4. Toggle debug logging OFF by sending the running automountd daemon another SIGUSR2 signal:

   ```
   # kill -SIGUSR2 813
   ```

The default log file for both automount and AutoFS is "`/var/adm/automount.log`." A portion of a debug log file data is included in Figure 7.11.

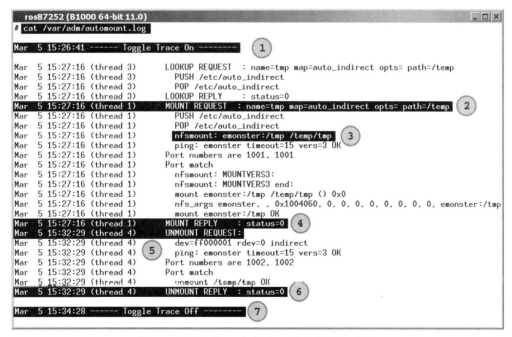

Figure 7.11   Sample Debug AutoFS Log File

It may not be immediately obvious what the contents of the debug log file indicate; however, this data provides a wealth of information about the current state of the automounter as well as a history of the requests it has serviced since debug logging was enabled. For example, the log file output in Figure 7.11 shows:

1. Debug logging was enabled on March 5th at 3:26:41 PM.
2. AutoFS received a MOUNT request at 3:27:16 PM.
3. The mount request was for server "emonster" and filesystem "/tmp." AutoFS is attempting to mount this remote filesystem to the "/temp/tmp" directory on the NFS client.
4. The MOUNT request completed successfully.
5. Approximately 5 minutes later at 3:32:29 PM, AutoFS launched thread number 4 to attempt to UNMOUNT this filesystem.
6. The filesystem was successfully unmounted.
7. Debug logging was disabled at 3:34:28 PM.

Again, the significance of the debug automounter log file contents may not be immediately obvious to someone without internal-level knowledge. However, in the right hands, this debug information can provide invaluable insight into understanding the sequence of events leading up to an automounter problem. Also, since each entry in the log file is time stamped, it is somewhat easy to locate any long delays occurring while the automounter is processing a request.

 KEY IDEA — The Importance of Patching the AutoFS and Automount Code

HP continually strives to improve the quality of HP-UX by distributing software patches containing both defect fixes and functionality enhancements. Many of these fixes and enhancements can significantly improve the performance and behavior of critical system components, such as the AutoFS and Automount code.

It is *strongly* recommended that the latest NFS patches be installed on every HP-UX system in order to take advantage of these improvements. Contact HP support to obtain a current set of patches for your specific operating system. You can also generate a current patch list using the tools available at HP's IT Resource Center: *http://itrc.hp.com*.

For a detailed discussion on the importance of keeping your HP-UX NFS client and server systems patched with current code, refer to Appendix B "Patching Considerations."

## CHAPTER 8

CacheFS

Ａs NFS is a *network*-based file access protocol, one of the primary goals of NFS performance tuning is to reduce the amount of network traffic required to satisfy NFS requests. One method of reducing redundant network traffic is to use main-memory caching mechanisms to store the most recently accessed data on the client. However, since available physical memory is limited in size, and HP-UX 11.0 NFS clients typically don't perform well when configured with a very large buffer cache,[1] the kernel often has to flush memory pages from the client's buffer cache and retrieve them again from the server, resulting in increased load on the server and the network. Also, as more and more clients are added to an existing NFS server, the file access times for each client is increased.

CacheFS (Cache File System) was specifically designed to address these problems. It is a filesystem caching mechanism that stores data retrieved from NFS servers to a local filesystem on the client. Any read requests for data residing in the client's cache can be retrieved locally, thereby eliminating the need for an NFS request and reducing overall server and network load. This reduction in server load can lead to an increase in server performance and allow the system to potentially serve a larger number of NFS clients. CacheFS also improves performance for NFS clients using slow network links.

CacheFS is *not* a pure NFS performance accelerator, in that it does not improve the performance of all NFS traffic. In fact, in many environments, CacheFS will yield slower performance than a standard NFS mounted filesystem. Before deciding whether CacheFS is worth investing in (in terms of local disk resources, configuration and administration time, etc.) a general understanding of the technology and its limitations is needed.

---

1. Refer to Section 11.2.3 for a discussion on why a large buffer cache can hinder HP-UX 11.0 NFS performance.

This chapter offers an overview of how CacheFS works and the potential benefits it can provide. This is followed by an explanation of how CacheFS caches are built and CacheFS filesystems are mounted. Following this is a technical discussion on how CacheFS is implemented on HP-UX systems and how to configure your systems for optimal CacheFS performance. Next is a description of an HP value-added feature — the *rpages* mount option — which allows HP's CacheFS product to outperform most other CacheFS implementations when serving remote application binaries. The final section outlines the various tools and methodologies available for quantifying CacheFS performance and behavior in your environment.

HP-~~UX~~11i   **Difference Between HP-UX 11.0 and 11i:**
CacheFS Support

CacheFS is not available on HP-UX 11.0. CacheFS is included in HP-UX 11i.

8.1 CacheFS Overview

This section outlines the many features of CacheFS. It also illustrates what happens during a "cache hit" and a "cache miss." Finally, it describes some of the design restrictions of CacheFS that can limit the types of applications that will benefit from CacheFS in your environment.

8.1.1 CacheFS Terminology

Throughout this chapter, several terms will be used when describing CacheFS behavior:

Back Filesystem   The filesystem that is being cached. On HP-UX systems, **NFS** is the only supported back filesystem type.[a]

Front Filesystem   The filesystem that contains the cached data. On HP-UX systems, **HFS** is the only supported front filesystem type.[b]

Cold Cache   A cache that does not yet have any data in its front filesystem. In this case, the cache must be populated by copying the requested data from the back filesystem. An attempt to reference data that is not yet cached is referred to as a "cache miss."

Warm Cache   A cache that contains the desired data in its front filesystem. In this case, the cached data can be returned without requiring any involvement from the back filesystem. An attempt to reference data that is already cached is referred to as a "cache hit."

a.   As of HP-UX 11i, HP's CacheFS product is only capable of caching **NFS** filesystems. Other vendors' implementations allow non-NFS filesystems to be cached, such as CD-ROMs formatted with the High Sierra Filesystem. HP will be adding support for caching non-NFS filesystems in a future OS release.

b.   As of HP-UX 11i, an **HFS** filesystem must be used to hold the local cache data on the client. HP will be adding support for VxFS-based front filesystems in a future OS release.

8.1.2 CacheFS Features

"Layered" filesystem   CacheFS is implemented as a "layered" filesystem, in that it caches data read from one filesystem (the "back" filesystem) onto another, local filesystem (the "front" filesystem).

Data remains cached after unmount or client reboot   Since the cache is maintained in a local client filesystem and not in memory, in most cases the cache contents will remain intact if the CacheFS filesystem is unmounted. In fact, the cache contents remain in the local filesystem even after the client system reboots.[2]

All file types are cached   CacheFS caches all file types, including: regular files, directories, symbolic links, special files, etc.

Contents are cached when referenced   Files and directories are populated in the cache as they are referenced. File contents are populated in "chunks" on an as-needed basis, as opposed to being copied to the cache in their entirety.[3] Given the manner in which client applications access files, it is not uncommon for most cached files to be sparse.

Cache contents are managed transparently   There is no need for user intervention when cache resources are exhausted. When a cache fills, cached files are discarded (on a least-recently-used basis) until sufficient space is available. In the unlikely event that no cache resources can be reclaimed, the cache is simply bypassed and CacheFS redirects all requests to the NFS back filesystem.

Cache consistency checking   By default, CacheFS maintains consistency with the back filesystem using a consistency checking model similar to that of NFS, i.e. periodically polling for changes in file attributes. Consistency checking semantics may be changed by using special CacheFS mount options (see the `mount_cachefs(1M)` man page for details).

Existing HFS filesystems can be used to hold a cache   There is no special disk partitioning requirements for CacheFS. Any existing HFS filesystem may hold a cache. However, there are performance benefits to creating separate HFS filesystems for caching purposes. These benefits are described in Section 8.2.1 "Creating a Cache."

Cache sharing   Multiple NFS filesystems may share a single CacheFS cache. However, there are performance benefits to creating separate caches for each NFS filesystem. These benefits are detailed in Sections 8.2.1 and 8.3.1.

---

2.   There are several situations where cache contents will be forcibly removed when a CacheFS filesystem is unmounted or the client system is rebooted. These scenarios are outlined in Section 8.1.4 "CacheFS Limitations" and Section 8.3.2 "The 32-Slot Allocation Map."

3.   When a CacheFS filesystem is mounted with the HP-specific *rpages* mount option, any application binaries executed via the CacheFS mount point are populated in their entirety. For more information about the *rpages* mount option, and the reasons HP developed this enhancement, refer to Section 8.4.

8.1.3 Cache Hits and Misses

Figure 8.1 shows an NFS client using a CacheFS filesystem and experiencing a "cache hit" — meaning the data requested by a client-side application was found in the local cache.

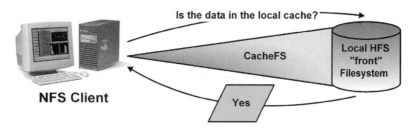

Figure 8.1 CacheFS "Cache Hit"

In the "cache hit" scenario, no NFS request is needed to satisfy the application's read request. This reduces the load on both the network and the NFS server. Figure 8.2 shows what happens during a "cache miss."

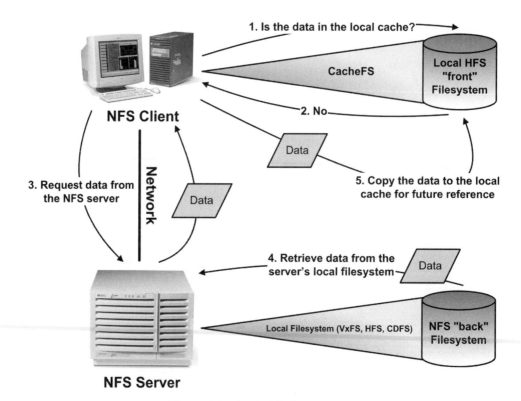

Figure 8.2 CacheFS "Cache Miss"

1. An application issues a read request for data residing in a cached NFS filesystem. The kernel attempts to read the data from the CacheFS front filesystem (i.e. local HFS).

2. In this case the data *is not* found in the front filesystem, indicating that the data has not yet been read across this NFS mount point and cached in the client's local filesystem.

3. The kernel issues an NFS read request to retrieve the data from the back filesystem.

4. The data is retrieved from the server's local exported filesystem and sent to the client.

5. The client kernel places a copy of the data in the front filesystem to satisfy any future requests for this data. The requested data is then returned to the application.

As Figure 8.2 illustrates, both networking and server system resources were required to satisfy the read request. There is some overhead associated with the initial reference to data in the cached filesystem (the cost of populating the cache), but subsequent references to the same data can be satisfied from the local disk instead of the remote server.

8.1.4 CacheFS Limitations

CacheFS provides an effective means of reducing NFS network traffic and server load when used in the right circumstances. However, there are cases where the performance benefits of CacheFS will likely be negligible. For instance, a single NFS client may not get much of a performance boost from caching, particularly on a lightly loaded fast LAN where the server is a powerful machine with a fast disk subsystem and is primarily idle.

Even when CacheFS is configured on multiple NFS clients mounting filesystems from heavily loaded servers across busy networks, there are situations where, due to design limitations, CacheFS may not provide much of a performance benefit. There are even situations where CacheFS can hinder performance compared to uncached NFS filesystems.

Only *read* performance is improved CacheFS improves *read* performance, but only for data that is accessed more than once. It can provide a tremendous performance boost to applications that spend a great deal of time accessing a common set of stable, read-only data over NFS filesystems. Good candidates for caching include man pages and application binaries,[4] which are read multiple times and rarely modified. Caching a directory like /var/mail is not a good idea since the /var/mail directory contents are modified frequently and e-mail messages are typically read only once and then discarded.

CacheFS does not improve *write* performance at all. In fact, when caching a filesystem where NFS writes are occurring frequently, CacheFS can hinder performance compared to uncached NFS. When an application attempts to write to a cached file, CacheFS is forced to invalidate the entire file contents from the local cache and re-direct the request to the back (i.e. NFS) filesystem. In addition, the kernel disables caching for this file, meaning the file cannot be

---

4. Caching application binaries is an ideal use of CacheFS, but it requires special consideration and planning to work effectively. To understand the issues surrounding caching application binaries, see Section 8.4.1 "The Application Caching Dilemma" and especially Section 8.4.5 "HP's Solution — the rpages Mount Option."

considered a candidate for caching until the CacheFS filesystem is unmounted and re-mounted. This additional overhead of invalidating the cache, disabling caching for the file, and redirecting write requests to the back filesystem can add significant overhead to a writing application.

CacheFS effectiveness depends on client's disk subsystem   CacheFS stores data to local filesystems on the NFS client. Thus, CacheFS performance is tied directly to the performance of the client's disk subsystem. If a client machine is configured with slow disks but has a fast network connection (such as 100BT or Gigabit Ethernet), then accessing data from the local CacheFS filesystem may actually be slower than accessing the same data via a standard uncached NFS mount. It is therefore recommended to configure your CacheFS clients with a fast local disk subsystem.

Loose synchronization with "back" filesystem   As stated in Section 8.1.2, CacheFS maintains consistency with the back filesystem using a consistency checking model similar to that of NFS — polling for changes in file attributes. This "polling" behavior can lead to inconsistencies among CacheFS clients when the contents of the remote NFS filesystem are changing frequently. Attribute or data changes made on the server by one client may take some time to propagate to the cache on other clients. For this reason, it is recommended that CacheFS not be used to cache NFS filesystems where data files are modified frequently.

8.2   Using CacheFS

This section outlines the steps involved in creating a local cache directory on an HP-UX client. All of the configurable parameters that control the behavior of the cache are described. Finally, it explains how to mount a CacheFS filesystem.

8.2.1   Creating a Cache

Before a CacheFS mount can be performed, a cache must be created in a local filesystem via the `cfsadmin(1M)` command. This command initializes the cache in the specified directory, and it determines how much of the front filesystem's resources the cache is allowed to consume, in terms of disk space and inodes (i.e. number of files).

Table 8.1 describes the various parameters used to control cache behavior that are configurable via `cfsadmin(1M)`. The table also denotes these parameters' default values.

Table 8.1   `cfsadmin(1M)` Parameter Descriptions and Defaults

Parameter	Description	Default
maxblocks	The *maximum* amount of disk space, expressed as a percentage of the total number of blocks in the front filesystem, that CacheFS is allowed to consume.[a]	**90%**

Table 8.1 `cfsadmin(1M)` Parameter Descriptions and Defaults

Parameter	Description	Default
minblocks	The *minimum* amount of disk space, expressed as a percentage of the total number of blocks in the front filesystem, that CacheFS will *always* be allowed to consume without being limited by the built-in sizing mechanisms (i.e. the size of the cache will never be decreased below *minblocks* blocks.)[a]	0%
threshblocks	The *upper threshold* percentage of total used disk space in the front filesystem, at which point CacheFS will stop consuming disk space resources. For example, if *threshblocks* is set to 85, then once 85% of the total disk space in the front filesystem is utilized (either by CacheFS or by other applications sharing the front filesystem), CacheFS will stop allocating disk space to the cache. This value is only enforced once the amount of disk space consumed by the cache grows beyond *minblocks*, since CacheFS is always permitted to allocate at least *minblocks* blocks of disk space.	85%
maxfiles	The *maximum* number of files that CacheFS may consume, expressed as a percentage of the total number of inodes in the front filesystem.[a]	90%
minfiles	The *minimum* number of files, expressed as a percentage of the total number of inodes in the front filesystem, that CacheFS will *always* be allowed to consume without being limited by the built-in sizing mechanisms (i.e. the cache will always be allowed to hold at least *minfiles* number of files).[a]	0%
threshfiles	The *upper threshold* percentage of total used inodes in the front filesystem, at which point CacheFS will stop adding new files to the cache. For example, if *threshfiles* is set to 85, then once 85% of the inodes in the front filesystem are utilized (either by CacheFS or by other applications sharing the front filesystem), CacheFS will stop adding new files to the cache. This value is only enforced once the number of files in the cache grows beyond the number specified by *minfiles*, since CacheFS is always permitted to cache at least *minfiles* number of inodes.	85%

Table 8.1 `cfsadmin(1M)` Parameter Descriptions and Defaults

Parameter	Description	Default
maxfilesize	The largest file size CacheFS is allowed to cache. This parameter is completely **ignored** by CacheFS. Setting it has *no effect* on caching behavior.	3MB (N/A)

a. If the local HFS filesystem housing the cache is not dedicated for CacheFS usage, then there is no guarantee that the cache will be able to grow to the size specified by this parameter.

In most cases, it is recommended to leave these `cfsadmin(1M)` parameters set to their default values. It is also recommended that a separate HFS filesystem be created to hold the cache, but this is not a requirement — a cache may be created in any existing HFS filesystem with sufficient available disk space and inode resources. If CacheFS is sharing an HFS filesystem with other applications, you may need to lower the *maxblocks* and *maxfiles* parameters from their default values to ensure that CacheFS leaves enough room for other applications.

Once you have identified an existing HFS filesystem to use as the front filesystem, or created a new filesystem for this purpose,[5] a cache may be created by issuing the `cfsadmin(1M)` command with the "`-c`" option, as shown in Figure 8.3. This example illustrates how `cfsadmin` may also be used to interrogate existing caches, via the "`-l`" option, in order to determine what parameter values the cache is currently using.

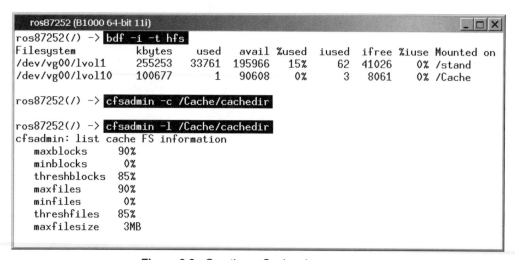

Figure 8.3 Creating a Cache via `cfsadmin`

5. Refer to the *HP-UX System Administration Tasks* manual for more information on creating and mounting HFS filesystems. This manual is available online at *http://docs.hp.com*.

In Figure 8.3, the "`cfsadmin -c`" command creates a directory called "`cachedir`" in the "`/Cache`" filesystem containing the data structures necessary to allow a CacheFS mount. The "`-l`" output confirms the cache was created using the default parameter settings. The `bdf(1M)` output indicates that the "`/Cache`" filesystem is not currently used by any applications (i.e. 0% used space and 0% used inodes). Assuming no other applications begin using this filesystem, CacheFS will be allowed to consume up to 85% of the disk space (*threshblocks*) and 85% of the inodes (*threshfiles*) in this filesystem.

Again, this single cache directory may be used to cache multiple NFS filesystems; however, it is important to understand that CacheFS resources are managed on a per-*cache* basis, not a per-*mount* basis. Thus, if a single cache directory is shared by multiple NFS mounts you can get into a situation where one cached NFS filesystem consumes so much of the shared resources that it forces CacheFS to remove files previously cached by another filesystem.

 KEY IDEA — Create a Separate Cache for Each Cached NFS Filesystem

The recommendation is to create a *separate cache* for each CacheFS mount point, thus avoiding the case where data from one NFS filesystem forces CacheFS to remove files cached by another NFS filesystem when the cache disk space or inode resource thresholds are reached.

8.2.2 Mounting an NFS Filesystem Using CacheFS

Once a cache has been successfully created via the `cfsadmin(1M)` command, an NFS filesystem may begin caching data to the local filesystem by invoking CacheFS. This can be done manually via the `mount(1M)` command, or automatically via AutoFS.[6] The typical syntax used to mount an NFS filesystem via CacheFS is:

```
mount -F cachefs -o backfstype=nfs,cachedir=<cache>
NFSserver:filesystem local_mount point
```

The "`-F cachefs`" option tells the `mount` command this is a CacheFS mount request. The "`backfstype`" field indicates the type of filesystem being cached.[7] The "`cachedir`" keyword specifies the location of the cache created via the "`cfsadmin -c`" command. Figure 8.4 shows an NFS filesystem being mounted referencing the cache built in Figure 8.3.

---

6.   For a detailed explanation of how to configure AutoFS maps to manage CacheFS filesystems, refer to the *Installing and Administering NFS Services* manual, available online at *http://docs.hp.com.*

7.   As of the time of this writing, HP's CacheFS product is only capable of caching NFS filesystems. HP will be adding support for caching non-NFS filesystems in a future OS release.

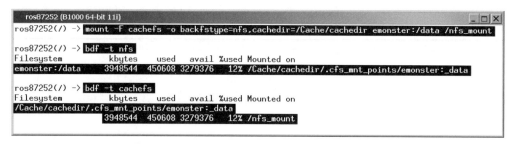

Figure 8.4 Sample CacheFS Mount Command

In this example, the "/data" directory on server "emonster" is mounted to the local directory "/nfs_mount." At this point, "/nfs_mount" can be accessed just like any other mounted filesystem. As data in "/nfs_mount" is read for the first time, a copy will be placed in the cache located in the "/Cache/cachedir" directory.

Figure 8.4 also illustrates the "layering" used by CacheFS when caching NFS filesystems. CacheFS mounts the requested NFS filesystem inside the specified cache directory, as shown by "bdf -t nfs." In the above example, the NFS filesystem "emonster:/data" is mounted as "/Cache/cachedir/.cfs_mnt_points/emonster:_data." The "bdf -t cachefs" output shows how a CacheFS mount point is created between the mounted NFS filesystem and the requested local directory. In this example, a CacheFS mount is created between "/Cache/cachedir/.cfs_mnt_points/emonster:_data" and "/nfs_mount." Any request to access files in "/nfs_mount" will go through the CacheFS front filesystem before looking in the NFS back filesystem.

As Figure 8.4 shows, the client system created two mount points when processing the specified CacheFS mount command. Each of these mount points will have an associated mnttab(4) entry, so it is expected behavior to see two /etc/mnttab entries representing a cached NFS filesystem — one for the remote NFS mount and one for the local CacheFS mount.

8.3 CacheFS Internals

This section describes several of the kernel mechanisms used to implement CacheFS on HP-UX, and how these mechanisms can dramatically affect both CacheFS behavior and performance. This section also explains how you can configure these kernel mechanisms, either directly or indirectly, to optimize CacheFS performance.

8.3.1 cachefsd Daemon and Kernel Thread Pools

The first time a CacheFS mount is processed on the client, the kernel launches a special daemon process called *cachefsd*. This is a multi-threaded process used by the client system to manage the contents of CacheFS local caches. A separate pool of cachefsd threads is created to service each cache, and each pool can have a maximum of 5 cachefsd threads associated with it at any time. The kernel launches new threads as requests for cached data increase.

All running cachefsd kernel threads are associated with the single cachefsd daemon. These threads can be examined using tools capable of displaying kernel threads, such as GlancePlus. Figure 8.5 shows a sample GlancePlus Thread List screen displaying the running cachefsd kernel threads.

TID	Process Name	PID	CPU %	Phys IO Rt	Stop Reason	Pri
2231	cachefsd	2182	0.0	0.0	NFS	153
2232	cachefsd	2182	0.0	0.0	SYSTM	152
2233	cachefsd	2182	0.0	0.0	SYSTM	152
2312	cachefsd	2182	0.0	0.0	SYSTM	152
2313	cachefsd	2182	0.0	0.0	SYSTM	152
2319	cachefsd	2182	0.0	0.0	SYSTM	152
2320	cachefsd	2182	0.0	0.0	SYSTM	152

GlancePlus - Thread List

File   Reports   Configure   Help

System: ros87252   Last Update: 12:14:07   Int: 15 sec

Thread List: 7 of 137 Selected   Users: 2

Figure 8.5 GlancePlus Thread List Displaying cachefsd Threads

In this example, the cachefsd daemon has a PID of 2182, and there are currently 7 cachefsd threads running. The fact that more than 5 cachefsd threads are running indicates that multiple CacheFS caches are in use. We know this because the kernel allocates a maximum of 5 cachefsd threads to each cache being serviced, so this client must be using more than one cache.

KEY IDEA   — cachefsd Kernel Thread Pools Are Created on a *Per-Cache* Basis

It is important to understand this distinction of how the kernel creates cachefsd thread pools on a per-*cache* basis — not a per-*CacheFS mount* basis. In other words, if three NFS filesystems share a single cache, all requests for these cached resources will be serviced by a single pool of cachefsd threads. If, however, there are three separate caches configured, and each of the NFS filesystems is mounted using different caches, then each cached filesystem will be serviced by its own pool of threads.

The recommendation is to create *separate caches* for each CacheFS filesystem, allowing the kernel to create dedicated pools of cachefsd threads to service each CacheFS mount point.

8.3.2 The 32-Slot Allocation Map

Each file stored in a CacheFS filesystem is represented by an internal data structure called an *allocation map*. This structure consists of 32 slots, where each slot represents a "chunk" of the cached file. What this implies is that each cached file must be stored in the front filesystem in *32 or fewer non-contiguous chunks.*[8]

Each allocation map slot contains a starting offset value and a length field, so there is no limit to the size of the chunk represented by a slot entry. In other words, if a client process opens a CacheFS-mounted file, begins reading at offset 0, and reads the entire file sequentially, then the entire cached file will be represented by a single slot in the allocation map (i.e. offset = 0, length = the size of the file). Conversely, if a client process opens a CacheFS-mounted file and reads variable sized portions of the file, each from a different non-contiguous location, then each of these read requests could potentially consume a separate allocation map slot entry.

Figure 8.6 shows an example of the allocation map for a cached file called "file1." In this example, a client process has read from three different locations of "file1." The first read request began at offset 0, where 2KB of data was requested. The next request was for offset 1024KB for 42KB, and then at offset 13MB for 1KB. These three read requests cause CacheFS to store a sparse copy of "file1" in the cache, as shown in Figure 8.6.

CacheFS Allocation Map for "file1"

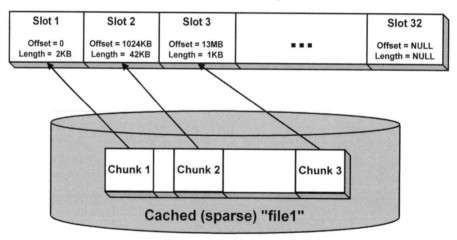

CacheFS "Front" Filesystem

Figure 8.6 32-slot Allocation Map for "file1"

---

8.   This 32-slot map structure is adequate for representing most cached files, as applications tend to read data files in sequential chunks. However, when CacheFS is used to cache NFS-mounted application binaries, this 32-slot allocation map design can be a serious limitation. Refer to Section 8.4 for more information.

At the point when the 33rd non-contiguous location of a cached file is referenced by a reading process, CacheFS concludes it is no longer capable of representing this file in its 32-slot allocation map and the kernel marks this file as being "uncacheable." Once a file is considered "uncacheable," all requests for this file are automatically re-directed to the back (i.e. NFS) filesystem, effectively nullifying any potential benefits from CacheFS. Also, whenever a CacheFS filesystem is unmounted, all files that have been marked "uncacheable" are removed from the cache directory, forcing the NFS client system to retrieve this data from the NFS server again the next time the CacheFS filesystem is mounted and the files are referenced.

 KEY IDEA — Cached Files May Be Removed from the Cache at Unmount or Reboot

There are three main reasons CacheFS will disable caching for a file:

- When a process on the NFS client *writes* to the cached file
- When a cache reaches its configured disk space or inode thresholds, the CacheFS *LRU algorithm* will select files in the cache to mark for removal
- When 33 or more *non-contiguous* chunks of the cached file are referenced

Once a file is flagged as "uncacheable," any read requests for this file must be serviced by the back (NFS) filesystem, effectively nullifying any CacheFS benefits for this file. All files that have been marked "uncacheable" are removed from the cache directory when the CacheFS filesystem is unmounted or the NFS client is rebooted.

Intelligent slot length adjustment and slot coalescing   The kernel makes every effort to represent each cached file in as few allocation map slots as possible by using intelligent coalescing mechanisms. As new regions of a cached file are read, the kernel checks the slots in the file's allocation map to see if any of the existing slots can be extended (by adjusting their length field) so that this new data can be represented without having to consume a new slot entry. For example, using the allocation map shown in Figure 8.6, if a client process requested 8KB of data from "file1" beginning at offset 2KB, the kernel would simply extend the length field in slot 1 from 2KB to 10KB, thus representing both the original 2KB of data and the new 8KB of data in this slot.

In addition, as existing slot entries are extended, the kernel analyzes the remaining slots in the map to see if this newly extended slot can be coalesced with any other slots, thus allowing the kernel to free up entries in the file's allocation map. These newly freed up slot entries can then be used to hold new non-contiguous regions of the cached file.[9] For example, Figure 8.7

---

9.   This CacheFS feature of coalescing across allocation map slots was added in patch PHNE_25627.

illustrates how the allocation map for "file1" shown in Figure 8.6 would change if a client process requested 1024KB of data from "file1" beginning at offset 2KB.

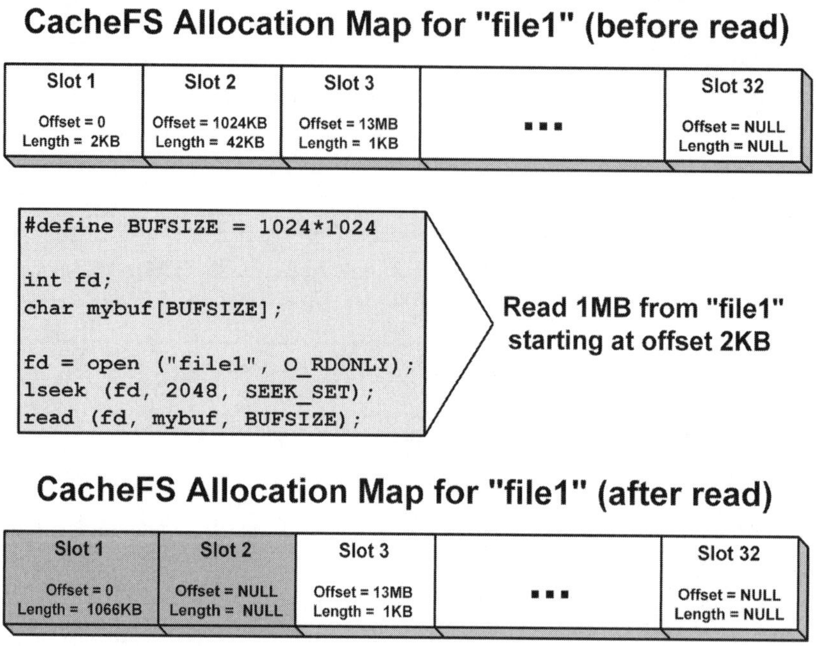

CacheFS Allocation Map for "file1" (before read)

Slot 1	Slot 2	Slot 3		Slot 32
Offset = 0 Length = 2KB	Offset = 1024KB Length = 42KB	Offset = 13MB Length = 1KB	▪ ▪ ▪	Offset = NULL Length = NULL

```
#define BUFSIZE = 1024*1024

int fd;
char mybuf[BUFSIZE];

fd = open ("file1", O_RDONLY);
lseek (fd, 2048, SEEK_SET);
read (fd, mybuf, BUFSIZE);
```

Read 1MB from "file1" starting at offset 2KB

CacheFS Allocation Map for "file1" (after read)

Slot 1	Slot 2	Slot 3		Slot 32
Offset = 0 Length = 1066KB	Offset = NULL Length = NULL	Offset = 13MB Length = 1KB	▪ ▪ ▪	Offset = NULL Length = NULL

Figure 8.7 CacheFS Allocation Map Slot Coalescing

While processing this 1024KB read request, the kernel recognizes this request as being contiguous with the data currently represented by slot 1. It therefore extends the length field of slot 1 to represent both the original 2KB of data and this new 1024KB of data (i.e. length changed from 2KB to 1026KB). The kernel then determined that slot 1 and slot 2 could be coalesced, since the starting offset of slot 2 (1024KB) fell within the range described by slot 1 (0KB — 1026KB). Consequently, slot 1's length is extended to 1066KB, which represents the data from the original 2KB contents, the new 1024KB read, and the 42KB of data originally represented by slot 2. The kernel then marks slot 2 as being "available," allowing a new non-contiguous chunk of "file1" to be represented in this slot if necessary.

8.3.3 The *maxcnodes* Kernel Parameter

Whenever a file or directory in a CacheFS filesystem is referenced on the client system, the kernel allocates a *cnode* data structure to uniquely identify the file/directory. A cnode is a CacheFS-equivalent of an `inode(4)`. The number of cnode entries available on HP-UX systems may be configured directly via the *maxcnodes* kernel variable. By default, *maxcnodes* is set to the same value as the *ncsize* variable, which is used to size the Directory Name Lookup Cache. Likewise, *ncsize* is sized based on the *ninode* kernel variable.

Sizing *maxcnodes* too low can have a disastrous effect on CacheFS performance. Since there are a limited number of cnodes available on the system, once the pool of cnodes is exhausted the client must begin reusing existing cnodes. In order to reuse a cnode, the kernel must locate and invalidate all memory pages associated with that cnode from the client's buffer cache. This invalidating of buffer cache pages associated with CacheFS cnodes can be an extremely system-intensive operation, and should be avoided whenever possible by appropriately tuning the *maxcnodes* variable.[10] Consider the following customer reported example.

NFS Performance Example: Caching a Large Directory

Problem: A customer reported that issuing the "`/usr/bin/ll`" command in a CacheFS-mounted directory containing approximately 20,000 files took over 11 minutes to complete.

The customer's NFS/CacheFS client system was configured as follows:

- 2-CPU system with 2GB of physical memory installed
- kernel variable *maxcnodes* set to 5000
- kernel variable *dbc_min_pct* set to 25 (500MB), *dbc_max_pct* set to 50 (1GB)

Symptom: After increasing *maxcnodes* to 25000, an "`ll`" command of the same CacheFS-mounted directory completed in approximately 90 seconds.

Question: Why did the original "`ll`" command take so long to complete, and why does the *maxcnodes* variable make such a significant difference in this situation?

Answer: When reading a CacheFS-mounted directory, the kernel allocates a *cnode* data structure for every entry in the directory. A cnode is the CacheFS-equivalent of an inode. There are a fixed number of cnodes available on the system — sized by the *maxcnodes* variable. Once all of the available cnodes have been used, the system must begin reusing cnodes, which involves invalidating all memory pages associated with these existing cnodes from the client's buffer cache. Unfortunately, HP-UX 11i currently does not keep track of which memory pages in the client's buffer cache are associated with each cnode. This forces the client to perform a *serial* search of the entire buffer cache looking for memory pages associated with the cnode being reused.

A system configured with 5000 cnode entries that is reading a CacheFS-mounted directory containing 20,000 files will need to reuse its cnode entries thousands of times, involving thousands of serial buffer cache searches. Increasing the pool of cnodes, by tuning the *maxcnodes* variable allows the client to allocate enough cnodes to complete this "`ll`" command without having to reuse any cnode entries or invalidate buffer cache pages.

---

10. Refer to Section 12.1.17 "ncsize" and Section 12.1.20 "ninode" for more information on what these kernel parameters are used for and recommendations on sizing them.

Configuring the *maxcnodes* Parameter   The *maxcnodes* parameter is not currently configurable via the standard kernel configuration tools (i.e. SAM, the /stand/system
file, kmtune(1M), etc.). It can only be sized directly via the adb(1) utility. Rather than sizing
maxcnodes directly, the recommendation is to configure it indirectly via the *ninode* parameter.

 KEY IDEA — **Configuring and Sizing the
maxcnodes Kernel Parameter**

The recommended method of sizing *maxcnodes* is via the *ninode* kernel variable. *ninode*
directly sizes the HFS inode cache and indirectly sizes the CacheFS cnode cache. Since
CacheFS caches must reside in HFS filesystems, configuring *ninode* correctly provides the
dual benefit of a well sized HFS inode cache and CacheFS cnode cache — both of which
are needed to achieve optimal CacheFS performance.

Refer to Section 12.1.20 "ninode" for recommendations on sizing this parameter.

8.4   HP CacheFS Enhancement — the *rpages* Mount Option

HP Labs recently added a new feature to our CacheFS offering called the *rpages* mount
option. This enhancement can potentially allow HP's CacheFS product to outperform other vendor's CacheFS implementations when serving NFS-mounted application binaries. This section
describes why the *rpages* mount option was developed and the benefits it provides.

8.4.1   The Application Caching Dilemma

When systems administrators first hear of the many benefits offered by CacheFS, one of
the first potential uses that comes to mind is to use CacheFS as a means of distributing applications to their NFS client base. Given the parameters under which CacheFS performs best (i.e.
read-mostly data that does not change frequently), caching application binaries would seem to
be an ideal use for CacheFS. After all, application binaries are almost exclusively read-only, and
once an application is installed the contents of the binaries typically do not change until a new
version is installed. The idea of installing an application once on an NFS server and then distributing the application to hundreds or thousands of remote clients simply by running the program
via CacheFS is extremely enticing.

The expectation of most systems administrators is that when an application is mounted
from an NFS server via CacheFS and executed for the first time, the client will store a copy of
the application in its local cache directory and never have to retrieve this data from the server
again. Since the cache resides in a local filesystem, another expectation is that these application
binaries will remain intact when the CacheFS filesystem is unmounted or the client system is
rebooted. Unfortunately, when caching application binaries, CacheFS rarely lives up to these
expectations.

8.4.2 The Influence of Demand Paging

We learned back in Section 8.3.2 about the 32-slot allocation map data structure used by CacheFS to represent locally cached files. We also learned that in order for a file to remain cached, it must occupy 32 or fewer non-contiguous chunks in the front filesystem. Ordinarily this is not a problem, since applications tend to read data files in sequential chunks. However, in the case of executing NFS-mounted application binaries via CacheFS, it is not uncommon for these files to exceed the 32-slot allocation map limit, forcing the kernel to flag these files as "uncacheable" and effectively nullify the benefits of CacheFS.

The reason application binaries are so susceptible to this 32-slot allocation map limitation is that UNIX systems, including HP-UX and Solaris™, use a feature called *demand paging* when launching programs. Demand paging allows the kernel to start an application by only paging in from disk those pieces of the binary that are absolutely required for execution. In other words, when launching an application, the kernel does not sequentially read the entire contents of the executable binary, it only loads those pieces that are needed to get the program running.[11]

While this demand paging mechanism allows applications to start much faster than if the entire contents of program files had to be loaded from disk, it absolutely wreaks havoc with CacheFS. Figure 8.8 shows an example of how demand paging influences CacheFS behavior.

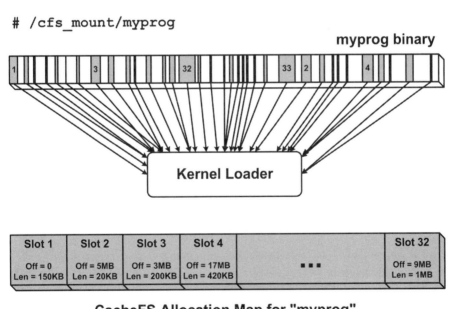

Figure 8.8 The Effects of Demand Paging on CacheFS

---

11.   To learn more about the demand paging mechanism, refer to the *HP-UX Memory Management White Paper*, available online at *http://docs.hp.com*.

In this example, a user launches a program called "myprog" residing in the CacheFS-mounted filesystem "/cfs_mount." The kernel begins the loading process, paging in only those portions of the "myprog" binary that it needs to begin executing the program. Throughout the loading procedure, the kernel actively works to coalesce any newly paged-in data into existing allocation map slots to avoid filling the map.

At some point during the loading process, the kernel has occupied all 32 available slot entries with non-contiguous data chunks. Once a 33rd non-contiguous piece of the "myprog" binary is requested, the kernel realizes it can no longer accurately represent this file in its associated allocation map and it marks the file "uncacheable." When this happens, the cached version of "myprog" is considered invalid, and all future requests for this file are re-directed to the back filesystem. The cached version of "myprog" will be discarded from the local cache directory the next time the "/cfs_mount" filesystem is unmounted or the client system is rebooted.

This example illustrates how the design of the demand paging mechanism allows applications to start faster (since the kernel only needed to load ~25% of the "myprog" binary file before launching the program), but can cause CacheFS to waste valuable system resources storing data retrieved from the NFS server only to have that data invalidated if the cached file exceeds the limits of the 32-slot allocation map.

There is currently no way to disable the demand paging mechanism on HP-UX systems.[12] That being the case, the only way to ensure that a cached application binary will not be marked "uncacheable" by the kernel and discarded when the CacheFS filesystem is unmounted is to somehow force the cached file to occupy a *single* contiguous chunk of disk space in the front filesystem, allowing the file to be represented by a single allocation map slot entry.

8.4.3 The cat(1) Solution

One way to guarantee that CacheFS stores an application binary, or any other type of file, in a single contiguous collection of disk space is to read the entire target file across the CacheFS mount point via the cat(1) command. For example:

```
cat /cfs_mount/myprog > /dev/null
```

Using cat in this manner forces CacheFS to read the entire "myprog" file sequentially, consuming only one slot in the allocation map. Remember, the map entries consist of a starting offset value and a length field. Therefore, if a 20MB file is read sequentially across a CacheFS mount, the file can be represented in one slot (i.e. starting offset = 0, length = 20MB). Once the cat command completes, the client system has a complete copy of the "myprog" binary in its local filesystem. This cached binary will survive a CacheFS filesystem unmount or a client

---

12.   Demand paging should not be confused with the DEMAND_MAGIC flag, which can be toggled on and off via the chatr(1) command. The SHARE_MAGIC and DEMAND_MAGIC flags are used to instruct the virtual memory sub-system how to lay out the four 1GB memory quadrants created when a 32-bit application is loaded, and whether the program's data and text regions are sharable between processes or not. These flags have nothing to do with how much of the binary will be read from disk before the program begins executing.

system reboot. The only time it will be removed from the cache is if the cache is destroyed, via the "cfsadmin -d" command, if a process attempts to write to this cached file, or if the configured disk space or inode thresholds of the front filesystem are reached and the LRU mechanism targets this file for deletion to make room for more recently accessed files.

While this cat solution does work around the 32-slot allocation map limitation, it is not a very practical solution. Most customers who wish to use CacheFS as a means of distributing applications have hundreds or thousands of clients to configure. The idea of logging into each of these clients and issuing a series of cat commands to populate the cache is not very attractive. Also, in most cases systems administrators are looking to distribute a variety of applications to their client base, which means that each group of clients would need to pre-load different application binaries. Keeping track of which clients need to pre-load which application binaries on hundreds or thousands of clients is a daunting administrative task.

8.4.4 Sun's Solution — the cachefspack(1M) Command

The 32-slot allocation map limitation is not specific to the HP-UX implementation of CacheFS. The Solaris™[13] version of CacheFS provided by Sun Microsystems also has this limitation, which means Solaris™ CacheFS clients will also flag binary files as "uncacheable" if they attempt to occupy more than 32 non-contiguous disk space chunks in the front filesystem, and they too will discard these "uncacheable" files during a CacheFS filesystem unmount.

Sun's solution to this problem is very similar to the cat workaround described in the previous section. Sun provides a utility called cachefspack(1M),[14] which can be used to forcibly populate the cache on a CacheFS client. The cachefspack command allows a systems administrator to configure a list of files or directories to pre-load into the cache once the CacheFS filesystem is mounted. The specified files/directories are read across the CacheFS mount point in sequential fashion, similar to the cat command, allowing each of them to occupy a single allocation map slot entry.

This method of populating a CacheFS front filesystem has similar drawbacks to that of the cat solution. With cachefspack, the systems administrator must pre-determine which files to populate on a per-client basis. If this is only required on a few NFS clients running a common application load, then this may not be a problem. However, in large and diverse NFS installations, where hundreds or even thousands of clients run a variety of different applications, the prospect of configuring a unique packing list for each client (or group of clients) is discouraging.

---

13.   As recently as Solaris™ 8, which uses the ONC 2.3 version of CacheFS.

14.   As of HP-UX 11i, HP's CacheFS implementation is based on the ONC 1.2 code provided by Sun Microsystems. This version of CacheFS did not include support for the cachefspack(1M) command. This feature was added after ONC 1.2. HP will be releasing a version of CacheFS based on the Solaris™ ONC 2.3 code, which includes support for the cachefspack(1M) command, in an upcoming OS release.

8.4.5 HP's Solution — the *rpages* Mount Option

HP recognized this 32-slot allocation map design as a critical CacheFS limitation. They concluded that this design inhibited CacheFS from easily and reliably distributing application binaries to clients, which is one of the primary advertised uses of CacheFS and the reason many customers investigate using it in the first place. After analyzing the existing solutions provided by other vendors, HP decided that the administrative overhead costs associated with the cat(1) and cachefspack(1M) models were too high. Also, we felt that having to pre-determine and configure which files to populate on a per-client basis ran contrary to many of the stated benefits of CacheFS — to provide *seamless* caching of data as files are *referenced*, with *minimal* administrative overhead.

HP's solution was to redesign the way CacheFS loads application binaries such that they will remain cached when the CacheFS filesystem is unmounted or the client system is rebooted. This new binary loading behavior is disabled by default and must be enabled on a per-mount basis through the use of a new CacheFS mount option called *rpages*.[15] The typical syntax used to mount a CacheFS filesystem with this option is:

```
mount -F cachefs -o rpages,backfstype=nfs,cachedir=<cache>
NFSserver:filesystem local_mount point
```

The *rpages* option instructs CacheFS to behave as follows: whenever an application residing in a cached NFS filesystem is executed, the kernel checks the front filesystem to see if a *complete* copy of the application binary is present in the local cache; if not, the client will sequentially read the entire application binary from the server and cache a local copy. This automatic caching of complete binaries occurs without any user intervention. Any future requests for this file are satisfied from the front filesystem, and this cached binary will remain intact during a CacheFS filesystem unmount or a client reboot.

The only situations where the client would need to retrieve this data from the server again is if the contents of the file on the server are modified (i.e. if a new version of the application is installed on the NFS server), if the file is written to by a process on the client (since writing to a cached file causes the file to be invalidated and flagged for deletion from the cache), or if the cached file was previously removed by the built-in LRU mechanism when the disk space or inode thresholds of the front filesystem were reached.

Only files that are *executed* are automatically fully populated An important point to understand about the *rpages* functionality is that it only forces the client to cache complete copies of application files that are *executed*. It does not automatically load entire copies of files that the client merely *reads*. For example, if a user on a client executes a CAD program via a CacheFS filesystem mounted with the *rpages* option, and a complete copy of the CAD application binary is not present in the client's cache, then the client will retrieve the entire contents

15.   The *rpages* functionality was added to HP's CacheFS implementation via patch PHNE_25627. This patch, or a superseding patch, is required to take advantage of this feature.

of this binary from the server and cache a local copy. If the user were then to open a CAD data file in the same CacheFS filesystem and began reading the file, CacheFS would *not* sequentially read the entire data file. It would only populate the cache with those portions of the data file that were actually *referenced* by the CAD application (in other words, normal CacheFS semantics).

Another important distinction with regards to caching applications is that the *rpages* option only forces the client to fully cache the application *binary* that is executed — not the entire remote *application*. Launching an application from a CacheFS client with *rpages* enabled will not magically cause the entire remote application (i.e. all binaries, shared libraries, help documents, etc.) to be installed locally on the client. Again, the only difference in CacheFS behavior with *rpages* enabled is that the client will automatically retrieve complete copies of any application binaries that are executed across the CacheFS mount.

Initial application load times vs. subsequent load times   The *rpages* feature may cause the initial application load time to be longer than it would be without *rpages* enabled. This is because *rpages* instructs CacheFS to read the entire binary file from the NFS server, forcing the client to potentially issue more NFS read requests than it would if *rpages* were disabled. However, since the client now has an intact copy of the binary, subsequent runs of the application are usually significantly faster — even after the CacheFS filesystem is unmounted and remounted or the client system is rebooted. Not only can the *rpages* feature increase long-term remote application loading performance on the client, it can also dramatically decrease the long-term load on the network and server since the client will not be needing to read the application binary from the server once its cache is populated.

Table 8.2 illustrates how the *rpages* mount option can influence both client behavior and performance when executing a CacheFS-mounted application. For this example, the Netscape Communicator™ program was executed once using a newly created (cold) cache, and a second time using the populated (warm) cache. The client system was rebooted before each run in order to eliminate any potential benefits of the client's buffer cache, and to force CacheFS to discard any cached files that were marked "uncacheable" during the previous run.

This table also includes the wall-clock time required to start Netscape™, as reported by the `timex(1)` command, as well as the number of NFS read calls issued during each run, as reported by `nfsstat(1M)`. In addition, the cache hit rates, as reported by the `cachefsstat(1M)` command (described in Section 8.5.1), are included.

Table 8.2 Influence of the *rpages* Option on Application Loading

Test #	rpages	Cache State	Cache Hit Rate	Elapsed Time	NFS Reads
1	No	Cold	18% (102 hits, 435 misses)	65 seconds	465
2	No	Warm	5% (27 hits, 452 misses)	55 seconds	452
3	**Yes**	Cold	**98% (902 hits, 12 misses)**	**84 seconds**	**597**
4	**Yes**	Warm	**100% (934 hits, 0 misses)**	**17 seconds**	**0**

The initial test results show Netscape™ started in 65 seconds and required 465 NFS read calls when *rpages* was not used. After rebooting the client and mounting the CacheFS filesystem, Netscape™ took nearly the same amount of time to start (55 seconds) and the NFS read calls were only reduced by ~3%. In other words, the second run consumed almost the same amount of network and server resources as the initial run, and took nearly as long to complete. These results suggest that the cached Netscape™ binary was discarded when the client was rebooted after the initial run and needed to be re-read from the server during the second run.

When the *rpages* feature is enabled, the initial test took somewhat longer to complete (84 seconds vs. 65 seconds) and issued more NFS read calls (597 vs. 465) than the initial run without *rpages*. However, the subsequent *rpages* test completed significantly faster (17 seconds) and required *no* NFS read calls. These results illustrate how effective CacheFS can be at caching applications when the *rpages* mount option is used. It also proves how the *rpages* feature allows CacheFS to significantly reduce network and server load once the client's cache is populated.

Which CacheFS filesystems are mounted with *rpages*? There currently is no CacheFS equivalent of the "`nfsstat -m`" command to display the mount options used on currently mounted CacheFS filesystems. Consequently, the only foolproof way to determine which filesystems are using the *rpages* feature is to examine the `mnttab(4)` entries and look for the string "rpages." This can be done by searching the `/etc/mnttab` file or by issuing the `mount(1M)` command and searching the returned `mnttab` entries, as shown in Figure 8.9.

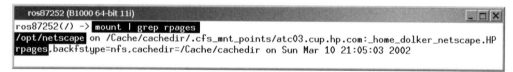

Figure 8.9 Identifying CacheFS Filesystems Mounted with *rpages*

8.5 Measuring the Effectiveness of CacheFS

As stated throughout this chapter, there are situations where CacheFS can provide numerous benefits. There are also cases where CacheFS provides little or no benefit. When deciding whether or not to invest the time and resources (i.e. additional client local disk resources, administrative costs, etc.) to deploy CacheFS throughout your environment, it is a good idea to begin by implementing CacheFS on a few clients and quantifying the effect CacheFS has on your client applications, your NFS servers, and your network.

Fortunately, there are several tools and methodologies available for measuring the effectiveness of CacheFS. The `cachefsstat(1M)` command can be used to display key statistics about how each cache is behaving. The `nfsstat(1M)` command can be used to calculate how many NFS read calls are saved by using CacheFS. `timex(1)` can measure the elapsed time of an application's execution in order to gauge any wall-clock time differences made by CacheFS. Finally, the contents of the local cache directory can be examined to verify which files truly remain cached following a CacheFS filesystem unmount or a client system reboot.

8.5.1 `cachefsstat(1M)`

The `cachefsstat(1M)` command is one of the utilities bundled with HP's CacheFS product. It displays statistical information about how the currently mounted CacheFS filesystems are performing, including:

cache hit rate   The percentage of cache hits over the total number of attempts, followed by the actual numbers of cache hits and misses.

consistency checks   The number of cache consistency checks performed, followed by the number that passed, and the number that failed.

modifies   The number of times a modify operation, such as write or create, has been issued in the cached filesystem.

garbage collection   The number of times the garbage collection mechanism has run, and the wall-clock time of the last run. Garbage collection is initiated when the front filesystem nears its threshold values for disk space and inode usage.

Figure 8.10 shows the `cachefsstat` results of running the Netscape Communicator™ application via a CacheFS filesystem mounted without the *rpages* option and using a newly built cache (i.e. Test #1 summarized in Table 8.2). This output reveals a cache hit rate of only 18%, which is not unexpected since an empty cache was used for this test.

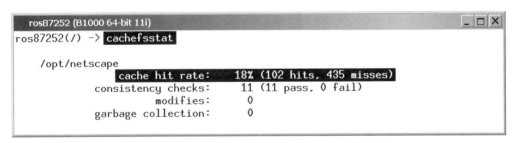

Figure 8.10   `cachefsstat` Output from Test 1 in Table 8.2

The output in Figure 8.11 is more revealing of the default CacheFS behavior (i.e. with *rpages* disabled). These results show the hit rate did not improve using the populated cache after rebooting the client. This indicates that the kernel discarded some cached data when the client rebooted, forcing the client to retrieve this data from the server again during the second test.

The `cachefsstat` results from the *rpages* tests (Test #3 and #4 in Table 8.2) provide still more evidence of the improved caching behavior when the *rpages* feature is enabled. Figure 8.12 shows the results of the initial *rpages* test using a cold cache and Figure 8.13 shows the `cachefsstat` output after launching Netscape™ using the populated cache.

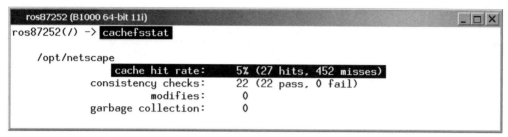

Figure 8.11 `cachefsstat` Output from Test 2 in Table 8.2

The initial *rpages* test results indicate a cache hit rate of 98%, which is understandable since the *rpages* option instructs the kernel to read the entire application binary into the local cache the *first* time it is referenced. Once a complete copy of the binary is cached locally, all future references to this file are satisfied from the cache, resulting in the high cache hit rate.

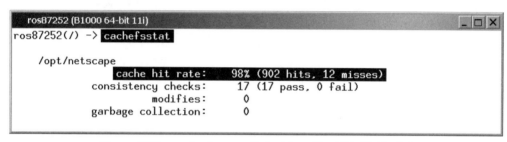

Figure 8.12 `cachefsstat` Output from Test 3 in Table 8.2

Using the populated cache (Figure 8.13) the cache hit rate is 100%, indicating that all data required to execute the Netscape™ application was located in the client's cache.

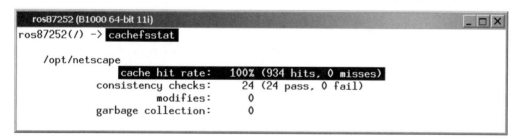

Figure 8.13 `cachefsstat` Output from Test 4 in Table 8.2

8.5.2 Compare Wall-Clock Times and NFS Read Calls

Cache hit rate statistics alone are not the best indicator of CacheFS performance. As an example, look at the results for Test #3 in Table 8.2. The `cachefsstat` output showed a cache hit rate of 98%, which would seem to indicate terrific caching efficiency and therefore great performance. However, the elapsed wall-clock time and the NFS read requests paint a different picture. These numbers indicate that Test #3 took the longest to complete and consumed the most network and server resources of all four tests.

When quantifying CacheFS performance, it is important to not only examine statistics like cache hit rates, but also to check "where the rubber meets the road":

• Do wall-clock times decrease when CacheFS is used compared to a standard NFS mount?

• Do your clients issue fewer NFS read requests when CacheFS is enabled?

timex(1)   In many cases, wall-clock time comparisons can be made by running your tests via the `timex(1)` command. `timex` is especially useful at measuring commands and applications that exit automatically upon completion since `timex` continues collecting elapsed time data until the process being measured exits. For example, the `ls(1)` command exits as soon as it returns the requested directory listing, and the `cp(1)` command exits once the requested files are copied, etc. These commands are ideal candidates for use with `timex`.

Even those applications that remain running can be timed with `timex`, as long as they are forced to exit as soon as they finish loading. For instance, `timex` was used to calculate the loading times for the Netscape™ tests summarized in Table 8.2 — even though Netscape™ remains running once it loads. For these tests, the browser window was killed as soon as it finished displaying the initial "splash" screen, at which point `timex` stopped measuring.

For those cases where you need to time a complex series of events (i.e. loading an application, followed by loading a data file, followed by rendering an image, etc.), a stopwatch or a clock with a second hand can be used. While these measurements may not be completely accurate, they should at least give you a sense of whether CacheFS is helping reduce the wall-clock time required of an operation.

nfsstat(1M)   Determining the number of NFS read calls required of an operation can be done easily using the "`nfsstat -c`" command. There are a couple of precautions you can take to simplify your `nfsstat` data collection efforts and ensure accurate results:

• Make sure no other NFS traffic is occurring on the client system during the tests.

• Re-initialize the `nfsstat` counters via the "`-z`" option before starting each new test.

One point to keep in mind — `nfsstat(1M)` statistics do not indicate how much data was actually sent over the network. Every NFS READ call will increment the `nfsstat` counter, regardless of whether the call is requesting 1KB or 32KB of data. The best way to determine the amount of data actually sent across the network is to collect a network trace and analyze the NFS request and reply traffic.

KEY IDEA — CacheFS Effectiveness Testing Tips

When measuring CacheFS performance it is important to test with a "warm" cache, since a "cold" cache is expected to add some overhead as the cache is populated. It is also important to unmount and re-mount the CacheFS filesystem before each test in order to nullify any performance benefits of the client's buffer cache or page cache mechanisms, and to force the kernel to discard any cached files from the front filesystem that were marked "uncacheable" during the previous test.

8.5.3 Examine the Contents of the Cache Directory

Throughout this chapter we've discussed three scenarios where CacheFS will forcibly and *silently* remove cached files from the front filesystem:

- When a process on the NFS client writes to the cached file
- When a cache reaches its configured disk space or inode thresholds
- When 33 or more non-contiguous chunks of the cached file are referenced

Since these situations cause files to be removed from the cache without any warning or notification, it can sometimes be difficult to determine which files are remaining cached after unmounting and re-mounting a CacheFS filesystem or following a client system reboot. One of the best ways of verifying which files are populated in the front filesystem is to examine the files in the cache directory and map them back to their equivalent files in the NFS back filesystem.

Locate the Cached Files   When mounting a CacheFS filesystem, one of the necessary components of the `mount(1M)` command-line syntax is the "`cachedir`" option, which identifies the location of the directory in the front filesystem where the cache resides. By looking in the specified directory, we can see the actual cached versions of the files that have been referenced via the CacheFS mount point. For example, the `mount` command syntax used during the first and second Netscape™ tests described in Section 8.4.5 was:

```
mount -F cachefs -o backfstype=nfs,cachedir=/Cache/cachedir
atc03.cup.hp.com:/home/dolker/netscape.HP /opt/netscape
```

This syntax instructs the kernel to store any cached versions of files or directories accessed via "`/opt/netscape`" into the cache located in "`/Cache/cachedir`." Looking in this directory, we can determine where these cached files are stored (see Figure 8.14). Inside this directory is a file whose name reflects the cached NFS filesystem in question:

```
atc03.cup.hp.com:_home_dolker_netscape.HP:_opt_netscape
```

The name of this file is generated by CacheFS at mount time. It contains the name of the NFS server and the filesystem mounted from the server, as well as the local pathname of the

CacheFS mount point. Any '/' characters are converted to '_' since '/' is considered a directory path component separator by most operating systems. This file is actually a symbolic link that points to a directory where the cache associated with this specific NFS filesystem is stored.

```
ros87252 (B1000 64-bit 11i)                                              _ □ X
ros87252(/) -> cd /Cache/cachedir/

ros87252(/Cache/cachedir) -> ll
total 300
-rw-------    1 root        users          48 Mar  9 13:39 .cfs_label
-rw-------    1 root        users          48 Mar  9 13:39 .cfs_label.dup
-rwx--S---    1 root        users           0 Mar  9 13:39 .cfs_lock
drwx------    3 root        users        1024 Mar  9 13:39 .cfs_mnt_points
-rw-------    1 root        users      139264 Mar  9 13:54 .cfs_resource
-rw-rw-rw-    1 root        users          34 Mar  9 13:39 .nsr
drwxrwxrwx    4 root        users        1024 Mar  9 13:40 00000180
lrwxrwxrwx    1 root        users           8 Mar  9 13:39 atc03.cup.hp.com:_home
_dolker_netscape.HP:_opt_netscape -> 00000180
```

Figure 8.14 Contents of `/Cache/cachedir` Directory

Remember, a single cache directory may be shared by more than one NFS filesystem. Each cached filesystem will have an associated symbolic link in "`/Cache/cachedir`" and a private directory to hold their cached files. In this example, the symlink points to a directory named "`00000180`,"[16] whose contents are shown in Figure 8.15.

```
ros87252 (B1000 64-bit 11i)                                              _ □ X
ros87252(/Cache/cachedir) -> cd 00000180/

ros87252(/Cache/cachedir/00000180) -> ll
total 20
drwxrwxrwx    2 root        users        1024 Mar  9 13:40 .cfs_attrcache
-rw-rw-rw-    1 root        users        8192 Mar  9 13:39 .cfs_option
drwxrwxrwx    2 root        users        1024 Mar  9 13:40 00000100
```

Figure 8.15 Contents of `/Cache/cachedir/00000180` Directory

Inside "`00000180`" is a subdirectory containing the cached versions of any files referenced via the "`/opt/netscape`" CacheFS filesystem. Figure 8.16 shows the contents of this directory after Netscape™ was launched via the "`/opt/netscape/netscape`" command. This directory contains seven files, indicating that a total of seven files or directories were referenced in the NFS back filesystem during the execution of the Netscape™ application.

---

16.   The name of the directory referenced by the symbolic link will not always be "00000180." The directory name will be different for each NFS filesystem sharing the cache directory.

```
ros87252 (B1000 64-bit 11i)                                                    _ □ ×
ros87252(/Cache/cachedir/00000180) -> cd 00000100/

ros87252(/Cache/cachedir/00000180/00000100) -> ll
total 10736
-rw-rw-rw-   1 root        users         8192 Mar  9 13:40 00000118
-rw-rw-rw-   1 root        users         8192 Mar  9 13:40 00000126
-rw-rw-rw-   1 root        users       278528 Mar  9 13:40 00000127
-rw-rw-rw-   1 root        users     18952192 Mar  9 13:40 000001dd
-rw-rw-rw-   1 root        users         8192 Mar  9 13:40 000001de
-rw-rw-rw-   1 root        users        57089 Mar  9 13:40 000001df
-rw-rw-rw-   1 root        users         8192 Mar  9 13:40 000001e5
```

Figure 8.16   `/Cache/cachedir/00000180/00000100` Contents

Because of the seemingly bizarre names assigned to these files by CacheFS, it is not obvious which files in the back filesystem are being cached. However, it is not too difficult to guess which cached file represents the Netscape™ binary — "000001dd" — since the `ll(1)` output shows this to be the largest cached file. To find out for certain which file "000001dd" represents, this cached file can be mapped to its back filesystem equivalent using the directions outlined in the next section.

It is important to remember that these cached files are most likely sparse, especially since the CacheFS filesystem was mounted without the *rpages* option. This can be verified by using the `du(1)` command, as shown in Figure 8.17.

```
ros87252 (B1000 64-bit 11i)                                                    _ □ ×
ros87252(/Cache/cachedir/00000180/00000100) -> du -k *
8         00000118
8         00000126
224       00000127
5096      000001dd
8         000001de
16        000001df
8         000001e5
```

Figure 8.17   `du -k` Output in Cached Directory

This output reveals that file "000001dd" only consumes a little over 5MB of disk space, even though the `ll(1)` output in Figure 8.16 indicated the file was over 18MB large. Again, it is normal for CacheFS to create sparse cached files since it only stores the portions of the files that are *referenced* by the client application.

Even when the *rpages* feature is enabled, CacheFS will still create sparse files except in the case of application binaries that are *executed* via the CacheFS filesystem. If "000001dd" is in fact the cached version of the Netscape™ binary, then the fact that this file is sparse would indicate that it was populated by a CacheFS filesystem that was not using the *rpages* feature.

Map cached files to their equivalent files in the back filesystem   Now that we know where the cached files reside, we can determine which files they represent in the NFS back filesystem. The naming convention used for the files and directories in a CacheFS front filesystem is fairly straight-forward — the names are the hexadecimal representation of the inode number of the file or directory they represent in the back NFS filesystem.

For instance, the file "000001dd" is the cached version of a file in the NFS filesystem whose inode is the decimal equivalent of 0x000001dd — 477. By searching the NFS back filesystem for a file whose inode number is 477, we can identify which file is represented by file "000001dd." The find(1) command can be used with the "-inum" option to search for a file with a specific inode number, as shown in Figure 8.18.

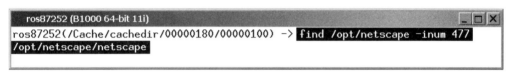

Figure 8.18   find Command Identifying File 000001dd

As suspected, file "000001dd" is the cached version of the Netscape Communicator™ binary "/opt/netscape/netscape."

Which files *remain* cached after the CacheFS filesystem is unmounted?
As discussed many times throughout Sections 8.4 and 8.5, if a cached file is written to or cannot be represented in 32 or fewer non-contiguous chunks it will be marked as "uncacheable" and removed from the cache directory when the CacheFS filesystem is unmounted or the client system is rebooted. Now that we know where the cached files are stored, and we know how to map these files to their back filesystem equivalents, we can verify which files truly remain cached after the CacheFS filesystem is unmounted.

Figure 8.19 shows an example of how the contents of a cache directory can be affected by unmounting its associated CacheFS filesystem. In this example, the contents of file "000001dd," which we've previously identified as the "/opt/netscape/netscape" binary, are destroyed (i.e. the file size is set to zero) after the filesystem is unmounted.

Based upon the fact that this cached file was sparse (see the du output in Figure 8.17), and the fact that this file was invalidated from the cache directory when the CacheFS filesystem was unmounted, we can conclude that the kernel loader must have been unable to represent the Netscape™ binary in 32 or fewer non-contiguous chunks in the front filesystem. We also know that this cached Netscape™ binary must have been populated by a CacheFS filesystem that was not using the *rpages* feature.

Examining the cache contents in this way is by far the most reliable method of determining exactly which files remain cached and which files are discarded when a CacheFS filesystem is unmounted or the client system is rebooted.

```
┌──────────────────────────────────────────────────────────────────────────┐
│  ros87252 (B1000 64-bit 11i)                                    _ □ X     │
├──────────────────────────────────────────────────────────────────────────┤
│ ros87252(/Cache/cachedir/00000180/00000100) -> ll                         │
│ total 10736                                                               │
│ -rw-rw-rw-   1 root      users        8192 Mar  9 17:07 00000118          │
│ -rw-rw-rw-   1 root      users        8192 Mar  9 17:06 00000126          │
│ -rw-rw-rw-   1 root      users      278528 Mar  9 17:07 00000127          │
│ -rw-rw-rw-   1 root      users    18952192 Mar  9 17:06 000001dd          │
│ -rw-rw-rw-   1 root      users        8192 Mar  9 17:07 000001de          │
│ -rw-rw-rw-   1 root      users       57089 Mar  9 17:07 000001df          │
│ -rw-rw-rw-   1 root      users        8192 Mar  9 17:06 000001e5          │
│                                                                           │
│ ros87252(/Cache/cachedir/00000180/00000100) -> umount /opt/netscape      │
│                                                                           │
│ ros87252(/Cache/cachedir/00000180/00000100) -> ll                         │
│ total 544                                                                 │
│ -rw-rw-rw-   1 root      users        8192 Mar  9 17:07 00000118          │
│ -rw-rw-rw-   1 root      users        8192 Mar  9 17:06 00000126          │
│ -rw-rw-rw-   1 root      users      278528 Mar  9 17:07 00000127          │
│ -rw-rw-rw-   1 root      users           0 Mar  9 17:09 000001dd          │
│ -rw-rw-rw-   1 root      users        8192 Mar  9 17:07 000001de          │
│ -rw-rw-rw-   1 root      users       57089 Mar  9 17:07 000001df          │
│ -rw-rw-rw-   1 root      users        8192 Mar  9 17:06 000001e5          │
└──────────────────────────────────────────────────────────────────────────┘
```

Figure 8.19   Cache Contents Before and After CacheFS Unmount

 KEY IDEA — The Importance of Patching the CacheFS Code

HP continually strives to improve the quality of HP-UX by distributing software patches containing both defect fixes and functionality enhancements. Many of these fixes and enhancements can significantly improve the performance and behavior of critical system components, such as the CacheFS product.

When CacheFS first shipped on HP-UX 11i, many of the features and core functionality were not working properly. Since that time, HP has resolved all known CacheFS defects and added several new performance features such as the *rpages* mount option. It is therefore *strongly* recommended that the latest NFS patch be installed on any 11i CacheFS client in order to take advantage of these new performance optimizations.

Contact HP support to obtain a current set of patches for your specific operating system. You can also generate a current patch list using the tools available at HP's IT Resource Center: *http://itrc.hp.com*.

For more information about the importance of patching HP-UX systems, refer to Appendix B "Patching Considerations."

## CHAPTER 9

NFS Protocol Version 2 vs.
NFS Protocol Version 3

T he NFS protocol continues to evolve over time. The original version of NFS, Protocol Version 1, existed only inside Sun Microsystems and was never released to the general public. Protocol Version 2 was introduced in 1984 as RFC1094.[1] PV2 has enjoyed a good deal of popularity as a file access protocol, and many customers continue to use NFS PV2 in their environments today. As time went by, some of the limitations imposed by the original Version 2 protocol design necessitated the development of an newer version of NFS — Protocol Version 3. The PV3 specification was released in June 1995 as RFC1813.[1] This version addressed many of PV2's identified shortcomings and introduced several behavioral and performance improvements. Today, NFS PV3 is by far the most widely used version of the NFS protocol. Most NFS vendors, including HP, support both PV2 and PV3 and allow systems administrators to specify which protocol version to use on a per-mount basis via the *vers* mount option.

While PV2 enjoyed a ten-year run before PV3 came about, Sun Microsystems (in conjunction with other vendors) has already completed the initial specification for Version 4 of the NFS protocol (RFC3010).[1] Since production-quality implementations of NFS PV4 were unavailable at the time of this writing, this book will concentrate on NFS PV2 and PV3.

This chapter discusses the many differences between the PV2 and PV3 protocols that directly affect NFS performance. It explains why an NFS PV3 filesystem will typically outperform a similarly configured PV2 filesystem. This chapter describes several scenarios where an NFS PV2 filesystem *may* outperform a PV3 filesystem, and the ways to reconfigure the PV3 filesystem in these situations to match the performance and behavior of PV2. Finally, it explains the criteria for deciding which NFS protocol is more appropriate to use in your environment.

---

1.   All RFC documents may be downloaded from the Internet Engineering Task Force web site: *http://ietf.org*.

9.1 Differences between NFS PV2 and NFS PV3

This section describes many of the functionality improvements made to the NFS Version 3 protocol. Many of these PV3 enhancements have a direct influence on NFS performance, including safe asynchronous writing, increased read and write buffer sizes, file and directory attribute caching improvements, and the newly introduced READDIRPLUS procedure. Other improvements affect the behavioral capabilities of the NFS client and server, such as support for large files and filesystems.

9.1.1 Maximum Supported File and Filesystem Sizes

PV2   The NFS PV2 protocol represents file offsets as signed 32-bit integers. This limited a PV2 client to accessing files up to 2GB. One of the primary design considerations for Version 3 was to increase this limit and allow clients to access much larger files.

PV3   The PV3 file offset fields were changed to unsigned 64-bit integers, which means the protocol allows a theoretical maximum file size of 16 exabytes (18,446,744,073,709,551,615 bytes). Of course, most of today's NFS server operating systems don't support creating files or filesystems anywhere near that size.

When discussing this topic, it is important to make a clear distinction between the supported maximum size of a *file* and the supported maximum size of a *filesystem*. While a system may only be able to create a *file* of a certain size, it may be able to create those files in a *filesystem* that is much larger. It is also important to understand the difference between the largest supported file or filesystem accessible by an *NFS client* and the largest file or filesystem supported on the *NFS server*.

HP-UX NFS Clients   An HP-UX 11.0 NFS client only supports accessing *files* as large as 1 terabyte.[2] This 1TB limit applies even when the 11.0 client has mounted an NFS filesystem from a server that supports files larger than 1TB. The largest supported *filesystem* an 11.0 NFS client may access is 2TB.[3] An HP-UX 11i client supports accessing NFS-mounted *files* as large as 2TB.[4] Again, this limit applies even when mounting filesystems from an NFS server that supports files larger than 2TB.

---

2.   Since the NFS PV3 protocol theoretically allows NFS clients to access files larger than 1TB, it may be *possible* for an HP-UX 11.0 client to access files larger than 1TB. However, HP only *supports* accessing files as large as 1TB from HP-UX 11.0 NFS clients.

3.   HP's NFS lab has fully tested both HP-UX 11.0 and 11i clients using 2TB NFS-mounted filesystems. At the time of this writing, HP was in the process of testing clients with filesystems mounted from a third party server that exceed the current 2TB limit of HP-UX. Until the results of these tests are finalized, the supported configuration remains accessing remote filesystems as large as 2TB from HP-UX NFS clients.

4.   Since the NFS PV3 protocol theoretically allows NFS clients to access files larger than 2TB, it may be *possible* for an HP-UX 11i client to access files larger than 2TB. However, HP only *supports* accessing files as large as 2TB from HP-UX 11i NFS clients.

HP-$u\mskip\!/\!x$11i	Difference Between HP-UX 11.0 and 11i: Maximum Supported NFS File Size

The largest file size currently supported by HP-UX 11.0 NFS clients is **1TB**. HP-UX 11i NFS clients may access files as large as **2TB**.

The differences between HP-UX versions that allow an 11i NFS client to access a 2TB file while limiting an 11.0 client to 1TB are not due to variations in the NFS implementations used by these operating systems, but rather differences in the supporting protocols that NFS is dependent on. For example, the Network Lock Manager protocol shares key kernel variable definitions with underlying local VxFS filesystem data structures. NLM is therefore subject to the same file size limitations as VxFS (VxFS file and filesystem limitations are discussed below).

In other words, an HP-UX 11.0 NFS PV3 client may be able to *write* to a file larger than 1TB,[5] but the client would not be able to set a *lock* on the file at an offset greater than 1TB. Again, this is not a limitation of the NFS protocol, but of HP's implementation of the Network Lock Manager protocol. Since NFS relies on NLM for file locking semantics, this NLM limitation does impose a limit on the maximum file sizes supported by HP-UX NFS clients.

HP-UX NFS Servers   The supported file and filesystem sizes on HP-UX servers depends upon the operating system running, and the local filesystem type (i.e. HFS or VxFS). Table 9.1 shows the various operating system and filesystem combinations available on current[6] HP-UX systems, as well as their associated limitations for supported file and filesystem sizes.

As Table 9.1 shows, HFS[7] filesystems are limited to a maximum size of 128GB on HP-UX 11.0 and 11i systems. Also, files built in an HFS filesystem are limited to a maximum size of 128GB. This implies that any NFS client accessing an exported HFS filesystem can only build files as large as 128GB.

Table 9.1 Maximum File and Filesystem Sizes Supported by HP-UX

HP-UX Release	FS Type	FS Version	Disk Layout	Max File Size	Max FS Size
11.0	HFS	N/A	N/A	128GB	128GB
11i	HFS	N/A	N/A	128GB	128GB

5.   Assuming the 11.0 client is writing to a file residing in an NFS PV3 filesystem that supports files larger than 1TB.

6.   The limits in Table 9.1 are for 11.0 and 11i. HP will be increasing these size limits in a future HP-UX release.

7.   For more information about the differences between HFS and VxFS filesystems, refer to Chapter 2 "Local Filesystem Considerations."

Table 9.1 Maximum File and Filesystem Sizes Supported by HP-UX

HP-UX Release	FS Type	FS Version	Disk Layout	Max File Size	Max FS Size
11.0	VxFS	3.1	2	2GB	128GB
11.0	VxFS	3.1	3 [a]	1TB	1TB
11.0	VxFS	3.3	2	2GB	128GB
11.0	VxFS	3.3	3	1TB	1TB
11.0	VxFS	3.3	4	1TB	1TB
11i	VxFS	3.3	2	2GB	128GB
11i	VxFS	3.3	3	2TB	2TB
11i	VxFS	3.3	4[a]	2TB	2TB

a.   This combination of VxFS filesystem version and disk layout version is the default for this HP-UX release.

VxFS filesystems allow for much larger files and filesystems, but only when using a VxFS disk layout Version of 3 or higher. This table shows that an HP-UX 11.0 server may build a VxFS filesystem as large as 1TB, while an 11i server may build VxFS filesystems as large as 2TB. Again, this implies that any NFS client accessing an exported VxFS filesystem (built using disk layout Version 3 or higher)[8] residing on an HP-UX 11.0 server can only build files as large as 1TB. Likewise, clients accessing an exported VxFS filesystem (using disk layout Version 3 or higher) residing on an HP-UX 11i server can build files as large as 2TB, providing the NFS client is capable of building files this large. Remember that HP-UX 11.0 NFS clients are only supported accessing files as large as 1TB, while 11i clients may access 2TB files.

HP-UX 11i **Difference Between HP-UX 11.0 and 11i: Maximum Supported VxFS File Size**

As of this writing, the largest file size supported by HP-UX 11.0 NFS servers is **1TB**. These 1TB files can only be created in VxFS 3.1 (or higher) filesystems using VxFS disk layout Version 3 or higher.

As of this writing, HP-UX 11i allows files as large as **2TB** to be created in VxFS 3.3 filesystems using disk layout Version 3 or higher.

---

8.   For more information about the various supported versions of VxFS and the available disk layout options, refer to the *HP JFS 3.3 and HP OnLineJFS 3.3 VERITAS File System 3.3 System Administrator's Guide for HP-UX 11.00 and HP-UX 11i* manual available online at *http://docs.hp.com*.

While this ability to access large files and filesystems is not directly related to NFS performance, it is one of the most prominent differences between NFS versions, and one of the most common reasons customers upgrade from NFS PV2 to PV3.

9.1.2 Safe Asynchronous Writing

PV2 "unsafe" asynchronous writing   When NFS Version 2 was introduced, one of the key features it offered was guaranteed data integrity when servicing write requests. It accomplished this by forcing the server to service all write requests with *synchronous* disc I/O, meaning that the server's nfsd would not reply to any write request until all the data and metadata associated with the request had been safely posted to disk.

Applications running on an NFS PV2 client did not need to specifically request synchronous write semantics to get this behavior. In fact, unless a PV2 client application opens the target file with the O_SYNC, O_DSYNC, or O_RSYNC flag, or the application locks the NFS-mounted target file,[9] it will write data for this file *asynchronously* to the client's local buffer cache. Again, it is the NFS PV2 server that enforces the synchronous write behavior by not allowing the nfsds to respond to write requests until the data has been safely written to the server's disks. While this synchronous approach guarantees data integrity for applications residing on NFS PV2 clients, the write performance of PV2 servers is generally considered poor.

After several years of enduring this synchronous behavior, systems administrators clamored for better write performance, even at the risk of possible data corruption. Many NFS vendors, including HP, made the decision to customize their PV2 server offerings to allow them to provide *asynchronous* write semantics.

In HP's PV2 implementation, the *async*[10] flag was added as an available exports(4) option. This new option instructed the server to relax the requirement of posting data to disk before replying by allowing the server's nfsd to reply to a write request as soon as the data in the request is copied to the server's buffer cache. The posting of data to physical disk takes place in the background on the server after the write reply is sent to the client. By letting the server reply prior to posting data to disk, the NFS client is able to send new write requests sooner, resulting in significant write performance gains.

Unfortunately, this improved write performance comes at a price. Since the server replies to write requests before safely posting the data to physical disk, a timing window exists where a client application could experience unreported data loss. If the server crashes after replying to a write request, any data blocks associated with this request that are queued for the server's disk, but have not yet been written to the disk, will be lost.

---

9.   HP recently modified this behavior of forcing all write requests to locked files synchronously. To learn more about configuring an NFS client to write asynchronously to locked files, see Section 3.3.4.

10.   For more information on exporting filesystems with the *async* option, refer to the exports(4) man page.

 KEY IDEA — The PV2 *async* Export Option

The resulting PV2 write performance gains seen using the *async* option are tremendous, in some cases increasing 20 times over the default synchronous behavior. The only downside of exporting filesystems in this manner is the slight potential for data loss during a server system crash.

Realistically, the window of opportunity for data loss is extremely small, so most NFS PV2 customers are willing to risk the outside chance of data corruption to gain the write performance benefits.

Strictly from a performance standpoint, the recommendation is to export any filesystems that will be mounted by NFS PV2 clients with the *async* option. However, the decision to export a filesystem with the *async* option should only be made after carefully weighing the performance benefits against the potential risk of data corruption.

The *async* export option has no effect on NFS PV3 client or server semantics. This option only affects NFS PV2 write requests.

PV3 "safe" asynchronous writing   While customers loved the performance gains provided by asynchronous NFS write semantics, they complained about having to compromise data integrity to get this performance benefit. NFS developers took this matter into consideration while designing the Version 3 protocol and came up with a "safe" method of performing asynchronous writes. This "safe" writing method became the default write semantic used by NFS PV3 clients and servers.

The main design premise of the PV3 write mechanism is to force the NFS client to maintain a copy of any data it sends to the server in its local buffer cache memory and only discard this local copy once it is certain that the data has been safely posted to the server's stable storage, and that the server did not reboot while writing this data. If the client learns that the server crashed while servicing the WRITE requests, it will re-send the data and once again wait for confirmation that the data is safely on the server's disks before discarding the local copy.

Figure 9.1 shows an example of an NFS PV3 client writing to a server that remains running while servicing the client's WRITE requests. Figure 9.2 depicts the same client writing to a different file on the same server, and it demonstrates how the Version 3 protocol handles the case where the server reboots while processing WRITE requests. These two examples reveal the many changes made to the PV3 protocol to implement the "safe" asynchronous writing mechanism, including the addition of the *stable*, *committed*, and *verf* fields to the PV3 WRITE request and reply packets, and the new COMMIT procedure.

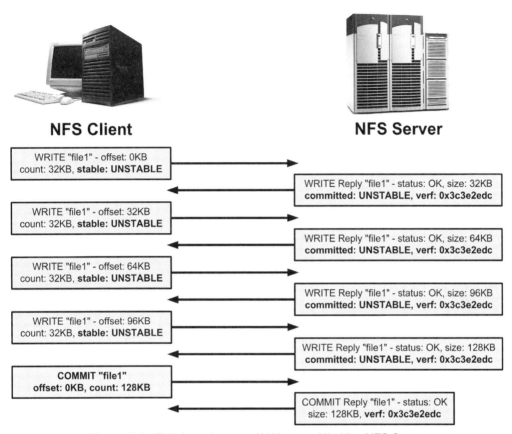

NFS Client   **NFS Server**

WRITE "file1" - offset: 0KB
count: 32KB, **stable: UNSTABLE**

WRITE Reply "file1" - status: OK, size: 32KB
committed: UNSTABLE, verf: 0x3c3e2edc

WRITE "file1" - offset: 32KB
count: 32KB, **stable: UNSTABLE**

WRITE Reply "file1" - status: OK, size: 64KB
committed: UNSTABLE, verf: 0x3c3e2edc

WRITE "file1" - offset: 64KB
count: 32KB, **stable: UNSTABLE**

WRITE Reply "file1" - status: OK, size: 96KB
committed: UNSTABLE, verf: 0x3c3e2edc

WRITE "file1" - offset: 96KB
count: 32KB, **stable: UNSTABLE**

WRITE Reply "file1" - status: OK, size: 128KB
committed: UNSTABLE, verf: 0x3c3e2edc

COMMIT "file1"
offset: 0KB, count: 128KB

COMMIT Reply "file1" - status: OK
size: 128KB, **verf: 0x3c3e2edc**

Figure 9.1 PV3 Asynchronous Writing to a Working NFS Server

stable The *stable* field was added to the PV3 WRITE request packet, allowing the client to instruct the server how it should handle the task of committing the data contained in the request to stable storage before replying. Possible values for this field include:

- FILE_SYNC — the server ***must*** commit all data contained in the request plus all filesystem metadata to disk before returning results. This corresponds to the PV2 write semantics.
- DATA_SYNC — the server ***must*** commit all of the data to stable storage and enough of the metadata to allow retrieval of the data before returning. The server is not required to commit all filesystem metadata, as in the FILE_SYNC case; however, NFS PV3 server vendors are free to implement DATA_SYNC in the same fashion as FILE_SYNC.
- UNSTABLE — the server is free to commit any part of the data and the metadata to stable storage, ***including all or none***, before returning a reply to the client. There is no guarantee whether or when any uncommitted data will subsequently be committed to stable storage.

committed   The *committed* field was added to the PV3 WRITE reply packet, allowing the server to inform the client how much of the data contained in its WRITE request, and any associated filesystem metadata, was committed to stable storage before the server replied. Possible values for this field include:

- FILE_SYNC — the server committed all data and metadata to stable storage before replying. If the client requested FILE_SYNC semantics via the **stable** flag, then the server is required to send back a **committed** status of FILE_SYNC.
- DATA_SYNC — the server committed all data and enough metadata to allow retrieval of this data to stable storage before replying. If **stable** was set to DATA_SYNC, then **committed** may be FILE_SYNC or DATA_SYNC.
- UNSTABLE — the server did not commit all data and metadata to disk before replying. If **stable** was set to UNSTABLE, then **committed** may be either FILE_SYNC, DATA_SYNC, or UNSTABLE.

The PV3 protocol allows a server to commit *more* data to disk than the client requested (i.e. a client may request DATA_SYNC semantics and the server is allowed to return a committed status of FILE_SYNC), but the server is never allowed to commit *less* data than requested by the client.

verf   The *verf* (*verifier*) field was added to the PV3 WRITE reply packet, which contains information that the client can use to determine whether the server has crashed and recovered while servicing the client's WRITE requests. The client stores the verifier value along with its local copy of the WRITE data, and it compares these WRITE verifiers against the verifier it eventually receives in a COMMIT reply (COMMIT is explained in the next section) to determine whether the server system rebooted while servicing these WRITE and COMMIT calls.

The verifier must be a unique value that only changes when the server system reboots. For this reason, HP (and most other NFS vendors) use the server system's boot time as the verifier value, as this is a unique value that is guaranteed to change when the server system reboots.

COMMIT   The COMMIT procedure was added to the PV3 protocol to allow an NFS client to instruct the server that it *must* post all data referenced in the request to stable storage. The NFS server is not allowed to reply to the COMMIT request until all data, and any associated filesystem metadata, are committed to disk.

The COMMIT reply contains the same *verf* field as the WRITE replies. When the client receives the COMMIT reply, it compares the COMMIT verifier against the verifiers returned previously in the WRITE replies. If the WRITE verifiers match the COMMIT verifier then the client is confident that all data has been safely written to the server's stable storage, and that the server did not reboot while servicing these requests. If the verifiers do not match, the client knows it must re-send the data and wait for confirmation that the server successfully posted the data to disk without rebooting.

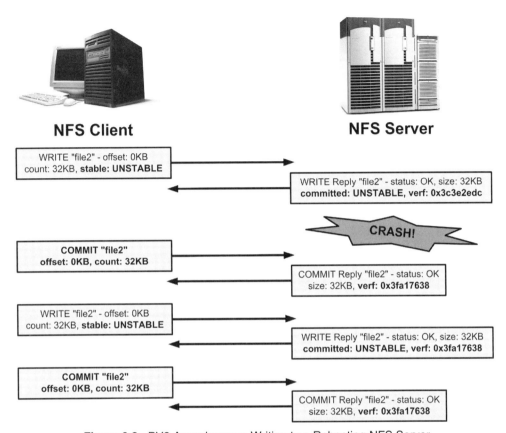

Figure 9.2 PV3 Asynchronous Writing to a Rebooting NFS Server

In the examples shown in Figure 9.1 and Figure 9.2, the client uses the stable field to request UNSTABLE semantics, allowing the server to commit all or none of the data to disk before replying. In most NFS PV3 implementations, including HP-UX, the NFS server will reply to an UNSTABLE WRITE request as soon as it has stored the data from the request into its buffer cache memory. Looking at the WRITE replies in these examples, the server responds with a committed value of UNSTABLE, indicating that the client's data was not posted to disk before the server's reply was sent. The server's kernel will subsequently schedule this data to be written to disk after replying.

This behavior of replying before the data is posted to physical media provides the same performance benefit of PV2's "unsafe" asynchronous writing method, as it allows greater parallelism between the client, the server, and the server's storage. Also, by scheduling the data to be written to stable storage after replying, the hope is that by the time the client sends a COMMIT request — demanding that the server post all remaining data to disk before replying — the server will have already stored most or all of the client's data to disk, and will therefore have little work to do before replying to the COMMIT.

In Figure 9.1, the verifier value remains consistent throughout all WRITE and COMMIT replies, letting the client know that the server successfully posted all data to disk and it did not reboot while doing so. The client therefore knows it can safely discard its copy of this data from the local buffer cache. In Figure 9.2, the initial COMMIT reply contains a different verifier than the preceding WRITE reply, indicating that the server must have rebooted while processing these requests. The client knows it must send this data again and wait for confirmation that the data was safely posted to the server's disks (via matching WRITE and COMMIT verifier values) before discarding the local copy.

The PV3 asynchronous write mechanism is especially effective when writing large files. As Figure 9.1 shows, a client may send many WRITE requests followed by a single COMMIT to flush the entire file to disk when it closes the file. This allows the server to potentially post the file data to stable storage in a single contiguous chunk, which most local filesystems (VxFS included) handle more efficiently than a series of small writes.

 KEY IDEA — PV3 *write()* vs. *close()* Delay Times

An interesting side effect witnessed by many customers who have migrated from NFS PV2 to PV3, and use applications that write data asynchronously across NFS-mounted filesystems, is an increase in the delay experienced by these applications when closing the files to which they write. To understand why a longer *close()* delay may be expected with NFS PV3 you need to first understand the difference between how the NFS client handles the *write()* system call versus how the *close()*, *sync()*, and *flush()* system calls are handled.

When an NFS client application issues a *write()* system call, the call completes as soon as the data is written to the client's local buffer cache. The client's biods take this data from buffer cache and send it to the server asynchronously in the background. It is only when the application later calls *sync()*, *flush()*, or *close()* against this file that the client must send any remaining data in its buffer cache to the server, and wait for notification that the server has received the data and committed it to stable storage, before the system call can complete. This explains why an application writing asynchronously to an NFS filesystem will see very fast *write()* system call completion times (assuming there is sufficient room in the client's buffer cache to store the data) and then experience a comparatively long delay when closing the file.

With this in mind, it is understandable that a PV3 client would experience longer delays at file *close()* time than a PV2 client writing asynchronously, since the posting of data to a PV2 server is considered complete once the server copies the data into its buffer cache and replies, whereas posting data to a PV3 server is not considered complete until all data is committed to physical disk and the server replies to the client's final COMMIT request. In other words, the *close()* system call can complete on an NFS PV2 client while the PV2 server is still posting data to stable storage, but this system call will not complete on a PV3 client until the PV3 server has finished posting all data to stable storage.

9.1.3 Increased `READ` and `WRITE` Request Sizes

PV2 The maximum size of an individual `READ` or `WRITE` request on an NFS PV2 filesystem is **8KB**. This is also the default size of PV2 `READ` and `WRITE` requests.

PV3 In HP's NFS PV3 implementation, the maximum `READ` and `WRITE` size is increased to **32KB**.

HP-UX 11i   **Difference Between HP-UX 11.0 and 11i:**
PV3 Maximum and Default I/O Request Sizes

When HP-UX 11.0 was released, an 11.0 PV3 *client* was only capable of issuing `READ` and `WRITE` requests as large as **8KB**, while an HP-UX 11.0 PV3 *server* was capable of handling 32KB `READ` and `WRITE` requests issued by non-HP clients. Support for 32KB PV3 client requests was added to HP-UX 11.0 via patches in March 2000.

Even with the latest NFS patches installed, the default size of `READ` and `WRITE` requests made by 11.0 clients remains **8KB**. The *rsize=32768*[a] and *wsize=32768*[a] mount options must be used to force an 11.0 client to issue 32KB `READ` and `WRITE` requests respectively.

HP-UX 11i shipped with full support for **32KB** requests, both as a PV3 client and server. The default size of `READ` and `WRITE` requests issued by 11i PV3 clients is **32KB**.

---

a.   Refer to the mount_nfs(1M) man page for more information about the *rsize* and *wsize* mount options.

9.1.4 Improved Attribute Retrieval and Caching

Attribute caching has long been a feature used by NFS clients to improve performance. By keeping a local cache of file and directory attributes, the client avoids making `LOOKUP` and `GETATTR` calls over the wire prior to every file access. Although these attributes are cached on the client, the client still needs to get the initial values for these file and directory attributes from the server when accessing an object on the server the first time. Additionally, the client needs to update its cache whenever it modifies an object on the server.

PV2 The PV2 server only returns updated attribute information when a client request results in modifying the contents of a server's file or directory. Only post-operation attributes are returned by the server in these case — i.e. the state of the file or directory after the server finished processing the client's request.

PV3 Every reply packet returned by a PV3 server includes current attribute information for the file or directory referenced in the client's request, thus eliminating the need for a subsequent `GETATTR` call to update the client's attribute cache. In cases where a client's operation results in modifying the attributes of both a file and a directory, the server's reply includes updated attribute information for both the file and the directory objects. Also, in cases where a client's request causes the contents of a server's file to be modified (such as a WRITE or SETATTR request), the server's reply contains two sets of attribute data for the file:

- **Pre-operation attributes** — the state of the file *before* the file was modified
- **Post-operation attributes** — the state of the file *after* the file was modified

Figure 9.3 and Figure 9.4 contain examples of NFS PV2 and PV3 WRITE reply packets respectively.

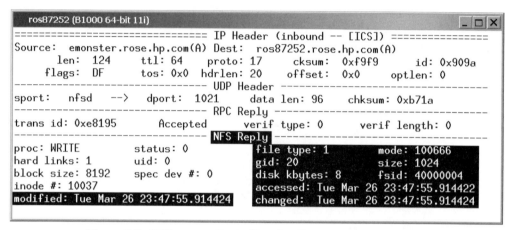

Figure 9.3 PV2 WRITE Reply Showing Post-operation Attributes

Weak Cache Consistency   PV2 and PV3 clients cache both file attributes and data to improve performance. The way a PV2 client determines whether its cached copy of a file is up-to-date is by sending GETATTR requests and comparing the file modification times it receives in the GETATTR reply against its cached file's attributes. If the modification time in the GETATTR reply matches the modification time in the attribute cache, then the client assumes its cached data is accurate. If the modification times do not match, the client assumes that the server's file contents must have changed and the client should invalidate its cached copy.

This mechanism of comparing modification times works well in most cases, but poses a dilemma in the case where an NFS client is modifying file data on the server. For example, the PV2 WRITE reply packet shown in Figure 9.3 illustrates how the PV2 server's reply only contains the attributes of the file after the file was modified. With only these post-operation attributes as a guide, the PV2 client has no way of knowing for certain whether its locally cached copy of this file is valid. For example, if a client writes to one part of a file, the cached data for the remainder of the file is probably still valid but the client cannot be sure since the client's own WRITE request updated the file's modification time. At this point, the PV2 client does not know whether it should keep the remaining cached data and risk potential data corruption, or discard its cached version and risk degrading performance.

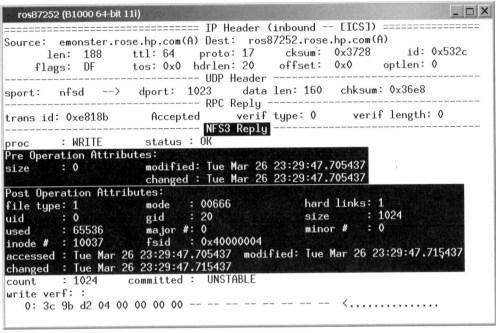

Figure 9.4 PV3 `WRITE` Reply Showing Pre and Post Attributes

As Figure 9.4 shows, the reply packet for each PV3 `WRITE` request includes the attributes of the file from just before the server performed the operation and the attributes from just after the operation completed. By using these pre-operation and post-operation file attributes, the PV3 client is able to determine when *its own request* is the one that caused a server's file attributes to change, allowing the PV3 client to intelligently determine when to invalidate its cached data. This mechanism is commonly referred to as *Weak Cache Consistency*.

In other words, if the modification time in the pre-operation attributes matches the client's cached modification time for this file, then the client knows its cache was up-to-date at the time the server performed its request. The client therefore knows its request caused the file's modification time to change in the post-operation attributes, and the client should update its local attribute cache with these new post-operation attributes. If the pre-operation attributes contained in the server's reply do not match the client's cached attributes for this file then the client knows the server's file must have been modified before the server received its request, and the client should therefore invalidate its cached version of this file.

9.1.6 The `READDIRPLUS` Procedure

PV2   When a user issues the "`ls -l`" command in an NFS PV2 filesystem, the client system must not only read the contents of the server's directory (i.e. the list of file names and their associated inode numbers) but also retrieve the attributes for every file in the directory. The

PV2 client uses READDIR calls to obtain the list of files and inodes, and then issues a LOOKUP call for each file in the directory to retrieve the file's attributes. In directories containing hundreds or thousands of files, a single "ls -l" command may require thousands of NFS requests to retrieve the directory contents and attribute data.

PV3   The designers of NFS PV3 created a new procedure called READDIRPLUS that combines the functionality of the READDIR and LOOKUP operations. When the "ls -l" command is issued on a PV3 client, it generates a READDIRPLUS call, instructing the server to return not only the list of files in the directory, but all of their accompanying attributes as well. In directories containing hundreds or thousands of files, READDIRPLUS can dramatically cut down on the number of NFS requests needed to retrieve the list of files and their attributes.

Since a READDIRPLUS reply packet contains substantially more information about each file than a READDIR reply, fewer files can be represented in a READDIRPLUS reply than a READDIR reply. Thus, a PV3 client may need to issue more READDIRPLUS requests than a PV2 client issuing READDIR requests to traverse a given directory. However, by avoiding the subsequent LOOKUP calls, the PV3 client greatly reduces the load on the network and the server.

Even with relatively small directories, the READDIRPLUS mechanism requires fewer NFS transactions to complete, saving client and server overhead and decreasing overall network utilization. Consider the following "ls" command issued in an NFS mounted directory:

```
# ls -l /nfs_mount
-rw-rw-rw-    1 root  users       111599 Apr   7 12:27 testfile1
-rwxr--r--    1 root  users         4836 Apr   7 12:27 testfile2
-rw-rw-rw-    1 root  users            6 Apr   7 12:27 testfile3
```

A network trace, shown in Figure 9.5, reveals the amount of PV2 network traffic required to complete this simple "ls" command.

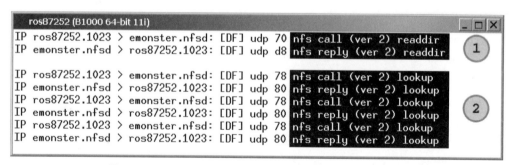

Figure 9.5   NFS PV2 nettl Trace of "ls -l" Command

The PV2 client was able to retrieve all 3 file names and inode numbers with a single READDIR call (section 1 in Figure 9.5), but then needed to make three LOOKUP calls (section 2 of Figure 9.5) to retrieve their extended attributes. A total of eight NFS PV2 request and reply packets were used to generate this "ls -l" screen output.

An NFS PV3 client reading the same directory via the "ls -l" command needs to issue only a single READDIRPLUS call to retrieve the list of three files, their inode numbers, and their extended attributes, thus reducing the number of NFS packets required to complete the "ls" command from eight (READDIR/LOOKUP) to two (READDIRPLUS).

Figure 9.6 shows both a one-line formatted version of a network trace of the single READDIRPLUS request (section 1 of Figure 9.6) and several of the formatted file entries contained in the READDIRPLUS reply (section 2).

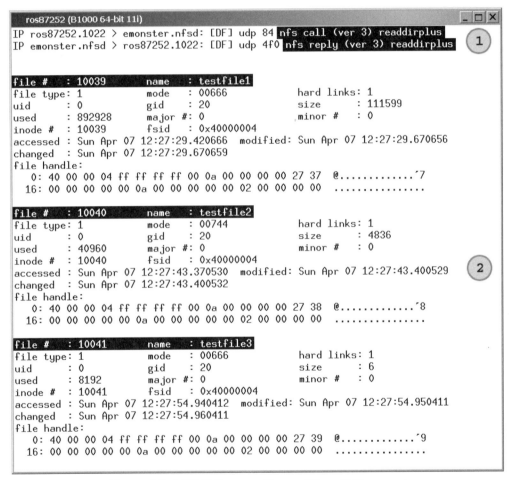

Figure 9.6 NFS PV3 nettl Trace of "ls -l" Command

Even this simple example shows how the READDIRPLUS procedure can reduce network traffic and client/server overhead. Again, the effect of READDIRPLUS becomes even more prominent when traversing large directories containing hundreds or thousands of files.

NFS Performance Example: READDIR vs. READDIRPLUS

The find(1) command is one of the most frequently issued systems administration tools on UNIX-based systems. It is used to locate files or directories within a specified filesystem, and it is supported on most UNIX and Linux-based platforms, including HP-UX. Prior to the release of NFS Version 3, a common customer complaint regarding the find(1) command was the amount of time and resources (both system and network) it consumed when traversing very large NFS-mounted filesystems.

Consider the following example:

```
NFS PV2> timex find /nfs_mount/20K_Files > /dev/null

real      6:44.53
user        0.21
sys         2.55

NFS PV2> nfsstat -c
Client nfs:
lookup                          readdir
19905 99%                       60 0%
```

In this example, an NFS filesystem containing 19,903 files was mounted using PV2 and searched using the find(1) command. The command took nearly 405 seconds to finish and it required nearly 20,000 NFS calls — 19905 of them being LOOKUP calls.

When this same filesystem is mounted using NFS PV3, the following results are achieved:

```
NFS PV3> timex find /nfs_mount/20K_Files > /dev/null

real       47.19
user        0.16
sys         1.58

NFS PV3> nfsstat -c
Client nfs:
lookup                          readdir+
1 0%                            478 84%
```

The find(1) command is able to traverse the same filesystem in only 47 seconds when PV3 is used. The PV3 test required less than 500 NFS calls to complete — 478 of which being READDIRPLUS calls. This is a good example of how the PV3 READDIRPLUS procedure can dramatically reduce network overhead (500 PV3 calls vs. 20,000 PV2 calls) and wall-clock time (47 seconds vs. 405 seconds) in these situations.

9.2 Will a PV3 Installation *Always* Outperform PV2?

Given all of the performance enhancements added to the Version 3 protocol, it should come as no surprise that PV3 will usually outperform similarly configured PV2. However, this is not always the case. There are situations where a PV2 filesystem may provide better performance than a PV3 counterpart. Fortunately, even in these rare cases, there are ways to configure the PV3 client and server to match or exceed the PV2 performance.

9.2.1 Asynchronous WRITE Performance

We learned all about the PV3 "safe" asynchronous writing mechanism back in Section 9.1.2, and how this model differs from the "unsafe" method used by PV2. The PV3 write method guarantees data integrity and dramatically improves write performance over the conventional PV2 *synchronous* writing method. While PV3 write performance is comparable to PV2 *asynchronous* write speed, writing asynchronously on a PV2 filesystem may yield higher throughput than PV3, since PV2 writing is not subject to any of the overhead associated with the PV3 "safe" mechanism, including maintaining local copies of data in the client's buffer cache, processing write verifiers, generating commit calls and replies, comparing commit verifiers, etc.

Configuring PV3 to meet or exceed PV2 performance Any overhead added by the PV3 "safe" mechanism can usually be offset by utilizing the larger WRITE buffer size available to NFS PV3 filesystems. Remember that PV2 WRITE requests are limited to 8KB of data, while PV3 filesystems allow WRITE requests containing up to 32KB of data. This larger request size allows a PV3 client to complete an I/O-intensive operation, such as writing a large file, in fewer requests than a PV2 client requires to complete the same operation.

As an example, Table 9.2 summarizes three test results of writing a 1GB file to an NFS filesystem using various mount option combinations. The table shows the NFS protocol version, the size of the WRITE requests, the number of WRITE requests, and the elapsed time of each test.

Table 9.2 Results of 1GB Asynchronous Write via PV2 and PV3

NFS Version	*wsize* Value	WRITE Requests	Elapsed Time
2	8192 Bytes	131072	79 Seconds
3	8192 Bytes	131072	94 Seconds
3	**32768 Bytes**	**32768**	**70 Seconds**

This table shows that a sample NFS client was able to write a 1GB file approximately 16% faster on a PV2 filesystem than on a PV3 filesystem when 8KB WRITE requests were used. When the client wrote the same 1GB file to a PV3 filesystem using 32KB WRITE requests, the test completed more than 11% faster than the PV2 test, illustrating how the larger WRITE requests available in PV3 more than compensate for the overhead added by the "safe" asynchronous writing mechanism.

Keep in mind that NFS throughput varies based on numerous factors, including the systems and networks used, so your WRITE throughput results will definitely vary from those shown in Table 9.2. These results are presented merely to illustrate the beneficial effect of 32KB WRITE requests on the PV3 "safe" asynchronous writing mechanism.

 KEY IDEA — The Influence of I/O Request Sizes on NFS Retransmissions

When sending an NFS request or reply on the network, the IP code on the sending system will fragment the outbound NFS message into IP datagram fragments based on the MTU (Maximum Transmission Unit) size of the network interface being used, and the size of the network protocol headers (i.e. IP, UDP, TCP). For example, Ethernet networks typically use an MTU size of 1500 bytes, a typical IP header is 20 bytes, and a typical TCP header is 20 bytes, so the maximum amount of application data (NFS, in this case) contained in a typical IP datagram is 1460 bytes.

That being the case, an 8KB NFS message would need to be broken down into 6 separate IP datagrams (8192 bytes / 1460 = 6 datagrams). Likewise, a 32KB NFS message would require 23 IP datagrams (32768 bytes / 1460 = 23 datagrams). Thus, as the size of NFS requests and replies increases, so too does the number of individual network packets needed to transmit these messages.

This increase in network packets is an important consideration in NFS environments where packet loss is occurring — especially those environments where NFS filesystems are mounted using **UDP** as the underlying network transport protocol.

It is important to understand how NFS deals with request retransmissions differently depending upon whether the UDP or TCP transport is used.[a] The TCP protocol includes a guaranteed notification mechanism that informs the sending and receiving systems of the successful delivery of their data. If a single **TCP** packet of an NFS message is lost, the **TCP transport on the sending system will re-send only the missing TCP packet**.

The UDP protocol has no such guaranteed notification mechanism, so if any of the **UDP** packets of an NFS message are lost, **the entire NFS/UDP message must be retransmitted by the sending system**. In other words, if an 8KB NFS/UDP request is lost, all 8192 bytes must be re-sent. Similarly, if a 32KB request is lost, all 32768 bytes must be re-sent.

If an existing NFS/UDP PV2 environment is currently experiencing timeouts and retransmissions (which can be determined via the nfsstat(1M) command), moving to 32KB PV3 requests will likely cause the number of NFS/UDP retransmissions to increase, resulting in a decrease in NFS throughput. In this case, NFS/TCP may be a better solution.

---

a.   This issue of how NFS handles retransmissions and timeouts differently for UDP and TCP, as well as many other differences between the UDP and TCP network protocols, is covered in detail in Chapter 10.

9.2.2 32KB I/O Requests and UDP Retransmissions

The test results shown in Table 9.2 illustrate how the larger request sizes supported by PV3 will generally result in better NFS throughput than PV2. However, there are situations where these large PV3 requests can be detrimental to NFS throughput. Any NFS/UDP environments that are susceptible to network packet loss would be poor candidates for using the larger PV3 request sizes, including:

- Heavily Congested Networks
- Overloaded NFS Servers
- Wide Area Networks

Configuring PV3 to meet or exceed PV2 performance   If the use of 32KB PV3 requests causes NFS/UDP timeouts and retransmissions to increase, the *rsize=8192* and *wsize=8192* mount options[11] can be used to tune the size of NFS READ and WRITE requests respectively to match the PV2 8KB sizes. Alternately, you can configure your NFS filesystems to use the TCP network transport protocol by specifying the *proto=tcp* mount option,[11] so that if network packets are lost, only those individual packets need to be re-sent.

9.2.3 Directory Retrieval where Attribute Data *Is Not* Needed

Back in Section 9.1.5 we learned how the READDIRPLUS procedure was added to PV3 to eliminate the need of sending LOOKUP requests for every file in a directory to retrieve its attributes. In large directories this can save hundreds or even thousands of LOOKUP calls. However, in cases where the application requesting the directory data needs only the list of files and their inode numbers and has no need for the extended attribute data, READDIRPLUS can add a tremendous amount of unnecessary overhead and cause applications to perform significantly worse on PV3 clients than on PV2 clients.

Many users have reported experiencing a decrease in application performance after migrating their clients and servers from NFS PV2 to PV3. Upon analyzing these environments, it is usually discovered that their applications are retrieving the contents of NFS-mounted directories containing hundreds (and in some cases many thousands) of files, and these applications have no need for the extended file attributes associated with these files. This is a classic example of READDIRPLUS adding unwanted overhead by retrieving file attributes when they are not required by an application.

Unfortunately, there is no way to configure an NFS client to automatically know when it is preferable to issue a READDIR call to retrieve the list of files and inode numbers, as opposed to making a READDIRPLUS call and retrieving the files and all attribute data. This unwanted READDIRPLUS overhead has caused many PV3 customers to consider reverting to PV2.

---

11.   Refer to the mount_nfs(1M) man page for a detailed explanation of these NFS mount options.

Configuring PV3 to meet or exceed PV2 performance This issue has prompted many PV3 users to ask: *"How can I continue using NFS PV3, which I need to take advantage of features like large file support, without paying the* READDIRPLUS *performance penalty?"* Fortunately, HP provides a solution — allowing READDIRPLUS to be disabled on the NFS server.

 KEY IDEA — Disabling NFS PV3 Server-Side
READDIRPLUS Support

On HP-UX 11.0 and 11i systems, the server-side READDIRPLUS feature may be disabled by modifying the undocumented ***do_readdirplus*** kernel variable. This variable is not currently configurable via the normal supported methods such as sam(1M) or kmtune(1M). The only way to change this variable is via the adb(1) command.

When READDIRPLUS is disabled using the procedure described below, the server will respond to any inbound READDIRPLUS request with the error NFS3ERR_NOTSUPP (operation is not supported). This causes the PV3 client to revert to the PV2 READDIR/LOOKUP method of obtaining directory contents for the specific filesystem that returned NFS3ERR_NOTSUPP. This client will continue to use the READDIR/LOOKUP method until the filesystem that returned the error is unmounted and re-mounted. At that time, the client will begin sending READDIRPLUS requests again.

Of course, if READDIRPLUS support is still disabled, the server will reply with an NFS3ERR_NOTSUPP error, forcing the client to once again revert to the PV2 READDIR/LOOKUP method.

WARNING — This procedure should be used with caution, as it disables READDIRPLUS functionality for any NFS PV3 client (HP or otherwise) that mounts filesystems from the server.

To disable READDIRPLUS on an HP-UX 11.0 or 11i server, log into the server as root and issue the following commands:

```
# echo 'do_readdirplus/W 0d0' | adb -w /stand/vmunix /dev/kmem
# echo 'do_readdirplus?W 0d0' | adb -w /stand/vmunix /dev/kmem
```

Two separate adb commands are used in this case to modify both the on-disk kernel file (?W syntax) and kernel memory (/W syntax). This allows the change to take effect immediately and remain in effect even if the server is rebooted.

The *do_readdirplus* parameter will be reset to 1 if the kernel is re-built, either manually (via the mk_kernel(1M) command) or by installing a kernel patch. This should be kept in mind when installing kernel patches on a system where *do_readdirplus* is intentionally modified.

9.3 Should You Use NFS PV2 or PV3 in Your Environment?

Given all of the enhanced functionality and new features introduced in NFS Version 3, most NFS environments will benefit from using PV3 rather than PV2. From a performance perspective, there are very few cases where an NFS PV2 will outperform similarly configured PV3, and even in those rare situations the PV3 client or server can be configured to match or exceed the performance of PV2. The recommendation is to use **NFS PV3** wherever possible.

 KEY IDEA — The Importance of Patching PV2 and PV3 Kernel and User-space Code

HP continually strives to improve the quality of HP-UX by distributing software patches containing both defect fixes and functionality enhancements. Many of these fixes and enhancements can significantly improve the performance and behavior of critical system components, such as the NFS PV2 and PV3 kernel and user-space code.

When HP-UX 11.0 first shipped, the PV3 implementation did not support features like 32KB READ and WRITE requests. Since that time, HP has added support for these large I/O requests and resolved many other functionality issues affecting both PV2 and PV3 performance and behavior. It is therefore *strongly* recommended that the latest NFS patch be installed on every HP-UX system in order to take advantage of these new performance optimizations.

Contact HP support to obtain a current set of patches for your specific operating system. You can also generate a current patch list using the tools available at HP's IT Resource Center: *http://itrc.hp.com*.

For more information about the importance of patching HP-UX systems, refer to Appendix B "Patching Considerations."

NFS/UDP vs. NFS/TCP

W hen NFS Version 2 was first being developed in the early 1980s, the majority of network-connected computer systems resided in local-area networks. This being the case, NFS designers selected the *User Datagram Protocol*, or *UDP*,[1] as the network transport on which to implement NFS. The *connectionless* semantics of UDP provided a lightweight and efficient mechanism for sending and receiving transactions in a local-area network. In fact, the Remote Procedure Call protocol (RPC) used by Sun Microsystems' initial NFS Version 2 implementation specifically assumed that the underlying network transport protocol would be UDP.

Over time, as client and server systems became geographically dispersed across wide-area networks, it became increasingly apparent that a better method of guaranteeing data delivery in these distributed environments was needed. While NFS PV3 was under development, a "transport independent" version of RPC (TI-RPC) was introduced, allowing NFS to take advantage of *connection-oriented* network transports, such as the *Transmission Control Protocol*, or *TCP*.[2]

The TCP transport protocol is available in most NFS implementations, including HP's, and it is considered an integral component of the overall infrastructure needed to support today's distributed applications. HP-UX 11.0 and 11i systems fully support both the UDP and TCP transports in conjunction with NFS PV2 and PV3 filesystems. The systems administrator may specify the desired network transport protocol on a per-mount basis via the *proto* mount option.

Since both UDP and TCP protocols are supported by HP's NFS implementation, the question is: "Which one should you use?" Most systems administrators tend to assume that UDP

1.   The User Datagram Protocol is documented in RFC768.

2.   The Transmission Control Protocol is documented in RFC793 and later RFCs.

should always be used in local-area networks and TCP should be used in wide-area networks. While there are definite advantages to using UDP in LANs and TCP in WANs, there are many situations where TCP may be a better choice in a LAN environment. Therefore, when deciding which underlying network protocol to use for a specific NFS-mounted filesystem, it helps to have a good understanding of the differences between these two transport mechanisms and how these differences can benefit or hinder NFS performance in your environment.

This chapter explains the many ways in which NFS behaves differently when used with the UDP and TCP transport protocols, and how these differences can influence NFS performance. It begins by describing many of the behavioral characteristics of UDP and TCP, such as how connections between client and server systems are managed, and how these characteristics contribute to the amount of overhead induced by each protocol. This is followed by an explanation of how NFS retransmissions and timeouts are handled differently by UDP and TCP, and the potentially dramatic effect this can have on NFS throughput. Finally, several typical NFS environments are presented, each denoting whether the UDP or TCP transport would likely yield superior NFS performance.

HP-11i   **Difference Between HP-UX 11.0 and 11i: NFS/TCP Support**

When HP-UX 11.0 released, the only network transport supported by NFS was **UDP**. HP added support for NFS/TCP via patches introduced in March 2000. Even after installing these patches on both client and server systems, UDP remains the default protocol used by NFS until NFS/TCP is manually enabled via the `setoncenv(1M)` command. The following screen shot shows the syntax used to enable NFS/TCP on HP-UX 11.0 systems.

```
 atc01 (L2000 64-bit 11.0)                                            _ □ X
atc01(/home/dolker) -> setoncenv NFS_TCP 1
The write to /etc/rc.config.d/nfsconf with NFS_TCP=1 succeeded

You must stop and restart the NFS Server and
NFS Client to take advantage of NFS over TCP.
This can be done by using the NFS client script.
/sbin/init.d/nfs.client.  Issue the following
commands:

        /sbin/init.d/nfs.client stop
        /sbin/init.d/nfs.client start
```

Once TCP is properly enabled on both the client and server, *TCP becomes the default network transport protocol used for all HP-UX 11.0 NFS mounts.*

NFS/TCP support is included and enabled on HP-UX 11i systems by default. **TCP** is the default transport protocol used for NFS mounts on 11i.

10.1   Overview of UDP and TCP

UDP is commonly described as a *connectionless* or *unreliable* network transport. It is a very lightweight protocol designed to quickly and efficiently deliver IP datagrams between systems. The term "unreliable" is used because UDP does not notify the sending system when an IP datagram fails to arrive at its destination. The term "connectionless" indicates that the client and server do not establish a lasting connection with each other. It is up to the application, NFS in this case, to make sure that data arrives, and take appropriate action when it does not.

TCP is a *connection-oriented* transport that maintains established connections between systems and guarantees *reliable* notification when delivery of data fails for any reason. As you might expect, the reliability provided by TCP does not come without some overhead. There is connection management overhead (i.e. connection establishment and tear down), tracking of sequence and acknowledgement information, congestion control, error recovery, etc. All of these features make TCP a superior protocol for high latency links such as wide-area networks; however, in the local-area network environments, where latency is low and collisions are few, the overhead imposed by TCP can be detrimental to NFS performance.

TCP Protocol Overhead   How much overhead does the TCP protocol add to NFS? As with most performance related questions, the answer is "it depends." Many factors can influence the performance of UDP and TCP in a given network, making it extremely difficult to predict how big of an effect converting to TCP will have to an existing NFS/UDP installation.

One potential source of objective data to gauge the effect of TCP in local-area networks is the SFS97_R1 benchmark test data maintained by the Standard Performance Evaluation Corporation, or SPEC. The SPEC SFS97_R1 (System File Server) test suite was created to allow NFS vendors to measure the maximum performance and throughput of their NFS PV2 and PV3 server offerings.[3] All submitted results are reviewed by SPEC, and if approved, are posted to the SPEC web site: *http://www.spec.org*. Many vendors, including HP, submit SPEC SFS97_R1 results for all possible test combinations (i.e. PV2/UDP, PV2/TCP, PV3/UDP, and PV3/TCP) for specific NFS server configurations. In cases where both UDP and TCP results for a server are available, the results show UDP performance exceeding the corresponding TCP results by anywhere from 2%[4] to 17%.[5]

While these SPEC results alone will not tell you how big of an effect TCP will have to your specific NFS environment, they do illustrate the potential overhead TCP can add to an existing local-area network-based NFS/UDP installation. The actual effect on your NFS environment can be accurately determined only via thorough testing.

---

3.   The SPEC SFS test suite measures only NFS server performance, not NFS client performance. There is currently no equivalent industry-standard test suite available for benchmarking NFS client throughput.

4.   PV2 UDP results vs. PV2 TCP results using an 8-CPU HP Surestore NAS-105LC Failover Cluster.

5.   PV2 UDP results vs. PV2 TCP results using a 4-CPU HP rx4610 Server.

10.2 Connection Management

UDP and TCP manage network communications between NFS clients and servers very differently. Some background on how these two protocols behave with regards to connection management can help in deciding which protocol is more appropriate for your environment. It is also useful to know what tunable kernel parameters exist that allow you to change the default connection semantics of NFS/TCP clients.

10.2.1 UDP *Unlimited* Data Flows vs. TCP *Single* Connection

As stated earlier, the UDP protocol is *connectionless* — meaning that client and server do not establish and maintain a lasting connection with each other. One potential benefit to this design is that there is no imposed limit on the number of data flows a UDP client can establish to NFS servers. TCP, on the other hand, is a *connection-oriented* protocol — meaning that client and server establish a connection and maintain this connection during the transfer of data.

NFS/TCP Single Connection Semantics By default, an HP-UX NFS client only creates a single TCP connection to each NFS server — regardless of how many NFS filesystems the client mounts from the server. Also, as we learned in Section 4.3 of the "nfsd Daemons and Threads" chapter, HP-UX NFS servers allocate nfsktcpd kernel threads on a per-TCP connection basis, and by default assign a maximum of 10 kernel threads for each NFS/TCP connection. Any threads allocated to a NFS/TCP connection are dedicated to servicing requests arriving on that specific TCP connection only — they are not shared among all active connections.

What this means is that if an NFS/TCP client mounted twenty filesystems from a single server, it would have to multiplex all requests and replies for these twenty filesystems across a single TCP connection, and the server would only dedicate 10 nfsktcpd threads to service the requests for these twenty filesystems. If that same client mounted twenty filesystems each from a different NFS server, it would instead open twenty TCP connections — one to each server, and each server would allocate a pool of 10 nfsktcpd threads to service requests for each connection.

In most cases this single TCP connection paradigm does not lead to performance problems because NFS clients tend to mount filesystems from many different servers. However, in the case where large multi-processor clients are mounting many NFS/TCP filesystems from a single server and multiplexing huge numbers of requests across a single connection, these defaults could introduce a performance problem.

Compare this behavior with a UDP environment — where the client is not restricted to a single connection, and where the server can be configured to run as many UDP nfsd daemons as it needs to handle the client's requests — and you can see where this single TCP connection/10 threads paradigm could lead to sub-optimal performance for some clients.

Fortunately, both the number of TCP connections opened by NFS clients and the number of kernel threads allocated to each connection by the server may be customized on HP-UX 11.0 and 11i systems.

10.2.2 Changing Client TCP Behavior via *clnt_max_conns*

The kernel variable on HP-UX 11.0 and 11i NFS clients that defines the number of TCP connections opened to each NFS server is *clnt_max_conns*. By default, this variable is set to 1, allowing clients to open only a single connection to each NFS server, regardless of how many NFS filesystems the client mounts from the server.

The *clnt_max_conns* variable is undocumented and is not currently configurable via the normal supported methods (i.e. `sam(1M)` or `kmtune(1M)`). The only way to change this parameter is via the `adb(1)` command.

 **KEY IDEA — Modifying the Undocumented
clnt_max_conns Kernel Parameter**

A great deal of care should be taken when increasing the *clnt_max_conns* parameter because it affects the number of NFS/TCP connections opened by HP-UX NFS clients to *every NFS server* — not just HP-UX servers.

In addition, changing this parameter will directly affect the number of NFS/TCP kernel threads launched by HP-UX NFS servers. Unless the server's kernel is tuned appropriately to handle these extra threads — specifically by adjusting *nkthread*, *max_thread_proc*, and *ncallout* — unexpected results can occur.[a]

WARNING — Modifying the *clnt_max_conns* variable from its default value of "1" is not currently supported by HP. Use the following procedure at your own risk.

To allow an HP-UX client to establish more than 1 NFS/TCP connection with each server, the systems administrator should issue the following commands on the NFS *client*:

```
# echo 'clnt_max_conns?W 0d2' | adb -w /stand/vmunix /dev/kmem
# echo 'clnt_max_conns/W 0d2' | adb -w /stand/vmunix /dev/kmem
```

In the above example, the "0d2" parameter instructs the client to open 2 connections per server. A value of "0d3" would specify 3 connections, and so on. A value of "0d1" would return the client to the default behavior of opening a single connection.

Two separate `adb` commands are used in this case to modify both the on-disk kernel file (?W syntax) and kernel memory (/W syntax). This allows the NFS/TCP connection semantics change to take effect immediately and remain in effect even if the client system is rebooted. This parameter will be reset to 1 if the kernel is re-built, either manually (via `mk_kernel(1M)`) or by installing a kernel patch. This should be kept in mind when installing kernel patches on a system where *clnt_max_conns* is intentionally modified.

---

a.   For a complete discussion on tuning the HP-UX kernel parameters that influence NFS, refer to Chapter 12.

10.2.3 Changing Server TCP Thread Pool Size via *maxthreads*

The kernel variable on HP-UX 11.0 and 11i NFS servers that defines the maximum number of threads allowed per NFS/TCP connection is *maxthreads*. By default, this variable is set to 10, allowing the server to allocate up to 10 threads per client connection, regardless of how many NFS filesystems the client mounts from the server.

The *maxthreads* variable is undocumented and is not currently configurable via the normal supported methods. The only way to change this parameter is via the adb(1) command.

 KEY IDEA — Modifying the Undocumented
**   *maxthreads* Kernel Parameter**

A great deal of care should be taken when increasing the *maxthreads* parameter because it affects the number of kernel threads allowed for *every NFS/TCP connection*, not just connections opened by HP-UX clients. In addition, changing this parameter can dramatically affect the total number of threads running on the server system. Unless the server's kernel is tuned appropriately to handle these extra threads — specifically by adjusting *nkthread*, *max_thread_proc*, and *ncallout* — unexpected results can occur.[a]

WARNING — Modifying the *maxthreads* variable from its default value of "10" is not currently supported by HP. Use the following procedure at your own risk.

To allow an HP-UX server to launch more than 10 kernel threads per NFS/TCP connection, the systems administrator should issue the following commands on the NFS *server*:

```
# echo 'maxthreads?W 0d20' | adb -w /stand/vmunix /dev/kmem
# echo 'maxthreads/W 0d20' | adb -w /stand/vmunix /dev/kmem
```

In the above example, the "0d20" parameter instructs the server to allow up to 20 threads per connection. A value of "0d30" would allow 30 threads, and so on. A value of "0d10" would return the server to the default 10 threads per connection.

Two separate adb commands are used in this case to modify both the on-disk kernel file (?W syntax) and kernel memory (/W syntax). This allows the NFS/TCP kernel thread semantics change to take effect immediately; however, it will have no effect on existing connections, as the thread pool limit is set when the connection is established. Only NFS/TCP connections established after the above commands are issued will use the new thread limit. The new settings will remain in effect even if the server system is rebooted.

This parameter will be reset to 10 if the kernel is re-built, either manually (via mk_kernel(1M)) or by installing a kernel patch. This should be kept in mind when installing kernel patches on a system where *maxthreads* is intentionally modified.

---

a.   For a complete discussion on tuning the HP-UX kernel parameters that influence NFS, refer to Chapter 12.

10.2.4 The Relationship between *clnt_max_conns* and *maxthreads*

It is very important to understand the relationship between the *maxthreads* parameter and the *clnt_max_conns* parameter. If *clnt_max_conns* has been increased above the default value of 1 on your NFS client systems, these clients will establish multiple TCP connections with the server when they mount NFS filesystems. Based on the load generated by these clients, this could result in the server launching more than 10 threads to service requests for each client. In this case, modifying *maxthreads* may not be necessary.

Similarly, if *maxthreads* has been increased above the default value of 10 on your NFS server, then increasing *clnt_max_conns* on your clients could have a significant effect on the total number of NFS/TCP kernel threads launched by the server. If the NFS server's kernel has not been tuned appropriately to handle these extra threads — specifically by adjusting *nkthread*, *max_thread_proc*, and *ncallout* — unexpected results could occur.

In a production environment, modifying *clnt_max_conns* should only be done in situations where the single NFS/TCP connection behavior appears to be causing a performance bottleneck. Likewise, *maxthreads* should only be modified in situations where the server's 10-thread limit seems to be yielding sub-optimal performance. Before changing either of these parameters in your production environment, extensive performance testing should be conducted using non-production systems to ensure that the desired results are achieved.

10.2.5 Idle TCP Connection Management — *Client* Side

Once an NFS client establishes a TCP connection to the server, this connection remains established until the client either stops using the connection for **5 minutes** or reboots. Even unmounting all NFS filesystems from the server will not cause the TCP connection to be torn down. The client leaves the connection intact in case new filesystems are mounted from the same server before the 5-minute idle timer expires. This design benefits clients using AutoFS, since it can un-mount and remount filesystems at any time. Once all of the filesystems from a specific server are unmounted, if no new mounts to the server occur within 5 minutes the client will destroy the connection.

The client can also destroy a TCP connection if no NFS requests have been sent between the client and a server, regardless of whether NFS filesystems are still mounted. If this occurs, the next NFS request from that client to the server will create a new TCP connection.

10.2.6 Idle TCP Connection Management — *Server* Side

The NFS server can also decide to tear down idle TCP connections. The server employs a **6-minute** inactivity timer (i.e. no outbound packets on the connection for 6 minutes). The benefit of having the server use a longer idle timer than the client is that it allows the NFS client to determine when it is appropriate to tear down a TCP connection. If, for some reason, the server does destroy a connection that the NFS client still wants to use, the next NFS request from the client will cause a new TCP connection to be established. The server will also tear down a TCP connection if it receives a disconnection event or unrecoverable error from the client.

10.3   Managing Retransmissions and Timeouts

One of the primary tools a knowledgeable NFS consultant will use when investigating a performance issue is the nfsstat(1M) command, and one of the first things he or she will typically check is the number of timeouts and retransmissions the NFS client systems are experiencing. Figure 10.1 contains an example of "nfsstat -cr" output, highlighting the number of TCP (connection-oriented) and UDP (connectionless-oriented) timeouts and retransmissions.

Some number of timeouts and retransmissions are expected, particularly in NFS/UDP environments. Too many of these events can be extremely detrimental to NFS throughput.

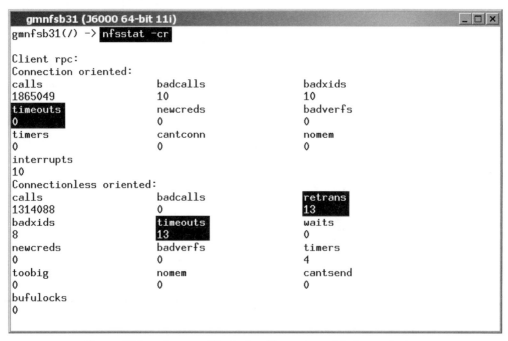

Figure 10.1   nfsstat Displaying Timeouts and Retransmissions

NFS retransmissions and timeouts are handled very differently depending upon whether UDP or TCP is used as the underlying network transport protocol. Understanding these differences can help you decide which protocol is better suited to your specific NFS environment.

10.3.1   When Would an NFS Client Retransmit a Request?

The initial NFS PV2 implementation was designed to use UDP as the sole underlying network transport. Given the semantics of UDP (i.e. unreliable), the NFS development team designed NFS with a built-in mechanism to guarantee data delivery. The client system keeps track of all requests and only discards this data once a response is received from the server. If the client does not receive a response within a specific time period, it reissues the request.

There are many situations where an NFS client would be forced to re-send data, including:

- **The client is temporarily unable to send the request.**
This could occur if a critical system resource is exhausted on the client, such as available system memory.

- **The request is dropped on the network before arriving on the server.**
If there is faulty hardware somewhere in the network path or a resource problem on an intermediate system separating the client and server (i.e. buffer overflows on a network switch), the request can be dropped before the server ever receives a copy.

- **The server is down or a network partition has occurred.**
When the server is down it obviously cannot reply to NFS requests. Also, if there is a network outage somewhere along the path between client and server causing packets to not be delivered, the client will not receive a reply.

- **The request arrives on the server but the server's UDP socket is full.**
All server-side NFS/UDP daemons establish UDP sockets where inbound requests are received. These memory buffers used by these socket can vary in size (i.e. one socket might use a 32KB buffer while another might use a 64KB buffer) but once established, they are fixed in size. During peak periods, when the NFS server is busy servicing existing requests and new requests are arriving at a high rate, it is possible for the inbound socket to fill up faster than the server can drain it. When the socket reaches its limit, the server will drop any request that cannot be appended to it.

- **The server receives the request but cannot process the request in time.**
Even if the server's queue is not filled, the server could still be busy to the point where it takes longer for it to process a request than the client is willing to wait. If the client has not received a reply before its retransmission timer pops it will re-send the request regardless of whether the server is still processing the original request.

- **The server processes the request but is unable to reply to the client.**
The reasons for this failure are similar to when the client is unable to initially send the request. If a resource failure occurs or a correct route to the client does not exist on the server, the server could be unable to respond to the client.

- **The server's reply is dropped in transit before arriving on the client.**
If the network is overloaded or a hardware failure occurs, a valid server reply could be dropped in transit before the client receives it.

10.3.2 How Much NFS Data Is Retransmitted?

UDP   When a retransmission occurs on an NFS/UDP filesystem, *NFS must re-send the entire request*. Depending on the *rsize* and *wsize* options specified at mount time, the client or server may need to re-send up to 32KB of data — even if only a single IP datagram is lost.

TCP   When TCP is used, the transport keeps track of how much data has been sent between the clients and servers by tracking the sequence and acknowledgement numbers in the individual packets. Therefore, if a single IP datagram of data is lost on the network, *TCP only resends the missing portion* of the overall NFS message.

 KEY IDEA — The Influence of I/O Request Sizes on NFS/UDP Retransmissions

When sending an NFS request or reply on the network, the IP code on the sending system will fragment the outbound NFS message into IP datagram fragments based on the MTU (Maximum Transmission Unit) size of the network interface being used, and the size of the network protocol headers (i.e. IP, UDP, TCP).

For example, Ethernet networks typically use an MTU size of 1500 bytes, a typical IP header is 20 bytes, and a typical TCP header is 20 bytes, so the maximum amount of application data (NFS, in this case) contained in a typical IP datagram is 1460 bytes.

That being the case, an 8KB NFS message would need to be broken down into 6 separate IP datagrams (8192 bytes / 1460 = 6 datagrams). Likewise, a 32KB NFS message would require 23 IP datagrams (32768 bytes / 1460 = 23 datagrams). Thus, as the size of NFS requests and replies increase, so too does the number of individual network packets needed to transmit these messages.

This increase in network packets is an important consideration in NFS environments where packet loss is occurring — especially those environments where NFS filesystems are mounted using **UDP** as the underlying network transport protocol.

It is important to understand how NFS deals with request retransmissions differently depending upon whether the UDP or TCP transport is used. The TCP protocol includes a guaranteed notification mechanism that informs the sending and receiving systems of the successful delivery of their data. If a single **TCP** packet of an NFS message is lost, the **TCP transport on the sending system will re-send only the missing TCP packet**.

The UDP protocol has no such guaranteed notification mechanism, so if any of the **UDP** packets of an NFS message are lost, **the entire NFS/UDP message must be retransmitted by the sending system**. In other words, if an 8KB NFS/UDP request is lost, all 8192 bytes must be re-sent. Similarly, if a 32KB request is lost, all 32768 bytes must be re-sent.

If an existing NFS/UDP PV2 environment (which only supports NFS messages as large as 8KB) is experiencing timeouts and retransmissions (which can be determined via the nfsstat(1M) command), moving to 32KB PV3 requests will likely cause the number of NFS/UDP retransmissions to increase, resulting in a decrease in NFS throughput. In this case, NFS/TCP may be a better solution.

10.3.3 How Do the *hard* and *soft* Mount Options Affect Timeouts?

The *hard* and *soft* NFS mount options are used to control the retransmission behavior of the NFS client when dealing with an unresponsive NFS server. Using the default *hard* behavior, an NFS client will continue to retransmit requests indefinitely until a response is received from the server. If the *soft* mount option is specified, NFS is allowed to return an error message to the calling application in the event of a timeout.

The actual amount of time it takes for the client to return an error to the reading or writing application will vary depending upon several factors:

- The current calculated minimum timeout value (explained further in Section 10.3.4)
- The number of retransmission attempts requested via the "retrans" NFS mount option
- The network transport protocol used by the mounted filesystem (i.e. UDP or TCP)
- The type of NFS call itself (refer to Table 10.1 for information on the default minimum timeout value used for specific types of NFS calls)

KEY IDEA — The Potential Risk of Using the *soft* Option on read/write Filesystems

Using the *soft* mount option on read/write filesystems can be dangerous if your applications are not designed to gracefully handle receiving a timeout error for operations such as *read()* or *write()*. With certain applications, allowing an NFS *write()* call to return an I/O error can lead to data corruption if the client application assumes that its data has been successfully written to the server when in fact the *write()* call timed out. For this reason, the *hard* mount option (default) is recommended whenever any *write()* operation will be performed on the mounted filesystem.

10.3.4 How Does the NFS/UDP Retransmission Mechanism Work?

The `mount_nfs(1M)` man page states that the minimum timeout value used by NFS is seven tenths of a second. While this was true for the NFS implementation on HP-UX 10.20, it does not accurately reflect how timeouts are calculated by HP-UX 11.0 and 11i systems. As of HP-UX 11.0, NFS uses different timeout values depending upon the type of request being sent. Under normal circumstances, the initial amount of time a client waits before retransmitting a given NFS request is the shown in the "Min. Timeout" column of Table 10.1.

The various NFS calls are broken down into three general categories — *Lookups*, *Reads*, and *Writes*. Each category has its own associated initial minimum timeout value. This categorization is necessary because some NFS requests will naturally take longer to complete than others — especially those calls that involve modifying data on the server's disks — and they should therefore be granted a longer grace period to reply.

Table 10.1 UDP Timeout Values for Various NFS Call Types

Call Category	NFS Procedures Calls	Min. Timeout	Max. Timeout
Lookups	NULL, GETATTR, LOOKUP, ACCESS, READLINK, FSSTAT, FSINFO, PATHCONF	.75 seconds	20 seconds
Reads	SETATTR, READ, READDIR	.85 seconds	20 seconds
Writes	WRITE, COMMIT, CREATE, MKDIR, LINK, SYMLINK, MKNOD, REMOVE, RMDIR, RENAME, READDIRPLUS	1.25 seconds	20 seconds

In other words, it is expected that the server will require more time to complete a WRITE (Writes category) than a LOOKUP (Lookups category), since the WRITE call involves modifying the server's filesystem and LOOKUP does not. Similarly, a READDIR (Reads category) consumes far fewer server resources than READDIRPLUS (Writes category), since READDIR only returns a list of files and inode numbers, whereas a READDIRPLUS call returns the files, their inode numbers, and their extended attributes. It is therefore important for the NFS clients to allow the servers sufficient time to respond to these resource-intensive requests before retransmitting them.

It is also important to note that Table 10.1 contains only the *initial* minimum timeout value for each call type. When timeouts do occur, the minimum timeout value is increased to ensure that the client will not flood an already overloaded server with retransmitted requests. These timer adjustments are made using an exponential back-off algorithm, which is discussed in greater detail later. All NFS requests share the same maximum timeout value — 20 seconds. This 20-second maximum value is fixed and cannot be overridden by applications or system administrators.

To better understand how this timeout mechanism works, let us look at a few sample scenarios. The NFS timeout and retransmission mechanism used when UDP is the underlying transport behaves differently depending upon the network's and the NFS server's responsiveness. The most common scenarios are listed below. All of the following examples assume the client mounted the NFS filesystem using *hard* semantics, and thus will not give up and return an error to the calling application.

"Normal" case The first scenario is the "normal" case where the server is responding to requests within the timeout period used by the client.

• Client sends a LOOKUP request and waits up to .75 seconds for a reply.
• Server sends a LOOKUP reply within .75 seconds.
• Client sends a WRITE request and waits up to 1.25 seconds for a reply.
• Server sends a WRITE reply within 1.25 seconds.

In this scenario, the client did not experience any timeouts, and so the retransmission timers remained set to their minimum values specified earlier in Table 10.1. This example also illustrates how the minimum timer values vary based on the type of NFS request being sent (i.e. the LOOKUP call uses a .75 second timer, while WRITE is allowed 1.25 seconds to reply).

"Down Server" case   Now let us look at the "down server" case where the client receives no replies:

- Client sends a READ request and waits up to .85 seconds for a reply.
- Client receives no reply; retransmits the READ request and waits 1.7 seconds.
- Client receives no reply; retransmits the READ request and waits 3.4 seconds.
- Client receives no reply; retransmits the READ request and waits 6.8 seconds.
- Client receives no reply; retransmits the READ request and waits 13.6 seconds.
- Client receives no reply; retransmits the READ request and waits 20 seconds.
- Client receives no reply; retransmits the READ request and waits 20 seconds.

In this example the client never received a reply from the server and it was forced to re-send the request many times — each time doubling its timeout value using an exponential back-off algorithm, until it reached the maximum timeout value of 20. Once reaching the maximum value, the client will continue to wait 20 seconds between retransmissions until a response is received from the server.

"Heavily Loaded Server" case   Finally, let us examine the "heavily loaded" server case, where the server is responding to requests but timeouts are still occurring either due to server or network load. Let us take the previous example and imagine that the server finally responded to the READ request after the client had reached the maximum timeout value:

- Client receives no reply; retransmits the READ request and waits 20 seconds.
- Client receives no reply; retransmits the READ request and waits 20 seconds.
- Server sends a READ reply within 20 seconds.
- Client sends a new READ request and waits a *calculated* number of seconds for a reply.

This example shows how the client *calculates* a new timeout value for the next READ request once the server begins responding. The client's kernel determines this new timeout value by using an exponential back-off algorithm. This algorithm calculates timeout intervals based on the average round trip times observed on a given NFS mount point (i.e. how long does a request/reply sequence take to complete).

Just as the client uses different initial minimum timeout values for the three different classes of NFS call types — Lookups, Reads, and Writes (refer to Table 10.1 for more information), the client also maintains separate "smooth round trip timers" for each of these NFS call classes on a per-mount basis. These calculated round trip timer values can be displayed via the "nfsstat -m" command. Figure 10.2 contains an example of this output.

```
ros87252 (B1000 64-bit 11i)                                        _ □ X
ros87252(/) -> nfsstat -m
/nfs_mount from atc01.cup.hp.com:/jamaica   (Addr 15.4.64.24)
 Flags:    vers=3,proto=udp,auth=unix,hard,intr,link,symlink,devs,rsize=32768,
wsize=32768,retrans=5
Lookups: srtt= 14 ( 35ms), dev= 4 ( 20ms), cur= 3 ( 60ms)
Reads:   srtt= 15 ( 37ms), dev= 4 ( 20ms), cur= 3 ( 60ms)
Writes:  srtt= 15 ( 37ms), dev= 4 ( 20ms), cur= 3 ( 60ms)
All:     srtt= 14 ( 35ms), dev= 3 ( 15ms), cur= 3 ( 60ms)
```

Figure 10.2 nfsstat -m Displaying Smooth Round Trip Timers

nfsstat displays the calculated smooth round trip time (srtt=), the estimated deviation from the calculated srtt (dev=), and the current calculated retransmission value (cur=) for each NFS call type. The kernel uses the "srtt=" and "dev=" values when calculating an appropriate value for the retransmission timer to use in a new outbound request (cur=). If the calculated value falls between the minimum and the maximum timeout value for that category of call, then the calculated value is used for the next request. If the calculated value is greater than 20 seconds (the maximum timeout value) then a timer value of 20 seconds is used. If the calculated value is less than the minimum value defined for the specific category of calls (refer to the "Min. Timeout" column of Table 10.1), the minimum timer value for that call category is used.

Over time, if the server continues responding quickly to client requests, this congestion avoidance algorithm will eventually lower the retransmission timer until this NFS mount point is once again using the minimum timeout values for each call type.

10.3.5 How Does the NFS/TCP Retransmission Mechanism Work?

Unlike UDP, the TCP/IP protocol was designed to provide reliable notification of when data is successfully delivered or not. It does so by verifying how much data has been sent, received, and acknowledged on both the sending and receiving systems. TCP has built-in mechanisms designed to retransmit data packets that have not been acknowledged within a given time period. This effectively eliminates the need for NFS to perform these tasks. When TCP is used, NFS leaves the responsibility of retransmitting data to the TCP transport layer.

NFS/TCP does still maintain the concept of a timeout — meaning NFS can decide that a request has taken too long to complete and it will force the client to perform the request again. However, since TCP guarantees data delivery and handles retransmissions of data packets so well, the likelihood of having to force the client to do this under normal circumstances is remote. For this reason, NFS uses a 60-second timeout value for retransmitting entire NFS requests.

There are still many cases where an NFS/TCP client would need to re-send entire requests (refer to Section 10.3.1 "When Would an NFS Client Retransmit a Request?" for more details), but under normal circumstances, 60 seconds should be more than enough time to send and receive any NFS request — even across wide-area network links. This 60-second timer value is hard-coded in the kernel and can only be changed via the *timeo* NFS mount option.

10.3.6   How Does the *timeo* Mount Option Affect UDP and TCP?

UDP   In HP-UX 11.0 and 11i, the *timeo* mount option is effectively ignored for UDP-based NFS filesystems. This value is enforced for the very first NFS request on a newly mounted filesystem, but any subsequent requests will use the algorithms listed in Section 10.3.4 "How Does the NFS/UDP Retransmission Mechanism Work?" Since HP ported the NFS code from Sun Microsystems, their implementation behaves the same in this regard.

 KEY IDEA — The Effect of the *timeo* Mount Option on NFS/TCP Filesystems

Using the *timeo* mount option with NFS/TCP filesystems can lead to disastrous NFS performance when misused.

There have been many cases seen in HP's labs and at customer installations where existing HP-UX 11.0 NFS/UDP clients are upgraded to 11i and begin mounting NFS filesystems using TCP (since TCP is the default protocol in 11i), and suddenly the clients begin experiencing hundreds of NFS timeouts. After analyzing these environments, it is discovered that the clients are mounting their TCP filesystems with the *timeo* mount option and forcing entire NFS/TCP requests (not just missing IP datagrams) to be frequently retransmitted.

The *timeo* option did not affect NFS/UDP clients because the *timeo* value is effectively **ignored by NFS/UDP**. However, when NFS/UDP clients switched to NFS/TCP, this option forced them to **re-send any entire NFS/TCP request** that did not complete within the specified time interval. The additional network overhead caused by these retransmissions led to more dropped network packets, resulting in an even higher number of NFS request retransmissions. In busy networks, the level of dropped packets and retransmitted NFS requests can get so high that the entire NFS environment nearly grinds to a halt.

The recommendation is to **avoid specifying the *timeo* option at all times**. This mount option serves no useful purpose with UDP filesystems, and it can absolutely destroy TCP performance when configured too aggressively. For TCP filesystems, it is best to let the TCP transport ensure that IP datagrams arrive safely on the client and server systems rather than force the client or server to frequently re-send entire NFS messages.

This *timeo* mount option issue is very important to keep in mind when converting existing UDP clients to TCP. It is especially important to remember to check any **AutoFS maps** used by NFS/TCP clients (both local maps and those distributed by NIS or NIS+) for occurrences of the *timeo* option and remove them. Again, removing this option from the maps should not affect NFS/UDP filesystems, since the option is ignored by NFS/UDP, and it avoids this potential NFS/TCP performance problem.

In addition to AutoFS maps, the /etc/fstab file should be checked to make sure that any NFS filesystems specified in this file do not include the *timeo* option.

TCP   With NFS/TCP filesystems, the *timeo* option can have a significant effect on the number of timeouts experienced, as well as the overall NFS performance of the mount point. When the *timeo* option is used on an NFS/TCP filesystem, the specified value (entered in tenths of a second increments) overrides the default 60-second retransmission timer and forces the client to re-issue entire NFS requests that have not completed in the specified interval.

For example, if an NFS/TCP filesystem is mounted using the option *timeo=10*, the client will re-issue any NFS request that does not complete within 10-tenths of a second, or 1 second. This effectively overrides TCP's built-in retransmission mechanism, which monitors the state of sent and received IP datagrams and only re-sends those datagrams that have not been acknowledged in a timely manner. When the *timeo* interval expires, the client disregards any information about sent and received IP datagrams and forcibly re-sends the entire NFS request. This could potentially result in the client or server having to re-send as much as 32KB of data, instead of re-sending only a missing network packet.

The TCP retransmission algorithm has been used and refined over many years and it works very well in most network environments. It is therefore desirable to let the TCP protocol handle the burden of making sure that IP datagrams are sent and received successfully, and not force NFS to interfere by shortening the retransmission interval via the *timeo* option.

10.4   Network Interconnect Device Buffering Considerations

An interesting phenomenon was recently witnessed at one of HP's largest NFS customer installations. The customer reported seeing large numbers of UDP packets being dropped, leading to unusually high numbers of NFS retransmissions and timeouts on UDP-based filesystems. Interestingly, this same customer reported that their NFS/TCP filesystems were not experiencing this packet loss problem. Their TCP connections, both those used by NFS and other applications like `telnet(1)`, experienced very few dropped packets, allowing their NFS/TCP performance to remain consistently stable and good while their NFS/UDP performance suffered dramatically.

After much investigation, it was determined that UDP packets were being discarded by one of the network switches used in this customer's network. When the switch vendor was engaged, and the hardware log files were analyzed, the vendor discovered that the UDP buffers in the switch were overflowing, which led to the dropped packets. When asked why the switch was not also dropping TCP packets, the vendor explained that they configure their switches with 75% of the buffer memory allocated for TCP packets and only 25% for UDP data. The switch therefore had enough memory to service the TCP traffic but not enough to handle the UDP load.

Whenever the switch dropped UDP packets it forced the clients to re-send entire NFS requests. As this customer uses 32KB `READ` and `WRITE` buffer sizes for their NFS mounts, their clients were continually retransmitting 32KB requests to the server only to have a portion of the request dropped in transit, and force the client to re-send the entire 32KB again. During peak network load periods, this packet loss problem caused a vicious cycle to occur where more and more NFS requests needed to be re-transmitted, resulting in very poor NFS/UDP performance.

KEY IDEA — Check for Network Interconnect Device Buffer Overflows

While investigating a severe NFS/UDP performance problem, it was discovered that a customer's network interconnect device was discarding UDP packets but not TCP packets. The network hardware vendor confirmed that their equipment allocates **75%** of the available buffer memory for **TCP** packets and only **25%** for **UDP** data.

It is likely that many network hardware vendors configure their device buffer memory in this manner, so this problem is not confined to large-scale implementations using a specific vendor's equipment. In these environments NFS/TCP has a distinct advantage over NFS/UDP, albeit a hardware-imposed advantage. This network hardware memory configuration issue should be kept in mind when investigating NFS/UDP timeout and retransmission problems.

10.5 Should You Use NFS/UDP or NFS/TCP in Your Environment?

Traditionally the decision to use UDP or TCP was determined solely by geography (i.e. local-area networks use NFS/UDP, wide-area networks use NFS/TCP). However, as stated throughout this chapter, there are situations where a LAN environment could benefit from TCP.

Even in the scenarios outlined in this section, where one protocol would seem to have a clear advantage over the other, there is no guarantee that the recommended protocol will always outperform the other protocol in every situation. Whenever possible, both protocols should be evaluated before making a final decision on which protocol to use for a specific NFS filesystem.

Table 10.2 Recommended NFS Network Transport Protocol

NFS Environment Description	Recommended Protocol
Local-Area Networks experiencing few NFS retransmissions	UDP
Wide-Area Networks or High Latency Links	TCP
Local-Area Networks experiencing many NFS retransmissions	TCP
Networks using hardware configured to favor TCP traffic	TCP

10.5.1 NFS Environments that May Benefit from UDP over TCP

LAN experiencing few NFS retransmissions Given the additional overhead induced by the TCP protocol, NFS will typically perform better using UDP in LAN environments where the number of NFS retransmissions is small.

10.5.2 NFS Environments that May Benefit from TCP over UDP

WAN or High Latency Links   TCP was specifically designed to work well in WAN environments and across high latency links. Many of TCP's built-in features, such as congestion control, window scaling, keeping track of which packets have been acknowledged successfully, etc., make it ideal for these types of network environments.

LAN experiencing many NFS retransmissions   As described in Section 10.3 "Managing Retransmissions and Timeouts" — UDP filesystems may perform significantly worse than similarly configured TCP filesystems in LAN environments where high numbers of NFS retransmissions are occurring. Remember that when a client needs to retransmit an NFS/UDP request for any reason (see Section 10.3.1 for a list of possible retransmission scenarios), the entire request must be re-sent — possibly containing as much as 32KB of data.

While TCP will not always outperform UDP in these situations, it is definitely worth experimenting with TCP to see if performance improves because of TCP's ability to retransmit only the missing portions of NFS requests rather than entire requests.

Networks using network interconnect devices configured to favor TCP   Some network hardware vendors configure the memory buffers in their devices to favor TCP traffic over UDP traffic. (For more details, refer to Section 10.4). In these situations the ideal solution would be to purchase a network interconnect device with a memory configuration that does not favor one network protocol data over another, or one that contains sufficient memory resources to handle all NFS traffic successfully regardless of the transport protocol used. However, since purchasing new equipment is not always an option, a possible workaround is to convert the NFS filesystems to use TCP.

 KEY IDEA — The Importance of Patching NFS and Network Transport Protocols

HP continually strives to improve the quality of HP-UX by distributing software patches containing both defect fixes and functionality enhancements. Many of these fixes and enhancements can significantly improve the performance and behavior of HP's NFS/UDP and NFS/TCP implementations, as well as the underlying network transport protocols. It is therefore *strongly* recommended that the latest NFS patch, as well as the latest network transport patch, be installed on every HP-UX system.

Contact HP support to obtain a current set of patches for your specific operating system. You can also generate a current patch list using the tools available at HP's IT Resource Center: *http://itrc.hp.com*.

For a detailed discussion on the importance of keeping your HP-UX NFS client and server systems patched with current code, refer to Appendix B "Patching Considerations."

## CHAPTER 11

Buffer Cache

Since NFS is a *network*-based file access protocol, one of the primary goals of NFS performance tuning is to reduce the amount of network traffic required to satisfy NFS requests. One common method of reducing redundant network traffic is to use main-memory caching mechanisms to store the most recently accessed data on the NFS client system. This is one of the primary roles of the buffer cache.

Buffer cache is a portion of physical system memory that is allocated for storing blocks of file data. It is used on the NFS client to store data retrieved from the server via NFS READ requests, and as a temporary storage site to hold data waiting to be written to the server via NFS WRITE requests. Buffer cache is used on the NFS server as a temporary storage facility to hold any write data sent by NFS clients waiting to be posted to physical media.

Sizing buffer cache correctly on NFS clients and servers can be a time consuming endeavor, but one that can dramatically improve both NFS and overall system performance. Setting the buffer cache size too large on an HP-UX 11.0 client can result in disastrous NFS performance, as well as starve other system processes from memory that they could put to better use. Setting the buffer cache too small on clients or servers can hinder NFS performance by limiting the number of READ and WRITE requests that a client can satisfy locally without blocking and waiting for a network request to complete, or limiting the amount of asynchronous write data a server can store prior to posting to physical disk.

By default, buffer cache memory is dynamically allocated with the minimum size set to 5% of physical memory and the maximum size set to 50%. While these settings may be fine for most NFS servers, they may not be suitable for most NFS client systems. So what values are appropriate for a specific client or server and the applications running on it? To understand the intricacies and factors involved in correctly sizing buffer cache, some understanding of what butter cache memory is, how it is managed, and how it is searched is needed.

This chapter describes the buffer cache memory mechanism and explains why it is so important to NFS performance. It explains the difference between the "buffer" cache facility and the "page" cache mechanisms of HP-UX, and what each is used for. This chapter illustrates how allocating too much memory to the client's buffer cache can result in poor NFS performance on HP-UX 11.0 systems, and why the same problem does not exist on 11i systems. It describes the differences between configuring buffer cache in *static* and *dynamic* modes, and the reasons for selecting one allocation method over the other. This chapter provides several recommendations for determining the appropriate amount of buffer cache memory to use on a given NFS client or server system. Finally, it describes the tools available for measuring the utilization rate and effectiveness of buffer cache memory on your systems.

11.1   What Is the Buffer Cache?

As stated at the beginning of the chapter, buffer cache is a portion of physical system memory that is allocated for storing blocks of file data. HP-UX uses this memory to speed up file operations such as *read()* and *write()*. Since memory access times are so much faster than disk access times, generally the more filesystem requests that can be satisfied by buffer cache the better overall I/O performance will be. NFS READ operations can be satisfied without waiting for a physical disk I/O if the requested data is already residing in the client's buffer cache. NFS WRITE performance can be dramatically increased by allowing a writing process to post the data to local buffer cache and continue, letting the system send these memory pages to the server in the background.

11.1.1   How Does *Buffer* Cache Differ from the *Page* Cache?

HP-UX uses a split memory cache design where some memory pages are cached in the buffer cache and others in a page cache. It is important to understand the differences between these two mechanisms and how they are used by HP-UX.

Buffer Cache   The buffer cache is used to buffer and cache I/O requests made through the filesystem interface using the *read()* and *write()* system calls. With the exception of I/O flagged as "direct I/O" (see VX_DIRECT in vxfsio(7)), which are not cached, all data which passes through the read(2) and write(2) interfaces to a filesystem is copied between a user-supplied buffer and a kernel-cached copy in buffer cache. I/O is then performed between the device and the buffer cache buffer only. These buffers are cached based on the device and the offset within that device, and are reclaimed from cache by other *read()* and *write()* calls to the same offsets within that same device.

Page Cache   The page cache is used when pages are brought into or pushed out from memory using the paging interface, either explicitly by mapping a file into memory through a call to mmap(2), or implicitly for objects such as executable programs or shared libraries which are mapped into memory on behalf of a running program. For any of these memory mappings, an address range in virtual memory is mapped to correspond to a range of data within a file.

When a virtual address is referenced for the first time, a physical memory page is associated with the virtual page, and the data from the file is brought into this newly allocated physical memory from disk using the paging interface. As memory pressure increases, the system frees physical memory by reversing this process: paging memory back to disk (if modified), and removing the physical-to-virtual memory address mapping to free the physical page.

There is a large time window in this sequence between the times a virtual memory page has been designated as "old" or "unused" — and thus a target for paging — and has actually been written out to disk and the physical memory freed. During this time, that virtual memory page is said to be "in the page cache," because another reference to this virtual page during this time will bring it back from its nearly-paged state before it actually becomes free.

HP-UX is allowed to have a reference to the same file through both interfaces simultaneously, even in the same program. However, since the mechanisms are independent, the process involved must take special care to ensure that the data used by the different interfaces is kept consistent. This is done by flushing data from cache to physical media — the two caches' only common point. See the `msync(2)` and `fsync(2)` man pages for more details.

11.2 Why Not Allocate Lots of Memory for Buffer Cache?

From an I/O performance perspective, buffer cache seems to offer many advantages, so why not just dedicate gigabytes of memory for buffer cache and be done with it? There are several reasons why this is not such a great idea, particularly on an HP-UX 11.0 NFS client.

11.2.1 A Large Cache Does Not Guarantee a High Cache Hit-Rate

Just because you configure a large buffer cache, that does not guarantee that the data your application is looking for will be in the cache. Keep in mind that the buffer cache can only offset the need for an NFS READ request if the data requested is present in the cache, which would imply that it has been retrieved from the server prior to the current client process requesting it. Back in Chapter 3, we learned that biod daemons will only pre-fetch sequential data. If the client is performing reading data from non-sequential locations there is strong probability that the data being requested will not be in the buffer cache, regardless of its size.[1]

11.2.2 Wastes Memory that Could Be Better Used by the System

By reserving huge portions of physical memory for buffer cache (particularly in the "static"[2] buffer cache configuration, where all of the memory is reserved at boot time), you are effectively removing this memory from the pool available to applications. If insufficient memory resources remain for applications and kernel processes, the memory management

---

1.   Refer to the Section 3.1.4 "How Do biods Work in the READ Case?" for more information about the biod daemon's read-ahead algorithm and how it uses client-side buffer cache.

2.   The differences between the *static* and *dynamic* allocation models are described in Section 11.3.

daemon vhand[3] will begin aggressively stealing memory from the buffer cache (if the cache is configured in "dynamic" mode) or the kernel will start deactivating processes (if the cache is configured in "static" mode) in order to reclaim memory resources. In either case, overall system performance can be negatively affected by allocating too much memory to the buffer cache when it could be better used by applications.

11.2.3 11.0 Client Performance Suffers with a Large Cache

Probably the most compelling reason not to use a large buffer cache on an HP-UX 11.0 NFS client is that doing so may actually result in much worse performance than using a smaller buffer cache. The main reason for this is that buffer cache pages associated with NFS files on an 11.0 client are not tracked on a file-by-file basis. The result of this limitation is that whenever a file needs to be invalidated from the cache, the kernel must perform a linear search of the entire buffer cache looking for any pages associated with that file.

The buffer cache management routines were completely redesigned in HP-UX 11i to avoid these linear searches by the NFS client kernel, so performance on an 11i client should not significantly deteriorate with a large buffer cache.

 Difference Between HP-UX 11.0 and 11i: NFS Client Buffer Cache Management

The buffer cache management routines in HP-UX 11i have been enhanced to keep track of the buffers associated with files on a per-file basis. These new routines allow the NFS client to keep track of dirty and clean buffers associated with each remote file accessed on the client. Therefore, when a file needs to be invalidated on an 11i NFS client, the client's kernel simply invalidates the buffers in the clean and dirty lists associated with the file rather than walking the entire buffer cache looking for pages associated with the file to invalidate.

By eliminating this need to serially search all of buffer cache, NFS performance on an 11i client with a large buffer cache is dramatically improved in most situations.

When does the NFS client need to invalidate a file?   There are many reasons why the buffers associated with a given file could become invalid, including when a file is truncated, removed, renamed, a problem is encountered during the close of a file, the client needs to reuse an existing rnode entry, or the client unmounts an NFS filesystem. Also, if the contents of a NFS-mounted file change on the server, then the client system needs to invalidate its local copy of any buffers associated with this file.

---

3.   For more information about the vhand daemon and how it works, refer to the *HP-UX Memory Management White Paper* available online at *http://docs.hp.com*.

NFS Performance Example: Reading a Large Directory

Problem: Soon after HP-UX 11.0 shipped, a customer reported that issuing an "ls -l" command in an NFS-mounted directory containing more than 20,000 files took approximately 30 minutes to complete and consumed 98% of the client's CPU resources.

The customer's NFS client system was configured as follows:

- V-Class system with 12GB of physical memory installed
- kernel variable *ninode* set to 2000
- kernel variable *dbc_min_pct* set to 3 (368MB), *dbc_max_pct* set to 10 (1.2GB)

Symptom: After changing the buffer cache configuration to only use 8MB of memory (as opposed to 1.2GB), an "ls -l" command in the same directory completed in 90 seconds.

Question: Why would a simple "ls -l" command issued in a large NFS-mounted directory take so long to complete and consume huge amounts of system resources, and why would the size of the client's buffer cache make such a significant difference?

Answer: When reading an NFS-mounted directory, an *rnode* structure must be allocated for every entry in the directory. The number of rnode entries available on the system can be sized directly via the *ncsize* kernel variable (see Section 12.1.17 "ncsize") or via the *ninode* variable (see Section 12.1.20 "ninode"). Once all of the available rnodes have been used, the system must begin reusing existing rnodes. In order to reuse an rnode, the system must first invalidate all memory pages associated with that rnode from the buffer cache.

The HP-UX 11.0 NFS client kernel does not keep track of which pages in buffer cache are associated with each file, requiring the client to perform a *serial* search of the entire buffer cache looking for pages associated with the existing rnode to invalidate. Fortunately the buffer cache subsystem was redesigned in HP-UX 11i to keep track of the memory pages associated with NFS files on a per-file basis.

On an NFS client system configured with 2000 rnode entries, whose application is traversing an NFS-mounted directory containing 20,000+ files, the kernel will need to reuse rnodes thousands of times, involving thousands of serial buffer cache searches. With a large buffer cache configured, these serial searches can consume high amounts of CPU resources and take a long time to complete.

Solutions: There are many potential solutions to this problem:

- Reduce the number of files in the NFS-mounted directory.
- Configure a relatively small buffer cache on HP-UX 11.0 NFS clients
- Configure the *ncsize* or *ninode* kernel variables so that enough rnode structures are allocated to avoid having the client need to frequently reuse them.
- Upgrade to HP-UX 11i where the buffer cache subsystem has been redesigned.

Another case where buffer cache pages need to be invalidated is to synchronize files that are mapped into memory via the mmap(2) call. Since memory mapped files reside in the page cache and non-memory mapped files reside in buffer cache, for cache consistency reasons the kernel needs to make sure that only one copy of the file resides in memory at any one time. Therefore, any time a file is memory-mapped, any buffers associated with the file need to be invalidated from the buffer cache.[4]

11.3 How Do *Dynamic* and *Static* Buffer Cache Mechanisms Differ?

Two methods for configuring buffer cache are supported: *static* and *dynamic*. The static method allocates a fixed number of 4KB buffers and buffer header structures at system boot time. The dynamic buffer cache mechanism allocates buffer space and supporting data structures as they are needed, using specified minimum and maximum values to establish the overall buffer cache limits. As the names imply, a static buffer cache never grows or shrinks in size, while a dynamic cache can grow to consume a designated maximum percentage of memory or shrink to a designated minimum percentage as the demands for memory resources fluctuate.

11.3.1 Kernel Parameters Used to Configure the Cache

Dynamic Cache   There are two kernel variables used to configure the size of the dynamic buffer cache: *dbc_min_pct* and *dbc_max_pct*. The *dbc_min_pct* variable defines the minimum percentage of overall system memory that the buffer cache will *always* be allowed to consume. At system boot time, the kernel dedicates *dbc_min_pct* percentage of memory to the cache, and the size of the cache cannot shrink below this amount. The *dbc_max_pct* variable defines the maximum percentage of system memory that the cache may eventually grow to consume as the demand for buffer cache resources increases.[5]

For example, on a system with 1GB of physical memory installed, if *dbc_min_pct* is set to its default value of "5" and *dbc_max_pct* is set to its default value of "50," then the kernel will dedicate 50MB of system memory to the dynamic cache at boot time and the cache will be permitted to consume up to 500MB of memory if needed.

Static Cache   There are two primary kernel variables used to configure the size of the static buffer cache: *bufpages* and *nbuf*. The *bufpages* variable defines the number of 4KB

---

4.   HP-UX uses a split memory cache design, employing both a buffer cache and a page cache. Some UNIX implementations use a single unified page cache that holds program binaries and libraries, application data, memory mapped files, etc. UNIX versions with a unified cache are not burdened with the overhead of synchronizing memory buffers between separate caches during an *mmap()* call, and therefore may outperform an HP-UX client when running applications that are heavily dependent on *mmap()*. HP will be migrating to a unified page cache design in a future release of HP-UX.

5.   For more information about the *dbc_min_pct* and *dbc_max_pct* variables and how to configure them, refer to Chapter 12 "Kernel Parameters."

memory buffers allocated to the cache. For example, if *bufpages* is set to a value of "131072" then the kernel will allocate 512MB of memory to the static buffer cache (i.e. 131072 buffers * 4KB per buffer = 512MB). Alternately, the *nbuf* variable may be used to specify the number of buffer header structures assigned to the static cache, where each header structure represents two 4KB buffers. For example, if *nbuf* is set to a value of "32768" then the kernel will allocate 32768 header structures, representing a total of 65,536 buffers, for a total cache size of 256MB (i.e. 32768 header structures * 2 buffers per header * 4KB per buffer = 256MB).[6]

The relationship between *bufpages* and *nbuf* is rather complicated, where the kernel will build the static cache differently depending upon whether one of these variables is defined, both are defined, or neither is defined. Table 11.1 summarizes the possible combinations of *bufpages* and *nbuf* values, and describes the static cache limits resulting from each combination.

Table 11.1 Relationship between the *bufpages* and *nbuf* Parameters

bufpages	nbuf	Resulting Static Buffer Cache Configuration
0	**0**	Enables the dynamic buffer cache mechanism and sizes the cache based on *dbc_min_pct* and *dbc_max_pct* (**Default**)
> 0	**0**	The kernel creates *bufpages*/2 buffer headers and allocates (*bufpages* * 4KB) of buffer cache memory at system boot time.
0	**> 0**	The kernel allocates *nbuf**2 pages of buffer cache memory and creates *nbuf* buffer headers at system boot time.
> 0	**> 0**	The kernel allocates *bufpages* pages of buffer cache memory and creates *nbuf* buffer headers at boot time. If the two values conflict such that it is impossible to configure a system using both specified values, *bufpages* takes precedence.

There is one additional way to create a static-sized cache on HP-UX systems: set the *bufpages* and *nbuf* parameters to "0" and set *dbc_min_pct* and *dbc_max_pct* to the same value. By configuring your system in this manner, the kernel will effectively create a static-sized cache (i.e. the kernel will allocate *dbc_min_pct* of memory to the cache at boot time, it will be unable to grow the cache since the size is already at *dbc_max_pct*, and it will be unable to shrink the cache since the size is already at *dbc_min_pct*). Given the complex relationship between the *bufpages* and *nbuf* parameters, most systems administrators wanting to use a fixed-sized cache may find it easier to calculate the size of the cache based on a percentage of physical memory rather than determining an appropriate number of 4KB buffers or buffer header structures.

---

6.   For more information about the *bufpages* and *nbuf* variables and how to configure them, refer to Chapter 12 "Kernel Parameters."

11.3.2 Behavior when the System Is Under Memory Pressure

As stated previously in Section 11.2.2, if system memory resources become exhausted, the vhand kernel daemon is invoked, whose goal is to identify and reclaim memory pages from areas where they are not immediately needed so that memory-starved processes can use them. Among the various places vhand looks for memory resources to reclaim are the dynamic buffer cache, ordinary processes, shared memory segments, shared libraries, and any memory pages associated with memory-mapped file regions.

Under severe memory pressure conditions, vhand will steal pages from the dynamic buffer cache three times more often than anywhere else on the system. If no buffer cache pages are available (i.e. the dynamic buffer cache has already been shrunk down to the size specified by *dbc_min_pct*), or if a static buffer cache is configured, then vhand will be forced to begin deactivating processes in order to reclaim their memory pages. In other words, vhand is allowed to steal pages from a dynamic cache until the cache consumes only *dbc_min_pct* of memory, but it is not allowed to steal pages from a static cache.

11.4 Should You Configure a *Dynamic* or *Static* Buffer Cache?

There are several factors involved in selecting which method of configuring buffer cache is more appropriate for your system.

11.4.1 Environments where a *Dynamic* Cache Is Recommended

Under most circumstances, the dynamic allocation method is the recommended method of allocating system memory to buffer cache. While there are some environments where the static allocation method might offer some benefits (described below), there are also environments where dynamic allocation should definitely be used.

Memory pressure or small memory systems As stated earlier, when a system is experiencing memory pressure the vhand daemon will begin looking for places to reclaim memory pages. If static buffer cache is used, vhand will not be allowed to steal pages from it and will be forced to deactivate processes in order to steal their pages. This is a very expensive system operation, and one that should be avoided at all costs. If dynamic buffer cache is configured, vhand will steal pages from the cache, aggressively shrinking the size in order to give these resources to other processes that need them, thereby avoiding the deactivation of processes. While allowing vhand to steal buffer cache resources on a system that has a valid need for the amount of buffer cache it is currently using may not be an optimal situation, from an overall system performance perspective, this stealing of pages is preferable compared to forcing vhand to forcibly deactivate processes.

Of course, the optimal solution in this situation would be to purchase additional memory for any system experiencing memory pressure so that the system has enough memory to allocate for maximum buffer cache performance without forcing vhand to steal memory pages or deactivate processes in order to help memory-starved applications.

11.4.2 Environments where a *Static* Cache Is Recommended

While the dynamic allocation method is recommended for most environments, there are situations where the static allocation method has advantages over dynamic.

You have determined the optimal cache size and have sufficient memory
If you have experimented with different amounts of buffer cache on a given client or server and have determined the optimal amount of memory to use for buffer cache (i.e. the amount that results in the best performance for your applications), then a good solution may be to fix buffer cache at that size and avoid any overhead associated with growing and shrinking a dynamic cache. Of course, this assumes that you have enough memory to dedicate this amount to buffer cache without starving the remaining applications and forcing vhand to deactivate processes.

You plan on adding or removing memory from your system   Once you have done the work of determining the optimal amount of buffer cache to use on a given system, the last thing you want is for the size of this optimized cache to inadvertently change without your consent. In situations where memory is being added to or removed from a system, this change in physical memory size will directly affect the size of the buffer cache if the dynamic allocation method is used, since the dynamic cache size is calculated as a *percentage* of physical memory.

For example, imagine you have a system with 1GB of physical memory and you have determined through rigorous testing that this system performs optimally with a 300MB buffer cache. Thus, you set the *dbc_max_pct* variable to "30." Some time in the future, the memory requirements of your applications increase and you determine that this system needs an additional 1GB of memory. As soon as this new memory is added, the maximum buffer cache size of the system doubles to 600MB, which could negatively affect this system's NFS performance.[7]

In this situation, a static-sized buffer cache would be a better choice because the size of the cache is not affected by changes to the amount of physical memory installed in the system.

Buffer Cache Fragmentation   On occasion, system administrators using dynamic buffer cache have reported cases where the performance of their system or applications[8] begins to degrade over time, especially on systems that experience periodic bouts of memory pressure. In some cases, the cause of this decrease in system performance is identified as being the result of the buffer cache memory becoming increasingly fragmented over time.

As stated previously, when the dynamic buffer cache method is used, the kernel allocates the specified minimum amount of memory (defined by *dbc_min_pct*) at boot time. This initial cache is allocated in contiguous memory regions, but as the size of the cache grows, new chunks

---

7.   Refer to Section 11.2 "Why Not Allocate Lots of Memory for Buffer Cache?" for an example of how a large buffer cache can negatively influence NFS performance.

8.   This is especially true of applications that take advantage of Performance-Optimized Page Sizing (POPS), also known as Variable Page Sizing. For more information about POPS, refer to the *Release Notes for HP-UX 11.0* document available online at HP's documentation repository web site: *http://docs.hp.com*.

of memory are added to the cache using any available regions. Over time, as the dynamic cache grows and shrinks as memory demands fluctuate, it is not uncommon for the cache to occupy many small memory chunks rather than a few large contiguous chunks. In extreme cases, this increased fragmentation of buffer cache memory can lead to diminishing system performance.

Configuring a static-sized buffer cache avoids this potential fragmentation issue because the entire cache is configured at system boot time in contiguous memory, and the size of the cache does not shrink or expand as the demands on system memory fluctuate over time.

TIP: Not every system that experiences a decrease in performance over time will be suffering from this buffer cache fragmentation problem. Only a qualified HP support engineer can accurately determine if this phenomenon is occurring on your system. If your system does period-ically experience a decline in performance over time, and it uses a dynamic buffer cache, it may be worth your time to experiment with a static-sized buffer cache prior to contacting HP support to see if switching to a static cache resolves your performance problem.

11.5 Interaction with the `syncer(1M)` Daemon

The `syncer(1M)` daemon is responsible for keeping the on-disk filesystem information synchronized with the contents of the buffer cache. The syncer process awakens at configurable intervals and scans the buffer cache contents looking for "dirty" memory blocks that need to be written to stable storage. The default syncer interval is 30 seconds, which is configured at system boot time in the `/sbin/init.d/syncer` script.

As we learned back in Chapter 4, NFS PV3 clients use a "safe" asynchronous writing mechanism when writing data to a PV3 server. A large component of this "safe" mechanism involves the NFS server placing the client's asynchronous WRITE data in its local buffer cache and marking the data with the B_DELWRI flag, indicating that the server should use "delayed write" semantics when posting this data to stable storage (i.e. allow the system to flush this data to disk in the background). This "delayed write" mechanism lets the server reply to the client's WRITE request as soon as the data is posted to the server's buffer cache, allowing the client to send new WRITE requests while the server posts the previously sent data to stable storage.

Given the nature of this "delayed write" mechanism, it is not uncommon for a busy NFS server to accumulate large amounts of asynchronous WRITE data needing to be posted to disk during a 30 second syncer interval — especially on NFS servers with very large buffer cache configurations.[9] When the syncer daemon flushes these large numbers of dirty buffers to disk,

---

9.   HP's Superdome servers can be configured with up to 256GB of main memory. Using the default buffer cache settings, this would allow the dynamic buffer cache to consume as much as 128GB of memory.

they transition to the disk's I/O queues where they have the potential of getting in the way of other I/O requests, such as *read( )* requests. Consequently there have been cases reported where *read( )* calls take many seconds to complete because they are blocked behind all of the delayed WRITE data being flushed from the server's buffer cache. This can make the NFS server appear to "hang" for short periods of time, which then causes the NFS clients to appear to hang as well. In these situations it may be desirable to modify the syncer interval on the NFS server.

 KEY IDEA   —   Modifying the NFS Server's Default `syncer(1M)` Interval

It is not uncommon for a busy NFS server to accumulate large amounts of asynchronous WRITE data needing to be posted to disk during a 30 second syncer interval — especially on NFS servers with very large buffer cache configurations. When the syncer flushes these large numbers of dirty buffers to disk, they transition to the disk's I/O queues where they compete with other I/O requests, such as *read()* requests. Consequently, there have been reported cases of *read()* calls taking many seconds to complete because they are blocked behind all of the delayed WRITE data being flushed from the server's buffer cache. In these situations it may be desirable to modify the syncer interval on the NFS server.

The syncer interval should only be modified on busy NFS servers with large buffer cache configurations servicing write-intensive workloads. As with any system configuration change, some experimentation should be done to find a syncer interval value appropriate for your server. In most cases a good starting point is to reduce the syncer interval to **20 seconds**. Because the syncer interval is not typically modified on HP-UX systems, there is no external parameter to control this interval. Consequently, the change must be made to the `/sbin/init.d/syncer` script file itself.

To change the syncer interval on an HP-UX 11.0 or 11i NFS server, the systems administrator should modify line 47 of the `/sbin/init.d/syncer` file as follows:

```
OLD              /usr/sbin/syncer && echo syncer started
NEW              /usr/sbin/syncer 20 && echo syncer started
```

In the above example, the "20" parameter sets the syncer interval to 20 seconds. Once this change is made, the syncer daemon needs to be stopped and re-started as follows:

```
# /sbin/init.d/syncer stop
# /sbin/init.d/syncer start
```

Stopping and re-starting syncer in this manner allows this change to take effect immediately. By changing the `/sbin/init.d/syncer` script, the new syncer interval remains in effect even if the server is rebooted. As with any important system configuration change, thorough testing should be done with the modified setting in a non-production environment, prior to implementing this change in your production environment.

11.6 Automounter's Influence on Client Caching

Back in the "Automount and AutoFS" chapter we learned about how memory pages in the client's buffer cache and page cache associated with an NFS filesystem are invalidated whenever an unmount is attempted on the filesystem. This invalidating of buffers occurs even if the unmount attempt fails because the filesystem is in use. The result is that the NFS client must re-populate its buffer cache and page cache by retrieving the invalidated data from the NFS server.

While this problem occurs with manually mounted NFS filesystems as well as auto-mounted filesystems, the likelihood of experiencing this problem is much higher when an automounter is used, since both the legacy automounter and AutoFS attempt to unmount the NFS filesystems they manage every 5 minutes.[10]

Although this topic is discussed in Section 7.2.4, the effects of this unmount behavior can be so devastating to NFS client caching performance that the key point bears repeating here.

 KEY IDEA — Unmounting Busy NFS Filesystems and Its Effect on Client Caching

One of the steps performed by the HP-UX kernel while processing an NFS filesystem unmount request is to search the client's buffer cache and page cache for any memory pages associated with the filesystem being unmounted. If the kernel finds any such pages it invalidates them. This step is done in order to accurately determine if the filesystem being unmounted is still in use by any client processes, and should therefore remain mounted. In other words, these memory pages are invalidated *regardless* of whether the NFS filesystem is successfully unmounted or not.

As you might imagine, this behavior can lead to a serious performance problem for applications running on the client that are actively using the NFS filesystem being unmounted. Although the filesystem will remain mounted if it is busy, all buffer cache and page cache memory buffers used by applications referencing this filesystem are invalidated. In other words, any memory buffers associated with application binaries that were executed across this NFS mount point will be removed from the page cache, forcing the client to re-acquire these pages from the server. Also, any data pages read across this NFS mount point will be removed from the buffer cache, forcing the client to get this data from the server again.

Given the serious performance implications of this problem, systems administrators are strongly encouraged to increase the unmount timer on any NFS client using either the legacy automounter (via the "-tl" option) or AutoFS (via the "-t" option).

---

10.   There are situations where AutoFS will not attempt to unmount an NFS filesystem after 5 minutes, even if the unmount timer has not been modified via the "-t" option. Refer to Section 7.1.3 for more information.

11.7 How Much Buffer Cache Memory Should You Configure?

After reaching a decision about whether to configure a static-sized or dynamically allocated buffer cache, the question remains: How much memory should you assign to buffer cache?

NFS Client Buffer Cache Sizing Recommendations Back in Section 11.2.3, we learned that configuring a large buffer cache on an HP-UX 11.0 client system can result in very poor NFS performance in certain situations. Although changes were made to the buffer cache code in HP-UX 11i that should allow an 11i client to better manage a large buffer cache, there is still the question of whether your NFS performance would actually improve from a larger client-side buffer cache, or whether these memory resources would be better utilized by the system for other purposes. This question can only be accurately answered through rigorous testing in your NFS environment, using your client's specific mix of applications.

Unfortunately, there is not one single buffer cache configuration that will always produce optimal results on every NFS client system. The best approach to sizing the cache on an NFS client is to configure a reasonable initial amount of memory, measure your application performance, and then try increasing or reducing the size of the cache and measure again until the optimal number is identified. A good initial starting point for sizing the buffer cache on most HP-UX NFS clients is **400MB or 25% of physical memory — whichever is *LESS*.**

On most client systems, creating a cache that consumes 25% of memory should only require setting the *dbc_max_pct* variable to "25." However, on client systems with more than 8GB of main memory installed, limiting the buffer cache to 400MB will require changing both the *dbc_min_pct* and *dbc_max_pct* variables from their default values. For these clients, both *dbc_min_pct* and *dbc_max_pct* should be set to the number that computes closest to 400MB.

NFS Server Buffer Cache Sizing Recommendations Back in Section 11.5, we learned how busy NFS servers that frequently service write-intensive workloads may experience transient hangs when configured with a very large buffer cache. Of course, sizing the cache too small will also yield sub-optimal performance. The server's cache needs to be sized large enough to temporarily store any inbound NFS WRITE data so that the nfsd daemons can immediately reply to the client requests and let the server's kernel handle the task of flushing this WRITE data to stable storage in the background.

Just as with sizing the cache on an NFS client, there is not one perfect buffer cache configuration that will work best on every NFS server. Once again, the best approach is to configure the cache at a reasonable starting point, measure your application performance, and then try increasing or reducing the size of the cache and measure again until the optimal buffer cache size is identified. A good initial starting point for sizing the buffer cache on most HP-UX NFS servers is **1GB or 50% of physical memory — whichever is *LESS*.**

KEY IDEA — NFS Client and Server Buffer Cache Sizing Recommendations

When trying to determine the optimal buffer cache size for a specific NFS client or server, the best approach is to allocate a reasonable initial amount of memory to the cache, measure your application performance, and then try increasing or reducing the size of the cache and measuring again until the optimal number is identified.

Recommended *initial* size for clients: **400MB or 25% of memory — whichever is *LESS*.**

Recommended *initial* size for servers: **1GB or 50% of memory — whichever is *LESS*.**

Of course, not every server system will perform optimally with only a 1GB buffer cache. In fact, in order to achieve the SPEC SFS97_R1[11] results for HP's rp7410 server, the system was configured with 16GB of main memory and a buffer cache size of over 7GB. Similarly, not every client system will perform optimally with only a 400MB cache configured. However, the majority of system administrators who have tested NFS clients with varying amounts of buffer cache memory have reported getting similar performance results when testing with a cache containing multiple gigabytes of memory and with a 400MB cache. That being the case, would you not rather let applications and kernel processes use these memory resources instead of dedicating them to buffer cache, where they may yield little or no performance benefit?

11.8 Measuring Buffer Cache Effectiveness

After configuring your system with a reasonable amount of buffer cache memory, the next step in your pursuit of identifying the optimal cache configuration size is to run your applications and measure the performance results with these settings. There are many ways to evaluate the effectiveness of a specific buffer cache configuration.

Time the application A very simple and common method of judging the effects of buffer cache is to time the execution of your application, either how long it takes to load the application or perform routine operations. The time(1) and timex(1) commands can provide detailed reporting on execution times, or a manual stopwatch can be used.

Monitor cache hit rates with GlancePlus A good way to measure the true effectiveness of your buffer cache is to monitor the read and write cache hit rates using a performance measurement tool such as GlancePlus. Figure 11.1 shows a sample "Disk Report" screen.

---

11.   The SFS97_R1 (System File Server) test suite was created by the Standard Performance Evaluation Corporation, or SPEC, to allow NFS vendors to measure the throughput capabilities of their NFS PV2 and PV3 servers. All submitted results are reviewed by SPEC, and, if approved, are posted to the SPEC web site: *http://www.spec.org*.

```
GlancePlus - Disk Report                                                    _ □ ×
File  Reports                                                                    Help
System: ros87252    Last Update: 18:43:27   Int: 15 sec                          ?

Req Type          Requests      %     Rate    Bytes   Cum Req     % Cum Rate Cum Bytes

Local Logl Reads    17815     96.8%   1187.6  13.4mb    83753   68.6%  195.2    97.1mb
Local Logl Writes     585      3.2%     39.0  105kb     38411   31.4%   89.5    25.0mb

Local Phys Reads        7      9.7%      0.4   50kb       508   21.1%    1.1     5.8mb
Local Phys Writes      65     90.3%      4.3  456kb      1902   78.9%    4.4    29.7mb

Local User             10     13.9%      0.6  120kb       942   39.1%    2.1    26.1mb
Local Virtual Mem      51     70.8%      3.4  324kb       874   36.3%    2.0     7.6mb
Local System           11     15.3%      0.7   62kb       594   24.6%    1.3     1.8mb
Local Raw               0      0.0%      0.0    0kb         0    0.0%    0.0       0kb

Remote Logl Reads   212457    99.9%  14163.8  1.61gb   629485   99.8%  1467.3  799.5mb
Remote Logl Writes     198      0.1%     13.2  12.1mb    1224    0.2%    2.8    74.9mb

Remote Phys Reads       22      1.3%      1.4    0kb      1891   16.2%    4.4     3.4mb
Remote Phys Writes    1630     98.7%    108.6  12.5mb    9811   83.8%   22.8    75.0mb

Remote User           1597     96.7%    106.4  12.5mb   10044   85.8%   23.4    78.5mb
Remote Virtual Mem       0      0.0%      0.0    0kb         0    0.0%    0.0      0kb
Remote System           55      3.3%      3.6    0kb      1658   14.2%    3.8      0kb
Remote Raw               0      0.0%      0.0    0kb         0    0.0%    0.0      0kb

Event             Current      Cum   Curr %    Avg %   High %

Read Cache Hits    649865   2004710   100.0    100.0   100.0
Write Cache Hits     2251     52379    58.6     79.7
DNLC Hits           35076    186795    89.9     92.0    99.5
DNLC Longs              0         0     0.0      0.0     0.0
```

Figure 11.1 GlancePlus Disk Report Displaying Cache Hit Rates

Among the statistics displayed on this screen are the overall buffer cache hit rates, as well as a breakdown of the logical and physical disk read and write requests for both local and NFS-mounted filesystems. Looking at the output in Figure 11.1, the buffer cache read hit rate (Read Cache Hits) is at 100% for the time period GlancePlus sampled. This indicates that all read requests during this interval were satisfied from the buffer cache.

This screen data also allows you to isolate specific types of I/O requests and identify the effectiveness of the buffer cache to satisfy those requests. For example, by comparing the number of remote *logical* read requests (Remote Logl Reads) against the number of remote *physical* read requests (Remote Phys Reads) you can identify the effectiveness of the buffer cache when servicing only *read( )* requests against NFS-mounted filesystems.

Another useful GlancePlus feature is the "System Tables Report." This screen displays the utilization rates of various system resources, one of which being the buffer cache. Figure 11.2 contains an example of this GlancePlus screen. From this data, we can easily identify the minimum and maximum amounts of memory available to the buffer cache based on the current configuration, the current size of the cache, which is especially useful when the cache is configured in dynamic allocation mode, and the high water mark of buffer cache utilization from the time GlancePlus began monitoring the system. This information can be extremely useful in helping to determine whether the cache is sized too small or if buffer cache memory is not being utilized.

```
 GlancePlus - System Tables Report                          _ □ X

 File   Reports                                                   Help

 System: atc03     Last Update: 19:03:28    Int: 15 sec        ?

 System Table                    Avail    Used    Util%   High%

 Proc Table (nproc)               276      170     62%      62%
 File Table (nfile)               920      552     60%      60%
 Shared Mem Table (shmmni)        200        7      4%       4%
 Message Table (msgmni)            50        2      4%       4%
 Semaphore Table (semmni)       16384       25      0%       0%
 File Locks (nflocks)             200       23     12%      12%
 Pseudo Terminals (npty)           60        1      2%       2%
 Buffer Headers (nbuf)             na    76296     na       na

 System Table                    Avail    Reqs    Used    High

 Shared Memory                  12.5gb   11.4mb
 Message Buffers                 16kb              0kb      0kb
 Inode Cache (ninode)           20480               0        0
 DNLC Cache                     25600

                        Min     Max    Avail    Used     High

 Buffer Cache         512.0mb  1024mb 552.8mb 552.8mb 552.8mb
```

Figure 11.2 GlancePlus Reporting Buffer Cache Utilization

After collecting a baseline set of data using these tools, your next step should be to try increasing or decreasing the buffer cache size and test again. After a few attempts, you should be able to identify the buffer cache settings that allow your applications to run optimally.

 KEY IDEA — The Importance of Patching Buffer Cache and Virtual Memory Code

HP continually strives to improve the quality of HP-UX by distributing software patches containing both defect fixes and functionality enhancements. Many of these fixes and enhancements can significantly improve the performance and behavior of critical system components, such as the buffer cache and virtual memory management code.

It is therefore *strongly* recommended that the latest buffer cache and VM patches be installed on every HP-UX system. Contact HP support to obtain a current set of patches for your specific operating system. You can also generate a current patch list using the tools available at HP's IT Resource Center: *http://itrc.hp.com*.

For a detailed discussion on the importance of keeping your HP-UX NFS client and server systems patched with current code, refer to Appendix B "Patching Considerations."

## CHAPTER 12

Kernel Parameters

Throughout this book, many kernel variables have been discussed that can positively or negatively affect the performance of NFS on HP-UX clients and servers. This chapter summarizes these variables and introduces several others that have not been discussed previously in this book. In addition to describing these kernel parameters, this chapter discusses several tools available for inspecting the current values of kernel parameters. Also described are the tools that allow the systems administrator to monitor the utilization rate of many of these parameters.

Like most other facets of system performance tuning, there is not one universal setting for these kernel variables that will provide optimal behavior and performance on every NFS client or server in every environment. It should be clearly understood that any kernel tuning recommendations in this chapter, and summarized in Table 12.1, are intended solely as *recommended initial settings*. Extensive testing should be conducted in your NFS environment with your specific mix of applications to determine the optimal settings for these parameters on your systems.

It should also be understood that the parameters discussed in this chapter in no way constitute a complete list of the kernel parameters available in HP-UX 11.0 and 11i. The parameters documented here are the parameters that most directly influence NFS behavior and performance on HP-UX 11.0 and 11i clients and servers.[1]

Many of today's complex applications, such as CAD/CAE programs and database applications, require additional kernel adjustments for things like maximum process storage, text and data segment sizes, semaphores, shared memory, etc., in order to perform optimally. However,

---

1.   There are many additional sources of information available that describe the parameters discussed in this chapter, as well as the HP-UX kernel parameters that are not discussed here. Two of the better sources are the *Tunable Kernel Parameters in HP-UX 11i* document and the *Configurable Kernel Parameters* white paper available online at *http://docs.hp.com*.

these same applications can also be affected by changes to the variables discussed in this chapter. It is therefore a good idea to check the support literature that came with your software programs to understand any specific tuning requirements of your applications before making changes to these or any other kernel parameters.

Finally, systems administrators are *strongly encouraged* to modify only one kernel parameter at a time and test after each change whenever possible. It is not uncommon when making multiple simultaneous changes to a kernel that one modification will result in a performance gain while a second change will nullify the benefits of the first change. By making individual adjustments to the kernel and testing after each change, you can better identify those modifications that have a positive effect on your environment and those that produce negative results.

Table 12.1 Recommended Initial Values for NFS Kernel Parameters

Variable	Description	Client / Server	Default Value	Recommended Initial Value
bufcache_hash_locks	Specifies the size of the pool of locks used to control access to buffer cache data structures	Both	128	**4096**
bufpages	Defines the number of 4096 byte memory pages in the *static*-sized buffer cache	Both	0	**0 (Dynamic Cache)**
create_fastlinks	Enable or disable storing the link text for symbolic links in the disk inode (*HFS filesystems only*)	Both	0	**1 (Enabled)**
dbc_min_pct	Specifies the minimum amount of memory used for *dynamic* buffer cache	Both	5	**5 or *dbc_max_pct* — whichever is *LESS***
dbc_max_pct	Specifies the maximum amount of memory used for *dynamic* buffer cache	Client	50	**25 or 400MB — whichever is *LESS***
		Server		**50 or 1GB — whichever is *LESS***

Table 12.1 Recommended Initial Values for NFS Kernel Parameters

Variable	Description	Client / Server	Default Value	Recommended Initial Value
default_disk_ir[a]	Enable or disable immediate disk reporting	Both	0	**0 (Disabled)**
dnlc_hash_locks[b]	Specifies the number of hash chains the DNLC entries will be divided into, and the number of locks allocated to control access to the Directory Name Lookup Cache	Both	64 (11.0) 512 (11i)	**4096**
fs_async	Enable or disable writing filesystem data structures asynchronously (*HFS filesystems only*)	Both	0	**1 (Enabled)**
ftable_hash_locks	Specifies the size of the pool of locks used to control access to file table data structures	Both	64	**4096**
max_fcp_reqs[c]	Specifies the maximum concurrent Fiber-Channel requests allowed on any FCP adapter	Server	512	**1024**
max_thread_proc	Specifies the maximum number of kernel threads that can be associated with a process at any given time	Server	64	**1024 or (10 *Number of NFS/TCP Clients) — *whichever is GREATER***
maxfiles	Specifies the "soft" limit for the number of files that a given process can have open at any time	Both	60	**1024**

Table 12.1 Recommended Initial Values for NFS Kernel Parameters

Variable	Description	Client/ Server	Default Value	Recommended Initial Value
maxfiles_lim	Specifies the "hard" limit for the number of files that a given process can have open at any time	Both	1024	**2048**
maxswapchunks	Used to calculate the maximum amount of swap space that can be configured on the system. It does not actually allocate swap space, it merely specifies the maximum amount of swap space that can be configured.	Both	256	**8192**
nbuf	Defines the number of buffer headers to be allocated for the *static*-sized buffer-cache	Both	0	**0 (Dynamic Cache)**
ncallout	Specifies the maximum number of timeouts that can be scheduled by the kernel at any given time	Both	(16 + NPROC)	**(16 + NKTHREAD)**
ncsize	Directly sizes the Directory Name Lookup Cache and the NFS rnode cache; indirectly sizes the CacheFS cnode cache	Both	(NINODE + VX_NCSIZE)	**8192**
nfile	Specifies the maximum number of open files allowed on the system at any given time	Both	928	**8192**

Table 12.1 Recommended Initial Values for NFS Kernel Parameters

Variable	Description	Client / Server	Default Value	Recommended Initial Value
nflocks	Specifies the maximum number of file locks allowed on the system at any given time	Both	200	**2048**
ninode	Directly defines the size of the HFS inode cache; indirectly sizes the CacheFS cnode cache, the Directory Name Lookup Cache, the NFS rnode cache, and the VxFS inode cache	Both	476	**8192**
nkthread	Specifies the maximum number of kernel threads that can be running system-wide at any time	Server	499	**2048**
nproc	Specifies the maximum number of processes that can be running system-wide at any time	Both	276	**1024**
scsi_max_qdepth[d]	Specifies the maximum number of I/O requests that can be queued to a SCSI device at any time	Server	8	**90**
vnode_hash_locks	Specifies the size of the pool of locks used to control access to vnode data structures	Both	128	**4096**

Table 12.1 Recommended Initial Values for NFS Kernel Parameters

Variable	Description	Client / Server	Default Value	Recommended Initial Value
vnode_cd_hash_locks	Specifies the size of the pool of locks used to control access to the clean and dirty buffer chains associated with the vnode structures	Both	128	**4096**
vx_fancyra_enable[e]	Enable or disable intelligent read-ahead algorithm (*VxFS 3.3 filesystems only*)	Both	0	**1 (Enabled)**
vx_ninode[f]	Specifies the size of the VxFS-specific inode cache	Both	0	**8192**

a. Enabling the *default_disk_ir* feature can significantly improve *write( )* performance, but it has the potential of causing data corruption on systems using non-battery-backed storage, such as JBOD without UPS or disk arrays without battery-backed caches. As of this writing, all HP disk arrays provide battery-backed caches. This parameter should only be enabled on systems using battery-backed storage, or on those systems where the system administrator decides the *write( )* performance gain is worth the potential risk of data corruption.

b. The *dnlc_hash_locks* kernel variable did not exist when HP-UX 11.0 was released. It was introduced in patch PHKL_12965, which has since been replaced by patch PHKL_18543. Be sure to install patch PHKL_18543, and its dependent patches, before attempting to modify this variable on HP-UX 11.0 systems. This variable has a default value of 64 on HP-UX 11.0. The default value was increased to 512 in HP-UX 11i.

c. Tuning *max_fcp_reqs* is only applicable on NFS servers using Fibre Channel-based storage systems.

d. Tuning *scsi_max_qdepth* is only applicable on NFS servers using SCSI-based storage systems.

e. The *vx_fancyra_enable* kernel variable did not exist when HP-UX 11.0 was released. It was introduced in patch PHKL_22414. Be sure to install this patch before attempting to modify this variable on 11.0 systems.

f. The *vx_ninode* kernel variable did not exist when HP-UX 11.0 and 11i were released. It was introduced in patch PHKL_18543 (11.0) and PHKL_24783 (11i). These patches, or patches that supersede them, must be installed before attempting to tune *vx_ninode* on any 11.0 or 11i system.

12.1 Tunable Kernel Parameter List

12.1.1 bufcache_hash_locks

Default Value — 128   **Recommended Initial Value — 4096**

The HP-UX kernel uses many different types of locks to control access to critical system resources such as vnodes, buffer cache, the file table, and the Directory Name Lookup Cache

(DNLC). Earlier HP-UX versions allocated a fixed number of locks for all resources, but beginning with HP-UX 11.0, pools of locks can be allocated for each resource type to accommodate very large and complex systems.

The *bufcache_hash_locks* variable specifies the size of the pool of locks used to control access to buffer cache data structures. The recommendation is to increase this pool of locks to its maximum size (4096) in order to reduce the potential for lock contention when managing buffer cache resources on a multi-processor NFS client or server system.

12.1.2 bufpages

Default Value — 0   **Recommended Initial Value — 0**

The *bufpages* variable specifies the number of 4KB memory pages allocated to the filesystem buffer cache. These buffers are used for all filesystem I/O operations, as well as all other block I/O operations in the system (exec, mount, inode reading, and some device drivers). Table 12.2 describes the relationship between *bufpages* and the *nbuf* parameter.

Table 12.2 Relationship between the *bufpages* and *nbuf* Parameters

bufpages	nbuf	Resulting Static Buffer Cache Configuration
0	0	Enables the dynamic buffer cache mechanism and sizes the cache based on *dbc_min_pct* and *dbc_max_pct* (**Default**)
> 0	0	The kernel creates *bufpages/2* buffer headers and allocates (*bufpages* * 4KB) of buffer cache memory at system boot time.
0	> 0	The kernel allocates *nbuf*2* pages of buffer cache memory and creates *nbuf* buffer headers at system boot time.
> 0	> 0	The kernel allocates *bufpages* pages of buffer cache memory and creates *nbuf* buffer headers at boot time. If the two values conflict such that it is impossible to configure a system using both specified values, *bufpages* takes precedence.

To enable dynamic buffer cache, both *nbuf* and *bufpages* should be set to zero. To configure a static-sized cache, either set *bufpages* to the desired number of 4096-byte pages to allocate to the cache, or set *nbuf* to the number of buffer header structures to allocate for the cache.

If the value specified for *bufpages* is non-zero but less than 64, *bufpages* is automatically increased at boot time and a message is displayed on the system console announcing the change. If *bufpages* is larger than the maximum supported by the system, *bufpages* is automatically decreased at boot time and a message is displayed on the system console announcing the change.

The recommendation is to leave *bufpages* set to 0, allowing the use of dynamic buffer cache. For more information on configuring buffer cache and determining whether a dynamic or static cache is more appropriate for your environment, refer to Chapter 11 "Buffer Cache."

12.1.3 create_fastlinks

Default Value — 0   **Recommended Initial Value — 1**

When *create_fastlinks* is non-zero, it causes the system to create HFS symbolic links in a manner that reduces the number of disk-block accesses by one for each symbolic link in a path-name lookup. To provide backward compatibility, the default setting for *create_fastlinks* is zero, which does not create the newer, faster format.

This kernel variable is only used by HFS filesystems. The VxFS filesystem enables this fast link creation functionality by default. VxFS filesystems are strongly recommended over HFS filesystems for most applications, and especially for exported filesystems on NFS servers. However, some systems administrators continue to use HFS filesystems on both clients and servers. For this reason, enabling this feature is recommended to provide faster symbolic link resolution performance in the event that HFS filesystems are present.

12.1.4 dbc_min_pct

Default Value — 5   **Recommended Initial Value — 5**

The value of *dbc_min_pct* specifies the minimum percentage of physical memory that is reserved for use by the dynamic buffer cache. To use dynamic buffer caching, both the *bufpages* and *nbuf* kernel variables must be set to zero.

The recommendation is to leave this parameter set at its default value of 5, thus allocating a minimum of 5% of physical memory to the buffer cache. However, this value should always be less than or equal to *dbc_max_pct*. On large memory systems, it may be desirable to allocate less than 5% of physical memory to buffer cache to achieve optimal performance.

For example, if an NFS client has 16 gigabytes of physical memory installed, then leaving *dbc_min_pct* set to the default value of 5 would result in an 800 megabyte buffer cache, which may not provide optimal NFS performance. If a smaller buffer cache is required for performance reasons, it would be necessary to configure both *dbc_min_pct* and *dbc_max_pct* to values smaller than 5. These parameters can be set to the same value, but *dbc_min_pct* should never be set to a value larger than *dbc_max_pct*.

For more information on configuring buffer cache and determining whether a dynamic or static cache is more appropriate for your environment, refer to Chapter 11 "Buffer Cache."

12.1.5 dbc_max_pct

Default Value — 50   **Recommended Initial Value — 25 (Client)**
                                          Recommended Initial Value — 50 (Server)

The value of *dbc_max_pct* specifies the maximum percentage of physical memory that is reserved for use by the dynamic buffer cache. To use dynamic buffer caching, both the *bufpages* and *nbuf* kernel variables must be set to zero.

The recommendation for NFS clients is to assign a maximum of 25% of physical memory or 400MB to the buffer cache, *whichever is LESS*. The recommendation for NFS servers is to configure a maximum of 50% of memory (default) or 1GB to the cache, *whichever is LESS*.

For more information on configuring buffer cache and determining whether a dynamic or static cache is more appropriate for your environment, refer to Chapter 11 "Buffer Cache."

12.1.6 default_disk_ir

Default Value — 0   **Recommended Initial Value — 0**

The *default_disk_ir* variable enables or disables immediate disk reporting. With immediate reporting enabled, disk drives that have data caches return from a *write()* system call when the data is cached, rather than returning after the data is written on the media.

Enabling the *default_disk_ir* feature can significantly improve *write()* performance, especially sequential *write()* performance, but it introduces the potential of causing data corruption on systems that do not use battery backed up storage when a device power failure or reset occurs before the device flushes the cached data to physical media.

The recommendation is to enable this feature *only on NFS client and server systems that have battery-backed storage devices*, such as disk arrays, or on those systems where the system administrator decides the *write()* performance gain is worth the risk of data corruption. On systems without such protection, it is recommended to leave this feature disabled in order to preserve data integrity.

12.1.7 dnlc_hash_locks

Default Value — 64 (HP-UX 11.0)   **Recommended Initial Value — 4096**
Default Value — 512 (HP-UX 11i)

The *dnlc_hash_locks* variable specifies the size of the pool of locks used to control access to the Directory Name Lookup Cache, or DNLC. This variable also defines the number of times the DNLC entries will be divided into hash chains for searching purposes.

dnlc_hash_locks did not exist when HP-UX 11.0 released. It was introduced in patch PHKL_12965, which has since been replaced by PHKL_18543. Be sure to install patch PHKL_18543 before attempting to modify this variable on HP-UX 11.0 systems. This variable has a default value of 64 on HP-UX 11.0. The default value was increased to 512 in HP-UX 11i.

The DNLC is a very heavily used kernel resource since it is queried any time a file or directory is referenced on the system. That being the case, the recommendation is to increase this pool of locks to its maximum size (4096) in order to reduce the potential for lock contention when managing DNLC resources on a multi-processor NFS client or server system.

HP-*UX*11i   **Difference Between HP-UX 11.0 and 11i:**
The *dnlc_hash_locks* Kernel Parameter

The *dnlc_hash_locks* kernel variable did not exist when HP-UX 11.0 was released. It was introduced in patch PHKL_12965, which has since been replaced by patch PHKL_18543. *dnlc_hash_locks* has a default value of 64 on HP-UX 11.0. The default value was increased to 512 in HP-UX 11i.

12.1.8 fs_async

Default Value — 0   **Recommended Initial Value — 1**

The *fs_async* variable specifies whether or not asynchronous writing of HFS filesystem data structures is allowed. By default, HFS data is posted to disk synchronously. This option has no effect on VxFS filesystems.

Writing data synchronously makes it easier to restore filesystem integrity if a system crash occurs while filesystem data structures are being updated. Writing data structures asynchronously can improve HFS filesystem performance; however, this behavior can also leave these filesystem data structures in an inconsistent state in the event of a system crash.

VxFS filesystems are strongly recommended over HFS filesystems for most applications, and especially for exported filesystems on NFS servers. However, some system administrators continue to use HFS filesystems on both clients and servers. The recommendation is to enable this feature on NFS client and server systems using HFS filesystems.

12.1.9 ftable_hash_locks

Default Value — 128   **Recommended Initial Value — 4096**

The *ftable_hash_locks* variable specifies the size of the pool of locks used to control access to the system file table. The recommendation is to increase this pool of locks to its maximum size (4096) in order to reduce the potential for lock contention when managing file table entries on a multi-processor NFS client or server system.

12.1.10 max_fcp_reqs

Default Value — 512   **Recommended Initial Value — 1024**

The *max_fcp_reqs* parameter defines the maximum number of Fibre Channel I/O requests that may be outstanding on any Fibre Channel host bus adapter at any one time. Tuning *max_fcp_reqs* is only applicable on NFS servers employing Fibre Channel-based storage systems. On those systems, the recommendation is to increase *max_fcp_reqs* to 1024.

12.1.11 max_thread_proc

Default Value — 64   **Recommended Initial Value — 1024 or**
                                                (10 * Number of NFS Clients)

max_thread_proc limits the number of threads a single process is allowed to create. This protects the system from excessive use of system resources if a run-away process creates more threads than it should in normal operation.

When a process is broken into multiple threads, certain portions of the process space are replicated for each thread, requiring additional memory and other system resources. If a run-away process creates too many processes, or if a user is attacking the system by intentionally creating a large number of threads, system performance can be seriously degraded or other malfunctions can be introduced.

Selecting a value for *max_thread_proc* should be based on evaluating the most complex threaded applications the system will be running and determine how many threads will be required or created by such applications under heaviest load. The value should not be so large that it could compromise other system needs if something goes wrong. Keep in mind that applications written in Java™ and most HTTP servers tend to utilize a considerable number of threads. If you are unsure about your application's use of threads, contact your software vendor and get their recommendation for sizing this parameter.

As of HP-UX 11.0 and 11i, the NFS client code does not use kernel threads, so sizing *max_thread_proc* on the NFS client is primarily done to ensure that applications running on the client have the thread resources they need to perform optimally. The NFS server code on 11.0 and 11i systems does use kernel threads to service NFS/TCP requests. UDP requests are still handled by user-space nfsd daemons.

Adequately sizing *max_thread_proc* on NFS servers that will be servicing NFS/TCP requests is very important. This value needs to be large enough to allow the nfsktcpd process to launch as many threads as it needs to meet the demand from the NFS clients. By default, the NFS server is allowed to start up to 10 threads for each NFS client connection. That being the case, it is easy to see why the default number of threads (64) could be exhausted in an environment with many NFS clients. However, keep in mind that the server will not start all 10 threads for every client that mounts TCP filesystems. It will only launch the number of threads it needs to satisfy the demands of each individual client system.

A good starting point for this parameter is 1024. This should allow most NFS servers to handle requests from many NFS/TCP clients without reaching the *max_thread_proc* limit. If your NFS server is used by hundreds of clients, then you may need to increase this value above 1024 to allow the server to launch sufficient threads to effectively handle the client workload.

KEY IDEA — Avoiding NFS/TCP Hangs by Tuning the *max_thread_proc* Parameter

When NFS/TCP was first introduced to HP-UX 11.0 and 11i, a defect existed that caused the server system to stop servicing NFS/TCP requests when the nfsktcpd process attempts to launch more than *max_thread_proc* number of threads. This issue was resolved in HP-UX 11.0 via patch PHNE_22642 and in 11i in PHNE_23502. Be sure to install these patches, or their replacement patches, on all NFS/TCP servers in order to avoid this hang.

If for some reason you are unable to install these patches on your NFS/TCP server (possibly due to application or environmental constraints), be sure to configure *max_thread_proc* high enough that the nfsktcpd process will not reach this limit. NFS/UDP traffic was not affected by this defect, so another possible way of avoiding this hang is to use NFS/UDP.

One way to be certain that *max_thread_proc* is configured high enough to satisfy the NFS client workload would be to set this value to 10 * the number of NFS/TCP clients accessing the given server. This would allow the server to allocate the maximum of 10 threads for each NFS client and not hit the *max_thread_proc* ceiling.

This assumes that the server is configured to allow only 10 threads per TCP connection (configurable via *maxthreads*, described in Section 4.3.4), and that the clients are configured to open only a single TCP connection to each server (configurable via *clnt_max_conns*, described in Section 4.3.3). If either the *maxthreads* or *clnt_max_conns* kernel parameter has been modified above its default value, then *max_thread_proc* will need to be adjusted accordingly.

12.1.12 maxfiles

Default Value — 60   **Recommended Initial Value — 1024**

maxfiles specifies the "soft" limit for the number of files a process is allowed to have open at any given time. A process may call `setrlimit(2)` to increase its "soft" limit and open more than *maxfiles* files until the "hard" limit is reached, defined by *maxfiles_lim*. To be useful, *maxfiles* must be set less than the value of *maxfiles_lim*. The recommendation is to set *maxfiles* to 1024, allowing each process to keep 1024 files open without having to call `setrlimit(2)`.

12.1.13 maxfiles_lim

Default Value — 1024   **Recommended Initial Value — 2048**

maxfiles_lim specifies the "hard" limit for the number of files a process is allowed to have open at any given time. This parameter is useful only if it does not exceed the limits imposed by *nfile* and *ninode*. The recommendation is to increase *maxfiles_lim* to 2048, allowing each process the ability to open a maximum of 2048 files at any one time.

12.1.14 maxswapchunks

Default Value — 256   **Recommended Initial Value — 8192**

maxswapchunks is used (along with other kernel variables) to calculate the maximum amount of configurable swap space on the system. If *maxswapchunks* is not sized large enough to allow the system to address all of the physical swap space configured, a warning message will be displayed on the system console requesting that *maxswapchunks* be increased in order to fully utilize the configured physical swap space.

The maximum swap space in bytes is calculated using the formula: (*maxswapchunks* * *swchunk* * DEV_BSIZE). By default, HP-UX 11.0 and 11i systems are configured to allow ~537MB of swap space: *maxswapchunks* (256) * *swchunk* (2048) * DEV_BSIZE (1024). For many systems this amount of swap space is sufficient. On systems with very large memory configurations, where large amounts of swap space are required, the default *maxswapchunks* value can impede the system administrator from being able to configure sufficient swap space.

The *maxswapchunks* variable does not actually affect the amount of physical swap space configured; it merely establishes the maximum amount of swap space you are allowed to configure on the system. Therefore, sizing *maxswapchunks* larger than necessary should cause no negative effects. For this reason, the recommended size for this variable is 8192 — allowing the system to support a maximum of 16 gigabytes of swap space.

12.1.15 nbuf

Default Value — 0   **Recommended Initial Value — 0**

The *nbuf* variable specifies the number of buffer header structures to allocate for the static-sized filesystem buffer cache. Each header structure represents two 4096-byte memory buffers, so the resulting size of a static buffer cache that is configured via the *nbuf* variable will be: (*nbuf* * 8KB). These buffers are used for all filesystem I/O operations, as well as all other block I/O operations in the system (exec, mount, inode reading, and some device drivers). The relationship between *nbuf* and the *bufpages* parameter is described in Table 12.2 in Section 12.1.2.

To enable dynamic buffer cache, both *nbuf* and *bufpages* should be set to zero. To configure a static-sized cache, either set *bufpages* to the desired number of 4096-byte pages to allocate to the cache, or set *nbuf* to the number of buffer header structures to allocate for the cache.

If *nbuf* is set to a non-zero value that is less than 16 or greater than the maximum supported by the system, or to a value that is inconsistent with the value of *bufpages*, *nbuf* will be automatically increased or decreased as appropriate at boot time and a message will be displayed on the system console announcing the change.

The recommendation is to leave this parameter set to its default value of 0, allowing the use of dynamic buffer cache. For more information on configuring buffer cache and determining whether a dynamic or static cache is more appropriate for your environment, refer to Chapter 11.

12.1.16 ncallout

Default Value — (16 + NPROC)   **Recommended Initial Value —**
                                          (16 + NKTHREAD)

ncallout specifies the maximum number of timeouts that can be scheduled by the kernel at any given time. Timeouts are used by many subsystems, including:

- *alarm()* system call
- *setitimer()* system call
- *select()* system call
- drivers
- process scheduling

If the system exceeds the timeout table limit, it will crash and display the following error to the system console: "`panic: callout table overflow`." It is therefore important to configure the kernel with enough callout table entries such that the table will not overflow during normal system use.

The callout table has historically been sized based on the number of processes allowed on the system (16 + NPROC) as opposed to the number of kernel threads allowed on the system (*nkthread*). Since HP-UX NFS servers use kernel threads to service NFS/TCP requests, it is important to increase the system callout table appropriately when NFS/TCP is enabled. The recommendation is to size *ncallout* based on *nkthread* via the formula: (16 + NKTHREAD).

12.1.17 ncsize

Default Value —   **Recommended Initial Value — 8192**
(NINODE + VX_NCSIZE) +
(8*DNLC_HASH_LOCKS)

The *ncsize* variable is used to directly size both the Directory Name Lookup Cache (DNLC) and the NFS client's rnode table. It also indirectly sizes the CacheFS cnode cache.

The DNLC is used to store directory pathname information related to recently accessed directories and files. Each DNLC entry maps a file or directory pathname component to a cached copy of an inode. Retrieving this inode mapping information from memory allows the system to locate frequently accessed directory and file inodes without having to repeatedly access physical disk. The DNLC saves considerable system overhead, especially in large applications such as databases, where the system is repeatedly accessing a particular file or directory. HP-UX systems use a single DNLC to cache both HFS and VxFS filesystems. Currently, only pathname components which are less than 39 characters will be stored in the DNLC.[2]

---

2.   HP will likely increase this 39-character pathname component limitation in a future HP-UX release.

The DNLC was historically sized based solely on the *ninode* variable, whose primary function is to size the HFS inode table. As more and more system administrators migrated their systems to use VxFS filesystems, they increasingly requested a way to directly size the DNLC without having to configure a large *ninode* value and dedicate memory resources for the HFS inode table, which they were no longer using, in order to get the peripheral benefits provided by a large DNLC. HP therefore created the *ncsize* variable, allowing system administrators to directly size the DNLC without having to dedicate memory resources to a large HFS inode table.

The *ncsize* variable also directly sizes the NFS client rnode table. The rnode table is used to store information about open remote NFS files on the client. Whenever an NFS client needs to reference a remote directory or file on an NFS server, it will use an entry in the rnode table. Once all rnode table entries are used, an existing rnode entry must be re-used. This operation can be very expensive on HP-UX 11.0 NFS clients because it involves finding and invalidating all page cache and buffer cache pages associated with the file referenced by the rnode. The buffer cache mechanisms were redesigned in HP-UX 11i to allow rnodes to keep track of which memory pages in the cache are associated with each file, thereby eliminating the need for serial cache searches when an rnode entry needs to be reused. Refer to Section 11.2.3 "11.0 Client Performance Suffers with a Large Cache" for more information.

The rnode cache can quickly be depleted when an NFS client traverses remote directories containing large numbers of files. Even performing a single `ls(1)` command in a large NFS directory can cause the rnode table to thrash if it is sized too small. It is therefore important to appropriately size the rnode cache large enough so that entries in the table are not constantly being invalidated and reused.

On most clients and servers, a good starting point for *ncsize* is 8192. However, if you know that your clients access NFS directories containing more than 8000 files, you might see substantially better NFS performance by increasing *ncsize* on these clients to a value comparable to the number of files in the largest remote directory

Another recommended method of sizing the DNLC and the NFS client rnode table is to leave *ncsize* set to its default value and instead tune the *ninode* variable. *ninode* affects many system resources in addition to the DNLC and rnode table (such as the HFS inode table, and the CacheFS inode table). Since *ncsize* is sized based on *ninode* by default, many system administrators prefer to leave *ncsize* set to its default value and tune all of these various system resources indirectly via the *ninode* parameter. Refer to Section 12.1.20 "ninode" for more information on sizing this parameter.

12.1.18   nfile

Default Value — (16 * (NPROC + 16 +   **Recommended Initial Value — 8192**
MAXUSERS) / 10 + 32 + 2 * (NPTY +
NSTRPTY + NSTRTEL))

nfile defines the maximum number of files that can be open at any one time, system-wide. Be generous with this number because the required memory is minimal, and not having enough file table entries restricts system-processing capacity. If a process attempts to open a file when there are no remaining entries in the file table, the following message will appear on the console: "file: table is full." When this happens, running processes may fail because they cannot open files, and no new processes can be started.

The recommendation is to increase *nfile* to a value higher than your expected file usage to avoid the "file table full" scenario. A good starting value for this parameter is 8192.

12.1.19 nflocks

Default Value — 200   **Recommended Initial Value — 2048**

nflocks specifies the maximum number of file and record locks that are available system-wide. When choosing this number, note that a single file may have several regions locked simultaneously, and will therefore consume multiple lock table entries. Applications that make frequent use of *lockf( )* or *fcntl( )* calls may require a large number of lock table entries. Once the lock table limit is reached, no new file locks can be set until existing locks are removed. Typically this is done by having the application issue an unlock request via *lockf( )* or *fcntl( )*. Applications could exhibit "hangs" or other unexpected behavior if they are unable to obtain a file lock.

The recommendation is to select a value higher than your expected lock usage to avoid running out of locks and experiencing application "hangs." An NFS server will likely require a larger lock table than a client, since it will potentially be servicing lock requests for many NFS clients. A reasonable starting value for this parameter is 2048.

If you know that your NFS server is servicing lock requests for a large number of NFS clients, and those clients run applications that rely heavily on file locking, this value may need to be increased beyond 2048 on the NFS server. In this situation, a practical approach would be to determine the number of file locks held by a single client while running the locking applications and multiply this number of file locks by the number of client systems.

12.1.20 ninode

Default Value — ((NPROC + 16 +   **Recommended Initial Value — 8192**
MAXUSERS) + 32 + (2 * NPTY))

The *ninode* variable has many potential uses:

• It directly sizes the HFS-specific inode table, and thus specifies the maximum number of open HFS inodes that can be in memory at any given time, system-wide.

• It indirectly sizes the Directory Name Lookup Cache (DNLC). Alternately, *ncsize* can size this table directly.

• It indirectly sizes the NFS client rnode table. Alternately, *ncsize* can size this table directly.

- It indirectly sizes the CacheFS inode table. Alternately, *maxcnodes* can size this table directly. Refer to Section 8.3.3 "The maxcnodes Kernel Parameter" for more information about directly sizing the CacheFS inode table via *maxcnodes*.

- It indirectly sizes the VxFS-specific inode table. Alternately, *vx_ninode* can size this table directly. The VxFS inode table is normally calculated by the kernel based on the amount of physical memory installed in the system. The kernel will only use the *ninode* value to size the VxFS inode table if *ninode* is larger than the value calculated by the kernel based on the system's physical memory size. See Section 12.1.27 "vx_ninode" for more details.

The only system table that is directly sized by *ninode* is the HFS-specific inode table. HP strongly recommends using VxFS filesystems on all NFS clients and servers. If only VxFS filesystems are used on your system (with the exception of /stand, which must be an HFS filesystem in order for the system to boot properly), and the system is not a CacheFS client, then *ninode* can be left at its default value, and the remaining system tables that are indirectly sized by *ninode* may be sized directly by other parameters (i.e. use *ncsize* to tune the DNLC and client rnode table, and *maxcnodes* to configure the CacheFS inode table).

Many system administrators prefer to leave *ncsize* and *maxcnodes* set to their default values and tune the DNLC, the client rnode table, and the CacheFS inode table indirectly via *ninode*. In this configuration, the recommended initial size for *ninode* is 8192.

12.1.21 nkthread

Default Value — (((NPROC * 7) / 4) + 16)   Recommended Initial Value — 2048

nkthread limits the combined total number of threads that can be running at any given time from all processes on the system. This value protects the system against being overwhelmed by a large number of threads that exceeds normal, reasonable operation. It protects the system against overload if multiple large applications are running, and also protects the system from users who might maliciously attempt to sabotage system operation by launching a large number of threaded programs, causing resources to become unavailable for normal system needs.

Processes that use threads for improved performance create multiple copies of certain portions of their process space, which requires memory for thread storage as well as processor and system overhead related to managing the threads. The kernel parameter *max_thread_proc* limits the number of threads that a single process can create. On systems running large threaded applications, such as applications written in Java™ and most HTTP servers, a large number of threads may be required. If you are unsure about the thread usage of a specific application, contact your software vendor and get their recommendation for appropriately sizing this variable.

The default *nkthread* value allows an average of two threads per process plus an additional system allowance. If you think your system may require a larger *nkthread* value, there are many ways to determine an appropriate size:

- Determine the total number of threads required by each threaded application on the system, especially any large applications.
- Determine how many and which of these applications will be running at any given time.
- Add these together and combine with a reasonable allowance for other users or processes that might run occasionally using threads (*nproc**2 might be a useful number).
- Select a value for *nkthread* that is large enough to accommodate the total, but not so large that it compromises system integrity.

As of HP-UX 11.0 and 11i, the NFS client code itself does not use kernel threads. So sizing *nkthread* on the NFS client is primarily done to ensure that the applications running on the client are given the resources they need to perform optimally.

The NFS server code on 11.0 and 11i systems does use kernel threads to service NFS/TCP requests. UDP requests are still handled by user-space nfsd daemons. Adequately sizing *nkthread* on NFS servers that will be servicing NFS/TCP requests is very important. This value needs to be large enough to allow the nfsktcpd process to launch as many threads as it needs to meet the demand from the NFS clients, and still leave room for all other system processes — multi-threaded or otherwise. This is important to keep in mind, especially on NFS servers where the *max_thread_proc* variable is increased. A good initial starting value for *nkthread* is 2048.

12.1.22 nproc

Default Value — (20 + 8 * MAXUSERS)   Recommended Initial Value — 1024

The *nproc* variable is used to size many system parameters:

- It directly sizes the system process table, which specifies the maximum total number of processes that can exist simultaneously in the system at any given time.
- It indirectly sizes the following kernel variables: *ksi_alloc_max*, *ncallout*, *nfile*, *ninode*, *nkthread*, *nsysmap*, and *nsysmap64*.
- The kernel uses the value of *nproc* in many of its internal calculations as well.

nproc can be sized directly or it can be tuned by modifying the *maxusers* kernel parameter. In addition to *nproc*, *maxusers* also affects *nclist*, *nfile*, and *ninode*. Given the number of interdependencies between all these kernel variables, the recommendation is to tune *nproc* directly and avoid the use of *maxusers*. When the total number of processes in the system is larger than *nproc*, the system issues the following message on the system console: "`proc: table is full.`" If a user tries to start a new process when the proc table is full, the process will fail to start and the following message will be displayed: "`no more processes.`"

The NFS protocol does not create many processes on the client other than biod daemons. The NFS server can consume a large number of processes if UDP nfsds are used. It is not uncommon for busy NFS servers to run over 100 nfsds. The number of nfsds and biods should be taken into consideration when determining the appropriate value for *nproc* on your NFS client or server. A good initial starting value for *nproc* is 1024.

12.1.23 scsi_max_qdepth

Default Value — 8   **Recommended Initial Value — 90**

The *scsi_max_qdepth* parameter defines the maximum number of SCSI I/O requests that may be outstanding on any SCSI device at any one time. Tuning *scsi_max_qdepth* is only applicable on NFS servers employing SCSI-based storage systems. On those systems, the recommendation is to increase *scsi_max_qdepth* to 90.

12.1.24 vnode_hash_locks

Default Value — 128   **Recommended Initial Value — 4096**

The *vnode_hash_locks* variable specifies the size of the pool of locks used to control access to vnode (virtual inode) data structures. The recommendation is to increase this pool of locks to its maximum size (4096) in order to reduce the potential for lock contention when managing vnode structures on a multi-processor NFS client or server system.

12.1.25 vnode_cd_hash_locks

Default Value — 128   **Recommended Initial Value — 4096**

The *vnode_cd_hash_locks* variable specifies the size of the pool of locks used to control access to the clean and dirty memory buffer lists associated with each vnode data structure. The recommendation is to increase this pool of locks to its maximum size (4096) in order to reduce the potential for lock contention when managing these lists on a multi-processor system.

12.1.26 vx_fancyra_enable

Default Value — 0   **Recommended Initial Value — 1**

One of the exciting new features recently incorporated into HP's version of VxFS is a patented[3] read-ahead prediction algorithm that recognizes specific I/O patterns, predominantly used by technical computing applications such as Computer Aided Engineering (CAE), and automatically adjusts read-ahead behavior accordingly. *vx_fancyra_enable* enables or disables this new read-ahead mechanism. This feature is only available for VxFS Version 3.3 filesystems.

---

3.   For detailed description of this enhanced read-ahead algorithm, please refer to *Multi-threaded read-ahead prediction by pattern recognition*, patent number: 6,070,230.

HP-~~ux~~11i   **Difference Between HP-UX 11.0 and 11i:**
                         The *vx_fancyra_enable* Kernel Parameter

The *vx_fancyra_enable* kernel parameter did not exist when HP-UX 11.0 was released. It was introduced in patch PHKL_22414. This parameter was included in HP-UX 11i.

Technical applications, like MSC.Nastran, generate unique I/O patterns that are not usually explored by a generic filesystem such as VxFS. As such, performance for these technical applications is not optimized by using a filesystem that is only configured and tuned for general purpose system performance. The new read-ahead algorithm enabled via the *vx_fancyra_enable* parameter improves *read()* performance for these technical applications by recognizing their unique I/O patterns and triggering read-ahead requests in the following situations:

- Read-ahead for backward read
- Read-ahead for files read in stride
- Read-ahead for files read by multiple processes or threads
- Read-ahead for files read collectively[4]

The recommendation is to enable this new intelligent read-ahead mechanism by setting *vx_fancyra_enable* to 1. However, if your applications generate predominantly non-sequential read requests, then you may experience better performance with *vx_fancyra_enable* disabled.

12.1.27 vx_ninode

Default Value — 0   **Recommended Initial Value — 8192**

The *vx_ninode* variable is used to directly size the VxFS-specific inode table. It is the VxFS equivalent to the *ninode* variable, which directly sizes the HFS-specific inode table. However, unlike the HFS inode table, which can *only* be sized via *ninode*, HP-UX 11.0 and 11i systems offer several methods of configuring the VxFS inode table.

- At system boot time, the kernel checks to see if the *vx_ninode* variable is set to a non-zero value. If it is, then the VxFS inode table is created with *vx_ninode* number of entries.
- If *vx_ninode* is set to its default value of 0, then the kernel attempts to automatically tune the VxFS inode table to an appropriate size based solely on the amount of physical memory installed in the system. Table 12.3 lists the various combinations of installed

4.   A collective filesystem operation is where one process (or thread) reads one block of data, then another process (or thread) reads the next block of data, etc. This new read-ahead algorithm can detect that, as a whole, the file is being accessed sequentially, and generate read-ahead requests on behalf of the entire collection of threads.

memory and VxFS inode table configuration values. For example, a system with 2GB of memory installed would have a VxFS inode table containing 128,000 entries.

Table 12.3 VxFS Inode Table Sizing Based on Physical Memory

Installed Physical Memory	Resulting VxFS inode Table Size
8MB	400
16MB	1,000
32MB	2,500
64MB	6,000
128MB	8,000
256MB	16,000
512MB	32,000
1GB	64,000
2GB	128,000
8GB	256,000
32GB	512,000
128GB	1,024,000

• If the system contains *more* than 128GB of physical memory, then the kernel extrapolates the size of the VxFS inode table based on the largest table size entry (i.e. 1,024,000).

• If the table size calculated by the kernel (based on installed physical memory) is *less than* the value of *ninode*, then the VxFS inode table is created with *ninode* number of entries.

On many systems, the calculated size of the VxFS inode table is too large for practical use, and it needlessly consumes system memory resources that could be better used in other areas. For example, the majority of systems with 2GB of physical memory do not need to keep 128,000 VxFS files open simultaneously. Likewise, few systems with 128GB of memory will need to keep 1 million VxFS files open at any given time. For most systems, a reasonable starting point for the VxFS inode table is 8192.

The *vx_ninode* kernel variable did not exist when HP-UX 11.0 and 11i released. It was introduced in patches PHKL_18543 and PHKL_24783 for 11.0 and 11i systems respectively. These patches, or patches that supersede them, must be installed before attempting to tune *vx_ninode* on any 11.0 or 11i system.

KEY IDEA — Test and Tune, Test and Tune, etc.

It is important to stress, yet again, that any recommendations made in this chapter, and indeed throughout this entire book, are merely **suggested initial settings**. There is simply no way that a single set of kernel parameter settings will produce optimal NFS throughput results in every situation. The only way to determine the optimal settings for your specific NFS client or server is via thorough testing.

For example, looking at the configuration used during a recent SPEC SFS97_R1 benchmark run on an rp7410 server,[a] the kernel parameters were tuned as follows:

- bufcache_hash_locks=4096
- create_fastlinks=1
- dbc_min_pct=10
- dbc_max_pct=42
- dnlc_hash_locks=4096
- ftable_hash_locks=4096
- max_fcp_reqs=1024
- max_thread_proc=1000
- maxswapchunks=16384
- ncsize=2100000
- nfile=16384
- ninode=2100000
- nkthread=10000
- nstrpty=200
- scsi_max_qdepth=90
- vnode_hash_locks=4096
- vps_pagesize=4
- vx_fancyra_enable=1
- vx_ninode=2100000

Does this mean that these parameter settings should be used on every NFS server? Perhaps, if every NFS server were an HP rp7410 server with 8 CPUs, 16GB of memory, servicing a load similar to the load generated by the SPEC SFS97_R1 benchmark suite. Should these kernel parameter settings be used on any NFS client system? Given the size of parameters such as *ninode*, *vx_ninode*, and *dbc_max_pct* — highly unlikely.

Again, the best approach to identifying a good set of kernel parameters is to start with a good baseline configuration and then test and tune, test and tune, test and tune.

a.   The complete system configuration used during this test is available at *http://www.spec.org*.

12.2 Inspecting Kernel Parameter Settings

HP provides several tools for determining the current size of the kernel parameters on an HP-UX 11.0 or 11i system. Some of these tools also show the formulas used by the kernel when calculating the size of these parameters. Also, it is important to note that each of these tools may not display the same list of kernel parameters. Therefore, it may be necessary to use more than one of these tools to gain a complete understanding of the current kernel configuration used by your NFS client or server system.

12.2.1 sam(1M)

The sam(1M) utility is a general purpose system configuration tool. One of its many features is the ability to view and modify kernel parameters. A sample of the "Kernel Configuration" screen is included in Figure 12.1.

```
Kernel Configuration (ros87252)                                                    _ □ X

File   List   View   Options   Actions                                              Help

Pending Kernel Based Upon:   Current Kernel

Configurable Parameters                                                   0 of 173 selected

                  Current     Pending               Associated
Name              Value       Value      Type        Module     Description
maxssiz_64bit     8388608     8388608    Static      N/A        Max Stack Segment Size For 64-bit Processes (Bytes)
maxswapchunks     256         256        Static      N/A        Max Number of Swap Chunks
maxtsiz           67108864    67108864   Dynamic     N/A        Max Text Segment Size For 32-bit Processes (Bytes)
maxtsiz_64bit     1073741824  1073741824 Dynamic     N/A        Max Text Segment Size For 64-bit Processes (Bytes)
maxuprc           75          75         Dynamic     N/A        Max Number of User Processes
maxusers          32          32         Static      N/A        Value of MAXUSERS Macro (Does Not Affect Max. User Logins)
maxvgs            10          10         Static      N/A        Max Number of Volume Groups
mesg              1           1          Static      N/A        Enable Sys V Messages
modstrmax         500         500        Static      N/A        Max Size (Bytes) of Kernel-Module Savecrash Table
msgmap            42          42         Static      N/A        Max Number of Message Map Entries
msgmax            8192        8192       Dynamic     N/A        Message Max Size (bytes)
msgmnb            16384       16384      Dynamic     N/A        Max Number of Bytes on Message Queue
msgmni            50          50         Static      N/A        Number of Message Queue Identifiers
msgseg            2048        2048       Static      N/A        Number of Segments Available for Messages
msgssz            8           8          Static      N/A        Message Segment Size
msgtql            40          40         Static      N/A        Number of Message Headers
nbuf              0           0          Static      N/A        Number of Buffer Cache Headers
ncallout          515         515        Static      N/A        Max Number of Pending Timeouts
ncdnode           150         150        Static      N/A        Max Number of Open CDFS Files
nclist            612         612        Static      N/A        Number of cblocks for pty and tty Data Transfers
ncsize            5596        5596       Static      N/A        Directory Name Lookup Cache (DNLC) Space Needed for Inodes
ndilbuffers       30          30         Static      N/A        Number of DIL Buffers
nfile             910         910        Static      N/A        Max Number of Open Files
nflocks           200         200        Static      N/A        Max Number of File Locks
ninode            476         476        Static      N/A        Max Number of Open Inodes
nkthread          499         499        Static      N/A        Max Number of Kernel Threads Supported by the System
no_lvm_disks      0           0          Static      N/A        Boolean: Set Only If System Has No LVM Disks
nproc             276         276        Static      N/A        Max Number of Processes
npty              60          60         Static      N/A        Number of ptys (Pseudo ttys)
nstrpty           60          60         Static      N/A        Max Number of Streams-Based PTYs
nstrtel           60          60         Static      N/A        Number of Telnet Session Device Files
nswapdev          10          10         Static      N/A        Max Devices That Can be Enabled for Swap
nswapfs           10          10         Static      N/A        Max File Systems That Can be Enabled for Swap
nsysmap           800         800        Static      N/A        Number of Entries in Kernel Dynamic Memory Allocation Map
nsysmap64         800         800        Static      N/A        Number of Entries in Kernel Dynamic Memory Allocation Map
```

Figure 12.1 sam Kernel Configuration Screen

This sam screen lists all of the supported kernel parameters, their current value, any new pending value based on changes made in the current sam session, a brief description of each variable, etc. By selecting any of the variables in the list, sam allows you to see the formula used by the kernel to calculate the size of the variable.

12.2.2 `kmtune(1M)`

`kmtune(1M)` is a new kernel configuration utility introduced in HP-UX 11.0. It may be used to query, set, or reset kernel parameters. When run without any command-line arguments, `kmtune` displays the current values of all kernel parameters. The `kmtune` screen output was enhanced in 11i also include any pending changes to kernel parameters resulting from previous invocations of `kmtune`. Figure 12.2 contains a sample of `kmtune` output.

```
┌────────────────────────────────────────────────────────────────────────┐
│  atc03 (L2000 64-bit 11i)                                      _ □ ✕    │
├────────────────────────────────────────────────────────────────────────┤
│ atc03(/) -> kmtune                                                       │
│ Parameter              Current Dyn Planned              Module   Version │
│ ======================================================================== │
│ NSTRBLKSCHED              -   -  2                                        │
│ NSTREVENT                50   -  50                                       │
│ NSTRPUSH                 16   -  16                                       │
│ NSTRSCHED                 0   -  0                                        │
│ STRCTLSZ              1024   -  1024                                      │
│ STRMSGSZ             65535   -  65535                                     │
│ acctresume               4   -  4                                        │
│ acctsuspend              2   -  2                                        │
│ aio_listio_max         256   -  256                                      │
│ aio_max_ops           2048   -  2048                                     │
│ aio_physmem_pct         10   -  10                                       │
│ aio_prio_delta_max      20   -  20                                       │
│ allocate_fs_swapmap      0   -  0                                        │
│ alwaysdump               1   -  1                                        │
│ bootspinlocks            -   -  256                                      │
│ bufcache_hash_locks    128   -  128                                      │
│ bufpages                 0   -  (NBUF*2)                                 │
│ chanq_hash_locks       256   -  256                                      │
│ core_addshmem_read       0   Y  0                                        │
│ core_addshmem_write      0   Y  0                                        │
│ create_fastlinks         0   -  0                                        │
│ dbc_max_pct             50   -  50                                       │
│ dbc_min_pct             25   -  25                                       │
│ default_disk_ir          0   -  0                                        │
│ desfree                  -   -  0                                        │
│ disksort_seconds         0   -  0                                        │
│ dnlc_hash_locks        512   -  4*128                                    │
│ dontdump                 0   -  0                                        │
│ dskless_node             -   -  0                                        │
│ dst                      1   -  1                                        │
│ effective_maxpid         -   -  ((NPROC<=30000)?30000:(NPROC*5/4))       │
│ eisa_io_estimate         -   -  0x300                                    │
└────────────────────────────────────────────────────────────────────────┘
```

Figure 12.2   `kmtune` Output from an HP-UX 11i System

In this example, `kmtune` returned an alphabetized list of kernel variables, their current values, an indication of whether each variable is sized dynamically by the kernel or not, and any pending changes. For those variables that are sized based on a kernel formula, `kmtune` displays the current formula as well as the value resulting from that formula.

12.2.3 sysdef(1M)

Similar to kmtune(1M), the sysdef(1M) command analyzes the currently running kernel and displays information about the current state of the tunable configuration parameters. Unlike kmtune, sysdef is only capable of displaying parameters — not modifying them. For each kernel parameter, the following information is returned:

NAME	The name and description of the parameter
VALUE	The current value of the parameter
BOOT	The value of the parameter at boot time, if it is different from the current value
MIN	The minimum allowed value of the parameter, if any
MAX	The maximum allowed value of the parameter, if any
UNITS	The units by which the parameter is measured
FLAGS	Flags that further describe the parameter

An example of sysdef output is shown in Figure 12.3:

```
atc03 (L2000 64-bit 11i)                                        _ □ X
atc03(/) -> sysdef
NAME                  VALUE      BOOT      MIN-MAX        UNITS     FLAGS
acctresume              4          -       -100-100                  -
acctsuspend             2          -       -100-100                  -
allocate_fs_swapmap     0          -          -                      -
bufpages            141516         -         0-           Pages      -
create_fastlinks        0          -          -                      -
dbc_max_pct            50          -          -                      -
dbc_min_pct            25          -          -                      -
default_disk_ir         0          -          -                      -
dskless_node            0          -         0-1                      -
eisa_io_estimate      768          -          -                      -
eqmemsize              23          -          -                      -
file_pad               10          -         0-                       -
fs_async                0          -         0-1                      -
hpux_aes_override       0          -          -                       -
maxdsiz                 2          -       0-655360       Pages      -
maxdsiz_64bit        16384         -      256-1048576     Pages      -
maxfiles               60          -       30-2048                   -
maxfiles_lim         1024          -       30-2048                   -
maxssiz             65536          -       0-655360       Pages      -
maxssiz_64bit       262144         -      256-1048576     Pages      -
maxswapchunks        8192          -       1-16384                   -
maxtsiz              2048          -       0-655360       Pages      -
```

Figure 12.3 sysdef Output

Comparing this sysdef output to the kmtune output shown in Figure 12.2, you can see that kmtune returns a much more complete list of the available kernel parameters.

12.2.4 The /stand/system File

/stand/system is the configuration file used to build the HP-UX kernel. Among other things, it contains a list of the current set of modified kernel parameters used on the system. Since it is an ASCII text file, it can be viewed with any text editor. Changes to kernel parameters can be made directly in the /stand/system file; however, these changes do not take effect until a new kernel is built using the mk_kernel(1M) command and the system is rebooted.

For a complete description of the contents and syntax of the /stand/system file, refer to the config(1M) man page.

12.3 Monitoring Kernel Parameter Values via GlancePlus

While HP provides many tools that allow you to view current kernel parameter settings, only GlancePlus can report on the actual utilization of these parameters. The "System Tables Report" displays utilization rates of several critical kernel parameters, as shown in Figure 12.4.

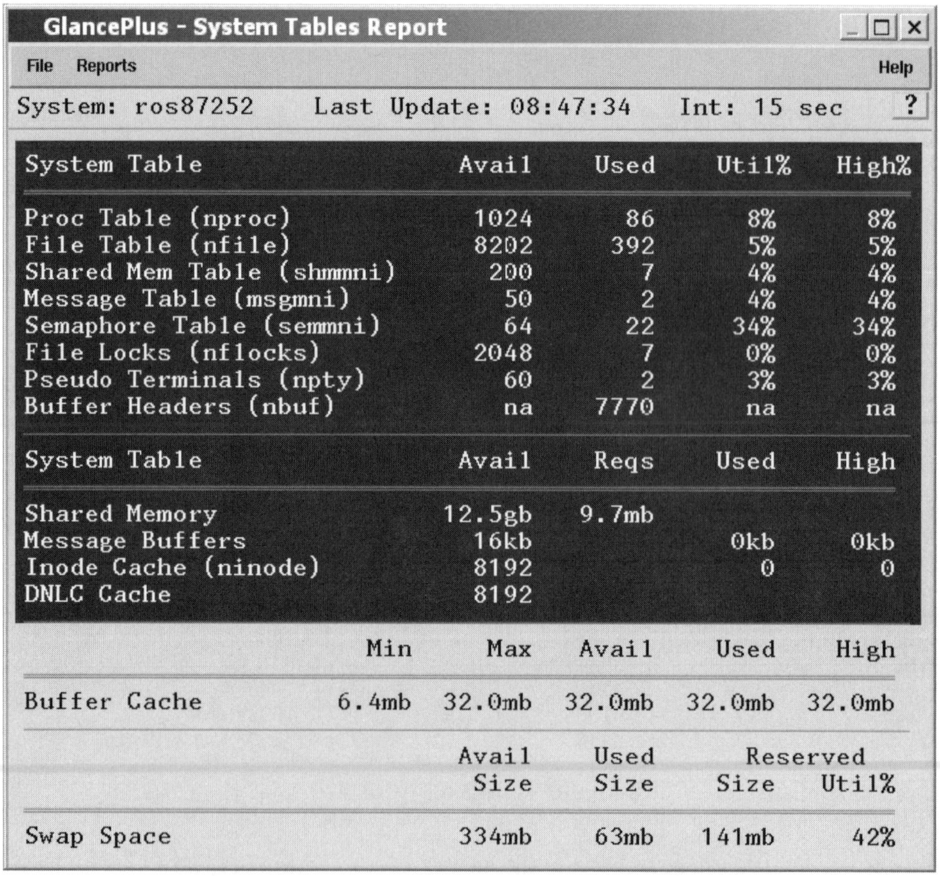

GlancePlus - System Tables Report   _ □ ×

File   Reports   Help

System: ros87252   Last Update: 08:47:34   Int: 15 sec   ?

System Table	Avail	Used	Util%	High%
Proc Table (nproc)	1024	86	8%	8%
File Table (nfile)	8202	392	5%	5%
Shared Mem Table (shmmni)	200	7	4%	4%
Message Table (msgmni)	50	2	4%	4%
Semaphore Table (semmni)	64	22	34%	34%
File Locks (nflocks)	2048	7	0%	0%
Pseudo Terminals (npty)	60	2	3%	3%
Buffer Headers (nbuf)	na	7770	na	na

System Table	Avail	Reqs	Used	High
Shared Memory	12.5gb	9.7mb		
Message Buffers	16kb		0kb	0kb
Inode Cache (ninode)	8192		0	0
DNLC Cache	8192			

	Min	Max	Avail	Used	High
Buffer Cache	6.4mb	32.0mb	32.0mb	32.0mb	32.0mb

	Avail Size	Used Size	Reserved Size	Util%
Swap Space	334mb	63mb	141mb	42%

Figure 12.4 GlancePlus System Tables Report Screen

While the list of kernel components monitored by GlancePlus is by no means exhaustive, this screen does display the utilization rates for many key system resources, including: the number of process table entries in use (*nproc*), the amount of file table entries consumed (*nfile*), the number of file locks currently held by all processes (*nflocks*), the current rate of buffer cache usage (*bufpages, nbuf, dbc_min_pct, dbc_max_pct*), etc.

This screen also reports the size of the Directory Name Lookup Cache (*ncsize*) and the HFS inode cache (*ninode*). Since both tables contain 8192 entries, this would indicate that either the DNLC is being sized via *ninode*, or that *ncsize* is also set to 8192. Another interesting statistic is the fact that the HFS inode cache appears to have a utilization rate of 0, indicating that HFS filesystems are not being used, and therefore the system must be using VxFS filesystems.

While the GlancePlus "System Tables" screen reports on the size of the DNLC, it does not show the hit rate of this important cache. Fortunately, this information is reported by GlancePlus in the "Disk Report" screen. An sample of this screen output is shown in Figure 12.5.

GlancePlus - Disk Report								_ □ ×
File Reports								Help
System: ros87252 Last Update: 18:43:27 Int: 15 sec								?
Req Type	Requests	%	Rate	Bytes	Cum Req	%	Cum Rate	Cum Bytes
Local Logl Reads	17815	96.8%	1187.6	13.4mb	83753	68.6%	195.2	97.1mb
Local Logl Writes	585	3.2%	39.0	105kb	38411	31.4%	89.5	25.0mb
Local Phys Reads	7	9.7%	0.4	50kb	508	21.1%	1.1	5.8mb
Local Phys Writes	65	90.3%	4.3	456kb	1902	78.9%	4.4	29.7mb
Local User	10	13.9%	0.6	120kb	942	39.1%	2.1	26.1mb
Local Virtual Mem	51	70.8%	3.4	324kb	874	36.3%	2.0	7.6mb
Local System	11	15.3%	0.7	62kb	594	24.6%	1.3	1.8mb
Local Raw	0	0.0%	0.0	0kb	0	0.0%	0.0	0kb
Remote Logl Reads	212457	99.9%	14163.8	1.61gb	629485	99.8%	1467.3	799.5mb
Remote Logl Writes	198	0.1%	13.2	12.1mb	1224	0.2%	2.8	74.9mb
Remote Phys Reads	22	1.3%	1.4	0kb	1891	16.2%	4.4	3.4mb
Remote Phys Writes	1630	98.7%	108.6	12.5mb	9811	83.8%	22.8	75.0mb
Remote User	1597	96.7%	106.4	12.5mb	10044	85.8%	23.4	78.5mb
Remote Virtual Mem	0	0.0%	0.0	0kb	0	0.0%	0.0	0kb
Remote System	55	3.3%	3.6	0kb	1658	14.2%	3.8	0kb
Remote Raw	0	0.0%	0.0	0kb	0	0.0%	0.0	0kb

Event	Current	Cum	Curr %	Avg %	High %
Read Cache Hits	649865	2004710	100.0	100.0	100.0
Write Cache Hits	2251	52379	58.6	79.7	
DNLC Hits	35076	186795	89.9	92.0	99.5
DNLC Longs	0	0	0.0	0.0	0.0

Figure 12.5   GlancePlus Disk Report Displaying DNLC Hit Rates

Looking at this example output, GlancePlus reports the DNLC hit rate for this system has averaged 92% since GlancePlus began monitoring the system. This information can be very helpful in determining whether the DNLC needs to be increased, either indirectly via *ninode* or directly via *ncsize*.

KEY IDEA — The Importance of Patching Prior to Tuning Kernel Parameters

Many of the kernel parameters discussed in this chapter did not exist when HP-UX 11.0 and 11i initially released. Support for these variables was added via patches. It is therefore very important to ensure that your systems have the appropriate patches installed before attempting to tune these kernel parameters.

Contact HP support to obtain a current set of patches for your specific operating system. You can also generate a current patch list using the tools available at HP's IT Resource Center: *http://itrc.hp.com.*

For more information about the importance of patching HP-UX systems, refer to Appendix B "Patching Considerations."

Summary of Tuning Recommendations

$\mathbf{T}$ his appendix summarizes many of the tuning and sizing recommendations made throughout the book. Keep in mind that these recommendations are intended merely as *suggested initial settings*. Only via thorough testing in your specific environment can you identify the optimal settings for these parameters for your NFS client and server systems.

In addition to the recommendations summarized here, there are 68 boxes located throughout the book labeled "Key Idea" or "NFS Performance Example" that explain important concepts for tuning HP-UX systems for optimal NFS performance. These tips are summarized in the table called "List of Key Ideas and NFS Performance Examples" located at the beginning of the book. Also situated throughout the book are boxes highlighting the differences between the NFS implementations on HP-UX 11.0 and 11i. These differences are summarized in the "List of NFS Differences Between HP-UX 11.0 and 11i" table, also located at the beginning of the book.

NOTE: This Appendix *Is Not* a "Quick Reference Guide"

This appendix is **not** intended as a "quick reference guide" for how to optimally tune your HP-UX 11.0 and 11i NFS systems. Before using any of the recommendations in this appendix, you are strongly encouraged to read the corresponding section of the book listed with each parameter in order to fully understand the implications of changing the parameter.

Much of the information in this appendix is displayed in tabular format; where each table contains a list of parameters, an explanation of how to modify each parameter (where applicable), a brief description, an indication of whether the parameter is applicable to an NFS client or server system (or both), the default value, the recommended initial setting, and the location in the book where you can learn more about the parameter.

A.1 NFS Client and Server Daemons

Table A.1 lists the configurable parameters that control the number of client-side block I/O daemons (biods) and server-side NFS daemons (nfsds) launched at system boot time.

Table A.1 Recommended Number of Client and Server NFS Daemons

Variable Name	Where to Modify	Description	Client / Server	Default Value	Recommended Initial Value	To Learn More
NUM_NFSIOD	/etc/rc.config.d/nfsconf	Number of biod daemons to start at system boot	Client	4 (11.0) 16 (11i)	16	Chapter 3
NUM_NFSD	/etc/rc.config.d/nfsconf	Number of nfsd daemons to start at system boot	Server	4 (11.0) 16 (11i)	64 or (8*CPUs) - whichever is *MORE*	Chapter 4

A.2 Supported NFS Kernel Parameters

Table A.2 lists the various kernel parameters that can directly influence the behavior and performance of HP-UX NFS clients and servers. These parameters are described in greater detail in Chapter 12.

Table A.2 Recommended Values for Supported Kernel Parameters

Variable Name	Description	Client / Server	Default Value	Recommended Initial Value	To Learn More
bufcache_hash_locks	Specifies the size of the pool of locks used to control access to buffer cache structures	Both	128	4096	Section 12.1.1
bufpages	Defines the number of 4096 byte memory pages in the *static*-sized buffer cache	Both	0	0 (Dynamic)	Section 12.1.2
create_fastlinks	Enable/disable storing link text for symbolic links in the on-disk inode (*HFS only*)	Both	0	1 (Enabled)	Section 12.1.3

302

Table A.2 Recommended Values for Supported Kernel Parameters

Variable Name	Description	Client / Server	Default Value	Recommended Initial Value	To Learn More
dbc_min_pct	Specifies the minimum amount of memory used for *dynamic* buffer cache	Both	5	5 or *dbc_max_pct* - whichever is *LESS*	**Section 12.1.4**
dbc_max_pct	Specifies the maximum amount of memory used for *dynamic* buffer cache	Client	50	25 or 400MB — whichever is *LESS*	**Section 12.1.5**
		Server		50 or 1GB — whichever is *LESS*	
default_disk_ir	Enable/disable immediate disk reporting	Both	0	0 (Disabled)[a]	**Section 12.1.6**
dnlc_hash_locks[b]	Specifies the number of hash chains the DNLC entries will be divided into, and the number of locks allocated to control access to the DNLC	Both	64 (11.0) 512 (11i)	4096	**Section 12.1.7**
fs_async	Enable or disable writing filesystem data structures asynchronously (*HFS only*)	Both	0	1 (Enabled)	**Section 12.1.8**
ftable_hash_locks	Specifies the size of the pool of locks used to control access to file table data structures	Both	64	4096	**Section 12.1.9**
max_fcp_reqs	Defines the maximum concurrent requests allowed on any Fiber-Channel adapter	Server	512	1024[c]	**Section 12.1.10**
max_thread_proc	Specifies the maximum number of kernel threads that can be associated with a process at any given time	Server	64	1024 or (10 * # of NFS/TCP Clients) – *whichever is MORE*	**Section 12.1.11**

Table A.2 Recommended Values for Supported Kernel Parameters

Variable Name	Description	Client / Server	Default Value	Recommended Initial Value	To Learn More
maxfiles	Specifies the "soft" limit for the number of files a process can have open at a time	Both	60	**1024**	**Section 12.1.12**
maxfiles_lim	Specifies the "hard" limit for the number of files a process can have open at a time	Both	1024	**2048**	**Section 12.1.13**
maxswapchunks	Used to calculate the maximum configurable swap space on the system. It specifies the maximum amount of swap space that can be configured.	Both	256	**8192**	**Section 12.1.14**
nbuf	Defines the number of buffer headers to be allocated for the *static*-sized buffer-cache	Both	0	**0 (Dynamic)**	**Section 12.1.15**
ncallout	Specifies the maximum number of timeouts that can be scheduled by the kernel at any given time	Both	(16 + NPROC)	**(16 + NKTHREAD)**	**Section 12.1.16**
ncsize	Directly sizes the Directory Name Lookup Cache and the NFS rnode cache; indirectly sizes the CacheFS cnode cache	Both	(NINODE + VX_NCSIZE)	**8192**	**Section 12.1.17**
nfile	Specifies the maximum number of open files allowed on the system at any time	Both	928	**8192**	**Section 12.1.18**
nflocks	Specifies the maximum number of file locks allowed on the system at any time	Both	200	**2048**	**Section 12.1.19**
ninode	Directly defines the size of the HFS inode cache; indirectly sizes the CacheFS cnode cache, the DNLC, the NFS rnode cache, and the VxFS inode cache	Both	476	**8192**	**Section 12.1.20**

Table A.2 Recommended Values for Supported Kernel Parameters

Variable Name	Description	Client / Server	Default Value	Recommended Initial Value	To Learn More
nkthread	Specifies the maximum number of kernel threads that can be running system-wide	Server	499	2048	Section 12.1.21
nproc	Specifies the maximum number of processes that can be running system-wide	Both	276	1024	Section 12.1.22
scsi_max_qdepth[d]	The maximum number of I/O requests that can be queued to a SCSI device at a time	Server	8	90	Section 12.1.23
vnode_hash_locks	Specifies the size of the pool of locks used to control access to vnode data structures	Both	128	4096	Section 12.1.24
vnode_cd_hash_locks	Specifies the size of the pool of locks used to control access to the clean and dirty buffer chains associated with vnodes	Both	128	4096	Section 12.1.25
vx_fancyra_enable[e]	Enable or disable intelligent read-ahead algorithm (*VxFS 3.3 filesystems only*)	Both	0	1 (Enabled)	Section 12.1.26
vx_ninode[f]	Specifies the size of the VxFS-specific inode cache	Both	0	8192	Section 12.1.27

a. Enabling the *default_disk_ir* feature can significantly improve *write()* performance, but it has the potential of causing data corruption on systems using non-battery-backed storage. This parameter should only be enabled on systems using battery-backed storage, or on those systems where the system administrator decides the *write()* performance gain is worth the potential risk of data corruption.

b. The *dnlc_hash_locks* kernel variable did not exist when HP-UX 11.0 was released. It was introduced in patch PHKL_12965, which has since been replaced by patch PHKL_18543. This variable has a default value of 64 on HP-UX 11.0. The default value was increased to 512 in HP-UX 11i.

c. Tuning *max_fcp_reqs* is only applicable on NFS servers using Fibre Channel-based storage systems.

d. Tuning *scsi_max_qdepth* is only applicable on NFS servers using SCSI-based storage systems.

e. The *vx_fancyra_enable* kernel variable did not exist when HP-UX 11.0 was released. It was introduced in patch PHKL_22414.

f. The *vx_ninode* kernel variable did not exist when HP-UX 11.0 and 11i released. It was introduced in patch PHKL_18543 (11.0) and PHKL_24783 (11i).

305

A.3 Undocumented NFS Kernel Parameters

Table A.3 lists the undocumented kernel parameters, discussed throughout the book, that can be used to control very specific NFS client and server activities. These parameters cannot be customized using the standard kernel configuration tools, such as sam(1M) and kmtune(1M). They can only be modified manually via adb(1).

Two of the parameters listed below — *async_read_avoidance_enabled* and *nfs_new_lock_code* — enable new performance-enhancing features that HP recently added to their NFS product via patches. The remaining kernel parameters control very specific NFS client and server behavior, and these should only be changed in certain situations. Before modifying any of the kernel parameters in Table A.3 from their default values, be absolutely certain you understand what they control and the potential implications of changing them. It is strongly recommended that you thoroughly test any changes to these undocumented parameters in a non-production environment before modifying your production systems.

Table A.3 Undocumented Kernel Parameters in HP-UX 11.0 and 11i

Variable Name	Description	Client / Server	Default Value	To Learn More
async_read_avoidance_enabled	Enable/disable the client's behavior of sending synchronous READ requests when buffer cache resources are unavailable	Client	0 (Disabled)	**Section 3.1.4**
clnt_max_conns	Specifies the number of TCP connections the client will open with each server it mounts NFS/TCP filesystems from	Client	1	**Section 4.3.2** **Section 4.3.3**
do_readdirplus	Enable/disable the NFS/PV3 READDIRPLUS procedure	Client	1 (Enabled)	**Section 9.1.5** **Section 9.2.3**
maxcnodes	Specifies the size of the CacheFS-specific inode cache	Client	*ncsize*	**Section 8.3.3**
maxthreads	Specifies the number of kernel threads the server will allocate to servicing requests on each NFS/TCP connection	Server	10	**Section 4.3.2** **Section 4.3.4**
nfs_new_lock_code	Enable/disable the client's behavior of writing asynchronously to locked NFS files	Client	0 (Disabled)	**Section 3.3.4**

306

A.4 NFS Mount and Exportfs Options

HP provides numerous NFS-specific mount options that allow a system administrator to control the behavior of client systems when accessing an NFS mount point. In addition, many exportfs options are provided to control the behavior of NFS servers when handling requests from NFS clients. Many of these options have been discussed throughout this book and are summarized in Table A.4. While this table is by no means an exhaustive list of the available options to the NFS mount and exportfs commands, these are the most commonly used options that can have a significant effect on performance. For more information about the available NFS mount and exportfs options, refer to the mount_nfs(1M) and exportfs(1M) man pages respectively.

The default values of many NFS mount options have changed in 11i. It is therefore important to understand which options have changed to know how a default NFS mount (i.e. a mount where no options are specified) will behave in 11.0 and 11i.

Table A.4 Recommendations for NFS Mount and Export Options

Option Name	Command	Description	Client / Server	Default Value	Recommended Initial Value	To Learn More
vers	mount(1M)	Specifies which version of the NFS protocol to use for a given NFS filesystem	Client	3	3	Chapter 9
rsize	mount(1M)	Specifies the amount of data an NFS client system requests when sending READ requests on a given filesystem	Client	8KB (11.0) 32KB (11i)	32KB	Section 9.1.3 Section 9.2.2 Section 10.3.2
wsize	mount(1M)	Specifies the amount of data an NFS client system includes in the NFS WRITE requests sent on a given filesystem	Client	8KB (11.0) 32KB (11i)	32KB	Section 9.1.3 Section 9.2.1 Section 9.2.2 Section 10.3.2
proto	mount(1M)	Specifies the network transport protocol to use for a given filesystem	Client	UDP (11.0)[a] TCP (11i)	See Section 10.5	Chapter 10

Table A.4 Recommendations for NFS Mount and Export Options

Option Name	Command	Description	Client / Server	Default Value	Recommended Initial Value	To Learn More
timeo	mount(1M)	Specifies the duration of time to wait for an NFS request to complete before retransmitting the request	Client	UDP (Ignored) TCP (60 Seconds)	**Do Not Use**	**Section 3.5.3** **Section 10.3.6**
noac	mount(1M)	Disables client-side caching of NFS file and directory attribute caching	Client	Attribute Caching Enabled	**Only use when required by applications[b]**	**Section 7.2.5**
async	exportfs(1M)	Instructs the NFS server to treat all WRITE requests received from PV2 clients as asynchronous requests (i.e. allows the server to reply to WRITE requests immediately as soon as the data is copied to the server's local buffer cache memory).	Server	PV2 WRITE requests are handled synchronously	**Enable *async***	**Section 7.1.4** **Section 9.1.2**

a. When HP-UX 11.0 shipped, the only supported network transport protocol available for NFS mounts was UDP. HP added support for NFS/TCP via patches in March 2000. Therefore, the default transport protocol used by HP-UX 11.0 systems depends upon whether NFS/TCP patches are installed and whether TCP support has been enabled or not. Once NFS/TCP patches are installed on a system and TCP support has been enabled via the setoncenv(1M) command, TCP becomes the default transport protocol used for new NFS mounts.

b. The *noac* option can have a dramatic effect on client performance because it forces the client to retrieve the attributes of any file or directory object it plans to access or modify prior to sending its request. This results in a huge increase in the number of LOOKUP and GETATTR calls performed by the client — calls which could be avoided if this data were cached. For this reason, the recommendation is to only use this option in application environments that absolutely require it. The types of environments that necessitate the need for the *noac* option are typically those where the contents of files and directories are changing constantly on the NFS server — either due to processes modifying these contents locally on the server or by sharing the contents with many NFS clients. In those cases, disabling client attribute caching is appropriate, since there is a strong likelihood that the client's cache would contain stale data anyway, which could lead to erroneous behavior or potentially data corruption. Unless your application environment is one where the server's contents fluctuate rapidly, the use of the *noac* option should be discouraged.

A.4.1 Verifying Mount Options for Mounted NFS Filesystems

The easiest and most accurate way to determine which NFS mount options are in effect on a per-mount point basis is to use the nfsstat(1M) command with the "-m" option. Figure A.1 shows an example of "nfsstat -m" output from an HP-UX 11.0 NFS client.

```
ros87252 (B1000 64-bit 11.0)                                              _ □ x
ros87252(/) -> nfsstat -m

/nfs_mount1 from emonster:/tmp  (Addr 15.32.72.208)
 Flags:    vers=3,proto=udp,auth=unix,hard,intr,link,symlink,devs,rsize=8192,wsize=8192,retrans=5
 Lookups: srtt=  7 ( 17ms), dev=  3 ( 15ms), cur=  2 ( 40ms)
 Reads:   srtt= 23 ( 57ms), dev=  4 ( 20ms), cur=  4 ( 80ms)
 Writes:  srtt= 28 ( 70ms), dev=  5 ( 25ms), cur=  6 (120ms)
 All:     srtt=  7 ( 17ms), dev=  3 ( 15ms), cur=  2 ( 40ms)

/nfs_mount2 from emonster:/home/dolker  (Addr 15.32.72.208)
 Flags:    vers=3,proto=udp,auth=unix,hard,intr,link,symlink,devs,rsize=1024,wsize=4096,retrans=5
 Lookups: srtt=  7 ( 17ms), dev=  3 ( 15ms), cur=  2 ( 40ms)
 Reads:   srtt=  9 ( 22ms), dev=  4 ( 20ms), cur=  3 ( 60ms)
 Writes:  srtt= 15 ( 37ms), dev=  3 ( 15ms), cur=  3 ( 60ms)
 All:     srtt=  7 ( 17ms), dev=  3 ( 15ms), cur=  2 ( 40ms)

/nfs_mount3 from emonster:/tmp  (Addr 15.32.72.208)
 Flags:    vers=3,proto=udp,auth=unix,hard,intr,noac,link,symlink,devs,rsize=32768,wsize=32768,retrans=5
 Lookups: srtt=  7 ( 17ms), dev=  6 ( 30ms), cur=  3 ( 60ms)
 Reads:   srtt= 14 ( 35ms), dev= 13 ( 65ms), cur=  8 (160ms)
 Writes:  srtt=103 (257ms), dev= 29 (145ms), cur= 27 (540ms)
 All:     srtt= 57 (142ms), dev= 35 (175ms), cur= 24 (480ms)

/nfs_mount4 from atc03.cup.hp.com:/export  (Addr 15.4.64.26)
 Flags:    vers=2,proto=tcp,auth=unix,hard,intr,dynamic,devs,rsize=8192,wsize=8192,retrans=5
 All:     srtt=  0 (  0ms), dev=4000 (20000ms), cur=1000 (20000ms)
```

Figure A.1 nfsstat -m Displaying NFS Mount Options

In this example, three of the four mounted filesystems are using NFS Version 3 — only /nfs_mount4 is using PV2. All filesystems except /nfs_mount4 are mounted from NFS server "emonster." The /nfs_mount3 filesystem is mounted with the *noac* option and is using READ and WRITE buffer sizes of 32KB, while /nfs_mount2 is using a READ size of 1KB and a WRITE size of 4KB. All NFS filesystems with the exception of /nfs_mount4 are using UDP as their underlying network transport, while /nfs_mount4 is using TCP. Finally, the output shows that both /nfs_mount1 and /nfs_mount3 reference the same remote filesystem from the same NFS server, but they are mounted on the client with different options.

This "nfsstat -m" information can be very useful, especially when determining why one NFS mounted filesystem performs better or worse than another.

A.4.2 Verifying Options for Exported Filesystems

There are many ways of determining which local filesystems on an NFS server are currently exported for client access, and with which options. The easiest and most accurate method is to simply issue the exportfs(1M) command with no command-line options, as shown in Figure A.2.

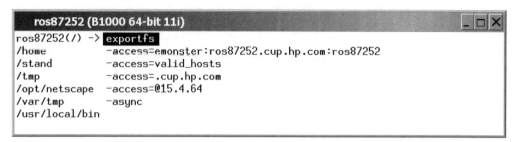

Figure A.2   Sample `exportfs` Output

In this example, there are six local filesystems exported for NFS client access, each using a different syntax. Four of the filesystems have specific access lists configured, allowing only certain clients access. The /var/tmp filesystem is exported with the *async* option, allowing the server to treat NFS PV2 WRITE requests for the /var/tmp filesystem asynchronously. For more information on exporting filesystems, refer to the exportfs(1M) man page.

Patching Considerations

NFS continues to evolve over time. The NFS product that shipped with HP-UX 11i is far superior in terms of functionality, stability, and performance compared to the product that originally shipped with the 11.0 release. This is not meant to imply that improvements in HP's NFS offering are only made as new versions of the operating system are introduced — far from it. HP continually strives to improve its existing products on supported OS releases by distributing software patches containing both defect fixes and functionality enhancements. Many of these fixes and enhancements can significantly improve NFS behavior and performance.

This appendix discusses the two primary reasons (from a performance perspective) why it is critical to keep your NFS client and server systems running current software: performance enhancing defect fixes and performance enhancing new functionality. It also explains the importance of keeping the many subsystems that NFS depends on patched, such as networking, filesystems, and the kernel.

B.1 Performance-Enhancing Defect Fixes

HP typically releases NFS patches on a quarterly basis. These patches are always cumulative, in that they include all fixes from previous patches. They also frequently contain defect fixes that improve NFS performance. Some recent examples of performance influencing fixes are described in Table B.1.

Table B.1 Performance-Enhancing Defects Fixed in Patches

Defect Number	Description
JAGad16541[a]	CPU time is wasted by unnecessary calls to the *compare_cred()* function in NFS PV3 client code.

Table B.1   Performance-Enhancing Defects Fixed in Patches

Defect Number	Description
JAGad14221[a]	Client performance is degraded, as shown by "nfsstat -c," by making unnecessary GETATTR calls for each read or write on files opened with synchronous I/O flags set. Synchronous I/O mode remains in effect for subsequent opens on an NFS file opened once with synchronous I/O flags set.
JAGad66201[a]	Performance degrades on systems with more than 1GB of physical memory installed.
JAGad72416[a]	A process sequentially reading a large file across an NFS mount runs extremely slowly if, at the same time, there is another process sequentially writing a large file to an NFS mounted directory, and one or more biods are running on the system.
JAGad15675[a]	The I/O throughput on a locked file is low compared to the throughput on an unlocked file.
JAGad48223[a]	Unnecessary NFS read before write is causing severe decreases in write performance.

a.   The defect numbers listed in the table represent the tracking numbers used by HP to monitor these defects. Customers can check the status of HP-UX defects by visiting the HP IT Resource Center web site: *http://itrc.hp.com.*

Table B.1 is by no means an exhaustive list of the performance-related fixes available in HP's current NFS patches; however it does illustrate the importance of keeping your client and server software up-to-date to optimize NFS performance.

B.2   Performance-Enhancing New Functionality

In addition to defect fixes, on occasion HP releases new NFS functionality via patches. Many of these new features (described in Table B.2) directly affect the performance of HP's NFS implementation.

Table B.2   Performance-Enhancing New Functionality in Patches

Feature	Release Date	Description
AutoFS[a]	August 1998	This feature is a newer version of the automount protocol, which includes many new features. For more information about AutoFS, refer to Chapter 7.

Table B.2   Performance-Enhancing New Functionality in Patches

Feature	Release Date	Description
NFS over TCP/IP[a]	March 2000	This feature allows NFS to run over the TCP/IP transport protocol. This allows NFS to work more reliably and perform better over wide area networks. For more information about NFS/TCP, refer to Chapter 10.
32KB read/write buffers[a]	March 2000	When HP-UX 11.0 shipped, NFS PV3 mount points only allowed read and write requests as large as 8KB. 32KB buffer size support was added in March 2000. For more information about read/write buffer sizes and their effect on NFS performance, refer to Chapter 9.
CacheFS[b]	September 2001	This feature allows NFS clients to keep copies of files read from NFS servers cached on their local filesystems, thus avoiding the need to re-read the information across the wire. Although CacheFS shipped with 11i, it was not enabled until the Fall 2001 patch, which shipped in September 2001. For more information about CacheFS, refer to Chapter 8.

a.   This feature was released via a patch for HP-UX 11.0. It was included in the 11i release.

b.   This feature is only available on HP-UX 11i.

This table shows that an HP-UX 11.0 or 11i system without current patches installed may not have all of the latest available NFS functionality, and therefore may not perform optimally.

B.3 Patching Dependent Subsystems

NFS relies on the health and well-being of many subsystems to function correctly and perform optimally. Chapter 1 and Chapter 2 discussed how NFS is dependent upon the networking and filesystems layers, but NFS is also heavily dependent upon many other subsystems, such as:

- OS Commands (i.e. `mount`, `umount`, `bdf`, `df`, `ls`, etc.)
- Libraries (i.e. libc, libpthread, libnsl, etc.)
- Kernel Mechanisms (i.e. Directory Name Lookup Cache, Buffer Cache, etc.)
- SAM (for NFS and kernel configuration)

Even in the networking and filesystems areas, there are many subsystems to consider:

- Network Transport (i.e. TCP, UDP, IP, ICMP, etc.)
- LAN Common (i.e. those functions common to all underlying network interface cards)
- Link-specific Drivers (i.e. 10BT, 100BT, Gigabit EtherNet, Token Ring, ATM, etc.)
- Filesystem Specific (i.e. VxFS, HFS, CDFS, LOFS, etc.)

Since NFS depends on all of these entities to perform optimally, it is very important to keep the patch levels of these underlying subsystems current, since a defect in any of those subsystems can negatively affect NFS behavior and performance. Given the list of dependent subsystems, it should come as no surprise that the list of dependent patches is lengthy. Table B.3 lists the HP-UX 11.0 NFS and dependent patches that were current as of the time of this writing.

> **TIP:** HP-UX patches are superseded on a regular basis, so *the list of patches listed in Table B.3 will undoubtedly be out of date by the time you read this book.* This table is provided merely as an example to show how many different subsystems (and patches) NFS depends upon for optimal functionality and performance.

Table B.3 Sample HP-UX 11.0 NFS Dependent Patch List

Patch Name	Patch Description
PHNE_25626	NFS Kernel and User-space Patch
PHCO_23117	bdf(1M) Cumulative Patch
PHCO_23651	fsck_vxfs(1M) Cumulative Patch
PHCO_23876	SAM/ObAM Cumulative Patch
PHCO_23963	libc Cumulative header file Patch
PHCO_25707	libc Cumulative Patch
PHKL_18543	Kernel Process Management, Virtual Memory, I/O Performance Patch
PHKL_20016	G70/H70/I70 Hardware Enablement Patch

Table B.3 Sample HP-UX 11.0 NFS Dependent Patch List

Patch Name	Patch Description
PHKL_22589	LOFS Cumulative Patch
PHKL_25613	IDS/9000; syscalls related to file/socket Patch
PHKL_24943	pthread, thread hang, nfs/tcp panic Patch
PHKL_27089	syscall, msem_lock, umask Cumulative Patch
PHKL_24027	VxFS 3.1 Cumulative Patch
PHKL_26800	Probe, IDDS, PM, VM, PA-8700, asyncio, T600 Cumulative Patch
PHNE_25116	Cumulative STREAMS Patch
PHNE_26771	Cumulative ARPA Transport Patch
PHCO_26000	libpthreads Cumulative Patch

Be sure to contact HP support to obtain a current set of NFS patches, and their dependencies, for your specific operating system. You can also generate a current list using the patch bundle tools available at HP's IT Resource Center web site: *http://itrc.hp.com*.

 KEY IDEA — **An Alternative to Individual Patches: HP-UX Quality Packs**

As an alternative to downloading individual patches, or sets of dependent patches, HP releases biannual Quality Packs for HP-UX 11.0 and 11i, which may be downloaded free of charge from HP's Software Depot web site: *http://software.hp.com*.

HP-UX Quality Packs include all stable defect fix patches for core HP-UX, graphics and networking drivers. HP thoroughly tests each Quality Pack and requires that it pass the same tests as would a new HP-UX operating system release. The HP-UX 11.0 Quality Pack updates every March and September and the HP-UX 11.11 Quality Pack updates every June and December.

B.4 Verifying Current NFS Patch Level

A critical step in the NFS patch analysis process is verifying which NFS patch is currently installed on your system. HP provides several tools for examining the installed software products, including patches, on HP-UX systems. Two of the most system commonly used utilities are `swlist(1M)` and `swremove(1M)`.

B.4.1 swlist(1M)

The swlist(1M) command is used to display information about installed software products. It can organize the contents in several formats: by bundles, by products, by subproducts, by filesets, or by patches. It offers many advanced capabilities as well, including the ability to:

- display the files contained in each fileset
- display all attributes for bundles, products, subproducts, filesets and/or files
- display the depots on a specified host
- list the categories of available or applied patches
- list applied patches and their state (applied or committed)

For the purposes of identifying the currently installed NFS patch on a system, swlist can be invoked using the syntax shown in Figure B.1. In this example, swlist lists all installed software organized by "product." The "-x show_superseded_patches=false" option filters the list of products and eliminates any superseded patches from the output, leaving only the current patch for each product in the resulting list. This output is then massaged by the grep(1) command to limit the list to only those patches containing the string "ONC," revealing the current NFS/ONC patch, which in this example is PHNE_25627.

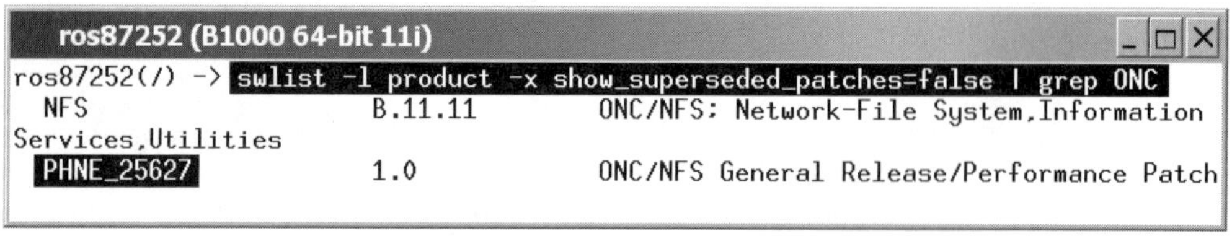

```
ros87252 (B1000 64-bit 11i)                                    _ □ ✕
ros87252(/) -> swlist -l product -x show_superseded_patches=false | grep ONC
  NFS                        B.11.11        ONC/NFS: Network-File System,Information
Services,Utilities
  PHNE_25627                 1.0            ONC/NFS General Release/Performance Patch
```

Figure B.1 Using swlist to Identify the Installed NFS Patch

For more information about swlist, refer to the swlist(1M) man page, the HP-UX 11.0 manual: *Managing HP-UX Software With SD-UX*, or the HP-UX 11i manual: *Software Distributor Administration Guide*.

B.4.2 swremove(1M)

The swremove(1M) command is primarily used to remove software products, patches, and bundles.[1] It graphically displays the list of installed software and allows the system administrator to select which components to remove. Since this list includes all installed software patches, including any patches installed via software bundles (such as HP-UX Quality Packs), swremove provides an easy way to identify the current NFS patch installed on the system.

---

1.   A single software bundle may contain filesets from several different products. Additionally, a single software bundle may contain dozens or even hundreds of individual patches.

swremove can be configured to display the installed software in two different formats: "top" view and "products" view. Changing the software view in swremove is done via the "View > Change Software View" menu item (see Figure B.2 for an example). The "top" view, shown in Figure B.2, displays the *names* of any installed software bundles; however it does not display the *contents* of these bundles. Additionally, the "top" view displays any products that were *not* installed as part of a bundle, including individually installed patches.

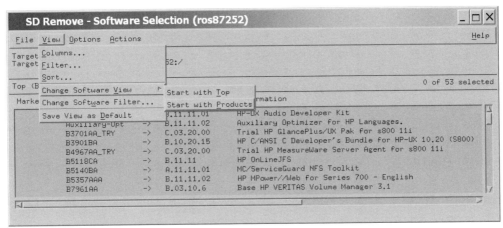

Figure B.2 Configuring swremove to Display by "Products"

The "products" view (Figure B.3) displays *all* installed software. Comparing this screen against the "top" view example in Figure B.2, you can see that the "products" view contains 163 items vs. 53 items in "top" view, indicating that many products and/or patches have been installed on this system via software bundles.

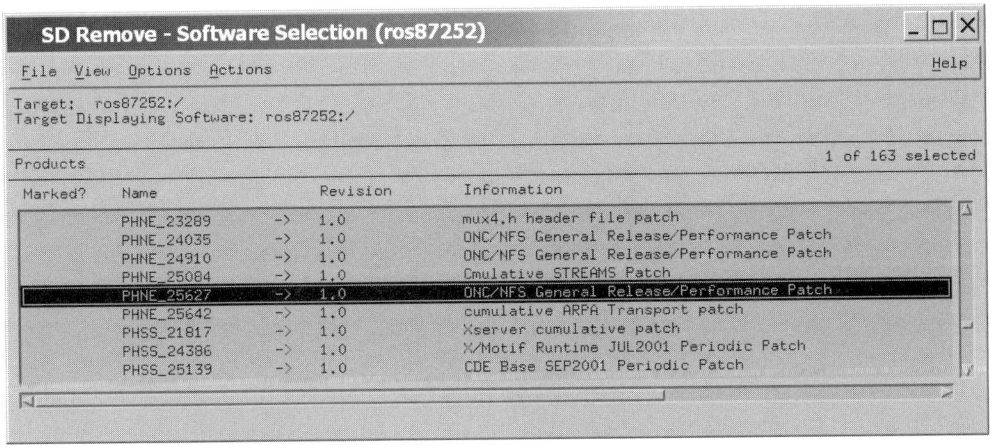

Figure B.3 Using swremove to Identify the Installed NFS Patch

The "products" view lists *all* installed patches, including any superseded patches. When using `swremove` to identify the current NFS patch, scroll down to the bottom of the listed "PHNE" patches and search upwards for the last patch containing the string "ONC" or "NFS." On this system, the last "PHNE" patch with the string "ONC" or "NFS" is PHNE_25627, which matches the patch `swlist` identified in Figure B.1.

For more information about `swremove`, refer to the `swremove(1M)` man page, the HP-UX 11.0 manual: *Managing HP-UX Software With SD-UX*, or the HP-UX 11i manual: *Software Distributor Administration Guide*.

BIBLIOGRAPHY

Callaghan, Brent, *The Automounter: Solaris 2.0 and Beyond*, October 1992

Callaghan, Brent, *NFS Illustrated*, December 1999

Co, Van, *The Mystery of NFS PV3 UDP Timeouts*, November 1999

Hewlett-Packard, *Installing and Administering NFS Services*, 2001

Hewlett-Packard, *Supported File and File System Sizes for JFS and HFS — White Paper*, 2001

Hewlett-Packard, *Tunable Kernel Parameters in HP-UX 11i*, 2002

Hewlett-Packard, Veritas, *HP JFS 3.3 and HP OnLineJFS 3.3 VERITAS File System 3.3 System Administrator's Guide for HP-UX 11.00 and HP-UX 11i*, November 2000

McNeal, T., Liu, L., *Implementing ONC+/NFS over the TCP/IP Transport Protocol*, 1999

Sun Microsystems, *Cache File System (CacheFS) White Paper*, February 1994

Sun Microsystems, *Network File System: Version 2 Protocol Specification*, 1984

Sun Microsystems, *NFS: Network File System Version 3 Protocol Specification*, February 1994

Sun Microsystems, *Systems Administration Guide, Volume 1*, February 2000

Pawlowski, B., Juszczak, C., Staubach, P., Smith, C., Lebel, D., and Hitz, D., *NFS Version 3 Design and Implementation*, June 1994

INDEX

HP's world-class education and training offers hands on education solutions including:

- Linux
- HP-UX System and Network Administration
- Advanced HP-UX System Administration
- IT Service Management using advanced Internet technologies
- Microsoft Windows NT/2000
- Internet/Intranet
- MPE/iX
- Database Administration
- Software Development

HP's new IT Professional Certification program provides rigorous technical qualification for specific IT job roles including HP-UX System Administration, Network Management, Unix/NT Servers and Applications Management, and IT Service Management.

become hp certified

http://education.hp.com

fulfill your needs

Want to know about new products, services and solutions from Hewlett-Packard Company — as soon as they're invented?

Need information about new HP services to help you implement new or existing products?

Looking for HP's newest solution to a specific challenge in your business?

HP Computer News features the latest from HP!

4 easy ways to subscribe, and it's FREE:

- **fax** complete and fax the form below to (651) 430-3388, or

- **online** sign up online at www.hp.com/go/compnews, or

- **email** complete the information below and send to hporders@earthlink.net, or

- **mail** complete and mail the form below to:

Twin Cities Fulfillment Center
Hewlett-Packard Company
P.O. Box 408
Stillwater, MN 55082

reply now to receive the first year FREE!

name

title

company

dept./mail stop

address

city

state

zip

email

signature

date

please indicate your industry below:

- ☐ accounting
- ☐ education
- ☐ financial services
- ☐ government
- ☐ healthcare/medical
- ☐ legal
- ☐ manufacturing
- ☐ publishing/printing
- ☐ online services
- ☐ real estate
- ☐ retail/wholesale distrib
- ☐ technical
- ☐ telecommunications
- ☐ transport and travel
- ☐ utilities
- ☐ other: _____